THE EMERGING GODDESS

THE EMERGING GODDESS

THE CREATIVE PROCESS IN ART, SCIENCE, AND OTHER FIELDS

ALBERT ROTHENBERG, M.D.

THE
UNIVERSITY OF CHICAGO PRESS
CHICAGO AND LONDON

THE UNIVERSITY OF CHICAGO PRESS, CHICAGO 60637
THE UNIVERSITY OF CHICAGO PRESS, LTD., LONDON

Paperback edition 1982
Printed in the United States of America

89 88 87 86 85 84 83 82   2 3 4 5 6

Library of Congress Cataloging in Publication Data

Rothenberg, Albert, 1930–
The emerging goddess.

Includes bibliographical references and index.
1. Creative thinking. 2. Creation (Literary, artistic, etc.)
I. Title.
BF408.R683 153.3′5 78–26486
ISBN: 0-226-72948-6 (cloth)
0-226-72949-4 (paper)

To
JULIA
golden muse

CONTENTS

PREFACE

This is a book of findings. It has grown out of work with some very creative persons and out of a collaborative tracing of an evanescent, intractable, and unpredictable phenomenon. I have been privileged to have a sometimes heady, sometimes dazzling, and sometimes worrisome but interesting experience. In systematic explorations with these persons, or in a particular experiment or test, the data reported here have been collected and analyzed. Although all have been research subjects and collaborators, not patients in therapy, I have promised them confidentiality and anonymity unless they themselves suggested otherwise. Consequently, I believe that the data I am reporting here are as free as possible of the common distortions and omissions induced by concern for public scrutiny. Such a concern must often be quite acute in celebrated persons, especially persons in the arts whose public image is—and should be—defined by their works. Because of this confidentiality and anonymity, however, the subjects of my researches must, by and large, go publicly unacknowledged. The book itself is its own acknowledgement of their contributions and I hope they will find it a worthy one.

This is also a book of theory. Here I have undertaken an especially perilous task, for the theory encompasses matters involving the experience and intuition of artists, writers, scientists, and other creators, the developmental and personality constructs of psychoanalysis, and the concerns of cognitive psychologists, psycholinguists, and philosophers. The theory of creativity and of the creative process presented here pertains in one respect to an enduring scientific achievement of Freud's, the understanding of the structure of dreams, and it is consistent both with psychoanalytic knowledge about personality function and with experimental psychological and psychiatric approaches. Overall, there is no allegiance to any one theoretical position but an inductive development from the data, wherever it leads.

Why study creativity and creative processes? After all, great thinkers throughout the ages have already tried to understand these matters or else they have directly practiced them through art, investigation, leadership, theory, or construction. Over and over, they have proclaimed both the mystery and awe of creativity. And indeed, part of the glory of creativity inheres in its very mystery and awesomeness, the sense we get of a discrepancy between merely human faculties and an enormous achievement. We prize not knowing how it is done; we enjoy bestowing accolades on those who fill us with marveling wonder. Why then try to dispel the mystery? Is science driven to reduce and invade all bastions of human ineffability, to deprive mankind of the sense of having qualities that resist rational comprehension?

The answer, I think, is not that science must dispel this mystery, that scientific progress always takes precedence over any other value or morality, but that we are at a point in history where science may be better prepared to dispel some of the mystery. We are at a point in history where we possess far more systematic information about psychological approaches and psychological functioning—small as it still is in an absolute sense—than any of the thinkers possessed who approached this topic earlier. Furthermore, we are at a point in history where science needs to tell us more about creativity and creative processes because of the goals and approaches we have already developed. In psychiatry and psychology, we attempt to treat persons we consider to be ill without any clear notion of what it is to be a psychologically healthy individual, or group of individuals. We attempt to define and identify poorly functioning processes without any clear notion of what effective or better-than-effective processes might be. We try to change behavior or to ameliorate suffering without knowing whether our alternatives are better. And, as psychiatrists, or psychologists, or educators or whatever, we have had little idea of whether we encourage or whether we stifle creativity in the clinic, or in our schools, or in our homes. We have had little idea of whether suffering and illness are somehow intrinsic to creative capacity. But now, we do have some knowledge and tools and with them we can contribute to man's deep understanding of himself. To the extent that we can help artists, scientists, and other creators to know themselves and their psychological functions better, we can also perhaps contribute to the entire creative enterprise.

Some assumptions are necessary. I have defined creativity fairly strictly—the state or the production of something *both new and valuable*—and I have focused primarily on outstanding achievement. I have also restricted my use of such psychoanalytic concepts as primary process thinking to the well-established aspects of their functioning. Although there have been advances and modifications regarding this concept in recent years, there is solid substantiating data, clinical and other, of the basic core. To those who take a very broad view of what constitutes creativity and to those who emphasize the positive aspects of human processes and functions, including an emphasis on the revelatory and creative nature of dreams, I say that dreams do have high potential for revelation, a potential that depends however on the wisdom and sensitivity of the dream interpreter. I also focus here in general ways on the positive aspects of human functioning. I think it reasonable to consider a wide range of activities to be creative, but for scientific and methodological purposes, I restrict the field. To those who look here for scientific data pertaining to genetic and physiological functioning, I think the scientific skills and knowledge needed for obtaining such data are, unlike our psychological skills and knowledge, not now available. Moreover, I would caution against any heedless reduction of the highly complex and qualitative phenomenon of creativity at any time.

Throughout this book I am interested in all the adaptive and progressive aspects of the human psyche and in the skill and effectiveness of cognitive and perceptual structures. In art, I am interested in focusing on psychological factors pertaining to structure or form, not merely to content. It is the conscious willed aspect of creative functioning that takes center stage here. Creativity is a highly adaptive function. To approach it without such a recognition and methodological orientation is not to be scientifically neutral, but to be ensnared in reductionistic and ultimately blind perspectives and strategies.

A word about the approach to data. Included here are reports—one very extensive one—of the psychological information derived from interviews with creative persons. There are also reports of experiments and of systematic analyses of creative works of the past. In order to demonstrate the generality of my findings to fields other than those directly studied and to clarify the precise nature and operation of particular processes, I have also used published commentary by a wide variety of creative persons. When using such commentary, I have tried only to use material that was authentic within a total context of the person's life and work, rather than an incidental, or a highly dramatic, or a seemingly revealing statement. As a psychiatrist, I took nothing in the psychological realm at face value. To the extent possible, I exercised the same caution about motivation and indirect meanings in assessing public material as I did with the private material of interviews.

For the origins of my particular wide-ranging approach, I cite an early influence of my brother, Jerome Rothenberg, and his very broad interest and knowledge of the arts. The idea of empirical investigation began with my college exposure to Henry A. Murray, and my orientation to the particular combination of psychiatric interviewing together with the use of systematic and experimental techniques developed with the guidance and support of my teachers and colleagues, Theodore Lidz and George F. Mahl. Especially gratifying and helpful on the literary side has been the collaboration and support of Robert Penn Warren. The Research Scientist Career Development Award Program of the National Institute of Mental Health is responsible for enabling me to begin to work on this research on a full-time basis. They awarded me my first five-year grant for Studies in the Creative Process in 1964, and in 1969 they awarded me another. I owe a debt of gratitude both to the committees of this agency and to the late Bert E. Boothe, administrator of the program. Boothe was responsible for facilitating the development of many psychiatric researchers in the United States, and as a former English professor, he gave some special interest to my research. Since 1974, the research has been graciously and generously supported by the Estate of Gladys B. Ficke, administered by Ralph F. Colin, trustee. In the year 1974/75, I received a John Simon Guggenheim Memorial Foundation Fellowship, which allowed me time to work on this book.

For help with specific material in this book, I am grateful to Donald C. Gallup, curator of the Yale Collection of American Literature, for making available to me the manuscripts of Maxwell Anderson's *High Tor* and for comments about the extensive manuscripts of Eugene O'Neill's *The Iceman Cometh* earlier. Daniel P. Schwartz read the entire manuscript and Edward Casey did a careful reading of chapter 12 on time, space, and causality, and both made many valuable suggestions. Meredith Nunes and Brenda Casey did translations in German and French, respectively, and the latter provided counsel on a passage by Henri Poincaré in chapter 5. Eugene Shapiro, Maryan Aynsworth, and Robert Sobel all helped collect some of the data and illustrations used; Sobel particularly called my attention to some examples of fusion by Leonardo da Vinci. Others whom I thank for providing particular documents and information are René Dubos, John Wheeler, the late Carlotta O'Neill, Quentin Anderson, Philip C. Peters, Otto Nathan, Gerald Holton, and the American Institute of Physics. A very special debt of gratitude is owed to Marie LeDoux, who not only typed and organized all aspects of this manuscript but has devoted enormous energy to collecting data, and to researching bibliography, persons, dates, and quotations with her own special capacities for tracking down the obscure and difficult. I cannot meaningfully document here the spirit and degree of help provided by my wife, Julia, but I will say that her thoughtful comments and deep perceptions about style and content are reflected throughout.

INTRODUCTION
THE EMERGING GODDESS

Pallas Athena, the Greek goddess of wisdom and protectress of fortresses, is said to have been born by springing full-grown from the head of Zeus. So, too, great individual achievements in art, science, philosophy, theology, and other fields have often appeared to spring all at once from their creators. Like Athena, these grand works do not seem to traverse the ordinary pathways of gestation and delivery, and they appear before us as creations, entities with the qualities of completeness, vibrancy, and organic vitality. They are themselves the embodiment of wisdom, both rational and intuitive, and such creations possess the only tangible form of immortality we know.

The origins of this conception—not a myth in the sense of being false, but mythic in the sense of being both culturally and temporally a widely held and pervasive view—of human creativity and creations are not difficult to understand. Art especially has been a source of sustenance and deep gratification amidst the rigors of human experience; it has been a testification to the uniqueness of individuals, a source of ineffable wisdom, and a seeming buttress against the terrifying fact of mortality. Using the honorific term "creation" with respect to a work of art evokes an implicit and unavoidable connection with the beginning of the world and of life, the cardinal acts attributed to the divine. Moreover, the subjective experience for anyone working in the arts, regardless of level of competence, is of bringing forth something out of nothing: filling a blank page, producing sounds and rhythms out of silence, and so on. Such subjective experiences occur in other areas beside the arts, but in distinction there is often a keener sense of starting *somewhere,* with previous information or with materials already formed. Valued achievements in the arts therefore seem to be especially deserving of the honorific term. Great individual achievements in science or other fields often are considered creations precisely because they share the qualities of great works of art. They seem to leap far beyond the previously formed or known, or they seem to have been achieved in the scientist's mind by such extensive leaps. Our sense of the full-grown birth of these achievements is a crystallization of the feeling of extreme discrepancy between the unformed and the formed, the known and the unknown.

The persons responsible for individual achievements and creations, whatever the field, have themselves contributed to this mythic view. When asked about their achievements, or on voluntary report, they sometimes say that a full conception, a poem or other opus, came all at once. Or they say that critical aspects resulted from inspirations, the fully developed formulations that once were attributed to a muse or other divinity and nowadays are attributed to the workings of unconscious mental factors. When inspirations or other dramatic events are not reported, creators from ancient times up to the present have consistently and patiently explained that they do not know *how* their achievements came about. They may describe the circumstances, the steps they undertook, and, in the absence of inspirations, they may emphasize their hard work at every point of the way. In the case of scientists, they may explain the fully coherent and interlocking logic of the theory or of their experimental procedures, but they do not describe the exact type of thought processes, emotions, and life history factors leading to the creation—that is, the creative process itself. This is not due to some form of wantonness, lack of sophistication (psychological or otherwise), or even to a lack of observational power. Neither is it frequently due to a desire to increase the public's awe and admiration for their accomplishments nor a wish to contribute to the mythic view about creation nor, as some poets have confessed as an intention,[1] to give an aura of a spontaneous or mystical quality to their work. Creators, while they are engaged in the creative process, do not, and generally cannot, pay very much attention to keeping track of exactly what they think and do, or of the nature and origins of their thoughts and behavior. When they complete their work, moreover, they themselves are often awestruck by the immensity of their accomplishment and, standing back or introspecting, they too adopt the mythic view. In such cases, a view of the accomplishment as both inexplicable and arising virtually full-grown from an unknown or outside source seems somehow valid; such a view is at least more comfortable than fully bearing the otherwise weighty pride and responsibility.

To understand creating scientifically, then, requires some means of viewing or figuratively photographing the goddess as she is emerging. A large task it is, to be sure, but one that will be the major purpose of this book. The focus here will be on the creative process in the individual: the thought processes, the affects, the experiences, and the psychodynamic structure of the psychological events connected to creating. A good deal of attention will be paid to the types of creations constituting mankind's great accomplishments, although definite limitations will be necessary. For one thing, many such creations are the result of large-scale cultural factors operating during long periods of history or they arise from the tightly interlocking work of certain groups, such as the contributions among scores of scientific investigators over a period of several decades or centuries. These types of creations cannot be attributed to the particular contribution of a single individual. On the other hand, even when a creation can be connected to the thought or work of a single individual, as it can in the arts, many cultural and historical factors still play an important role. In science, accumulated knowledge and investigation is so important in any advance that it is difficult to define and isolate a particular individual's contribution even in famous cases. In focusing on the creative process in the individual, such limitations of scope and application will be taken for granted throughout and only discussed when they have particular bearing or seem to be modifying circumstances. The role of such factors as baroque style, cultural upheaval, modern theories of art, technological advance, and other such matters that are the important concern of the critic, the art historian, the sociologist, and the philosopher of art and science will not generally be discussed directly here. The influence of such factors will, however, dictate the manner of presentation of evidence. Individual creations from diverse cultures and diverse periods of history will be considered.

Another limitation, and an expansion, concerns the definition of what constitutes a creation. Though many of mankind's achievements have been called creations, the terms "achievement" and "creation" are not synonymous. In the most literal dictionary definition sense, creating is merely "bringing something into being." As generally used, however, the term almost invariably has a connotation of positive value. "Bringing something into being" does not include a specification that the "something" be new, but we must also add this specification if we are to draw distinctions between creations and mere productions, manufactured or spontaneously generated. The creative process,[2] as conceived and discussed here, consists of the series of thoughts, acts, and functions that results in a product with attributes of *both* newness and positive value. Consequently, included as creations will be neither automobiles, chairs, body secretions, nor imitations, reproductions, and achievements such as excellently worked items of craft. Many specific aspects of a work of art, though it be an immortal masterpiece, would also not necessarily be created according to this definition. Imitated features or representations of the style of a period, unless initiated by the author of that work, would not be new and would not in themselves be creations. The study of artistic creation, therefore, does not pertain to all aspects of art works and of aesthetics.

Many achievements would not qualify as having newness as well as positive value, but the definition allows for an expansion beyond great creations. As I have not included a designation of the degree of positive value in the definition, nor can I appropriately do so, many creations other than those constituting mankind's greatest achievements will be considered. Positive value is notoriously difficult to pin down and analyze. Who, for example, decides the degree of positive value in a particular accomplishment? Is it the contemporary society, the "judgment of history," the prize givers, the critics, the man on the street? Difficult as this question is for aestheticians, historians, and the like, it is even more difficult for the scientist investigating the nature of the creative process. The scientist requires an objective criterion and therefore the only solution from his point of view is to invoke the principle of consensus or consensual judgment. Products generally considered to be creations by consensus, products consensually determined to have both newness and positive value, either intrinsic or instrumental positive value,[3] will be discussed here. This approach ensures that many outstanding achievements will be included, as consensus about value and newness with such achievements is high, but it also allows for a consideration of a fairly wide range of creations. Though some will disagree about this wider range and challenge the consensus about some examples of creations and creators included in this book, such is the inevitable outcome of the complexity of the task.

Another limitation pertains to method. In order to get a complete view of the goddess emerging, the specific factors in the creative process, one might want perhaps to *be there* while the process is unfolding. Though this is clearly impossible with creations of the past, those that are said to "stand the test of time," one might conceive of some device, an apparatus of wires and tapes perhaps, that would allow such investigation with contemporary creators. On the basis that such direct observation would unduly influence the process being observed, not to mention the grotesquerie of a strapped up and plugged in creator, that particular method was not employed. Nevertheless, all the methods used—interviews, manuscript reconstructions, experiments, and analysis of primary source documentary evidence—have been geared toward getting as close to the unfolding process as possible. The photograph of the emerging goddess is therefore a composite one, developed from bits and pieces from different methods and perspectives. In the case that begins this volume, however, I attempt to present a detailed and extensive documentary motion picture of a particular instance of her birth.

Forms of Creativity

There are many possible approaches to creativity; why then has this particular focus been adopted? Why, for instance, have I limited the definition to the *production* of the new and valuable, a definition implying tangible accomplishments and tangible products? Taking an Eastern view of creativity, one could study subjective states said to be creative and avoid considerations of newness and value, as they would be unrelated or otherwise inapplicable to such phenomena. Or taking a view that has become increasingly popular in the United States, one could study a presumed potential for creativity in everyone and, also very popular, one could attempt to develop methods for maximizing such potential and facilitating its expression. As an initial answer, I believe that tangible artistic, scientific, social, and intellectual creations are highly important and of wide pervasive interest. The major reasons for adopting the focus on new and valuable tangible products, however, are scientific. To adopt the Eastern view, or any position—Western or Eastern—that defines creativity or a creation as a subjective state of mind, would make consensual validation and scientific assessment virtually impossible. Despite the current interest in what has been called "intersubjective validity," it is enormously difficult to formulate a satisfactory way of consensually assessing the meaning of a statement such as, "I feel more creative now," or of a description of a meditative state in which peace, harmony, and creativity are said to be achieved.

To adopt the view that the potential for creativity exists in everyone also raises problems of consensual assessment. As such a position begins with potential rather than realization, it is a matter of assumption and belief rather than demonstrated fact. Not that I mean to say that science does not, or should not, begin with assumptions—that would be patently false and fatuous—but I do mean that the particular assumption of everyone having potential for creativity is a diffuse and difficult one to operationalize. The term creativity is so honorific that it is often not clear whether those assuming this potential in everyone are referring to the basic worth or potential for growth of human beings or to some general capacity for high artistic and intellectual achievement. If it is the former, such worth and potential can surely be taken for granted, and can warrant separate study as well as nurturance. If the latter is the case, it would seem crucial first of all to define and to elucidate the processes involved in high artistic and other types of creation in order to know how to recognize them. If these processes are found to resemble certain general ones in everyone or, contrariwise, if they are found to be qualitatively different in a gifted few, a great deal of energy and effort can be saved. If a connection to yet another form of production or state is what is meant—for example, creative living, creative thinking, or a creative outlook—then the question of consensual agreement again arises. Despite the difficulty in obtaining consensual agreement about particular works in the arts, there is at least consensual agreement that such types of works deserve to be designated as creations. Also, in fields such as the arts, a person producing one creation, or two or more, can be operationally defined as having creative potential. Even though we cannot theoretically assume that such a person will always produce creations, most of us would call that person definitely creative, or a proven creator.[4]

Tangible products allow the scientist to compare, replicate, and discuss his findings. With this in mind, there is surely the possibility of studying such commonly designated creative activities as creative cooking, creative carpentry, creative sewing, creative ball playing, or creative performance in any field. The idea of a potential for creativity in everyone may indeed appropriately refer to such diverse manifestations. But again consensual validation can be a problem because social valuation of these activities is highly variable. There is no intrinsic reason not to study these more general types of production and I personally would endorse attempts to maximize and nurture creativity in such areas, as well as in thought, life-style, and so on, if it could be meaningfully defined there. Moreover, the findings presented in this book could, in ways that are suggested by the broad considerations at the end, apply in numerous areas. From my clinical work with patients, I already know the findings have pertinence to psychotherapy. The data presented here, however, are derived primarily from the fields of art, science, philosophy, social thought, and theology—fields consensually recognized as producing definite creations, that is, entities considered both new and clearly valuable.

Creativity and Its Discontents

Though creativity is a hallowed, honorific term, creative people are not always accepted and recognized. To some extent, the reasons for this are clear. Creative thinking deviates from ordinary modes and is sometimes at odds with standard rules and conventions. Creative people sometimes oppose and seriously criticize the dominant values of the society in which they live. Such deviance and confrontation can be so threatening as to preclude any social recognition of creative achievement. Even without direct confrontation and criticism, however, the appearance of anything moderately or radically new has, throughout all cultures and history, tended to produce an experience of discomfort and a pressure to resist it. A good deal of neglect has occurred. Mendel's work on genetics was not at all accepted until long after his death and Copernicus did not publish his work during his lifetime out of fear of serious reprisal and criticism. Galileo's travail, Mozart's, Rembrandt's, and Poe's ignominious deaths, and past rejection of many great creators is well known today. Resistance to change, resistance to the new, is strong. On the other hand, seeking out and accepting the new has also operated, and sometimes creators and creations have been immediately recognized. More of this is needed, but without a mindless advocacy. New theories, styles, or forms of behaviors should not be accepted merely because they are new. Routine and obsessive seeking for the new can be a way of denying the truly valuable. Merely seeking and accepting the new can be an avoidance of effort or thoughtful evaluation. As it then becomes fruitless, obsessively seeking the new can be an insidious way of maintaining the status quo.

Society and creative people tend to be ambivalent toward each other. On the one hand, society rewards creations with its highest honors and holds creators in awe and esteem. On the other hand, there is a tendency to suspiciousness and even fear because of the creator's deviance from rules and his emphasis on the new. Sometimes widespread jealousy of the immensity of an individual's achievement even operates. Creative people, in their right, tend to feel strongly about society. They tend to have strong positive feelings of concern for other human beings and strong personal idealism. From their point of view, severe criticism of a particular convention or of a factor of social order arises from such positive devotion to other people. While they sometimes seek change or novelty for its own sake and sometimes feel resentful about being unrewarded and unrecognized, they experience a severe discrepancy between their attachment for society and its reaction to them.

Related to this mutual ambivalence is an issue that constantly comes up in discussions about the psychology of the creative process, or of creativity: the relationship between creativity and psychological illness. Centuries ago, the Roman savant, Seneca, insisted that "the mind . . . cannot attain anything lofty so long as it is sane," and he referred both to Plato's connecting poetry with madness and quoted Aristotle—from an unknown source—as saying, "no great genius was without a mixture of insanity."[5] And Shakespeare, in *A Midsummer Night's Dream,* said: "The lunatic, the lover and the poet / Are of imagination all compact" (act 5, sc. 1, lines 7–8). Constant reference to the eccentricities and unusual behavior of geniuses and other highly creative people is made in both serious and popular writings and in common everyday conversation. In fact, there is fairly well documented evidence that several of these people, geniuses and highly creative persons in the arts, sciences, and other fields, have suffered from manifest psychosis at various periods of their lives.[6] The issue is a serious and complex one. Though there is mutual ambivalence between creative people and society, that alone does not account for the number who have been psychotic, nor for the widespread interest in this issue. I bring it up with respect to the mutual ambivalence, because the folkloristic connecting of creativity and psychological disturbance is clearly exaggerated. While it is difficult to carry out a full and thorough investigation of the matter, there has never been evidence to support such allegations. On the contrary, on the basis simply of numbers and percentages, a large majority of well-known creative people have shown no evidence of suffering from serious psychological disturbance. Society's ambivalence toward creative people has led to an overemphasis on supposedly detrimental information.

Yet, documented evidence of some psychosis and serious psychological disorder among creative people has been puzzling. As creations are very highly valued, and as creative activity seems to be a highly productive and psychologically adaptive aspect of personality functioning, how can these disorders be explained? For the creative person himself, working sometimes unrecognized and in opposition to society, how can he know whether his difficulties, or even his point of view, result from illness? While I would not presume, nor would it be medically meaningful, to provide an answer that would apply to each individual case, the understanding of the creative process emerging from the pages to follow has direct bearing on the matter. The creative process, as the evidence will show, is itself a healthy, adaptive personality function. Psychological disturbance, therefore, bears a complicated relationship to creativity, a relationship in which social factors play a role, though not necessarily a decisive one.

Investigatory Approach

Another problem stemming from the variable acceptance and recognition of creativity pertains to the investigatory approach to the phenomenon. When empirical research, such as this study, is based on evidence derived primarily from contemporary creators, there is the risk that some currently unrecognized but highly creative person may be totally missed or overlooked. There is also the risk of overemphasizing creative modes appropriate only to the contemporary scene. I attempt in part to overcome the latter risk and difficulty by presenting material from the work and thought of creators from diverse periods of history throughout this book. To some extent, this overcomes the implications of the former risk as well, because the creators cited include some who were recognized in their time and some who were not. The cardinal means used to overcome the pitfall of overlooking contemporary creative persons, however, have been the specific criteria used for selection of my research subjects.

The major evidence upon which this book is based was derived from numerous series of research psychiatric interviews. These interviews were carried out with subjects who were selected as being highly creative in the arts (literary and otherwise) and in science. Specifically designed to focus on the creative process as directly as possible, the interviews were regularly scheduled on a weekly or biweekly basis, were very intensive, and were carried out, in most cases, over an extended period of time. For the collection of data reported in this study, I have carried out over 1,690 hours of interviews with these research subjects, in several cases continuing regularly scheduled interviews over a period of three or four years. Selection of the subjects was based on a dual criterion which consisted of the following: recognition as creative by society and recognition as creative by peers.

The selection procedure involved the specific designation by a literary critic, eminent scientist, or other qualified person (not myself) of persons who were highly creative in their fields. In most cases, such persons had already received one or more major artistic or scientific award or honor: Nobel Prize, Pulitzer Prize; National Book Award; Bollingen Poetry Prize; Gold Medal for Poetry; designation as Poet of the Library of Congress; membership in the American Academy of Arts and Letters, the National Institute for Arts and Letters, the American Academy of Arts and Sciences, the National Academy of the Sciences, or the Royal Society of London. In a separate determination, I obtained assessments of these same persons by their artist or scientist peers. Hence, two independent ratings of highly creative persons were used. Many prominent and recognized creators were subjects in this research—many of the most outstanding American writers especially and several of the leading American scientists. Of the two criteria used for selection, assessment by peers was given greater weight, however, so that several subjects who were not major award winners were included. As a result, several creators, as yet unrecognized by society at large, were also studied.

Overall, fifty-seven highly creative men and women have been subjects in this interview research. Because they are guaranteed confidentiality at the outset and because of the sensitive and confidential nature of some of the material discussed in the interviews and reported here, their names cannot be given. Two other types of subjects have also been studied in a manner similar to that used with the outstandingly creative persons. One type of subject consisted of novice literary creators, persons who were identified by a teacher or a critic as having creative potential. Independent creativity assessments from peers were also obtained for these subjects who varied in age (young adulthood to middle age), sex, ethnic background, and socioeconomic status. The other type of subject studied consisted of noncreative persons—noncreative in literature—who agreed to attempt fiiction or poetry writing for a fee. All subjects of all types were offered a fee for participation in the research.

The overall design and purpose of the research psychiatric interview included the following: (1) systematic discussion of work in progress or recently completed with a focus on affects, motivations, and thought processes involved in carrying out the task; (2) systematic discussion of particular phenomena in the artistic, scientific, or intellectual process: initial ideas, new ideas during the course of the work, revisions or changes, and overall conceptions, along with dreams, associations, and life circumstances (present, past, or future) connected to any of these factors; (3) exploration and assessment of subject's verbal and nonverbal behavior in connection with descriptions, explanations, experiences, and associations pertinent to the work in progress; (4) exploration and evaluation of special issues and hypotheses: (*a*) adaptive and defensive operations during the creative process: appearance of anger, depression, happiness, anxiety, sexual arousal, and their effects; role of wish fulfillment, identity, development, specific defenses, attempts at mastery of present and future internal and external events; (*b*) nature of thought processes: use of imagery, special types of thinking, effect of drugs and alcohol, role of inspiration, state and condition of consciousness, function of peripheral thoughts and ideas; (*c*) communication functions: does the creator have a particular person or audience in mind during the process of creation? Is there evidence for an unconscious communication process? Is there a pure expression function in artistic creation? (5) at the end of the interview series, formulation of hypotheses about psychological processes operating during the work in progress, and direct discussion and assessment of these hypotheses with the subject.

As will be seen in the detailed report of interview findings contained in the first portion (chaps. 1, 3, 4) of this book, many other areas were also covered. I had originally adopted an interview approach to creativity in order to be able to capture as much of its freewheeling, unexpected, innovative pathways as possible. Therefore, although I kept the above overall design in mind, the interviews were conducted in an unstructured manner. In following the undulating, uncharted pathways of the process,[7] the research subject was a vital and full collaborator.

Other research methods have consisted of special reconstructions of the creative process through objective and statistical studies of archived literary manuscripts—a means of studying outstanding creations of the past—and of special psychological experiments designed to test specific hypotheses and carried out with subjects of the interview studies as well as with additional groups of creative and noncreative research subjects. The design of the overall research project has been presented elsewhere[8] and several specific studies will be described here.

Nature of the Findings

The picture of the emerging goddess described in this book is multidimensional and widely focused. Many fields and complex psychological issues are viewed. Reference to previous related research on creativity appears throughout this work. I shall not here present a comprehensive review of the literature, because I have done so previously.[9] Some brief comments about the hypotheses of previous investigators are necessary, however, in order to highlight the sharp differences from the findings presented here.

Drawing primarily on studies in perception, Frenkel-Brunswik and her associates described a personality trait or factor of "tolerance for ambiguity."[10] Such a factor surely has a broad and general relationship to creativity. Creative people are able to tolerate ambiguities in perception and in concepts, as are many other types of people, but there is no specific or necessary connection with creative functioning. Ambiguity is a general term referring to multiple meanings, but the term does not include a necessary or intrinsic relationship among these meanings. Although art products convey multiple meanings or multiple levels of experience, and this is surely a factor in their appeal, multiple meanings and levels in art are not merely randomly connected with each other. Ambiguity alone may be diffuse and chaotic. An ambiguous event, phrase, or form may be obscure rather than new and valuable. Even if the definition of ambiguity is modified to denote multiple *related* meanings, tolerance for such ambiquity would not necessarily be directly involved in creating. Producing ambiguity or multiple related meanings is not the same as tolerating such phenomena, the latter being only a receptive attitude. The specific types of thinking as shall be described in this book are *necessary* to produce creations. While the general type of flexibility of thought and perception involved in tolerance for ambiguity may in some broad way be related to creativity, flexibility of any type must still include specific factors producing new and valuable connections. As a personality trait or attitude, constant tolerance for ambiguity can even be countercreative. For some phases in the creative process an orientation to precision and an *in*tolerance for ambiguity and diffusion are vital.

The lack of specificity and of a necessary connection to creativity also differentiates Mednick's theory of remote associates from the findings to follow. Mednick proposed that creative thinking was based on the combination of elements that were remotely associated with one another. As he put it, "The more mutually remote the elements of the new combination, the more creative the process or solution."[11] The mechanisms he described for producing such combinations were the associational ones of serendipity (accidental contiguity of elements), similarity, and mediation. Rather than an associational meeting of contiguous, similar, or indirectly connected and mediated mental elements, the processes to be described here are active, directed forms of cognition in which the creator intentionally and in distinct ways brings particular types of elements together. Elements are juxtaposed, brought together, and/or integrated rather than being merely added or combined. Other sharp differences also obtain. Mednick's definition of remoteness is based on infrequent connection on word association tests, and his Remote Associates Test for Creativity assesses the ability to connect such rarely associated words. Rather than remoteness and rare association, distinct antitheses and oppositions as well as strong similarities and connections are involved in the creative operations presented in this book.

Arthur Koestler's theory of bisociation refers not only to thought processes but very broadly to any biological, psychological, or social phenomenon.[12] Bisociation consists of the coming together or association of two self-consistent but habitually incompatible frames of reference. Koestler considers creation to be a matter of a single act rather than a process, and his theory, like Mednick's, is based on the principle of association of elements or entire frames of reference. Rather than the several opposite or antithetical factors involved in the cognitive process to be described here, merely two habitually incompatible elements or frames of reference are Koestler's bases of creation. Postulating a combination of the two, rather than a juxtaposition, bringing together and positing of several, and describing habitual incompatibility, rather than active opposition and antithesis, are keenly and radically different. As will become clear here (chap. 8), opposition involves reciprocity within the same category as well as difference. Opposites are not merely incompatible, they are specifically different and specifically resistant to each other. Also, instead of being an intentional active process, bisociation results from the random concatenation and coming togther of habitually incompatible frames of reference. As a complete theory of creativity, it does not explain how new aspects of creations can result merely from a combination of previously existing and fully developed frames of reference.

Lateral thinking, a term introduced by DeBono,[13] refers to the capacity to shift the context of thought from ordinary or "vertical" progressions. This type of thinking is somewhat similar to tolerance for ambiguity in its shifting away from fixed, predefined concepts and it is also quite similar to the productive-thinking mechanism, the "breaking of old gestalts" or the shifting out of habitual formulations, ways of seeing, or contexts, proposed some time ago by Wertheimer.[14] Such formulations about creative thinking define its general direction away from ordinary thought, but in their generality they provide no way at all to draw a distinction with other aberrant or deviating modes such as, for example, the thinking of schizophrenia.

The divergent-production factor of Guilford[15] was derived from analyzing creativity tests and their responses. Operationally, capacity for divergent response to open-ended questions that have no single appropriate answer differs from convergent-production, appropriate response to questions with a defined solution. Guilford has also emphasized the importance of factors of fluency, flexibility, originality, elaboration, and evaluation in creative performance. In his model of the intellect, divergent production is the most relevant overall characteristic of creative thinking, but convergent production also plays some role. While the divergent-production construct has the advantage of being operationally defined, it primarily refers to a capacity to generate multiple alternates in a general way and to deviate from a focused or convergent mode of problem solving. There is no explanation of the appropriateness or of the effectiveness of any particular divergent response. In distinction to processes I shall describe, divergent production is quite general and nonspecific to creativity. Divergent production does not involve antithesis, contradiction, or opposition, and it is a factor or trait of intellectual functioning rather than a psychological process operating psychodynamically within a personality system.

Turning to aesthetics, or, more precisely, artistic criticism, I would emphasize to literary readers and to art and music historians that the findings presented here do not pertain solely to particular literary or artistic movements such as romanticism or surrealism. Antithesis, contradiction, and opposition are often considered to be guiding principles or attributes of romanticism, both within the late-nineteenth-century artistic movement described by that name and for artists from varying periods of history manifesting a romantic type of style. I would not quarrel with this precept of art history and criticism, and I would not deny that expression of antitheses may frequently have been an intentional goal of so-called romantic artists. I want to emphasize, however, that the evidence presented here comes both from romantic and classical periods and from artists operating in a so-called classical style. Furthermore, though attributes of the created product are frequently considered, my research is focused on the *process* of achieving creations. Factors operating during the course of the creative process, such as those to be described, can change and be transformed along the way. Their effects may or may not be manifest in the final product. Consequently, factors appearing early in the process can be distinctly independent from an intention to incorporate manifest antitheses in the completed work of art.

Similar considerations apply with respect to surrealism. Though depicting manifest opposites, antitheses, and spatial distortions in completed works have been intentional goals for artists of this school, thought processes involving such images and formulations have not in any way been their special province. Surrealists often attempt to produce art with a dreamlike content, but like all artists their attempts at a particular goal are not always effective. The creative thought processes described here, however, function in a structural way to produce effective art rather than only art with particular types of content, be it oppositional, antithetical, or dreamlike. Consequently, these thought processes operate to produce *successful* surrealist creations, just as they produce successful creations of other types.

Creativity is such an important phenomenon and so many thinkers have explored it that any claim for exhaustively unique findings would be presumptuous. Philosophers, artists, critics, and others concerned with aesthetics especially have, in their deep and penetrating studies of art, touched on aspects of what will be reported here. Some will see echoes of Blake's and Coleridge's formulations about the importance of form and of opposites[16] and of Kenneth Burke's "perspectives by incongruity"[17] in the material to follow. Others, because of my focus on opposites, will emphasize connections with Eastern philosophies; because of my use of the names of the Roman god Janus or of the Greek goddess Athena in my terms and references about creativity, they might insist on the deep wisdom incorporated in Greco-Roman mythology.[18] I would not deny the very broad and general relatedness of these sources nor, in my emphasis on distinctions from other positions, deny all validity to them. None of the findings were inspired by or at all derived from these sources or positions, however. They came originally from empirical studies of creators engaged in creating. I was not even familiar with most of these particular conceptualizations during the major portion of my investigations.

Many formulations about creativity, including those just mentioned, are so broad and all encompassing that they pertain to a wide variety of effects in art and in human behavior. They thus include aspects of art, problem solving, and achievements of many kinds. Such views of the goddess emerging are very very panoramic indeed, and they are therefore diffuse, misty, and blurred. In the specificity of data, results, and theory presented here is a scientific, naturalistic, and sharpened focus.

1

CREATION OF A POEM

I will attempt to illustrate the psychological processes involved in creativity through the analysis of the creation of a specific poem. The poem was written by a subject of mine and presented to me during a research interview, one interview in the course of a long series. The subject is a major American poet and, for my investigation, he has proved to be cooperative and insightful to an extraordinarily high degree. At the time the poem was written, I had worked with him for more than three years and so I knew him quite well at that point. The schedule had been two-hour weekly and biweekly appointments. At the beginning of each session, the poet presented to me the manuscript material of the work he had done since the last appointment and we then discussed this material. During the course of our meetings he had written and shown me many poems, from first draft to last, but the one I will discuss is the one I believe we learned the most about. This is partly because I had begun tape-recording our sessions some months before and therefore have an unusually detailed and accurate account of our discussion of this particular poem, and partly because we had been meeting for so long and knew and trusted each other so well that this discussion became especially deep and illuminating. But, most important of all, an event occurred during the writing of this poem which I had been waiting for all along: the subject reported a dream occurring shortly after he began the poem, a dream that offered information elucidating some of the psychological processes involved in the poem's creation.

Long before this, dream analysis had become a central focus of our discussions. The subject had, on his own, decided to keep a careful record of his dreams and a large portion of our weekly or biweekly sessions was devoted to trying to understand the relationship of his dreams with his poetry. The reasons for this mutual focusing on dreams and poetry will become clear in the discussion to follow. The point I want to emphasize now is that we had both become quite used to dream analysis in the sessions and, I believe, quite skilled in the practice of analyzing his dreams. Although our discussion of dreams had all along done much to elucidate various aspects of his poetic creation in progress, never before had he been able to describe the thoughts associated with the inception of a poem in minute detail and never before had he recorded a dream occurring shortly after beginning a poem.

Here is the final version of the poem presented to me:

In Monument Valley*

One spring twilight, during a lull in the war,
At Shoup's farm south of Troy, I last rode horseback.
Stillnesses were swarming inward from the evening star
Or outward from the buoyant sorrel mare

Who moved as if not displeased by the weight upon her.
Meadows received us, heady with unseen lilac.
Brief, polyphonic lives abounded everywhere.
With one accord we circled the small lake.

Yet here I sit among the crazy shapes things take.
Wasp-waisted to a fault by long abrasion,
The "Three Sisters" howl, "Hell's Gate" yawns wide.
I'm eating something in the cool Hertz car

When the shadow falls. There has come to my door
As to death's this creature stunted, cinder-eyed,
Tottering still half in trust, half in fear of man—
Dear god, a horse. I offer my apple-core

But she is past hunger, she lets it roll in the sand,
And I, I raise the window and drive on.
About the ancient bond between her kind and mine
Little more to speak of can be done.

To begin, we must agree that these lines constitute a poetic creation. I shall not here engage in a lengthy and digressive literary critique or dissertation in aesthetics, nor would it be appropriate to do so. As a scientist, my purpose is to discover the nature of the psychological processes leading to creations. The attributes of both newness and value, establishing that a particular product is a creation, are designated by consensus. Though admittedly the nature of this consensus is quite complex, it must be the scientist's guide. If I studied products that I alone judged to be creations, I would likely be choosing data

* This poem is protected by copyright and is reprinted by permission; the author's name is withheld upon request.

that fit my preconceived theories. I believe this poem to be new and to have intrinsic aesthetic value. I trust that the reader agrees.

Now, to the creation of the poem: where did it start? When all the facts are known, we may end up deciding that the poem started in the poet's childhood. Biologists might insist it began in the poet's genes and Jungians might heatedly argue for its origin in the Collective Unconscious. I would like first to make my goals more modest than those implied by such far-sweeping theoretical positions. I shall recount some of the information the poet gave me about the specific material in the poem and some other pertinent data; I shall then go further from there.

During an extended visit to the southwestern United States, the poet and a male friend made a visit to Monument Valley, Arizona. Named from the unusual natural rock formations resembling monuments or statues of humans and animals, this valley is located in the Colorado Plateau, east of the Grand Canyon and Rainbow Bridge, a bleak, arid region. Many of the rock formations have been given names, among which are Elephant Rock and Two Sisters. Although the two friends attempted to have a picnic while viewing the monuments, the wind, as is often the case in that sandstone desert site, blew stinging sand into their faces and food. It was an unpleasant ex-experience and, as they were about to gather up and leave, a small bedraggled dark brown horse—"tiny and shrunken," he said—appeared on the scene. The horse was alone, unsaddled, and it moved toward them. The poet's friend, who had had a good deal of experience with horses and felt strongly about them, was immediately moved. He was excited by the horse's presence and by the strange and sudden way it appeared. The poet, preoccupied and bothered by the sand, was less immediately impressed but, partly because of the dramatic qualities of the circumstance and his friend's reaction, he thought to himself that someday he might write a poem about the experience.

Although he wrote many poems after that, he actually gave little or no further thought to the horse until, one morning approximately a week prior to one of our interview sessions, the horse came to his mind and he wrote the following lines:

> Hot pumice blew
> Through Monument Valley.
> The Elephant Rock ached
> The Three Sisters wailed.
> It was not the place for a picnic
> We ate in the car's shade, hunched over, at top speed
> Looking up, there was our guest, our ghost.
> At death's door
> Slender, tottering, liquid-eyed . . . .

Strikingly, these first few lines are virtually a simple description of the scene. Except for the poetic references to the aching of Elephant Rock and the wailing of the Three Sisters, they are a dim shadow of the final poem he wrote. Do these lines represent the beginning of the poem? In retrospect, it is hard to retrace the exact temporal sequence of thought. But when I asked the poet how he got the specific idea for the poem, he said the idea of the horse linked up to a poem written by Edwin Muir—I will quote the poet subject's description—"in which civilization has been entirely destroyed and there's a little cluster of men without any tools or skills. And suddenly they look up and the horses had come, standing around waiting to be used. And it would be the lever somehow by which things would get going again. And this feeling you have about tameable animals; I feel it particularly about animals that they don't need to be tamed, really, like dogs and cats—the funny way that they've, you feel, renounced their own kind in order to live our lives." I will return to discuss the significance of this early thought later. Now, it should be noted that his central conception relating to the horse was: *horses live human lives.* A horse, as he later said, was not a "beast," nor was it human, but it was both human and beast together.[1]

With this thought in mind, he wrote the next version of the poem:

Hot pumice blew through Monument Valley
Causing the Devil Rock and the 3 Sisters to shriek
It was hardly the time or the place for a picnic
Hunched over in the car's shade we gobbled bread and butter.
When we looked up there at our door our guest
At death's door rather, tottering stunted
Liquid-eyed: a horse, between starvation and distrust
By then we had only an apple-core to offer it
A tradition in China as in modern verse
Gives to each age its emblematic beast.

This second version still bears little resemblance to the final completed poem. The cliché "at death's door" from the first version has been enlivened by a direct comparison to the door of the car. The offering of an apple core, an idea retained in the final poem, has introduced some possible metaphysical overtones—an allusion to apples in the Garden of Eden as contrasted with the allusion to death. This version is, however, still primarily descriptive and the language structure somewhat prosaic. But the organizing idea—some would say the inspiration—is now present: the horse will be the emblematic beast for the age.

After writing these lines, the poet stopped working on the poem for that day. In his notebook, there had been one further line after the above which he had crossed out soon after writing it. This line was: "Years have passed since that day." Thus, he had begun to think about introducing a lapse of time into the descriptive sequence, but for the moment he did not develop it. As we know from the final poem, he eventually reversed the time sequence of this latter idea—the experience at Monument Valley is the present event and his experience of riding a horse himself is antecedent—but the notion of passage of time was clearly present at this early phase.

Having the poem in this partially germinated and dynamic phase, the poet went about his various social and professional activities for the rest of the day. He knew he was not going to be able to get back to work on the poem for a while because he was expecting a visitor and had plans to spend the next several days in a large city nearby. But, during sleep that night, he had the following two dreams (I quote his own description):

> Dream 1. J.T. [pseudonym initials of the poet's male friend] and I are on a trip or a visit. We come to a soccer field and feel like playing, even though one must pay to do so. If we start at once, we shall have two hours worth for a few dollars apiece. But the other players delay. Next, indoors, we are shown a room with two day beds. Miriam [pseudonym for a female friend] enters and begins compulsively to make up my bed—rather, to tear it apart under the guise of making it. I keep asking her not to, and finally am angry. She falls back in a swoon, dressed only in underclothes. Other people enter slowly: J.T. in a sweatshirt and a boring old couple I am stuck with throughout the party. I have made my own bed by then.
>
> Dream 2. I've taken a position in a large comfortable house. I am to be the companion of a very old woman—at least 100. After many preliminaries I am led (by my mother among others; but we treat each other like polite strangers) through halls and up stairs to arrive at the invalid's apartments. I expect her to be bedridden but in honor of the occasion she has risen to meet me at the door—an ancient dwarf with my grandmother's face, head smiling and enlarged, in a blue dress. My mother, with a practiced movement, takes the old creature onto her shoulders. I touch her hands. They are horribly small, a baby's—no, hands made by a plastic surgeon—the last joints missing from the fingers, and little false nails attached. We sit down to supper—she in her chair, I on the end of a chaise longue. Her teeth have little secondary fangs attached, which enable her to eat. People are watching. It is clear that we are going to be delighted with each other. In an unused electric heater is mounted a bad copy of a copy of a portrait, coarsely colored and printed, of R.L. [pseudonym initials of an old family friend]. There's some question of destroying it.

Is there a relationship between these two dreams and the poem he began writing during that day? Without considering the poet's specific associations to the elements in the dreams, we cannot know for certain. But before doing that, it is important to note some interesting structural and manifest similarities between the dreams and the poetic fragment. Dream 1 begins with elements reproducing the original circumstances stimulating the writing of the poem, and J.T. is the same friend with whom the poet made the "trip or visit" to Monument Valley. Although the poet and J.T. are represented in the dream as coming to a soccer field rather than to that particular tourist site, the friends are clearly making a pleasurable stop outdoors, a circumstance resembling their plan to have a pleasurable open-air picnic on their visit. Also, the discomfort, the sense of pressure of time, and the aborted pleasure involved in having to eat quickly at Monument Valley are retained in the elements pertaining to playing soccer in the dream: they must pay for playing, must start at once, and, disappointingly, the other players delay. Next, the female friend Miriam is represented in the dream as entering the door of the room just as the horse is represented in the poem as appearing at the door of the car. While the poet and his friend had not been indoors, nor had they retreated to the inside of their car when the horse appeared, the animal's sudden appearance at the door of their car had been the telling aspect of the experience.

In its overall outline, the manifest content[2] of the first dream and the experience described in the poetic fragments written that day had much in common. As the first fragments of the poem went no further than the horse's appearance, there is little further analogy with the remainder of the dream. Miriam in the dream goes on to behave in a servile and perhaps a beastlike fashion, and her mistrustfully tearing up an already made bed—"under the guise of making it"—along with her swoon, a swoon incorporating both a sense of weakness and a seductive or needy type of behavior, are somewhat analogous to the horse's distrustfulness along with starvation. More direct and definite analogies obtain, however, between the remainder of this first dream and the final version of the last section of the poem written several days later.

Before going into these analogies, I want to point out that dream 2 also has overt structural similarities to the poem. This dream also begins with a trip of sorts—"through halls and up stairs"—in pleasurable surroundings. Again, a figure—the grandmother—appears at a door, and this time the figure more closely resembles the horse of the poem. Much as the horse appeared surprisingly at the door—"when we looked up"—the grandmother unexpectedly rises to meet the dreamer. She is an ancient dwarf—the horse was "tiny and shrunken" —and she clearly shares the descriptive adjectives for the horse, "small," "gaunt," "tottering," "stunted," which the poet had written in the first fragments of the poem and on the margins of the manuscript.[3] Also, just as there was a picnic at Monument Valley and in the poem, there is a supper in the dream. Structure and sequence in the second dream are not quite as close to the poetic fragment as in the first one, but particular elements are definitely shared. The significance of the parallels I have just drawn for both dreams will become apparent shortly.

When I asked the poet for his thoughts and associations regarding the first dream, he indicated that Miriam was a friend of his and a friend of his mother whom he had been expecting on a visit during the day following the dream. She lived several hundred miles away and, after a couple of days' visit, a group of friends, including Miriam and the poet, had all planned to spend time at the city together. Although he liked her, he felt she had been oversolicitous to him in the past, and in some ways reminded him of his mother. Interestingly, the last time he had seen Miriam was during his trip to the southwestern United States, the same trip occasioning the visit to Monument Valley. Both had been guests at J.T.'s house at the time and, though she then had left some time before the two friends had gone to Monument Valley, her currently expected visit was surely the immediate factor reviving that experience in the poet's mind. He insisted, however, that he was not consciously thinking about Miriam, or her intended visit, when he began the poem.

As for his associations to dream 2, he immediately referred to some conversations he and I had had about the burdens imposed on offspring by parents, a connection suggested to him by the image of his mother taking his grandmother onto her back. He elaborated this theme with remembrances and anecdotes about his mother caring for his grandmother during a good part of the latter's terminal illness.

Then, he began to talk about his own relationship to his grandmother and remembered a period in his life, after his parents divorced, when he lived alone with his mother, his grandmother, and his grandmother's sister. The grandmother's sister had not been an actual member of the household but, on occasion, she visited for long periods. It was a time of his life, he said, that was relatively happy and serene. Although he had often had the task of staying at home and amusing his grandmother by playing cards with her, or going out with her to lunch, he felt that the attention he received from one, two, and often three women during this period more than compensated for any burdens. He related such feelings directly to feelings in the dream, saying that despite his being hired to take care of the old lady in the dream, he enjoyed being made much of by the women. Spontaneously, he added that the idea of destroying the photograph of the old family friend in the dream would mean the removal of—his words—"the minimal male presence in the house," his only competition for the women. Within the dream itself, he said laughingly, the photograph was to be destroyed on "aesthetic grounds."

After giving his associations, he went on to analyze further the meanings of these dreams himself.[4] He felt that the situation in dream 2 provided the underlying reason for his rejection of Miriam in dream 1.[5] Dream 2 indicated his relationship with important women in his life. Everything was pleasant on the surface, but women often could be terrible burdens with their own little weapons (the grandmother's fangs). In dream 1, Mariam attempted, under the pretense of helpfulness, to make a bed that did not need fixing. She attacked the bed in a "feverish" way and was consequently destructive and burdensome rather than helpful. At the end of that dream, therefore, he went ahead and made his own bed. And that meant the same as the figurative expression "to make one's bed"—he would go his own way.

Dream Analysis

From his own dream analysis, therefore, there are definite substantive connections between the final poem and the dream. The poem ends with the lines "About the ancient bond between her kind and mine / Little more to speak of can be done." The relationship with the horse and her kind is renounced, much as his relationship with Miriam is renounced in the dream. He goes it alone in the poem, driving off in his car, much as he makes his own bed in the dream.

Considering the many parallels between the dream and the poetic fragment, it is hardly likely that these substantive connections between the final poem and the dream are accidental. The mental events are clearly related to one another in a less than haphazard way and, with all the information from the poet himself at our disposal, we may hope to understand some of the lawful aspects of this relationship.

For one thing, it appears that dream 1 helped to provide a solution to an aesthetic problem raised by the writing of the poetic fragment during the day. From what the poet said about his thoughts about the poem, and from what he had actually written that day, we know he did not have the final lines of the poem in mind when he went to sleep. Only much later, while fully awake in the daytime, did they occur to him. Hence, there was a psychological continuity between his dreams and his later waking thoughts. The precise nature of this continuity is, I would insist, largely unconscious for the poet himself. It is possible, of course, that the poet had been consciously influenced by his dreams and/or his interpretation of their meaning during the writing of the final lines of the poem. Many poets do try to use their dreams in such a conscious way when they create poetry. But even if this were so—the poet distinctly said that he was *not* thinking of

Miriam or of the dream when writing the poem, but he could have forgotten by the time we talked about it—there would still be an unconscious factor or set of factors linking the involuntary dream in a continuity to his voluntary decision to use the dream or its interpretation in the poem. No one would maintain, I am sure, that poetic decisions are dictated totally by conscious considerations.

To understand the nature of this continuity beyond merely saying that it is unconscious, let us look further at the psychological meaning of the dreams. Here, we are on surer ground than the still treacherous sands of the poem itself because psychoanalysis has established that the psychological function of dreams is the fulfillment of wishes.[6] Can we then establish a basic wish or wishes expressed in these dreams? Is the poet's insightful interpretation complete when he suggests that the psychological meaning of the dreams is the same as the statement of the final line of the poem, he will make his own bed and go his own way? It is important to ask this, because if "going his own way" were the basic wish expressed in both the dreams, the question about the nature of the continuity between dream and poem would be answered at the start. If the dreams merely functioned as a disguised expression of the poet's wish to be on his own or, more deeply, a wish to be free of bonds and encumbrances, then the poetic statement, as incorporated in the final line of the poem, would also be essentially an expression of wish fulfillment disguised in slightly different terms. Although many psychological analysts of poetry would be happy with a conclusion that art is essentially a form of wish fulfillment and directly analogous to dreams—they often assume this automatically when analyzing a finished poem or theorizing about creativity[7]—we cannot easily accept that conclusion here. Surely there is some element of wish fulfillment in the final aspect of dream 1, the poet's making his own bed, but to stop at that would ignore other important portions of the dreams and the poet's associations to them.

The poet himself, it will be remembered, sensed that the temporal sequence of the two dreams reversed an actual psychological sequence, that dream 2 represented the circumstances leading to the outcome in dream 1. Also, the poet's major association to dream 2 was that the content related to a discussion he and I had had, in our previous session together, about the burdens parents impose on children. Although he was specifically referring to the burden represented by the dream image of his grandmother upon her daughter's back, there was another burden represented for him as well, the burden of caring for the grotesque invalid old woman. But rather than experiencing distress about such an onerous burden, he was pleased, even delighted, at the prospect. What is the reason for such a paradoxical reaction? The answer—and the key to the major wish fulfillment of the dreams—lies in another portion of the same dream and the poet's associations to it.

Quoting directly from the poet's description of his dreams, "In an unused electric heater is mounted a bad copy of a copy of a portrait, coarsely colored and printed, of R.L. There's some question of destroying it." This, the poet suggested, indicated a minimal male presence in the house—a substitute for the artificial heat of the electric heater —who was the poet's only competition. R.L. himself was an old family friend (a little older than the poet's mother) whose wife had died. The poet's own father had died some years after divorcing his mother. Since his mother had remarried a man who also had died, this eligible widower had currently become a potential competitor for the poet's mother, a possible third husband. His picture was a "bad copy of a copy of a portrait," suggesting that, as a potential husband for the poet's mother, he was both a poor replica of the poet's own father (the real painting or "a portrait") and a symbol for the father himself. The "copy of a copy" construction also suggests other interpretations in terms of three levels of relatedness. Three male generations are suggested and therefore a two-generations-removed grandfather as competition for the poet's grandmother could inferentially be included, although there were no specific associations regarding this. With respect to his grandmother and the picture, then, this much is clear: the poet enjoys taking on the burden of his invalid grandmother because he has both women to himself. He has replaced all males in these women's lives, including (symbolically) his father, his recently deceased stepfather, R.L., and perhaps his grandfather, who are all relegated to an unused electric heater and will probably be destroyed. The primary or basic wish fulfillment, therefore, is the attainment of the major role in his mother's and grandmother's lives —with all its burdens—in order to receive the deep pleasure of being the major focus of their attention.

With this in mind, we can reconstruct the primary psychological meaning of the two dreams as follows: dream 2 represents the fulfillment of the forbidden oedipal wish, replacement of the father and sole possession of the mother (as well as the grandmother who is both a love object in her own right and, in all probability, a representation of the mother herself in advanced years). As the poet suggested, the situation in dream 2 leads to the outcome in dream 1. The realization of the oedipal wish in dream 2 is associated with guilt, and in dream 1 he has to pay the piper. He and his friend come to a soccer field (the only sport he enjoyed in school, he told me) but they must pay for the enjoyment. They plan to play but are prevented from doing so by the other players. Next, Miriam, who is a friend of the poet's mother and, as he said, shares features of his mother's personality, assumes a maternal helping role by making his bed but eventually becomes destructive and sexually seductive in a manipulative way. Then he experiences only the burden of such a relationship. The "boring old couple" he is stuck with throughout the party very likely represent the poet's own parents—unidentified old couples in dreams frequently represent the dreamer's parents—but, even without recourse to such a specific interpretation, the sense of burden he felt is surely represented by the emotional quality of this portion of the dream. Finally, more in an act of desperation than an act of wished-for independence, the poet makes his own bed.

I have developed this primary interpretation of the dreams solely on the basis of the dreams themselves, the poet's associations to them, and information about the poet's background. So far I have made no mention of the content of the poem. But now I will confess that I myself was driven to this interpretation partly on the basis of the content of the poem and partly because of some other knowledge I had about the poet's further thoughts about the poem, knowledge I have yet to reveal. I trust I will be excused for this seeming deviousness when I explain that my purposes are scientifically methodological as well as dramatic. I have separated the dreams from the poem in order to be able to specify the relationship between dreaming and creating poetry more precisely. To use the poet's thoughts about the poem or to use the content of the poem to explain the dreams would require an assumption that such thoughts or poetic lines are psychologically equivalent to direct dream associations. Since I myself did use them somewhat in that way, I would not argue strongly against such an assumption. When we analyze dreams in psychotherapy, we know that the patient's behavior in the days preceding and following a dream can contribute to an understanding of the dream. So, too, the poet's thoughts about the poem that precede and follow his dreams could, in a sense, be considered as a type of association to the dreams. Despite these points, I believe I have so far demonstrated that the dreams can be interpreted without any direct recourse to the poem itself. I will say more about the importance of this methodological matter later. As for the dramatic purpose, I withheld his thoughts about the poem in order that the reader might share the sense of surprise and discovery I have experienced in the unraveling of the dark and knotted skein of dream thought and poetic creation. So, now, without any further pause for digression or explanation, I will plunge into the thick of it.

The Dreams in Relation to the Poem

The very first lines of the poem, the first fragment, had been written in a special notebook the poet used for initial ideas and thoughts about his poetry. Sometimes these initial ideas were simple poetic phrases or prose statements about method, and sometimes they were extensive fragments. In this notebook, the poet made a later entry the morning after writing the first fragment and having the dreams I just discussed, as follows: "His rider—he had never had a rider."

As he reflected about the poem that next morning, he later told me, he had a complex thought and image connecting the horse with a rider and he wrote that entry in his notebook in order to remember it.[8] He had decided at that point to give the horse in the poem a rider but did nothing further about that for the remainder of that day. In fact, he did not begin working on the idea of the rider until the next day, and he only developed it in a version resembling the first stanza of the final poem several days later. Though the idea of the horse and rider dominates the whole first portion of the poem (i.e., the first two stanzas), it was, as we now see, conceived well after the second portion.

What is the significance of that particular thought connecting the horse with a rider on the day after starting the poem and having the dreams? Ultimately, this idea had an important influence on the entire structure of the poem. But in addition to revealing a crucial step in the development of the poem, his telling me about this thought alerted me to the importance of the second of the two dreams. When he mentioned the rider idea, I felt a flash of illumination. Suddenly I realized that, in the second dream, *the poet's mother was carrying her own mother on her back, just as a horse carries a rider.*

Could this have been an accidental connection? I hardly thought so. First, the poet thought of the rider the morning after the dream and went on to incorporate the idea in a major way into the final poem. Second, he himself felt that the dream concerning his mother and grandmother was the primary one in an emotional sense. Consequently, the wishes and concerns of that second dream—the parent-child relationship represented by the mother carrying her mother on her back—must have been the major underlying focus of his dreams and of his unconscious mental processes. The analogy between the dream image and a major idea used in the poem, the arresting image of the mother carrying her mother on her back in conjunction with the idea of a horse carrying a rider, suggested to me that these underlying concerns about the burdens and gratifications of the parent-child relationship might also be a significant underlying emotional issue relating to the overall creation of the poem.

The remaining history of the writing of the poem bore out my supposition further. Later in the day following the dreams, the poet worked on the lines he had written the day before and began to incorporate the idea of a horse with a rider. In the final version of that day, he tried the following lines after the phrase pertaining to the offering of an apple core:

A gentle broken horse
For all he knew it could have been I who first
Broke him, rode him, abandoned him
When I went off to study or to war.

When he returned the next day to his writing, he decided to shift the whole idea of himself as rider to the beginning of the poem. Starting anew, he wrote the following:

We live mostly in the past or in the future
These lines begin in one and end in the other
It was the first or second summer after the war
That I last found myself on horseback.

Then, progressing through several versions of the poem on this next day, he developed the following formulation of the first six lines, and he made an interesting change:

One spring dusk before I went to war
I found myself for the last time, as things turned out,
Riding bareback, at Shoup's farm north of Woodstock.
A stillness swarming inward from the first star
Or outward from the buoyant sorrel mare
Who moved as if not displeased by my weight on her back.

The horse, which had been clearly male from the beginning and had remained male throughout several rewritings of the poem, was at this point suddenly switched to female! And—a matter that carried a good deal of weight for this poet—the word used for the female horse is, of course, "mare," the English word that is pronounced exactly like the French word *mère,* meaning mother.

Poets are commonly highly sensitized to words having overtones and connections to languages other than their own. This poet was especially so: he spoke several languages fluently and intentionally included multilingual overtones in his poetry. He referred to them as "tenth-level associations."[9] In this case, however, he was not immediately aware of the connection between "mare" and *mère.* When I asked him why he had switched the horse's sex, he said that he had begun to have an erotic feeling about his relationship to the horse while writing those lines and a change of sex seemed appropriate. He added that he had not known the sex of the real horse he had seen in the desert, but had described the poetic horse as male in earlier versions without much deliberation. This alteration of a major characteristic of the horse, the primary subject of the poem, and the poet's unconscious use of a word linguistically connoting the idea of mother further emphasize a connection to the parent-child, or more specifically, the mother-child relationship. As the poet was initially unaware of the bilingual overtones of the word "mare," when ordinarily he would have been acutely so, the supposition of an underlying major concern with this relationship is considerably supported.[10]

Further events also had a bearing on this matter. One of the conscious influences on the creation of the first two stanzas of the poem, the poet told me, was a poem by Elizabeth Bishop, a poet he very much admires. Bishop's poem was about a mechanical horse with a little ballet dancer on top.[11] Always very fond of that poem, he had marveled at how lightly she had used this figure of a horse and rider; he felt there were overtones in philosophy—the relationship of the soul to the body.

Although it was difficult for the poet to ascertain exactly when the Bishop poem came into his mind, except that it was clearly after he had the conception of a horse and rider, Elizabeth Bishop herself appeared in one of his dreams during the period when he was working on the Monument Valley poem. The dream occurred six days after he began the poem, and—an important piece of evidence connecting it to the poem's creation—the next morning he returned after a three-day hiatus to write another version of the poem in his notebook. In this version, he moved the first two stanzas closer to their final formulation:

> One spring dusk before I went to war
> I found myself for the last time, as things turned out,
> Riding bareback, at Shoup's farm west of Troy.
> A stillness swarmed inward from the first star
>
> Or outward from the buoyant sorrel mare
> Who moved as if not displeased by my weight on her back.
> Her gait swung onto meadows framed by unseen lilac.

The dream—more sketchily remembered than the previous ones, he said—was the following:

> I may be going to Brazil again. J.T., Elizabeth Bishop, and I are at some seaside place here in the North. Elizabeth Bishop needs a doctor, her hands are covered with scabs and scales. She tells me that Marianne Moore is getting married to a much younger man. Now we glimpse Marianne Moore gallantly descending alone into a New York subway. The map of Brazil, retraced and colored, becomes the face and shoulders of an old woman wearing a cardigan. A telephone call. The trip is off. Some old person (woman? man?) did not renew the invitation.

Despite the sketchiness of this dream, there is again a manifest structural and sequential similarity to the poem. But now the structural similarity pertains to the entire poem and includes the first two stanzas. The dreamer is *anticipating* a trip, much as the rider of the horse is *anticipating* going to war. With the same friend of the Monument Valley trip and of the first of the previous dreams, and with

Elizabeth Bishop, he is making a visit prior to taking a trip. The rider of the poem is also on a visit.[12] Finally, the dream ends with the cancellation of an invitation by an old person, just as the poem ends with a nullification of an ancient bond between the rider and the horse (these final lines, close to the completed version, had actually been written by the time of the dream).

Associating to this dream, the poet immediately mentioned the similarity to the previous dreams; he suggested that the scabs and scales on Elizabeth Bishop's hands connected her with the grandmother in the previous dream because the grandmother also had unsightly hands. Also, the map of Brazil[13] that turned into a drawing of an old woman suggested his grandmother to him. Finally, he said he had thought that the question of the poet Marianne Moore's marrying a younger man was quite important and also was connected to the previous dreams. But the connection and the reason she was in the dream "eludes me," he said.

In the light of these dream associations as well as the information about the change of the horse's sex in the poem and about the associations to the previous dreams, it is now clear that the wish fulfillment of this later dream also is a forbidden oedipal one. The connection that "eludes" the poet is that the then seventy-year-old Marianne Moore's marrying a younger man in the dream represents his own desire to marry an "older" woman, his mother and/or his grandmother. Both the connection and the consummated wish "elude" him. The appearance of Elizabeth Bishop in the dream and the association linking her to the poet's grandmother indicate that his thoughts about Elizabeth Bishop's poem were therefore also related and connected to his underlying concern about his relationship to his mother and grandmother. As Elizabeth Bishop's poem directly influenced his writing of the first two stanzas of "In Monument Valley," the poet's associations to the dream provide further confirmation that his major underlying concern throughout the writing of this poem was the parent-child relationship, specifically his relationship to his mother.

The Creative Process

Establishing the role and significance of this theme of the poet's relationship to his mother in the creation of the poem will now serve well in a very complicated task. It will provide a clear, steady source of light whose shifts and permutations will illuminate some of the dark and murky corners of a poet's creating mind. Our following the shifts and permutations of this illuminating theme will, in part, provide a basis for some general formulations about the process of creation.

Retracing and summarizing the salient features of the history of this poem, we have the following: several months after an experience of seeing a lone horse in Monument Valley, Arizona, the poet began a poem with the horse as a central image. This poem was begun on the day prior to a visit from a woman with indirect, though definite, connections with the Monument Valley trip, a woman not consciously in his mind while writing the poem that day but represented in his dreams that night. His conscious thought while first writing the poem was that horses were included in and interposed between more than one species: they lived antithetical existences. They led human lives and not-human lives, and were therefore both beasts and not-beasts at once. This concept and its attendant images were the primary germinating ideas for the entire poem, and they were later elaborated and merged with other ideas.

Following the writing of the basic outline of what ultimately became the last two stanzas of the poem, the poet had two dreams indicating unconscious concerns and feelings about his relationship with his mother. The morning after the dreams, he had a thought that was the basis for the portion of the poem that ultimately became the first two stanzas: he connected the horse with a rider. Later, he was reminded of a poem by Elizabeth Bishop, a poem presenting a figure of a horse and rider in a manner having, for him, philosophical overtones. Before writing a version of the first two stanzas of the poem, a version containing all the essentials of this portion of the completed work, he dreamed about Elizabeth Bishop herself. This latter dream also indicated an unconscious concern with his relationship with his mother. Another important feature of the period between the writing of the outline of the last two stanzas and the adding of the first two stanzas, the period during which the essential structure of the final poem was determined, was the change of the horse's sex from male to female. And the word for female horse used in the poem was the English word with sound properties identical to the French word for "mother."

Throughout the preceding description of these salient features of the writing of the poem, two major points about the psychic life of the poet stand out in bold relief: (1) there is a continuity between the psychological substance of the poet's dreams and his waking thoughts pertaining to the poem; (2) there is wish fulfillment in the poem as well as the dream. Therefore, the dreams and the poem are related and are in some ways similar. But a detailed consideration of the nature of this psychological continuity between dreams and poem and a consideration of the specific way wish fulfillment influences the poem require an underscoring of some sharp, distinct, and important dissimilarities. They are, as follows: unlike the dream, the finished poem is not structured around wish fulfillment; its purpose is not to express the fulfillment of a wish. Also, unlike dreaming, the writing of a poem is not primarily a matter of disguising underlying wish fulfillments.

Surprising as these statements may seem to some, who may now wonder why I have just been at such pains to demonstrate the wish-fulfillment aspect of the poet's thought, they follow as initial conclusions from what has been said so far. For one thing, the poet's wish for care and nurturance from his mother is embodied in the first two stanzas of the poem rather than the concluding three. There is wish fulfillment relating to the figure of the horse and rider and the thoughts about Elizabeth Bishop; such fulfillment is conveyed in the contented, happy quality of the stanzas themselves. The point of the poem—if it is ever meaningful to make a fine poem like this one stand still long enough to talk about a single point; perhaps I should say the denouement or conclusion of the poem—is not, however, contained in these first two happy stanzas but in the final ones describing desolation and a broken bond. In simplistic terms, the poem does not have a happy wish-fulfilling ending. In fact, the ending is quite distinct from wish fulfillment; the last stanzas portray the loss of happiness, the ravages of time, and the breaking of a bond. Furthermore, there is no sense in which the poet's underlying wish could be discerned solely from his waking thoughts about the poem nor from a reading, or even an extensive analysis, of the finished poem itself. Nowhere does a parent-child relationship, nor even a relationship with another human being (except the glancing reference to Shoup—a person's name) manifest itself in the poem. I venture to say that even the most highly speculative psychoanalytic critic would be hard pressed to make a case for the horse as a clearly recognizable symbol for the poet's mother in the finished poem. To argue that from reading this poem, he would have to propose a general principle that female horses are always mother symbols, a highly doubtful assumption. The poem does not convey wish fulfillment to a reader and, as I will spell out extensively later, neither does it *primarily* express fulfillment of the creator's wish.

Probably the most important distinction between the role of wish fulfillment in this poem and its general role in dreams is that the particular manifestation of wish fulfillment in this poem contributed to coherency and aesthetic value. In dreams, wish fulfillment characteristically produces the reverse effect. As psychoanalysis has clearly demonstrated, over and over again, wish fulfillment in the dream requires disruption and incoherence in manifest content, the very disruption and incoherency characterizing the entire experience of dreaming.[14] The addition of the first two stanzas in the poem, the stanzas embodying the poet's wish fulfillment, clearly contributed to the coherency of the poem and, I think no one would disagree, increased its aesthetic value.

Now that I have said this, however, I must return to a device I used earlier in this chapter and promised to discuss again later. Although

I first discussed the dreams without referring to the content of the poem, there is now a new state of affairs. I have, in the interest of presenting evidence and facilitating identification of the poet's wish fulfillment, treated the contents of the poem as psychological material shedding light on the dreams. I begged for indulgence about the expository separating and then conjoining, but in my conclusions I have now strayed fairly far. A discerning critic may say: we've gone along with you up until now, but here you've tricked us. Didn't you yourself first come to an understanding of the early dreams by paying attention to the image of the horse and rider in the first two stanzas of the poem? Isn't the image of the female horse and rider actually a closer representation of the poet's wish for maternal care than the images in the dreams, by your own analysis? After all, as the rider of the horse, the poet puts himself on his mother's back. He is, therefore, supported, and, by extension, cared for by his mother. There is also a clear quality of emotional fulfillment in those first two stanzas. How can you now say that the purpose of the poem is not the expression of a wish? And why do you draw a contrast between poem and dreams in terms of disruption and distortion? Isn't there still distortion in the image of the poet on a horse's back? He isn't telling us or telling himself directly that he would like to be cared for by his mother, the wish is disguised by symbolization.

My reply to the critic is that he is correct on both counts: the horse and rider image is not an overt statement of the poet's wish; as in the dream, the wish is represented indirectly. The poem goes much farther than the dream; the horse and rider image embodies the content of the wish more closely and directly than any of the images in the poet's dreams. In fact, this latter point goes immediately to the heart of the matter: the image in the poem embodies the content of the wish more directly than the images of the dreams because of a major *difference* between the creative process and dreaming. This difference, a crucial one for understanding creativity, is that the creative process functions to reverse censorship, while dreams depend on it. The issues raised by the discerning critic do not invalidate our discussion of differences between the creative process and the dream, but these issues help to specify the nature of the differences further. Considering the dreams apart from both the poet's thoughts during the creation of the poem and the images in the poem itself, comparing dreams and creative process as independent psychological phenomena rather than overlapping routes of expression, reveals both striking similarity and striking difference, reciprocity as well as complementarity. Processes bear a marked resemblance to each other but they function in reverse. The image of the grandmother on the mother's back in the dream, the parent riding on the offspring, and the rider on the horse's back in the poem, the offspring on the parent, are reflecting ones: *the creative process is the mirror image of the dream.*

The mirror-image or enantiomorphic relationship between the dreams and the creation of the poem obtains in many ways at once. The horse and rider image in the poem is a homologous, and thereby a closer and a more direct, representation of the poet's wish for nurturance and care than the images in the dreams because the creative process turned backward and reversed an aspect of the censorship operation in constructing these dreams. The dream distortion was in part unraveled and the underlying wished-for structure of the relationship adopted. Also, the poet thought of the horse and rider image following a dream depicting his grandmother on his mother's back, but in the poem he reversed positions and reversed the offspring-parent relationship. Dream thoughts led to poetic thoughts, but the representation was reversed. Dreams and the creative process were functionally reciprocal and complementary, and there was reversal and reflection of similar content and imagery between dream and poem. There was also reversal and reflection of temporal sequence. The first of the two dreams occurring prior to the creation of the horse and rider image pertained, both structurally and emotionally, to the final stanzas of the poem. The second of the two dreams bore a structural resemblance to the final stanzas but emotionally pertained to what became the earlier ones. Dreams and creation mirrored each other in this poem, and dreams and the creative process universally bear a mirror-image relationship.

In the succeeding chapters of this book, I will describe two specific thought processes operating in creativity; I will explain in detail how these particular thought processes operated in the creation of "In Monument Valley" and how they operate in various types of creative processes, ranging from poetry, art, and music to science and intellectual endeavors. I will anticipate the full discussion now simply by saying that the psychological properties of these particular thought processes help account for the mirror-image relationship between dreams and the creative process I have just described. The properties of these thought processes account for such effects as the emergence of the horse and rider image with its close approximation to the poet's underlying wish. The structural aspects of these processes demonstrate the mirror-image relationship between dreams and the creative process even more precisely than I have already suggested; the thought processes themselves are mirror images of processes operating in dreams.

That the poetic image of the horse and rider is not an explicit or overt statement of the poet's wish and is therefore similar to the symbolic element in dreams is, as I said, a correct observation. Following this aspect of the discerning critic's challenge can perhaps now make clearer what I mean by mirror image. The poetic image is not an explicit statement of the poet's wish; it is representational or symbolic. If poetry characteristically contained such explicit statements, we would hardly ever find it interesting or aesthetically valuable. One of the characteristic features of art of all types is that the artist, unlike the neurotic or the psychotic, does not impose his wishes and needs directly upon his audience. He does not simply confess, nor does he make the demands of pure and explicit confession upon us. Primarily, he gives us something emotional as well as conceptual. With respect to "In Monument Valley," I believe that the shifting of the wish-fulfillment aspect into the first two stanzas had a good deal to do with its becoming a far better poem in its totality than was suggested by the early fragments alone. Not only was the personal wish embedded into an overall symbolic statement with universal significance, but a dynamic emotional sequence was produced.

The main point about the symbolic nature of the poetic horse and rider image is that there are definite similarities between dreaming and the creative process. Indeed, mirror images bear precisely such a relationship to each other: they are similar but reversed. Similar to dreaming, the creative process molds and structures deeply unconscious material and it produces affect laden and vivid images, symbols, and new connections. But it also functions to reverse the censorship, images, and other aspects of dreams; the results embody the creator's unconscious contents more closely and more directly than do dream constructions.[15] From this relationship of similarity and reversal between creative process and dreams has come the concept of the mirror image.

2

THE CREATIVE PROCESS AS THE MIRROR IMAGE OF THE DREAM

Creativity is such a value-laden topic that any new formulation about it runs the risk of being rejected out of hand. Creativity pertains to art, scientific discovery, even theology; it touches on the most cherished areas of life and the highest ideals. It is exalted and often mysterious. For many, the mysterious aspect of creativity constitutes an important part of its appeal. Any attempt to dispel even a portion of the mystery is, therefore, resisted. There is, in fact, reason to say, on philosophical grounds, that denying the mystery of creativity is a contradiction in terms.[1]

I am not concerned here with philosophical objections because I believe I can answer them and will do so later in this volume (chap. 12). My more immediate concern is with a widespread tendency to resist any formulation about creativity by insisting that it contains nothing new. After all, creativity has been thought about for a long time. Not only have philosophers, theologians, and scientists devoted a good deal of attention to it but, throughout the history of art, creative artists themselves have reflected on the nature of creativity, within the substance of their art works and in other forms of communication. Much of what is said about creativity, regardless of how new, will have some connections to what has been said before.

Dreams and Creativity

The idea of a connection between dreams and creativity is not new. As V. G. Hopwood points out: "Tradition joins dream, prophecy and poetry. The bard is both dreamer and seer, according to an association which goes back into mythology and persists into our own period."[2] Moreover, before Freud discovered and elaborated what is now accepted as the essential nature and function of dreams, artists and theorists drew analogies between dreaming and creating. So-called visionary poets—Blake, Coleridge—reported altered dreamlike states during the creation of poetry, and Blake insisted that an entire poem came to him word-for-word during sleep in a dream. For Blake, the source of dreams and of poetry was divine. The philosophers and critics Novalis (Friedrich von Hardenberg), Jean Paul Richter, and Friedrich Nietzsche also emphasized strong connections between dreams and art and between dreams and creativity.[3]

After Freud described wish fulfillment in dreams and the mechanisms of condensation and displacement, and developed the complete theory of primary process thinking as a form of mentation sharply distinct from the logical or secondary process thinking in waking life, a widespread interest in relating creativity and art to dreams developed.[4] The most elaborate early study was Marie Bonaparte's analysis of the life and works of Edgar Allan Poe. Making the explicit assumption that dream processes such as condensation and displacement operated directly in art, Princess Bonaparte related Poe's major themes and symbols to events and personages in his life. In Poe's story "The Black Cat," for example, she proposed that the author's mother was represented in several characterizations: the slayer's wife, the cat Pluto, and the second cat. Spelling out the analysis of the artistic work as equivalent to the dream, she stated the following: "Through *displacement,* the psychic emphasis that belongs to the mother is shifted on the unrecognizable cats or on the murderer's anonymous wife. Through *condensation,* in each of these three protagonists, the poet's mother Elizabeth has been fused with Virginia his wife and, what is more, has incorporated Catterina, Poe's cat, in two of them."[5] Other psychoanalysts became deeply interested in the symbolic content of art, both literary and visual art, and ingenious interpretations of artistic symbols, modeled after the interpretation of the symbolic content of dreams, abound in psychoanalytic writings.[6]

Freud himself made some tentative connections between the dream processes he had discovered and the creative process in art, although he purposely shied away from any overall formulations about creativity. Emphasizing the important role of daydreaming or fantasy in the creation of poetry and other types of fiction,[7] he pointed out that daydreams, like dreams occurring during the night, were motivated by unfulfilled wishes. Though daydream wishes were decidedly egoistic and therefore socially unacceptable, they were often not subject to the same degree of distortion as the personally unacceptable wishes of dreams. In creating literature, the manifestly egoistic or wish-fulfilling daydreams were, according to Freud, softened by the artist through the disguises and changes produced by formal aesthetic devices. The specific nature of the artist's disguises or the psychological properties of these formal aesthetic devices were never spelled out by

Freud. But with respect to the production of jokes, a matter indirectly connected to the production of art, he suggested that the dream mechanisms of condensation and displacement played a direct role.[8] Jokes, like dreams, contained unconscious material disguised by the primary process mechanisms of condensation and displacement.

Although Freud did extend some aspects of his analysis of jokes to an analysis of the psychodynamics of the comic and thereby entered the domain of the psychology of aesthetics, he steadfastly stayed clear of any systematic formulation about the creative process.[9] It remained for Ernst Kris, the illustrious psychoanalytic theorist of creativity, to bring together implications he saw in Freud's analysis of jokes and to coin the phrase "regression in the service of the ego" as a description of the creative process.[10]

Kris's widely touted concept emphasizes the daring free play in creative thinking and purports to explain the striking leaps of imagination, the intensity, and the emotional profundity in completed works of art. Like many of the psychoanalysts exploring art before him, Kris was struck by the way that art seemed to reveal unconscious material more readily than ordinary waking thought and it appeared, like dreams, to reveal such material through symbols, images, vivid sequences, and ambiguities that conveyed intense emotional charge. As Freud's theory of dream formation indicated that these types of effects in dreams were accomplished by primary process thinking, the primitive form of thinking also considered to be characteristic of infants, schizophrenics, and culturally primitive peoples, Kris, like his psychoanalytic predecessors, postulated that primary process thinking was responsible for the same effects in art. He proposed that, similar to the ordinary condition in dreaming, the creator's attention was withdrawn from objects in reality. Although convinced that something approximating dream thought occurred during the creator's waking state, he, unlike earlier psychoanalytic theorists of creativity, saw a sharp distinction between creative thinking and the thought of children, schizophrenics, and so-called primitives, and he therefore emphasized the concomitant role of mature ego adaptive processes. He said that the creator *temporarily* regressed to primary process thinking; that is, the creator adopted the developmentally primitive modes of thought characteristic of dreaming but this regressed type of cognition was controlled by the functioning of the ego. Such controlled regression was relatively easily reversed and it served the creator's ego, replenishing him rather than overwhelming him as with the insidious regression of schizophrenia.

Kris's formulation, the analyses of art by psychoanalysts before him, and the observations of many artists and writers both prior and subsequent to psychoanalysis clearly assume and emphasize a similarity between dreams and works of art. Even in music, musicologists such as Max Graf[11] have attempted to demonstrate similarities between dream processes and musical works, despite the absence of visual and linguistic representations characteristic of dreams. Scientific creation has also been linked to dreaming, despite the ordered, logical and seemingiy unemotional content of those productions.[12]

Another widely held conception about the creative process, a conception pertaining indirectly to the similarity between creating and dreaming, is that creation is largely due to unconscious processes. This conception, again, has primarily been an outgrowth of the work of the psychoanalysts. But before psychoanalysis—long before Freud formulated his notion of the Unconscious—artists had denied that their creations came solely from conscious thought and therefore implicitly suggested this type of conception themselves. For psychoanalysts, in fact, the high degree of psychological insight about unconscious processes embodied in works of art throughout history supported the same view. Freud consistently acknowledged his own great debt to art and literature for the wealth of psychological truth and knowledge contained therein. On several occasions, he insisted that he personally had merely achieved a systematization of artistic and literary knowledge accrued through the centuries before him. Psychoanalytic studies of art and literature by Freud and his disciples seemed to reveal the dynamisms seen in patients—Oedipus complex, repetition compulsion, separation anxiety—and the conviction grew that creative artists have some type of direct access to their own unconscious contents while creating. This conviction has persisted in modern psychoanalytic writings.

Among artists themselves, the idea that art consists of the revelation of unconscious material has influenced several modern movements, including: expressionism, dadaism, surrealism, and beat as well as confessional poetry and literature. Such a conception of art has been adopted fully by the beat writers Kerouac and Ginsberg as well as others who follow a model of writing out virtually everything that comes into their minds, in the style of free association in psychoanalysis. For these writers, the closer they could come to their inner or unconscious worlds, the closer they could come to truth. And truth, for them, was synonymous with art.

Scientists and investigators of scientific thinking also have emphasized the importance of unconscious processes in scientific creation and discovery although they have sometimes differed about the manner in which these processes operate. Poincaré thought there was an unconscious or subliminal self that played an important role in mathematical creation.[13] Cannon emphasized the role of what he called "extraconscious" processes in the development of scientific hunches.[14] And Graham Wallas, in a famous description of the phases of creative thought, discussed an early phase he called incubation, a phase in which thought went underground and, he believed, problems were worked on unconsciously both in scientific and in other types of creation.[15]

Although the emphasis on the role of unconscious processes or on the revelation of unconscious material in the creative process is not identical to the emphasis on dreams, dreamlike thought, or primary process thinking, there are many features in common, especially for psychoanalysts. Primary process thinking is the logic of the Freudian Unconscious. In the Unconscious, there are no boundaries of time or space and opposites are interchangeable. Primary process thinking functions to represent events and feelings without respect to time, space, or contradiction. Events and feelings both of childhood and of everyday adult life are represented in the same image or symbol. Church and boudoir, earth and water, are interchangeable or are represented as one. Primary process thinking is governed only by the principle of fulfillment of needs and wishes, and the primary process mechanisms of condensation and displacement function to express such fulfillment while evading internal censorship. In other words, if it were not for censorship, unconscious contents might be able to appear directly in waking or in sleeping consciousness (dream). Because primary process thinking is governed by the Unconscious, and because in waking life censorship is strongly operative, producing a virtually opaque and complete covering over unconscious contents, Freud considered dreams to be the royal road to the Unconscious. For the psychoanalyst, therefore, emphasizing the role of the Unconscious in creativity is virtually synonymous with emphasizing primary process thinking or the thinking occurring in dreams.

Before leaving this necessarily brief account of previous conceptions connecting the creative process to dreams, I must mention that another traditional perspective about creativity tends to connect nonrational processes, similar to unconscious ones, with the production of art. Affirming the nonrational quality of creative thinking has not by any means been the sole province of creative artists and psychoanalysts, but, beginning with Plato, philosophers have also emphasized nonrational, free, and sometimes dreamlike functions. Plato avowed that, while creating, the poet was possessed by "divine madness"; he was out of his mind and bereft of his senses.[16] Kant distinguished aesthetic thought from rational thought and described a soul-animating spirit as responsible for artistic creation.[17] Nietzsche, mentioned before, related both dreams and intoxication to artistic production—vision, association, and poetry with the former and gesture, passion, and song and dance with the latter. Apollonian and Dionysian principles, which according to Nietzsche are the driving forces of art and artistic creation, correspond with dream and intoxication, respectively, in everyday life.[18] Modern philosophers, such as

Brand Blanshard,[19] insist directly on the important role of unconscious or subconscious factors in creation.

The Mirror-Image Relationship: Similarity and Reversal

This summary of the impressive history of formulations, descriptions, and approaches relating creativity indirectly or directly to dreams should help clarify similarities and differences with the discovery I am presenting. All of these investigations have, I believe, been basically correct in recognizing the remarkable truthfulness of art. By truthfulness, I mean the way that art depicts or embodies psychological phenomena with extraordinary accuracy, not merely as verisimilitude or as imitating the elements of nature, but, in modern terms, as a presentation of the structure and content of the deepest levels of the human psyche. Because such a high degree of psychological truth is attained through artistic creativity (I will discuss the psychological truth in scientific creation in chaps. 6 and 13) it is reasonable to assume that the creative process has an intimate connection to unconscious processes. Further, all of these previous investigators seem to have recognized a *formal* similarity between dreams and works of art, whether or not they have spelled this out specifically. I have already alluded to some of the elements of this formal similarity such as use of symbols, ambiguity or multiple implication and meaning, wide-ranging types of structures and forms, and I would add the following: the primarily visual nature of dreams and the visual nature of painting, sculpture, etc.; the seeming novelty in the content of dreams and the novelty in art; the particularity and concreteness of dreams and art; the sense of story and sequence in dreams despite shifting time references and the similar sequential sense in art, especially in literature and music; the sharp contrasts and contradictions depicted in dreams and art; the extraordinary vividness of dreams and the vividness embodied in works of art. Also, of course, there is a crucial connection between the content of dreams and art: the sense —acknowledged explicitly by some of the theorists mentioned but also tacitly influencing others—that dreams, like art, have strong emotional connotations.

All of these similarities are, in part, the basis for saying that the creative process[20] is the mirror image of the dream. A mirror image must be similar to the object or process it reflects, but a crucially important point about the creative process is that, biologically, psychologically, and socially, it is the reverse or obverse of dreaming.

Creative Process as the Psychological Obverse of Dreaming

Let us take the psychological level first in order to consider the point more precisely: the creative process is the obverse of dreaming in that the creator consciously uses the mechanisms and processes characteristic of dream thought and dreaming for the purposes of abstracting, conceptualizing, and concretizing as well as reversing the effects of unconscious censorship.

As a key to much that will follow, I will discuss the elements of this statement separately. (1) "The creator consciously uses": This means that the creator actively, with full logic, and in a waking, conscious state employs thought processes structurally similar to unconscious dream processes. Thus, structurally similar processes operate in the obverse aspects of the psychic apparatus, conscious and unconscious. The creator consciously pays attention to factors that are also important in unconscious thinking such as sound similarities between words—that is, rhyme, homophony, and alliteration. He works with visual and with verbal symbols. He alters time sequences. He shifts and he compresses. And he uses two specific thought processes (to be described) that are both similar and obverse, mirror images, to dream processes.

This does not mean that creators necessarily are aware that they are using thought processes similar to the unconscious processes operating in dreams. If they had been traditionally aware of this, they might well have discovered a systematic interpretation of dreams long before Freud, or they would have long ago described this mirror-image factor in creativity. But it does mean that creative thinking is primarily a conscious process and not the welling up—temporary, ego controlled, or whatever—of unconscious psychological processes. (2) "For the purpose of abstracting, conceptualizing, and concretizing": In contrast to dream thought, which produces confusing, chaotic, and manifestly illogical images and sequences, the creative process produces order and meaningful images and metaphors, as well as tight conceptualizations. The creative person engages primarily in abstract thinking, hierarchically the reverse of the primitive literality of unconscious or primary process thinking. Concrete forms are used for abstract purposes. (3) "Reversing the effects of unconscious censorship": One of the psychological goals—not necessarily an intentional one—of the creative process, particularly the creative process in art, is reversal of unconscious censorship. Not a matter of mere catharsis, the expression and purgation of highly charged or forbidden emotional contents, there is an active unmasking and structuring of unconscious thoughts, feelings, and motives. Unconscious material is shaped and integrated into the resulting creation and, for the creator, some degree of awareness or personal insight usually occurs. This reversal of censorship accounts for the high preponderance of unconscious material in artistic creations, one of the factors contributing to the intrinsic value of art. In other types of creation, where integration of unconscious material into the product is of lesser, or of minor, importance, reversal of censorship primarily serves a function for the creator himself.

Reversing censorship is a direct result of the creator's conscious use of particular mirror-image processes. Used consciously, these processes tend to reveal unconscious material rather than to conceal and to distort, major features of the function of their primary process counterparts in dreaming. The structural reversal and similarity between the conscious mirror-image processes and the unconscious primary process counterparts are the properties responsible for the unmasking effect.

As the mirror image of dreaming, creative cognition is adaptive, progressive, and pervasively logical. It is not pervasively logical in the strict Aristotelian sense, though the creator constantly uses traditional types of Aristotelian logic along with the mirror-image processes, but logical in the sense that creative thinking is rooted in reality, and is clear about distinctions and similarities. It is capable of, and often permeated with, highly abstract formulations. According to a psychoanalytic model of thought, the mirror-image type of cognition must be considered an advanced type of secondary process rather than primary process functioning.

Because of the similarities between creativity and dreaming, previous investigators have erroneously considered creative thought processes to be identical with the primary process mechanisms responsible for dreams. Because unconscious material appears in art to a strikingly high degree, investigators have assumed that artists characteristically experience some type of altered state of consciousness in which there is direct access to unconscious material. They have assumed short and temporary or longer lasting states where so-called primitive thinking holds sway. Influenced by and in accord with Kris, most psychoanalytic investigators believe that critical thinking and other forms of secondary process cognition follow such states rapidly, or even after a time lag, and function to modify or transform the products of primary process thought. But if we link the creative process to the primary process or to a state where there is direct access to unconscious material, the core of creative thinking becomes a reversion to childlike, primitive, or psychotic modes of thought. Though Kris and others have recognized some of the adaptive features of the creative process, especially the adaptive nature of its results, the concept "regression in the service of the ego" tends to emphasize the primary process or regressive mode of thought.

Many efforts have been made to remove the pejorative sting of this assumption about regression to primary process thinking. Temporary regression, Kris argued, also occurs in sleep and in sexual orgasm.[22] Therefore, it could be considered a type of recharging mechanism necessary for mature functioning. Another approach has been to recast the basic psychoanalytic notion of primary process thinking or to propose other formulations of the way in which primary process thinking operates in creativity. A recent notable attempt to revise the classical conception of primary process was carried out by Pinchas Noy.[23] Noy argued that primary process thinking undergoes progressive development throughout life and functions side by side with secondary process rational thought in adult waking life. Primary and secondary process thought are therefore only distinguished because of having different functions. Formulations emphasizing the expansion of ego boundaries in creativity[24] or the creative process as connected to Winnicott's transitional phenomena[25] are attempts to relate primary process thinking to adaptation and maturation. Arieti's formulation of a tertiary process mode of thought, the "appropriate matching" of "primitive forms of cognition" with secondary process mechanisms, is another instance of this type.[26]

All of the attempts to recast the concepts of the primary process or of regression, or of the role of the primary process in creativity arise from a recognition of the essential difficulty in postulating a causal, unitary, or homologous connection between creativity and the Unconscious or between creativity and dreams. There is an intrinsic disjunction between the adaptive, primarily ordering, and revelatory processes characteristic of creative thought and the primitive, primarily disruptive, and obfuscating primary processes functioning in dreams. In psychoanalysis, some of the disjunction and the pejorative quality of the theories linking creativity to the primary process can be traced directly to Freud. Although highly respectful of creative artists and of the creative process, Freud had a decided tendency to overvalue language and to consider any form of visual thinking as primitive, and therefore regressive. This tendency was clearly operative in his formulations about the interpretation of dreams, and it also permeated his writings.[27] While there is no reason to doubt that the visual thinking characteristic of dreams is more primitive—or, at least, less communicative and precise—than waking thought, there is good reason to insist that aspects of the visual thinking occurring within the creative process, as well as other thinking characteristic of creativity, are not only *not* primitive but are consistently more advanced and adaptive than ordinary waking thought.

Later, in connection with the discussion of specific mirror-image thought processes, I shall clarify further the abstract advanced nature of these types of cognition. Now, I want to emphasize another feature of the obverse relationship between creation and dreaming, namely, reversal of censorship and its effect on anxiety. Structural reversal of primary process, or dream censorship mechanisms involves a reversal of their functions and effects. Where primary process operations allow distorted expression of unconscious material, operations mirroring these processes produce a degree of revelation of the actual nature of the material. This does not mean that the creator uses a mirror-image process to interpret the meaning of his or others' dreams. The functional method for interpretation of dreams has already been elaborated by Freud and his followers. That method makes use of the dreamer's direct associations to the dream, as well as other information. Reversal of dream censorship does mean that the mirror-image thinking of the creative process retraces steps and pathways also traversed by the primary process. The starting point of the creative process could include dream content: the poet starting a poem, for example, could be actively thinking about a manifest portion of a dream of the night before. But more often, it has nothing whatever to do with an actual dream; it includes other types of thought content such as words, concepts, vague emotions, remembered scenes, or mathematical symbols. Such types of thought content initiating the process are subjected to a mirror-image process tending, in some degree, to reveal underlying unconscious (as well as preconscious) preoccupations.

A patient of mine not too long ago indicated something of what I am describing here and, incidentally, also spelled out one of the differences between creative and psychotic thinking. This patient, a seriously ill but, I believe, potentially a very creative young girl, was describing some of her frustrated efforts at beginning a piece of creative writing, and she said: "The trouble is, when I try to describe her [referring to a girl to whom she had some homosexual attachment] I realize that I'm not simply describing her but I'm really revealing a good deal about myself. I think I'm frightened to find out the things about myself I might reveal." Psychotic thinking per se lacks any features of progressive or structured insight. Results of some experimental procedures with creative (research) subjects supporting this formulation of reversal of censorship with its concomitant instigation of anxiety will be presented in the final chapter of this book.

As the creative process progresses, censorship is increasingly reversed and the creative person experiences increasing anxiety. Opposite to the dream function of keeping the dreamer asleep and consequently expressing forbidden wishes in disguised form to avoid anxiety, the creative process functions to stimulate the anxiety of the wide-awake creator.[28] This function is not adventitious to creativity, but is intrinsic to its goal. Both the goal and the method of the creative process involve mirror-image relationships with dreaming. The function of increasing anxiety, as I shall discuss shortly, contributes to the value achieved within the creative process, particularly the process of artistic creation. And increasing anxiety also pertains to what might be called the creative impulse, a term that brings us to a consideration of the biological functions of creativity.[29]

Creative Process as the Biological Obverse of Dreaming

The biological functions of creativity are also the reverse of the biological functions of dreaming. Like sleep, dreaming seems to appear fairly early on the evolutionary scale and there is reason to believe that both sleep and dreaming are necessary to life. Relatively recent research, for example, has demonstrated that rather simple animals seem to dream, and it has been postulated that dreaming is not only the guardian of sleep, as Freud said, but that it serves a crucial type of biological discharge function.[30] In any event, dreaming is a spontaneous involuntary process and, unlike creativity, it is suppressed with difficulty, if indeed it can be suppressed at all. Although it could be argued—weakly, I believe—that it is also impossible to suppress human creativity, taking human beings as an aggregate, creativity clearly is quite fragile and rather easily suppressed in individuals. Indeed, one of the cardinal issues about creativity is that the converse is markedly apparent; it is difficult, if not impossible, to stimulate creativity. Creativity appeared fairly late in human evolution. Although one could possibly consider man's first construction of tools or his first use of language as creative acts, it is difficult to discuss creativity as we conceive of it today prior to the time of the first cave drawings. In all likelihood, creativity could not become manifest in human affairs until some amount of leisure time was available. Also, man's brain surely needed to evolve to a point where it was capable of creative activity. In both circumstances, creativity could not be an automatic spontaneous activity like dreaming, but intentional, even arduous, application and invocation were required.

Dreaming is an involuntary biological activity while creativity must be invoked, an aspect of the obverse relationship between dreams and creativity. Only when considering human beings in the aggregate could it possibly be argued that the creative impulse was a spontaneous involuntary outgrowth of social functioning. From the viewpoint of the individual creator, however, the thought processes and acts leading to a creation must always be intentionally invoked. This is simply saying that creating is always motivated, strongly so in fact. Though there are times during the creative process when thought seems to flow spontaneously and effortlessly, even to approach some type of automaticity, the reverse characteristically is the case. Extreme effort and definite conscious application and intention characterize the creative process more than other types of cognitive activity. This automatic phase resembling the automatic quality of dreams always follows effort, whereas on the other hand spontaneous and automatic dream activity may often instigate effort because of a push toward understanding, curiosity, or anxiety.

Why did human beings begin to invoke creative processes? Are there biological reasons for individuals to engage voluntarily in creative activity unconnected to the psychological motivation to produce something with important social value? A complete answer is not currently available, but one clear reason seems to be the biological factor of *arousal,* the intensification and activation of physiological processes. While engaging in the creative process, the creator is stimulated and aroused. Though this arousal occurs in different ways, one manifestation is readily apparent on superficial observation of persons while they are creating. While painting, an artist is clearly highly stimulated; he is hypersensitive and hyperalert. Easily bothered by the slightest interruption or distraction, he appears to be carried along by the impetus of the project. As he progresses in his work, enormous reserves of energy appear, energy that was not available at the beginning. He does not, in other words, necessarily begin his day's work with a good deal of energy—my creative writer subjects, for example, report that they usually take a long time to "warm up" before they get into their creative work—and energy is generated by engaging in the creative process itself. Partly because of this hyperalert and aroused state, most creative people require solitude to carry out their work. There are other reasons for the solitude as well, such as concentration and internalized communication, but it is strongly plausible to assume that solitude is required because of arousal. Solitude not only facilitates concentration on difficult intellectual work, but it is needed because of the irritability and intensity of the hyperalert and aroused state. The temperamental artist who flies into a fury when frustrated or distracted is a caricature, but it is a caricature based on an intrinsic difference between the creative process and other types of intellectual work. A major reason for this difference is the high degree of anxiety generated by creative activity.

Biologically, this anxiety is an aspect of the protective state of physiological readiness engendered by internal or external threat. This internal and external threat in creative activity is, paradoxically, produced by the creator himself; he engages in a process of unearthing[31] unconscious material and seeking the internal and external new and unknown. These factors, as well as others, engender anxiety and a protective state of alertness.

Dreaming and creativity, therefore, function in reverse biological directions. While dreaming functions to keep the dreamer asleep, the creative process functions to arouse and alert the creator. On a biological continuum from sleep to wakefulness, the creative process operates at the wakefulness end. It functions to keep the creator awake. It is no accident, I believe, that we, the appreciators of art and literature, speak figuratively of "having our eyes opened," "being waked up" by a book or painting or musical work, or being aroused. Our figurative language is derived from a subjective perception of the biological nature of creativity. The creator's own arousal is preserved in the product he creates. When the full biological story of creativity is told, I believe that factors involving the reticular activating system of the brain, the system responsible for biological arousal and activation, will be demonstrated. Berlyne, whose work is discussed at some length in the final chapter, has already shown some connections between the reticular activating system and the experience of aesthetic pleasure.[32]

Among animals, birds, insects, and plants, the closest thing to art in human terms is the decorative coloring or intricate sound patterns that play a role in the propagation of the species. Among animals, birds, and insects, the male's decorative colors attract the female for fertilization, and musical mating sounds and calls are used in many species. Among plants, decoration is not sex-related but functions to attract insects, who help facilitate plant fertilization. While animals, birds, insects, and plants certainly do not create their own decorations or mating calls in any way analogous to human creating, these attributes indicate a widespread connection between art and physiological arousal. For Darwin, art or sense of beauty was preserved in evolution because of its apparent role in the propagation of species.[33] As there are reasons to challenge some aspects of this particular hypothesis, such as the fact that decorated male animals commonly seek out undecorated females rather than vice versa, arousal of a more general type could probably be considered to be a more crucial factor than sense of beauty alone in the evolutionary development of creativity. In addition to the connection between decorations and musical sounds and sexual arousal leading to fertilization, general physiological arousal involving hyperalertness and readiness has considerable survival value in its own right. Even hunters temporarily engaged in doing cave drawings might very well have been more aroused and better prepared for danger than others not similarly occupied. A more parsimonious explanation of the relationship between art and natural decorations is that humans are themselves aroused by the decorations and musical patterns in nature and consequently try to emulate them. This more psychological explanation should not, however, exclude the possibility that humans are also consciously or unconsciously aware of some direct connection between art and sexual arousal and attraction in nature. Surely, bird feathers have been used for decoration and sexual attraction from time immemorial. If Freud's famous assertion that the goal of the (male) artist is the attainment of "honor, power and the love of women"[34] has any validity, real or intuitive, it points to the partial connection between art and sexual attraction in nature.

The Role of Arousal: Anxiety and Control

Anxiety is the cardinal form of arousal involved in the creative process. Not a purely biological matter, to be sure, the mirror-image relationship of creativity and dreaming with respect to anxiety pertains also to complex psychological and social factors. Dreams function to express forbidden wishes but, because of censorship, dream mechanisms and processes distort and disguise these wishes in order to reduce the anxiety connected with their expression. Anxiety-producing dreams, or nightmares, occur only when the wish is too strong or when its expression threatens to evade disguise and censorship. The creative process is the obverse or mirror image of the dream with respect to anxiety because processes structurally similar to condensation, displacement, and other disguising mechanisms function to reverse censorship and to arouse anxiety. On a figurative scale of low to high anxiety intensity, dream processes point toward reduction and inhibition, while creative processes point toward increase and stimulation.

The creator's motivation for engaging in such a process might well seem puzzling. Why stimulate anxiety and potential discomfort rather than maintain a steady biological and psychological state? Partly, the motivation is to experience an alerted, awakened state, a state that could be biologically particularly necessary for an individual creator. As this state is also transmitted through and stimulated in others by the creator's products, it may also be necessary—or, at least, valuable—for the species as a whole. But there is another more clear-cut factor motivating the creator, a factor that definitely is highly important to society as well. This is the factor of *control.*

Much about the nature of creativity either tacitly or explicitly indicates the importance of control. The clearly magical function of artistic creation in the early phases of human history, for instance, emphasizes the essential role of control. Invariably, the subject matter of surviving primitive cave drawings were the beasts of prey or animals of the hunt which were the sources of food or the competitors for survival. Consequently, gaining magical control over such animals was very likely an important purpose of making such drawings. Dance, theatre, music, and literature as well grew directly out of magical, prophetic, or religious rituals designed to evoke some power and to gain control over the environment. In modern times, the importance of scientific creativity as a means of gaining control over nature is self-evident and requires no further elaboration. But the control function of creativity with respect to internal psychological phenomena, particularly anxiety and the reversal of censorship, may not be immediately obvious.

Though he is generally not aware of it, the person engaged in creative activity is attempting to reverse censorship of unconscious material in order to gain increased conscious control of his inner psychological world. One of the (usually unconscious) universal motives for engaging in the creative process is to gain some personal understanding, or, at least, to impose some order on inner confusion and chaos. Despite increased anxiety, or sometimes in order to gain the experience of heightened anxiety followed by relief, the creator plunges forward in a psychologically perilous activity. Anxiety is aroused and reduced, and some order is attained. The quest for truth that we know to be so characteristic of artistic creativity is partly just such a quest for control. The artist actually reveals more about his inner world than the rest of us, excepting perhaps a patient in psychotherapy, and, at the same time, he often reveals truths about the the world of men and nature. There is some relationship between revelations about his inner world and revelations about the external world of nature and society, because the structure of truth in both domains seems, in some ways, to be homologous. Partly because of this homology, the scientific creator is, in ways that will become clearer in subsequent chapters, also unwittingly motivated by a need to reveal and thereby to control his inner world. In saying this, I do not intend to declare that all creators have a higher degree of chaos in their inner world than the rest of us. The pressure toward revelation, arousal of anxiety, and subsequent control is universal. Creators, however, have a greater capacity to engage in the mirror-image process and they are usually better able than others to tolerate the attendant anxiety.

The universality of the motive to arouse and control anxiety is indicated by the widespread appeal of art itself. No one would question the proposition that a basic feature of many forms of entertainment, such as riding roller coasters or watching acrobats or stock car racers, consists of the experience of anxiety stimulation followed by relief and a renewed sense of control. An intrinsic feature of good art, not generally recognized or acknowledged, consists also of the induction of an experience of anxiety arousal followed by relief and increased control. A simple example is the pleasure engendered by suspense in literature, or in music. Tension associated with suspense is unquestionably a mild to moderate form of anxiety. More complex examples are the experiences of anxiety aroused by new perceptions engendered by every type of art. In fields outside of art, new perceptions are frequently considered valuable and accepted because of their applications to tangible matters and affairs. A new way of understanding the functioning of the cell, a new twist on a technological matter, or a new perception of a personnel problem are sometimes immediately useful. In art, however, usefulness is not a major value or an immediate concern. New perceptions are valued more for intrinsic reasons related to the experience of having and attaining them. Yet, regardless of whether or not they directly pertain to unconscious psychological material, new perceptions engender a certain amount of anxiety because they always challenge habit. The aesthetic experience of anxiety arousal followed by relief and control or anticipation of control when confronted with a new perception constitutes one of the intrinsic values of art.

Most readily apparent in attending a theatrical performance is this relationship between anxiety relief and anxiety arousal characteristic of all forms of art. At the end of a good play, there is a fair amount of relief of anxiety and tension due to resolution of suspense. But, concomitantly, there is an arousal of further anxiety as well. We all know that a really good play stimulates us to continue talking with our friends and companions for some time afterward and, after talk has ceased, to think about it for quite a while. While this has something to do with the intellectual content of the play, emotional factors significantly enter in. We are somewhat shaken up and anxious in our intrigued and thoughtful state.[35]

Of course, many other factors beside anxiety arousal are involved in the social value and appeal of art. But saying this, I now shall rapidly culminate this outline of the obverse relationship between creativity and dreaming, for I have brought matters into the relativistic realm of sociology, the realm where absolute assertions are quickly challenged with counter examples and where the observer himself is inevitably biased by his own cultural view. Though many professionals have been able to overcome this, the problem is especially acute with respect to the sociology of art. Consequently, I shall state only the most glaring and global social level antitheses between creativity and dreaming, because they appear so self-evident and because they follow from and, in reciprocal and circular fashion, also help determine the psychological and biological circumstances I have mentioned so far.

Creativity and Dreaming in Society

With respect to social value and to communication, creativity and dreaming tend to be at opposite poles. Earlier, when I stressed the enormous aura of value associated with the topic of creativity, I anticipated no contradiction from even the most skeptical sources. The term "creative" is so heavily embued with positive value that it is virtually synonymous with "good" or "worthwhile" and, in virtually all societies, the term "creation" is almost synonymous with positive achievement. No such social value is universally and consistently conferred upon dreaming, however. In ancient times, of course, and sporadically among various groups up to the present day, dreams have been considered portents of the future or directives from a deity. But even when such beliefs are held, they seldom confer a specific value to dreaming. Most often, special persons in the society are considered to be endowed with the capacity to receive prophetic and divine dreams, or, like Joseph, specially able to interpret the meaning of such dreams. Dreaming is only one of a series of mental phenomena, including hallucinations and telepathy, considered to be endowed with such special properties. In rationally oriented, so-called civilized societies, interest in dreams has generally been relegated to the realm of superstition, astrology, and other derogated orientations. While creativity has been accorded high esteem in such societies, dreams have often been on the reverse end of the continuum. The general social viewpoint, even in these societies, has been an ambivalent one, of course, just as the general social viewpoint about creativity has been ambivalent, but by and large dreams have been very low in the hierarchy of valued mental activities.

When Freud wrote the "Interpretation of Dreams," the predominant scientific view of dreams was that they were nonsensical and consequently without any value whatsoever.[36] The modern resurgence of interest in dreams is, as we know, a direct result of Freud's work, as well as that of Jung. But the history of hostile rejection of both Freud's and Jung's theories of dreams, when first presented and continuing into the present day, demonstrates in part a traditional reluctance to accord special value to dreaming. That such reluctance still exists is demonstrated by an instance from the modern everyday practice of psychoanalysis. Practitioners of psychoanalysis, that veritable bastion of dream valuation, have, in recent years, begun to deemphasize dream analysis because patients find it too easy to abjure responsibility for their dreams.[37] After going through a full and extensive analysis of the underlying meaning of a particular dream, patients still find it relatively easy to insist "but it was just a dream." Or else they insist the dream was involuntary and the underlying wishes out of their control. My point is not that such denials are motivated by a desire to avoid the important truths concealed in dreams, although I certainly believe that to be the case, but that dream denigration occurs even in the psychoanalytic setting because of deeply imbued social conventions and beliefs.

I have no intention of being polemical about according value to dreams, but I intend only to describe the social value polarity between dreaming and creativity. Freud directly referred to such a polarity when he quoted Virgil at the beginning of his book on dreams, "Flectere si nequeo superos, acheronta movebo" [If I cannot bend the Higher Powers, I will move the Infernal Regions].[38] There is, moreover, a clear social rationale for the value polarity between dreaming and creativity: dreams tend to conceal, while creativity tends to reveal and to elaborate both truth and meaning. In more sociological terms, creativity, especially artistic creativity, tends to communicate while dreaming tends to distort communication.

Now that Freud (and Jung as well) has given us the tools for understanding the communication in dreams, we can, of course, say that some of the polarity between dreaming and creativity has been reduced. We know, too, that patients in psychoanalysis often produce dreams that seem geared to communicate something to their analyst.[39] Kanzer and others have spelled out some of the other communication functions of dreams.[40] But, as Kanzer cogently points out, dreaming is the quintessential narcissistic psychological activity. Regardless of the skills of the analyst or the interpreter of dreams, dreams function primarily to keep the dreamer at rest by concealing truth and meaning from the dreamer and from other people.

Creativity communicates in many ways and on many levels at once. Even art that is very difficult to understand, or is supposedly produced for art's sake alone, has important communication aspects. Difficult art is directed at some audience, even if only a potential one, and it communicates values, emotions, complicated ideas, and, frequently, new and unprecedented principles and forms. Art produced for the artist's own sake, if there really is such a type, that is, art produced without any concern whatsoever for an audience, is either a kind of communication to the self, a personal externalization having high communication potential for others, or, despite the art-for-art's-sake artist's disclaimer, it is intended as a communication to future generations. Scientific creations must be communicated to others, and the scientists' creative thinking is so geared to a rational, communicative context it seems, in a broad way, to be the extreme antithesis of dreams.

Creativity as the mirror image of dreaming means that creativity has both social and personal value. By reversing the censorship in dreaming, the creator is engaging in an attempt to unearth unconscious material, and he is embarking on a process of gaining insight and understanding about himself, albeit in a limited way. He is also experiencing arousal and anxiety. By reversing the censorship in dreaming and by the use of the mirror-image processes involved in creating, he reveals truths in a structured and organized way. Especially important in artistic creativity, this organization and structuring of inner truth also plays a significant role in scientific creativity. Creative thoughts in science are deeply emotionally gratifying to a scientist and scientific creations often have distinct aesthetic qualities of economy and elegance. These emotional gratifications and aesthetic qualities, as well as some aspects of the practical achievement, have roots in the mirror-image-of-dreaming processes. While engaged in the creative process, the scientist uses a daring and orderly type of thought; as a mirror-image process, this thought is extremely disparate in orderliness but matched in daring with the thinking in dreams.

As the mirror image of dreaming, creativity is one of the highest, if not the highest, kind of adaptive mental process. It is not regressive, irrational, a concrete type of thinking, or even a radically altered state of consciousness. The creator, in full consciousness, purposefully attempts to produce the most socially valuable products possible and he uses the highest mental function he possesses.

3

THE MIRROR-IMAGE PROCESSES

In order to show how the mirror-image process functions, its specific forms and operations, I shall return and examine further the creation of "In Monument Valley." The wide generality of the process illustrated here in a particular case shall be demonstrated later. In other chapters of this book, I shall consider a variety of cases and I will present some of the evidence, both clinical and experimental, supporting the conclusions to follow.

Janusian Thinking

When I traced the development of "In Monument Valley," certain salient factors emerged. The poet's relationship to his mother constituted an underlying unconscious and preconscious theme, and two particular conscious thoughts played critical roles at certain junctures in the poem's creation. The first of these pertained to a characteristic of horses: horses lived human lives. This formulation played an important role in the early phases of the writing and it guided the creation of what eventually became the last two stanzas of the poem. The second thought pertained to the horse in relation to a rider and it guided the creation of what became the two earlier stanzas. Together, these particular thoughts determined major features of both form and content and were crucial to the creation of the entire poem.

I will begin with the first of these, the idea that horses lived human lives. Previously, I called this thought the germinating idea for the poem despite its not technically being the very first one the poet had—remember both the first words he wrote, "Hot pumice blew in Monument Valley," and the original experience of seeing the horse—because it was, by the poet's own statement, the idea that propelled the poem forward. No explicit reference to this idea appears in the final poem but it is both implied and indirectly incorporated overall. Special connections between horses and humans are suggested in the reference to a bond between "his kind and mine" and in the narrative progression from a horse and rider together, a later meeting between them, and a final separation. That the horse as an intermediate species is a very important idea in the poem is further demonstrated by its forming the basis for the conception of the horse as an emblematic beast of our time—creating emblems and metaphors for the time and culture is, of course, the very stuff of which poetry is made.

Some would describe this thought or idea as the "inspiration" of the poem, but I will refrain from using that problematic term. The term "inspiration" has many misleading connotations and there are many misconceptions about the role of inspiration in creativity.[1] Described more simply as an important early thought or as a germinating idea, it is less clothed in myth or mystery than described as an inspiration; nonetheless, it is a critical aspect of the creative process. As such a critical aspect of the creative process is seldom definitely and precisely identified or reported, it bears careful scrutiny.

In order to clarify the salient features of the formulation, "horses live human lives," I will focus on its structure. Rather than analyzing or discussing the particular perspective or bit of knowledge contained in the poet's conception of horses, as would usually be done in an aesthetic approach, I shall be primarily concerned with a formal property of the thought, a property that may not be immediately apparent and one that the poet himself may not have noticed when embroiled in the writing of the poem. I am interested in properties that poets have not noticed because that is the point of the exercise. If poets and other creators characteristically stopped during the process of creating to examine the structure or formal properties of their thinking, they would hardly progress with the business at hand. If creators could have done the job themselves, the psychological story of the creative process would have been told and would be well established by now. Another reason for focusing on formal properties derives from a special feature of creative processes and their outcomes. Not uncommonly, the content of creative thoughts seems self-evident retrospectively or a posteriori. After a creative idea is posited and elaborated, after its *plausibility* is demonstrated through logical explanation or presentation in a poem or other work of art, we sometimes find it to be remarkably apparent or true; sometimes we even believe that we ourselves might have arrived at such an idea, had we "merely" known to look at things in that particular way. Consequently, if we focus on content alone, it might be difficult, even impossible, to recognize that the initial creative thought may not have been so plausible or necessarily conforming to the format of ordinary logic; it might be difficult to recognize that the initial thought may have been quite different in structure. It might be hard to realize that the particular thought was actually based on an apparent *implausibility*.

In the case of "horses live human lives," the basis of the thought was such an apparent implausibility. More specifically, the formulation was structurally self-contradictory. Note carefully the specific aspects of the idea: horses do not only share the human experience nor are they simply subjected to the wishes and needs of humans, they *live* human lives. Horses bridge the barrier separating humans from beasts, not in this case through an evolutionary relationship but because of their living their lives in the human sphere. Tameable animals renounce their kind in order to live human lives, the poet told me in our discussion of the idea. Yet the horse continues to be a beast and to retain his animal nature despite his *living* a human life. The idea was not that horses were equivalent to human beings, but that they lived their lives. As the poet conceived it, two opposite and contradictory propositions were true of the horse *at the same time*. A horse was human and a horse was a beast simultaneously. A horse was also simultaneously not-a-human and not-a-beast. The poet formulated a concept emphasizing distinctly antithetical aspects of the horse rather than a concept involving mutual modification of certain aspects or a compromise formation. Horses were not humanly beasts nor beastly humans, nor were horses thought of as related to humans on an evolutionary scale. He did not think of a combination of horses and humans such as the centaur, the mythical entity composed of the torso, arms, and head of a man merged with a horse's body. In the context of the poem, the horse assumed no human characteristics nor a human any horselike features, nor, as in fable and myth, did the horse speak as humans do. The formulation consisted of a logical contradiction and the postulation of a simultaneous antithesis.

I designate this process[2] of actively formulating simultaneous antitheses "janusian thinking," a term based on the qualities of the ancient Roman deity Janus, the god whose many faces looked in several opposite directions at the same time. Janusian thinking consists of *actively conceiving two or more opposite or antithetical ideas, images, or concepts simultaneously*. Opposites or antitheses are conceived as existing side by side or as equally operative and equally true. Such thinking is highly complex. It is intrinsic to creativity and it operates widely in all types of creative processes, intellectual and pragmatic as well as artistic. It is different from dialectical thinking, ambivalence, and the thought processes of children or of schizophrenics. It is the mirror image of a dream quality and of primary process thought.

Keeping to the context of the creation of this particular poem, I shall specify the mirror-image quality of janusian thought. The poet's thought of a horse as both human and beast simultaneously occurred in full consciousness and in a totally rational context. There was nothing altered about his state of consciousness, as in hypnosis, drug intoxication, dreams, or other so-called altered states—nor was there any indication of an upsurge of unconscious thought. The poet's thinking was goal directed, clear, and he was fully cognizant and aware of logical connections and distinctions. He knew that horses did not actually live as humans; the idea was only figuratively true.

According to psychoanalytic theory, a cardinal feature of unconscious thinking is that opposites represent each other and operate interchangeably with no contradiction whatsoever. In the dream, something may be turned into and represented by its opposite. Such reversal and representation by opposites are considered to be characteristic of the primary process cognition responsible for dreams. There is a good deal of clinical evidence supporting these theoretical formulations about dreaming and unconscious processes. But, although opposites represent each other without contradiction in the Unconscious, or in unconscious thinking, and although primary process operations defy such opposition and contradiction, it does not follow that all interchangeable opposition or defiance of contradiction in thinking is a direct manifestation of the contents of the Unconscious, or of unconscious thinking, or of the primary process. On the contrary, in creative thinking, simultaneous opposition or antithesis, rather than interchangeable opposition, occurs as a function of a secondary process type of cognition. Secondary process cognition obeys the rules of ordinary logic—psychoanalysts refer to Aristotelian logic—and it is characteristic of conscious thinking. Janusian thinking occurs during full consciousness with full rationality and logical faculties operating at the moment simultaneous oppositions and antitheses are formulated. Janusian thinking is a special type of secondary process operation.[3] It is a mirror-image process in that its contents resemble the reversals and multiple opposites found in dreams, but its psychological charactertistics and functions are the obverse of dreaming. The creator's thinking is goal oriented and directed, he is concerned with secondary process tasks in the aesthetic and scientific realm, and he produces images and thoughts that superficially appear to be similar to some spontaneously formed images in dreams. And, although he does not realize it, he reverses the psychological function of dreaming.

With respect to the aesthetic task, the janusian thought of a horse as simultaneously human and beast functioned to produce a fundamental tension undergirding the poem, "In Monument Valley." Guided by this thought, the poet introduced the idea of an ancient bond between man and beast, and later in the writing process he elaborated the making and breaking of this bond. The janusian thought also functioned to unify the poem because the relationship between man and beast complemented the idea of the weird blending of animate and inanimate in the shrieking rocks of Monument Valley.[4] Furthermore, the idea of the human-beast horse as emblematic for the modern age was one of the factors giving the poem universal meaning beyond the particular experiences described.

But the janusian thought was derived from other psychological sources beside purely intellectual deliberations about the horse as emblematic of the modern age and even aside from purely aesthetic considerations such as providing contrast and unification within the structure of the poem. There is no doubt that the poet himself was aware of the intellectual implications of his thought and some of the aesthetic functions that it served, and there is also no doubt that he was *not* aware of some of the emotional roots of his thought at the time it occurred to him. He was not aware that the thought of a horse as human and beast simultaneously, or not-human and not-beast simultaneously, had roots in his own personal conflicts. And he was not aware that this janusian thought also served to bring some of the elements of these conflicts to the surface during the writing of the poem. This function or quality of janusian thinking, together with the quality of similarity to dream representation, constitutes the essential enantiomorphic relationship with dreaming. A janusian formulation superficially resembles a dream image but it functions in unearthing unconscious processes rather than in keeping them submerged and hidden.

Because of our unique knowlege of the emotional and unconscious material relating to this poem, we are in a position to trace this process quite specifically. The janusian thought, like all conscious secondary process thought, is accompanied by or merges with[5] preconscious and unconscious affects, wishes, and defense mechanisms. Thus, we can immediately see that the structure of the janusian thought, the simultaneous antithesis, coincided with the structure of an emotional process going on outside of the poet's awareness. The janusian thought consisted of mutually contradictory or conflicting intellectual elements relating to and merging with mutually contradictory or conflicting emotions and wishes. From the analysis of the poet's dream and other data, an analysis concerning the unconscious processes relating to the poem, we know that the poet was dealing with a conflict between wanting to be cared for and wanting to be free and independent. The conflicting qualities of the horse in the janusian thought represent this emotional conflict closely. As part of the human sphere, a horse is a beast of burden, supporting and taking care of the needs of humans as well as (by implication) being cared for by them. As a wild beast, a horse is free and independent.

Many other levels of conflict could also be considered to be incorporated and impressed into the image, depending on interpretations of other aspects of the poet's conflict. For example, the poet's conception of the horse-human relationship as pertaining to philosophical issues about the body and the soul could be considered a reflection of a conflict about sex, that is, whether sex is beastly or sublime. The poet's dream concerning Miriam contained definite sexual elements, she swooning in her underclothes, and both the remaining content of the dream and his later associations about Miriam's demanding qualities indicate he was conflicted about these elements. As Miriam was intimately connected to the underlying thoughts of the poem, an associated sexual conflict must have been incorporated there as well.

Simultaneous opposition suggests unconscious processes because it is structurally congruent with emotional conflict. Janusian formulations have roots in unconscious conflicts. The function of revealing and unearthing these unconscious conflicts and other unconscious material is due to a particular factor directly associated with janusian thinking. This factor is a specific mechanism of psychological defense, *negation.*

Janusian Thinking and Negation

First described by Freud in 1925,[6] the negation defense has a special position compared to other defense mechanisms in psychoanalytic practice and theory. More than any other defense mechanism, defensive negation seems widely accepted in psychoanalytic practice and so much taken for granted that it has become a virtual hallmark of psychoanalysis among the laity. A popular caricature of psychoanalysis is to describe it as the psychological theory asserting that a person spontaneously saying "no" really means "yes." Shakespeare's famous reference to the same defense—"methinks the lady doth protest too much"—is often cited not only as an instance of Shakespeare's psychological acuity but particularly of his having anticipated Freud by many centuries. Yet, very little specific attention has been paid to defensive negation in psychoanalytic theory, while there has been a good deal of theoretical discussion about virtually every other psychological defense.[7]

When Freud first described the negation defense, he cited the example of the patient who tells the analyst, "I had a dream last night, but it was *not* about my mother." Sagely, Freud pointed out that such a gratuitous comment, an introduction despite its negative form of the thought of the mother, indicated that the dream most certainly *was* about the patient's mother. He went on to point out a most intriguing aspect of this defensive act—defensive because the negative form is used in order to avoid and protect against the anxiety attendant on entry of the content into consciousness; he stated that the defense overcomes the *effects* of repression without actually removing repression. Preconscious or unconscious material is allowed to appear in a person's conscious thought directly without that person recognizing or acknowledging its source. Negation sidesteps repression rather than overcoming it and, consequently, unconscious and preconscious material can appear in consciousness without anxiety. Like all ego defense mechanisms, negation functions unconsciously to protect against anxiety but influences and distorts conscious processes. All defenses potentially disrupt reality-oriented thinking to some degree. Negation is not a mechanism of primary process thought; it influences secondary process thinking as an ego defense. Despite some defensive distortion of secondary process thinking, negation functions indirectly to reveal and thereby to unearth unconscious and preconscious concerns more than other defense mechanisms.[8] Bringing unconscious material into consciousness albeit in negative form is a step in an unearthing process.

Just such a defense mechanism operates in janusian thoughts. The psychological function of simultaneous and mutual contradiction, the function allowing unconscious and preconscious material to appear in consciousness without excessive anxiety, is defensive negation of content in janusian thoughts. With respect to the particular janusian formulation of the horse as not-human and not-beast simultaneously, defensive negation operated in the following way: the horse as *not*-human indicates that the horse actually did represent something human. A male horse at the time of the conception, the horse represented the poet himself. The horse as *not*-beast, or not a member of a wild beast species, indicates that the horse did represent something wild or beastly. This was the poet's own beastly nature; the poet was also a beast. Represented in part was the poet's wish to be free and independent like the wild beast, but the unconscious identification of himself with a beast or animal pertained to deeper and more unacceptable feelings. The double negation indicates that the poet unconsciously saw himself as a beastly human or a humanly beast. Given our previous analysis of his unconscious yearnings, he felt, "I am a beast who wants to be cared for by his mother." Both the human and beast aspects of the horse were figurative aspects of the poet's unconscious concerns.

Defensive negation operates widely in the artistic creative process in other operations beside janusian thinking. Broadly speaking, it is the mechanism that allows a creator to incorporate into a work of art aspects of personal unconscious content without recognizing that he is doing so. When describing the feeling and perceptions of a specific character in a literary work, for example, the writer often uses negation when he tells himself (and the carping critics) that he is not representing any of his own feelings in the description. Another more dramatic example of the effect of negation in the creative process is the frequently reported experience of arriving at a point in artistic activity where "the work creates itself." At such a point, the work flows extraordinarily freely and the experience is exceptionally gratifying. Artists characteristically look forward to such gratifying occurrences, and they and others often term them as inspirations or believe the experience to consist of an altered state of consciousness; in many quarters such experiences are considered to be the sine qua non of creativity. Significantly, material produced in such a state often seems to be full of overt preconscious and unconscious content, one of the reasons many theorists proclaim that creativity involves a direct outpouring of unconscious material. But rather than such direct outpouring, these experiences are due to defensive negation; they occur at a phase when defensive negation is in full sway. According to both public and private testimony (collected in my own researches) of countless writers, the literary work only "writes itself" in a relatively late phase of the creative process, at a point when characters and situations have become quite sharply drawn. Characteristically, the writer avers to himself that the actions and emotions he constructs have *no relationship to himself,* that they belong to the characters alone and it seems that the work is writing itself.[9] Another observation bearing on this point is that writers almost invariably reveal more of their unconscious and preconscious concerns in their fiction than in their direct autobiographical accounts. This was demonstrated in a study comparing Strindberg's autobiographical writings with his fiction[10] and, more widely, it was suggested by data bearing on the psychodynamics of the creation of fiction in general.[11] It appears that the virtually intrinsic negation of fiction—"this is not about me, it is about imaginary people"—allows for the inclusion of unconscious and preconscious material without the accompaniment of excessive anxiety.

The function of defensive negation helps clarify an essential mirror-image characteristic of janusian thinking, the active postulation of simultaneous opposition or antithesis on a conscious, secondary process level; janusian thinking reverses the concealing operation of representing opposites interchangeably by the primary process. Janusian thinking brings opposites or antitheses together in order to produce aesthetic effects, to solve conceptual and scientific problems, and it helps to reveal unconscious material without producing excessive anxiety. The defense mechanism of negation facilitates this revelation of preconscious and unconscious material in janusian thinking. Simultaneous opposition and simultaneous antithesis are accompanied by simultaneous negation, an operation allowing the creator to unearth unconscious and preconscious contents without becoming overwhelmed.[12]

What happens to the unconscious and preconscious material revealed by janusian thinking? Does such material simply appear and remain unacknowledged and inaccessible to the creator because of defensive negation? No, as a reversal and a fully reflective mirror image of dreaming, the creative process continues to make unconscious material increasingly accessible to consciousness. A specific example from "In Monument Valley" to follow will serve to illustrate how this continuation occurs.

Janusian Thinking and the Unearthing of Unconscious Material

Janusian formulations frequently occur early in the creative process and serve to guide ensuing ideas and developments. Often, therefore, they are changed and elaborated and are not clearly identifiable in the completed work. Some formulations, however, emerge later in the process and remain intact and unchanged at the end. In the final version of "In Monument Valley," the first stanza lines "Stillnesses were swarming inward from the evening star / Or outward from the buoyant sorrel mare" constitute an intact janusian formulation. These lines describe a simultaneous opposition pertaining to the source of the quality of stillness, a suggestion that the stillnesses arise from two opposing directions—inward and outward—at once. In case that is not immediately clear, note a slightly ambiguous use of the conjunction "or" in the second of the two lines. In contrast to a conjunction such as "and," the "or" serves to produce a sense of simultaneity rather than sequence. The source of the rider's subjective sense of stillness is identified as being the evening star or the mare. As the subjective stillness is constant, the impact is that the rider does not precisely know where it comes from because it comes from both at once. With "and" the source of the feeling of stillness would seem sequential: first from the star and then from the horse and so on. With stillnesses swarming inward or outward, they swarm from both directions at once. Though a literalist might insist that the "or" merely indicates an alternative source of the stillnesses, and such a meaning is also included, the primary thrust of the lines in context surely conveys simultaneous opposition.

I choose this example partly because these lines were not conceived all at one time, but achieved in a stepwise fashion. Hence, there is an opportunity to look closely at the process of janusian thinking as it unfolds, rather than only considering a fully formed result. I also choose this example because the formulation of the particular janusian construct is followed by the unearthing of some particular unconscious material. In the working manuscripts of the poem, the development of these lines occurred in the manner and the sequence to follow.

The poet made the first reference to "stillness" in this early version of the first stanza:

We live mostly in the past or in the future
These lines begin in one and end in the other
The evening a summer or two after the war
That I last found myself on horseback
A swarming stillness under

After writing the beginning fragment of the line referring to stillness, the poet could not continue. Instead of going on, he recopied and revised the entire first stanza and, after many changes and revisions, his next version of the same line was: "A swarming stillness. A first star . . . ." Making an attempt to begin another line after this one with a reference to "a strong and gentle animal," he soon got stuck and again tried to start anew. Then he wrote:

One summer dusk a year or two after the war
I found myself for what would be the last time
On horseback, at Shoup's farm north of Woodstock
A stillness swarming inward from the first star
The world expanding buoyantly upheld
By the strong and patient animal
Who seemed himself to be enjoying things, his gait
Opening vistas of the absolute

Here again, he stopped and turned to work on the second stanza and, leaving the first stanza as above, he changed the second stanza to the following:

Or outward from the strong and fragrant animal
Who seemed to find sufficient my weight
Upon his back, just as I did his gait
Opening buoyant vistas of the

With this, he arrived at the janusian formulation, "A stillness swarming inward from the first star / Or outward from the strong and fragrant animal."

We must immediately consider several things at once. It is important to notice that the horse in this version is still referred to as male, a stallion, just as he had been in the other stanzas of the poem written up to this point. No reference to the "mare" of the completed poem, the word connected to his underlying wish, has yet appeared. Also, it should be clear that the very first thought referred only to a sense of stillness and that the rest of the formulation developed through a slow, erratic accretion of ideas. Early, the stillness was connected to a star, a far away and virtually abstract thing that conveyed expansiveness to the scene. The succeeding reference to "a strong and gentle animal" in the very next version indicates that the horse was thought of next, but the idea of opposing the stillness of the horse to the stillness of the star did not occur until two versions later. Only then could the stillness *also* come from something near, concrete, and relatively small. The transitional idea leading to the stillness emanating from the horse, it appears, was contained in the phrase describing the horse's gait "opening vistas of the absolute." Relating the horse to something "absolute" connected, or led back, to the star. It suggested, or otherwise developed into, the janusian formulation of stillness coming from inward and outward sources simultaneously. But before this formulation was constructed, the heavenly star and the earthly beast had already been connected together.

Another point to bear in mind is that the wordplay involving the homophonic term "gait" provided the means whereby the horse could be connected to the absolute. The use of "gait" in the version just presented is somewhat like a pun; it refers both to the horse's stride and to the identical sounding word, "gate." Thus, the horse's gait is itself a gate opening vistas of the absolute. I shall shortly refer again to this particular punning-like connection in relation to another type of mirror-image process in creativity.

I also want to call attention to the phrase "strong and fragrant animal" used in this version of the stanza. Although the qualities of strength and fragrance together are not exactly antithetical or oppositional, especially in reference to an animal, there is a slightly jarring or arresting note introduced by the use of these two adjectives together. After all, the word "fragrance" does usually apply to delicate and pleasant odors and it is seldom used to describe a horse's smell except in a joking or ironic way. I am suggesting that the description of the horse as both strong and fragrant is the beginning of a janusian thought. I do this, not to push the idea of seeing opposition or antithesis to an unwarranted excess—I realize some such objection might be raised at this point—but to prepare for a full appreciation of the steps taken by the poet in the next version of this stanza. We are now ready to understand how the poet progressed to the virtually final formulation of these lines and to follow the operation of janusian thinking with respect to the unearthing of unconscious processes.

The next change the poet made in these lines was to substitute the words "sweet smelling" for the word "fragrant." The phrase became, "the strong and sweet smelling animal," a much more definite simultaneous antithesis and a janusian formulation.

Next, he rewrote the entire stanza, changing the horse's sex, as follows:

> Or outward from the strong and gentle mare
> Who moved as if not displeased by my weight on her back
> While I—a buoyant present entered through a gait
> Bordered as by thick hedges of invisible lilac

Finally—that is, his final change before retyping and starting to work on the entire poem again from the beginning—he changed the words "strong and gentle mare" to "buoyant sorrel mare," the description he used in the completed version.

Now we have observed in detail the specific point at which the change of the horse to a mare occurred! This important change occurred after two particular janusian thoughts had been defined. Earlier, it will be remembered, I strongly emphasized the importance of the poet's changing the horse's sex during the writing of the poem because, as I also emphasized, the word "mare" was homophonic with the French word, *mère,* meaning mother. I pointed out that this change provided evidence that the poet was unconsciously preoccupied with wanting to be cared for by his mother while writing this poem. Now I must emphasize that the use of this word also led to the unconscious preoccupation coming close to and finally appearing almost fully in consciousness. The poet, who is highly sensitive to homophonic qualities of words—note the punning use of "gait" just considered—and highly fluent in French, was not initially thinking of the specific homophony of the word "mare" while writing the poem. Later, however, when he focused on his use of the word, he himself immediately adopted the idea that the poem had a great deal to do with his mother. The overlooking of the homophony while writing the poem could hardly be attributed to anything but psychological blocking—especially in view of the dream evidence linking the poem to his mother—but his use of the word and his later quick acceptance of the link to his mother also indicates that the idea of mother was very close to his awareness. The rapid achievement of insight at that point indicated that the unconscious issue was at the threshold of consciousness.[13]

The janusian process, therefore, functioned in two interrelated modes at once: the aesthetic and the psychological. It gave structure, coherence, and abstract implication to the lines,[14] and it served to unearth the poet's unconscious concerns. The probable psychodynamic sequence was as follows: the janusian formulation of the stillness coming both from a heavenly body and a supporting animal involved an initial double defensive negation indirectly revealing that the source of the feeling of contentment was an unconscious element having dual characteristics. It was an element often considered both absolute—brilliant, all embracing, heavenly, might be better words—and supporting at the same time: namely, a parent. Although I lack the poet's specific associations to this line in order to corroborate such an assumption, I am influenced by my previous knowledge that a star has been an unconscious image for the poet's mother in other poems he has written.

The element suggested by the operation of defensive negation in this general formulation is, however, vague and only dimly revealed. The next janusian formulation began to make it clearer and more specific. When the poet referred to a strong and fragrant horse, he began to reveal, through defensive negation, that the horse not only unconsciously represented a person, but a very specific person. Only his mother could be the one strong enough to support and care for him and to be fragrant and female at the same time. When he developed the full-blown janusian formulation through the substitution of "sweet smelling" for "fragrant," he was unaccountably moved—that was the way he explained it, "not really sure why"—to change the horse to a mare, a direct but not yet quite conscious representation of his mother.

I would not insist that the janusian process was exclusively responsible for the poet's progress toward unearthing his unconscious concern while writing these lines. As I have stated, the entire creative process is the mirror image of dreaming, and other as yet unidentified processes played a role. Of additional interest regarding the poet's production of the janusian formulation in this stanza is the first construction of an image directly connecting the poem to the unconscious wish of his dreams. Beside using the word "mare," he also constructed an image related to being cared for. Immediately following his writing the line, "Or outward from the strong and fragrant animal," he referred to his weight on the horse's back, the first time he made a concrete reference in the poem to the idea of being a burden and being supported. As I have previously suggested, this reference is a representation of the feeling of being cared for. Interestingly, too, he initially used the understated wording "who seemed to find sufficient my weight / Upon his back" and then changed it to the slightly stronger, "who moved as if not displeased by my weight on her back." In the change, the horse is satisfied with her burden.

The poet mentioned these lines to me in connection with changing the horse's sex, a fact lending support to the supposition that this latter aspect of this version also touched on and began to unearth his unconscious concerns. He said he began to feel a sort of sexual relationship with the horse while describing his weight on its back. This feeling led him to make the horse female. The reference to a sexual relationship with the horse certainly recalls the oedipal aspects of the dreams I mentioned earlier.

Homospatial Thinking

The germinating idea for the poem was a janusian thought of a horse as not-human and not-beast and this thought became transmuted, transformed, and elaborated throughout the poem. Primarily, this janusian thought influenced the content of the last three stanzas of the poem and it is implied both in the line referring to "the ancient bond between her kind and mine," and in "tottering still half in trust, half in fear of man." Janusian thoughts are often implied or transformed in the final versian of a poem, as well as in the final versions of other types of creations, because the simultaneous opposition is integrated into a unified structure such as an image, metaphor, or a complete poem or theory. Sometimes, especially in poetry, a janusian thought is manifestly expressed in the final product without transformation. The lines just discussed specifying an inward and outward source simultaneously are examples of such untransformed and manifest janusian constructions in the completed poem. Most often, however, janusian constructions are integrated into the final creation and are difficult to recognize. The integration of these constructions is produced, in part, by an entirely different thought process, a process that is also an enantiomorph or mirror image of dream processes and operations. This distinct and second type of thinking operates very extensively in the creative process. Not only does it integrate janusian thoughts, but it also produces a variety of other types of created phenomena. Like janusian thinking, this other, second type of thinking functions to unearth unconscious material during the process of creation.

To describe this other type of thinking, I shall return to consider the second important formulation influencing the creation of this poem. This was the poet's thought the day after he began the poem, the idea occurring on the morning after having the dreams concerning the playing field and the invalided grandmother. The poet described this thought in his notebook with the words: "His rider—he had never had a rider," and the idea strongly influenced the writing of what later became the first two stanzas of the completed poem. These stanzas, as the poet later told me, were intended to provide a history of the rapport between man and horse. The aesthetic intent was to sharpen the intensity of the final point of the poem. As I pointed out in chapter 1, these stanzas also contain the wish-fulfilling image relating to the poet's unconscious preoccupation. The mood is idyllic and the rider is supported by the horse much as the poet wished to be supported and cared for by his mother.

It will probably surprise no one familiar in the slightest way with creative thinking, or for that matter any type of productive thinking, that the poet's thought about the horse and rider came to him originally as a visual image. After all, the word we always use in connection with creative and productive thought is imagination, a word originally referring to visual experience. Scientific studies of creative thinking have been strongly influenced by this root meaning of the word "imagination," and some have discussed or attempted to assess the role of visual imagery in the thoughts of both artists and scientists.[15] The poet's first mental formulation consisted of a visual image pertaining to a horse and rider and, unsurprisingly, he then took up his notebook to write the words mentioned above. However, the specific nature of this image should be surprising, because it was quite unusual and it has never been previously documented or described. The poet's mental image of a horse and rider was of *two discrete entities occupying the same space.* He did not see a clear image of a specific horse with a specific rider, the poet himself for example, on its back. He did not visualize a remembered scene, say a landscape, with horse and rider in it, nor was there even any definitely clear outlines of a horse and a rider. Instead, he referred to the image as a "double thing," a vague undefined whole with two aspects. Human and horse were diffusely represented together. Difficult as such an image is to describe, he told me that he imagined "both the riderless horse and the horse as he would be with a rider." The diagrammatic representation in figure 1 will give only an approximation of the nature of this mental event.

Because conscious visual experiences such as this may only occur during the creative process, it is possible that persons who have not engaged in highly creative thinking will have difficulty grasping the actual construction of this mental formulation. Even creative persons seldom focus on their thoughts while creating to the extent that we are doing here and they have therefore not themselves ever documented such a type of thinking. The poet visualized the horse alone riderless and unsaddled, and in the same mental space, he visualized the horse with a rider fully astride. In such an image, the horse alone and the horse with the human become fused and superimposed upon one another. Trying to comprehend this image probably leads one immediately to think of representations in dreams because dream representations do not respect ordinary conceptions of space. Neither does the type of thinking I am describing. But there is an immediate and major difference between dream representations and the poet's waking thought of both a horse alone and a horse with a rider occupying the same space: dream images and events are sharp and vivid but this waking thought was vague and diffuse. Whereas dreams might convey the *sense* of a horse without a rider occupying the same space as a horse with a rider by means of an image of a horse accompanied by a vivid feeling of an invisible rider's presence, or by means of a distorted but vivid compromise formation of horses and a rider merged, the poet's waking thought is rooted in reality and consists totally of a necessarily vague superimposition or fusion of discrete entities. To reemphasize, the illustration presented here is a diagrammatic representation of the poet's thought, not a picture of the actual image in his mind. It is impossible to present two or more discrete entities occupying the same space concretely because such an event never oc-

Fig. 1. An artist's conception of the nature of the mental image alluded to by the words, "His rider—he had never had a rider." Drawing by Robert C. Morris.

curs in concrete experience. The actual image is necessarily a vague and abstract representation.

This type of experience occurs regularly in all types of creative processes. It occurs in full consciousness and leads to aesthetic constructions and to solutions of scientific problems. It is somewhat similar to a dream experience but is not a manifestation of dream thought or dreaming in waking life. In a psychodynamic reversal of the function of dream processes, it serves to unearth, reveal, and neutralize unconscious material rather than to disguise and hide it. This type of thought is a manifestation of "homospatial thinking" (from the Greek *homoios,* meaning "same"), a mirror image of dream process.

Homospatial thinking consists of *actively conceiving two or more discrete entities occupying the same space, a conception leading to the articulation of new identities.* Concrete objects such as rivers, houses, and human faces, discrete sensations such as wet, rough, bright, and cold, and also sound patterns and written words are superimposed, fused, or otherwise brought together in the mind and totally fill its space.[16] Although the process is often visual, it may involve any of the sensory modalities: auditory, tactile, olfactory, gustatory, or kinesthetic. A visual image may be accompanied by another type of sensory impression or factor, or a homospatial thought may consist of nonvisual entities and their sensations and qualities exclusively. Two or more discrete entities are conceived as occupying the same space as a preliminary step toward producing a new unity or a new identity. Because discrete entities cannot remain in this preunified state for very long, even in the mind, the homospatial thought is held as a rapid, fleeting, and changing mental impression or conception that soon leads to separating out of various components. As with janusian thinking, the creator is fully conscious and rational while having homospatial thoughts and he thinks of connecting links and plausible circumstances to express them. Thus, the poet thought of the "double thing," a diffuse image both of horse alone and of horse and human, and this led directly to the formulation of a horse with the poet (the poetic "I") as a rider when he "went off to study or to war."

The Creative Function of Homospatial Thinking

The specifically creative aspect of homospatial thinking is that components separated out of the fleeting conception are new ones, they are not simply *aspects* of the original discrete entities considered stepwise or independently. Homospatial thinking is not synonymous with analogic thinking, the stepwise comparing of partial similarities between two or more independent things. Homospatial thinking consists of the superimposition or fusion of whole entities rather than a side by side consideration of their aspects or parts. For example, the poet's conception of a horse alone and of a horse and rider both together did not result from a search for entities with mutual attributes such as: horse and man are both alone; both carry burdens, give and need support and nurturance; both are mortal, and so on. Such analogues emerge from the homospatial conception after it occurs rather than initially producing it. Nor was there a simple association of a horse and a rider because of their commonly being found together in experience. The homospatial conception is based on the creator's idea that two or more entities *ought* to or *should* have mutual attributes. Hence, the poet thought of bringing together and superimposing an unridden wild unbroken horse and a horse gentled and ridden. Riderless horse, human rider, and ridden horse were all occupying the same space. Such entities are brought together for abstract and emotional purposes, and concrete images emerge. Furthermore, homospatial thinking is not simply a type of gestalt process where the formulation of new wholes or new contexts is the primary thrust. Homospatial thoughts effect the filling of gaps and formulations of wholes as a by-product; the wholes are produced because of the filling of mental space.

Homospatial thinking operates throughout the creative process, in its earliest phases as well as its later ones. In the creation of the "In Monument Valley" poem, the homospatial conception fusing and superimposing the riderless horse and the human rider on the horse functioned to integrate into an effective literary construction the previous janusian thought of a horse as simultaneously not-beast and not-human. Indeed, one of the important functions of homospatial thinking is to integrate janusian thoughts occurring early in the creative process. The poet's first formulations pertaining to his janusian thought in this poem were the lines, "A tradition in China as in modern verse / Gives to each age its emblematic beast." Although these lines do not explicitly spell out the idea of a horse as not-human and not-beast, the reference to an "emblematic beast"—that is, the horse as an emblem of the nonbelongingness and personal alienation characteristic of our times—strongly implies it. But these early lines are really rather prosaic and heavy, as the poet himself would be the first to agree, and the presentation of poetic imagery rather than explicit ideas improves the poem enormously. Through poetic imagery, the horse is shown to be an emblem and the point is conveyed emotionally. Also, the poetic statement is made through emotionally effective and structural changes.

The homospatial thought led to poetic images, structural changes, and the construction of lines integrating the janusian thought into the fabric of the entire poem. There is, first, a sense of temporal development and change: as a result of the homospatial idea, the poem begins with a relationship of harmony between man and beast in the first two stanzas; it moves to a later chance encounter, followed by a breaking of a bond. Second, the presentation of horse and rider virtually merged together in the first two stanzas (e.g., "with one accord we circled the small lake") was derived from the human and horse occupying the same place within a portion of the homospatial conception and resulted in a vivid representation of the janusian thought about the kinship between horses and humans. This representation or poetic construction (image or metaphor) is necessary as a background for the explicit reference to the paradoxical nature of this kinship in the lines of the last stanza, "still half in trust, half in fear of man." Both the poetic image and the explicit reference together state the theme; neither would be sufficient alone. Finally, the poetic image of the horse and rider together allows for a peaceful idyllic emotional tone in the first two stanzas contrasting sharply with the turbulent tone of the last three stanzas and especially with the statement of emptiness and renunciation at the finale. There is a strong emotional impact and a sense of climax.

Homospatial thinking is a type of cognition best described as a mode of spatial abstracting. The conception of two or more entities occupying the same space is an abstraction from nature, not a form of concretion or a concrete mode of thinking. It functions to integrate janusian thoughts and it also functions in many other aspects of the creative process. One of its chief effects is to produce metaphors, artistic metaphors as well as those used in scientific theory. It produces these metaphors sometimes in combination with janusian thinking and sometimes in a more direct way. Saying this, I have begun to anticipate the discussion in a later chapter (chap. 10) of some of the wide-ranging manifestations of this thought process; rather than go on, I will return to my theme and to the spelling out of how homospatial thinking operated as a mirror-image process of dreaming in the poem we are considering.

Homospatial Thinking as a Mirror-Image Process

Following his homospatial thought of the horse alone and the horse and rider together, the poet had not immediately had the idea of reformulating the beginning of the poem. Later that day, he sat down to work and began another version starting with his original line, "Hot pumice blew . . . . ." In this version, he described the meeting with the horse in Monument Valley and, after referring to the gift of an apple core, he brought in the horse and rider relationship with lines that tended to reproduce the structure of the homospatial conception. I present these lines again in figure 2 to show what I mean.

The denotation of each of the aspects of the conception, a riderless horse and a horse with a rider, leads into lines indicating an interaction and relationship.

Poetic Lines, Second Version	Aspects of the Homospatial Conception
A gentle broken horse	[the horse alone]
For all he knew it could have been I who first	[the horse and rider together]
Broke him, rode him, abandoned him	[development of the image]
When I went off to study or to war.	[development of the image]

Fig. 2. Lines from the second version of "In Monument Valley" are on the left; the column on the right identifies the aspects of the structure of the homospatial conception explicated in each corresponding line.

He did no further work on this idea that day, and on the next he worked sporadically on various parts of the poem. But his work was interrupted by the planned trip to the city, and so he did not fully develop the horse and rider relationship as contained in the final version of the first three stanzas until four days later. He wrote the fully developed version on the day after his having the dreams about Elizabeth Bishop and Marianne Moore.

The main point about this sequence is that the homospatial conception continued to be in some form in his mind—a portion of the poetic image had been constructed and specified—and it facilitated the process of unearthing his unconscious concerns, an unearthing that had begun with the janusian thought of the horse as not-human and not-beast simultaneously. I have already pointed out that the idea of the poet himself on the horse's back, the offspring supported by the parent, was a more direct representation of the poet's unconscious wish than the dream presentation of a parent on an offspring's back. But lest I be accused of a tautology here, because I have used the poetic construction of the horse and rider as a means of interpreting the wish fulfillment of the dream, I will marshall final and telling evidence for a mirror-image unearthing process in the creation of the poem as follows: the first written material derived from the homospatial conception contained an allusion to a time in the poet's life when *his wish to be cared for by his mother*—or at least to be the center of his mother's, as well as his grandmother's, attention—*came closest to being realized.* He referred in this first formulation to a time before "I went off to study or to war." From facts gathered in our later discussions, it is clear that the phrase referred to a very important period in his life. During this period (mentioned in chap. 1), his relationship to his mother and grandmother had a very special character.

The poet had a brief sojourn in the army in his late teens which interrupted his college education. Prior to his college experience (before going "to study"), there was a series of summers and shorter holidays, as well as some short holidays during his first college year (a time prior to his going "to war"), which he spent almost exclusively in the company of his mother, his grandmother, and his grandmother's sister. His parents had gotten divorced some years before and his father had moved away. The poet's sibling was older than he and no longer lived at home. The maternal grandmother, an on-and-off resident from the time her own husband had died, had by then moved in with the poet and his mother permanently. The grandmother's sister, whom the poet "adored," was also a widow and she visited for the entire summer each year. It was a time when the poet was the only male in a house of women. He remembered especially being with his grandmother constantly during this time because his mother was away from home running a small business. Although the grandmother was somewhat of a burden, there were important emotional compensations.

As a period of his life during which there was no male competition in the house, the years including these summers and holidays provided the closest realization of his wish for exclusive nurturance he ever experienced. He was the sole object of attention of the three women and it was a period of relative peace and gratification compared to a stormy earlier time. If he were not totally cared for by his mother, he at least had a good deal of her attention. This period of his life was clearly the latent reference of the manifest imagery in the second early dream, the actual time during which he had been responsible for his grandmother and had felt pleasure at the prospect. The actual ride on Shoup's farm—there was one, a very happy one—took place several years later, during the summer.

The poet did not consciously think of these summers with his mother, grandmother, and the grandmother's sister while writing the lines designating the time before "I went off to study or to war," but he did think of words referring to himself as the rider of the horse and also referring virtually directly to this important period of his life. The homospatial thought led to a more direct connection to the latent reference and the underlying wish of his dream. It brought close to consciousness the time of his life when his wish to be the sole object of his mother's and his grandmother's attention came nearest to being gratified.[17]

After the poet wrote the lines connecting the horse to himself and to the wish-fulfilling time of his life, the process of unearthing unconscious material continued. His dreams of several days later pertain to the same issues and they develop the unconscious themes further. In the dream prior to his writing the full and definite version of the first two stanzas of the poem, there is a fairly direct representation of an oedipal wish. Marianne Moore, the aged and respected poetess, was to marry a younger man; this younger man, it is fair to assume, was the poet himself, while Marianne Moore represented his mother and/or grandmother. His underlying wish, therefore, consisted of wanting to marry his mother and/or his grandmother, a further extension and development of the desire to be the sole focus of female attention.

On the day after this dream, the process of unearthing unconscious material continued with the writing of the first two stanzas of the poem. In working out the homospatial thought concerning the horse and a rider, the poet came even closer to unearthing the nature of the unconscious connection to his mother; he changed the horse's sex to female at a moment when, as he put it, he began to feel a sexual relationship or sexual overtone between the rider and the horse. In other words, he more consciously experienced sexual feelings related to his mother, and came closer to a full recognition of the oedipal attachment. Previously, I explained the manner in which a janusian thought facilitated the unearthing process during the writing of this section of the poem; now, the phenomenon of unearthing can be seen as a combination of the effects of both janusian and homospatial thinking. One other example from these stanzas, an example of another homospatial process functioning to unearth the poet's unconscious concerns, shall at this point further clarify the mirror-image operation and the particular psychodynamic factors that facilitate unearthing.

I have mentioned the punning use of the word "gait" in the initial formulation of the poem's second stanza. I pointed out that the words "gate" and "gait" were homophones and that the overlapping sound of these words allowed for a connection between "the horse" and "the absolute" as well as "the horse" and "a star" ("his gait opening vistas"). The overall conception and the use of this homophonic connection in the poem is also an example of homospatial thinking.[18] Having conceived of the words "gait" and "gate" together—he had used each of the spellings in different manuscript versions of the poem—the poet experienced two discrete kinesthetic sensations occupying the same space in his consciousness. He thought of both the up and down rolling motion of the horse and the opening motion of an entrance way together. The word "gate/gait" allowed two discrete entities, or discrete sensory qualities of entities, to emanate from and occupy the same space. He did not, to be sure, invent or create this double meaning for the word "gate/gait"; it was already present in the English language. Unlike the previously described homospatial thought of the riderless horse and the horse and rider together, an unusual type of conception helping to integrate a janusian idea, there is nothing strikingly unusual or even inventive about recognizing that gait/gate has a double reference. What is unusual, and what is part of the creative process, is actively conceiving and using the two sensory references of the word together. That the two sensations were jointly present in the poet's mind in the manner I have just described is evident from the phrase, "his gait / Opening buoyant vistas of the . . . ," the participle "opening" clearly referring to the entrance way meaning of the word and the adjective "buoyant" clearly referring to the horse's stride. Horses' gaits cannot open anything, nor can gates be buoyant unless floating on water.

At this point in the writing, however, the phrase read mostly like a bad pun. But punning—either good or bad—and homospatial thinking are not the same; the homospatial process functions as an integrating factor and it functions to unearth unconscious material. There is more at stake than simply demonstrating a double meaning for the word gait/gate and, as a pun does, producing pleasure through the recognition of the familiar.[19] There is a unifying purpose and a special congruence between the elements of a homospatial conception and the context from which it develops. There is additionally a special congruence between the original psychological context and the unconscious material unearthed by the homospatial process. Like janusian thoughts, homospatial thoughts may also not appear directly in the final version of the creation. The double reference of gate/gait does not appear directly in the final version of this poem, but it served to stimulate the following sequence:

1. After the version of the phrase employing "gait" just mentioned, "his gait / Opening buoyant vistas of the . . . ," the poet tried:

> While I—A buoyant present entered through a gait
> Bordered as by thick hedges of invisible lilac.

The earlier connection of the gait/gate to "the absolute" was dropped; the word and idea "buoyant" was connected to the rider rather than to "vistas," and a new idea of a "gate" bordered by lilac was introduced.

2. Following this, he tried another version using the "gate" spelling of the word and describing an affect of happiness, rather than the buoyant kinesthetic experience:

> While I—Happiness had entered through a gate
> Burdened by thick hedges of invisible lilac.

3. Next, he decided to consolidate the two lines into:

Her gait swung onto meadows heavy with unseen lilac

4. Finally, he decided to drop completely the idea of using the double meaning of gate/gait in these lines, changed "heavy" to "heady," and produced the essentially finished version of the line:

Meadows welcomed us, heady with unseen lilac.
(Final: "Meadows received us, heady with unseen lilac.")

The progression has, it is clear, gradually led to a description and an overt formulation of a sense of peace and happiness in these first two stanzas. The series of lines starting from "Meadows received us, heady with unseen lilac" to the end of the second stanza surely intensify the sense of fulfillment expressed in the poem. These lines were definitely derived from the homospatial conception with fused discrete kinesthetic sensations in the idea of the double word gate/gait, despite the final disappearance of the explicit idea. As we know, the image of the rider on the female horse represented the poet's unconscious wish in this portion of the poem, and now we see that the homospatial conception consisting of gate/gait has functioned to produce specific lines and to unearth an affect of happiness and fulfillment which was surely connected to that basic image. But the unearthing process did not stop there. The poet continued to think about using gate/gait, and while deciding to drop it from the line above referring to the meadows, he thought of putting it into another place.

He thought of using the word "gate" as part of the name of another natural monument in Monument Valley. Turning at that point to his earlier written line, referring to the "Three Sisters" as a natural monument, which read, "Shreik the 'Three Sisters!' No place for a picnic," he added the phrase "St. Peter's Gate." Dissatisfied, he then tried "Gates of Heaven" and soon he arrived at the particular construction he used in the final version, "Hell's Gate." He cast the entire line into its final form as: "The 'Three Sisters' howl, 'Hell's Gate' yawns wide"—an effective change, I believe all would agree.

In a strange but rather dramatic way, this change represents another instance of the unearthing of unconscious material: when the poet and I had discussed the phrase "Hell's Gate," he told me that he had been thinking of the Rodin sculpture "Gate of Hell" in Paris as well as of the German word *hell* meaning "light." Also, he laughingly (and anxiously) told me about another connection—his mother's Christian name was a fairly common one with an unusual spelling. Her name was spelled, "Hellen," and he had been conscious of this double "l" spelling of her name since he was a child. In his words, "once I had even teased my mother about the 'hell' portion of her name."

The path leading from the homospatial thought of gate/gait to a manifest reference to the mother's name and thereby to the mother herself was not accidental. As I have repeatedly emphasized, the mother was an important underlying focus of this poem. Moreover, given the libidinal emphasis of the underlying oedipal wish, the presence of an erotic connotation in "Hell's Gate yawns wide" (mother's vagina opening) constituted another aspect of the progression toward unearthing unconscious meaning. The homospatial process unearths these aspects of the underlying ideas and helps to unify the poem in structure as well as emotional content.[20]

Psychodynamics of Homospatial Thinking

With regard to the unearthing of unconscious material, psychodynamic factors involved in the homospatial process differ from those operating in the janusian process. Fusion of drives and resultant neutralization of drive energy rather than defensive negation play a major role in the homospatial process. Such drive fusion and neutralization function to overcome repression and to unearth unconscious material.

Psychodynamically, the process generally responsible for the release of adaptive or neutralized energy is the fusion of affects and drives, particularly sexual and aggressive drives, usually as a result of a working through of unconscious conflicts. Drive fusion and neutralized energy are, as is well recognized in modern psychoanalytic theory,[21] necessary for ego adaptive activity. Such ego adaptive activity involves a wide range of positive psychological functions and it includes the development and use of insight, a progressive unearthing and integration of unconscious and preconscious material by the conscious ego. Through neutralized energy, repression can be increasingly overcome. Although fusion of drives and adaptive or neutralized energy play an important role in the general adaptive functioning of every individual, I shall here merely point out how a particular drive fusion is a direct result of the homospatial process and the factor responsible for unearthing unconscious material.

When discrete entities are brought together in the mind to occupy the same space, fusions of cognitive and perceptual elements are surely taking place. Elements must be thought of and perceived as fused to some degree in the vague and diffuse homospatial experience. This fusion is not, however, restricted to the cognitive and perceptual realm. As I pointed out previously in connection with the janusian process, conscious (secondary process) thinking involving cognitive and perceptual events is not separated from affects and drives. Affects and drives accompany the cognitive and perceptual events within the homospatial process, and the fusions on the perceptual and cognitive levels also involve these accompanying drives and affects to some degree. Although this fusion of affects and drives does not necessarily result from a working through of unconscious conflicts and does not produce real resolution of conflicts between affects or drives, basic sexual and aggressive factors are always represented in the homospatial conception and some drive neutralization therefore occurs. As a result of the bringing together and fusion of the sexual and aggressive aspect of the content, and a concomitant fusion —even to a minimal degree—of unconscious sexual and aggressive drive, neutralized energy is available to the creator's ego. This neutralized energy facilitates overcoming repression in the same manner as neutralized energy functions to facilitate overcoming repression in the achievement of emotional insight, such as in psychoanalytic treatment or, for that matter, in any form of adaptive psychological activity. Moreover, neutralized energy is available for further ego adaptive activity. The homospatial process, therefore, facilitates all types of ego adaptive activity involved in the creative process. In this way, the creative process becomes self-generating with respect to neutralized energy and ego adaptive functioning.

Both of the cited examples of homospatial thinking in the creation of the poem illustrate fusion of unconscious sexual and aggressive content. From our analysis of both of the dreams of the night before the poet conceived the riderless horse and the horse and rider together, we know that the riderless horse—the horse of the final stanzas—initially represented the poet's wish to be aggressively free and independent, to make his own bed and go his own way. Hence, the riderless horse was a representation of his aggressive impulses. The horse with rider aspect of the homospatial conception was, on the other hand, perfused with sexual content. As evident from the dreams, the horse and rider represented his oedipal attachment to his mother, an attachment that—as we later saw—was highly eroticized. Horses, it should be added, are frequently the objects and representations for sexual feelings, for persons of both sexes. This homospatial conception, therefore, actively fused sexual and aggressive content. The fusion of impulses in the conception provided some of the neutralized energy to enable the poet to think more concretely of a wish-fulfilling time before he went "to study or to war" and to unearth, in part, the connection of his poetic thoughts to his mother in the change of the horse to a mare.

The use of the homophonic words "gait/gate" in a homospatial process also served to produce a degree of fusion of unconscious sexual and aggressive content. There can be little doubt that the sensations of an opening gate conjured up in the poet's formulations had sexual overtones. The early line, "While I—A buoyant present entered through a gait / Bordered as by thick hedges of invisible lilac," is readily suggestive of sexual intercourse; the idea of a "gait / Bordered as by thick hedges" readily arousing an image of pubic-hair-surrounded vaginal orifice. Focusing directly on the word "gait" referring to the horse's stride, there seems to be a definite representation of aggressive feelings. Although I cannot prove this particular premise from the poetic material itself, a horse's gait is so vigorous and powerful that it is difficult to imagine its not representing aggressive qualities to some degree.

To my emphasis on psychodynamic fusion involved in the homospatial process, some might raise an objection and insist that the mental events I have described do not indicate adaptive fusion but a wish for primitive or regressive fusion on the poet's part. Reversing the psychodynamic sequence in a sense, they would propose that the dreams as well as the horse and rider image in the poem derive from the poet's primitive wish to fuse with his mother. The genesis of the homospatial conception, according to this, would be the poet's attempt to effect a symbolic fusion between himself the rider and the horse his mother, through his daytime waking fantasy. The poetic creations following this fantasy then would result from some form of elaboration and, as Freud put it, "changes and disguises" and the offer of a "purely formal, that is, aesthetic pleasure."[22] Such an objection and explanation would categorize the homospatial conception as a manifestation of primary process thinking and it would conform to traditional explanations of creative thinking as manifestations of "regression in the service of the ego"[23] or narcissistic fusion states.[24] But, just as Freud's emphasis is on disguise and change or on the mysterious invocation of what he called "formal . . . pleasure," these explanations do little to advance our knowledge of the specifics of creative processes and, more importantly, they neglect the quality of the poet's waking thought and the crucial sequence of mental events I have described.

There was a progression from the initial waking thoughts about the poem to the dream thoughts and back again to the thoughts about the poem, a progressive unearthing rather than a disguising, of unconscious meaning. The homospatial conception was not an eruption of primary process material into consciousness which was then mysteriously controlled by some undefined ego operation. The homospatial process is itself an ego operation and a form of secondary process thinking. The conception did not occur during a period of "withdrawl of cathexis," a decrease of attention in the environment or an immersion in fantasy as required by Kris's concept of regression in the service of the ego.[25] It occurred when the poet was fully aware of his environment and *beginning* to think of how to modify his poem in process. Finally, two points of crucial importance derived from the data. (1) The homospatial conception was a conscious, intentional superimposing and fusing of two images in which the overall configuration was vague and diffuse; in distinction, primary process symbolization results in vivid sharp images in which compromise formation, e.g., a horse with a human head, occurs. (2) The horse was clearly considered to be a *stallion* rather than a mare *at the time of the homospatial conception;* only later was it changed to a female representation of the mother. Consequently, even if fusion with his mother was the poet's underlying wish, it would be erroneous to consider the particular homospatial conception to be merely a disguised representation of that wish. Psychodynamic fusion is a function of the homospatial process, but it is not merely a representation of primitive or regressive function; it is an active cognitive and affective function that is adaptive and energy neutralizing.

Neutralized energy is the factor fueling the ego in all its healthy and adaptive functions. I do not mean to say that the neutralized energy produced directly in the creative process by homospatial thinking is necessarily as stable or as generally available to the individual himself as that produced directly through processes such as conflict resolution, skill development, or psychological maturation. The homospatial conception is a temporary fusion of cognitive and perceptual elements accompanied by temporary drive and affect fusion. Therefore, it always has limited albeit valuable success; the fusion is temporarily effective only within the creative process, that is, energy is provided for creative work. Just as the success of the fusion is limited, the degree to which unconscious material is unearthed and meaningful insight occurs is also limited. The writing of "In Monument Valley" brought the poet's wish in relation to his mother closer to consciousness, but he did not become fully aware of it until after he finished the poem, analyzed his dreams, and so forth.

The limited effectiveness of the fusion in homospatial thinking explains, in part, how it is that some creators behave healthily in the creative process—the process clearly requires good reality testing while it is going on—and also may behave in quite an unhealthy manner in their everyday lives. There may be little carryover between the spheres of creative activity and of everyday interpersonal relationships. The creative process generates its own neutralized energy and sometimes provides real psychological insights to the creator. However, creativity does not necessarily lead to psychological health. A healthy person is not necessarily a creative one; there is reason to believe that psychological health is helpful and important for creativity, but it is still necessary to have the capacity to use the mirror-image processes.

There are other mirror-image processes operating in the creative process besides the ones I have mentioned, but I must first recapitulate and spell out a fuller psychodynamic understanding of the writing of "In Monument Valley" before all the threads are lost. In the course of this recapitulation and extension, some of these other mirror-image processes will emerge and become clear.

4

L'ENVOI: PSYCHODYNAMICS OF THE CREATION OF A POEM

Now that various connections to the poet's life and to his psychological preoccupations have been revealed, revealed not merely to satisfy curiosity-seeking into the affairs of the outstanding, and surely not for the purpose of debunking or reducing the creative process to some simplistic series of formulations, I shall give this necessarily disjointed narrative some coherence and order. I shall recapitulate the information pertaining to the creation of "In Monument Valley" and provide some additional information about the poet's thoughts pertaining to the poem, information that will fill some of the gaps produced along the way. I shall, in essence, tell the story of the creation of this poem—the psychological story—to the extent that such a story can be told.

First, to review the pertinent life history and factual circumstances concerning the writing of the poem, as follows:[1] approximately six months after the trip and encounter with a horse at Monument Valley, the poet was expecting a visit from Miriam, a friend who had also been a guest at J.T.'s house in the southwestern United States. On the morning prior to her visit, the poet formulated specific poetic lines about a horse appearing suddenly among Monument Valley rock formations.

During the writing of these preliminary lines, he thought of a poem by Edwin Muir pertaining to horses and human survival, the idea of a horse as emblematic of the modern age, and he conceived of horses sharing and figuratively living human lives while remaining beasts and not-humans. After writing some tentative formulations, he stopped working on the poem for the remainder of the day.

While asleep that night, he had two dreams in sequence. The first manifestly portrayed both J.T. and Miriam, and the persons in the second were the poet's mother, his grandmother, and, represented by a picture, an old male friend of the family. In the second dream, the poet's mother carried his grandmother on her back, much as a horse carries a rider.

The next morning, the poet thought of the horse in the poem and a visual image briefly came to mind of both a riderless horse and a horse with a rider. He decided to incorporate this image into the fabric of the poem and, as a means of establishing a prior relationship between the horse and the human meeting in Monument Valley, he began to include a previous experience of riding. He did some preliminary work on this idea that day and on the next, beginning to connect a happy period of his own life with the riding of the horse. Temporarily discontinuing his work on the poem because of a visit of several days to a nearby city, he resumed on his return following a night of dreaming about Elizabeth Bishop, Marianne Moore, and an old unidentified lady. At that point, he constructed its overall final structure as follows: the first two stanzas were to describe the rider and horse on an idyllic ride in a pastoral setting and the last three were to describe the meeting of horse and man in Monument Valley. He essentially finished the poem within the next few days and briefly returned to it some months later for some minor final changes.

With respect to the relationship between the poem and the poet's life, it is certain that the poem was derived from the actual incident of meeting a lone horse at Monument Valley and that it had connections to both his friends, J.T. and Miriam. Although the poet consciously focused both on the incident at Monument Valley and on J.T. during the writing of the poem, he did not think at all about any connections with Miriam. Only after he had virtually completed the poem, during his conversation with me, did he connect together his dream about Miriam and her indirect association with the incident at Monument Valley by virtue of being a guest at J.T.'s house. Then, he began to consider her prospective visit to his home to be the probable instigation for the writing of the poem. This, of course, should be no surprise. The poet was consciously after other game than thinking through or even expressing something about his relationship to particular friends; he was writing a poem concerning a meeting with a horse and making a statement having universal effect and meaning.

The poet's relationship to me also constituted a connection between the poem and his life, although very indirectly so. Here, too, he did not at all consciously focus on me or on anything he and I had discussed while he was writing the poem, but, when analyzing his dreams and relating them to the poem, he thought of an issue he and I had been discussing previously, the burdens parents impose on children.[2] Underlying all these connections to the poet's life—both direct and indirect connections—was the relationship between the poem and the poet's unconscious feelings about his mother and his grandmother. Strong evidence for this assertion consists of the manifest appearance of his mother and grandmother in his dreams and the detailed collaborative analysis of the poet's associations and of the meaning of those dreams.

So far, I have added no new information or formulations to the account. I have brought together some disconnected data pertaining to the writing of the poem in order to pave the way for an exposition of the psychodynamics of the poem's creation. Before that, I will briefly mention some other pertinent facts.

In addition to the poet's closeness to his grandmother throughout his youth, another factor in that relationship bears on the creation of this poem. When his grandmother died, several years after the gratifying period of summers of regular and intensive contact, the poet had his very first direct experience with death. Prior to the burial, the grandmother's body had been dressed in a red velvet gown and lay in stately splendor in the bedroom of her house. Here, the poet visited her and, never having seen a dead body before, he remembered thinking about how prettily she had been made up. While telling me his associations about his grandmother, he also described undergoing the very disturbing experience of sitting alone beside her bed for many, many hours, imagining to himself that she wasn't dead.

The psychological theme of a parent becoming a burden to a child had deep roots in his actual life experience. He witnessed such a relationship between his mother and his grandmother. Failing gradually during her last years, the grandmother had imposed a heavy physical and psychological burden on the poet's mother. The latter cared for the grandmother constantly and bore the burden well, but it was an extraordinarily difficult time for all, including the poet.

A specific association to a line in the completed poem connects that line directly with the poet's mother and indirectly with his experience with his grandmother's death. With no prompting from me, he at one point began to wonder and to talk about the line, "Brief, polyphonic lives abounded everywhere." He felt it had some particular emotional importance to him. After some tentative attempts to connect the line to other poems he had written, he suddenly realized that the idea related specifically to his mother. Remembering an incident when he was fairly young, he became aware that the idea of brief lives connected to the word "ephemeral," a word that had strong associations with his mother. Never having heard the word before, he had been introduced to it in a conversation with his mother about insects. He asked her at that point what it meant. When she told him, spontaneously and forcefully he said to her, "I'm glad *you're* not ephemeral." She was, he said, enormously pleased and he had always remembered the incident with great pleasure himself. It is of special interest—exactly why I will explain shortly—that the conversation in which this word came up pertained to insects. The idea of insects had played a role in his thinking of the phrase "brief polyphonic lives" during the creation of the poem. In arriving at the final poetic line pertaining to this remembrance, the poet progressed through the following formulations, all after the line, "Burdened by thick hedges of invisible lilac" (sequence numbering added):

1. A frog unheeded sang 'Plaisir d'Amour . . .'
2. The katydid sang Plaisir d'Amour
3. Tree toads in thin polyphony sang 'Plaisir d'Amour'.
4. Where lives abounded, brief and polyphonic.

Another sequence in the creation of the poem that I have not mentioned previously, but is of interest, pertains to the very first thoughts the poet had about the poem. On the morning he wrote the first lines about the incident of the horse appearing while he was picnicking at Monument Valley, the poet was reminded of Edgar Allan Poe's story, "The Fall of the House of Usher." He thought that the horse appearing suddenly on the scene was reminiscent of the figure of Madeline Usher in that story looming up suddenly from the dead, looming up while the House of Usher was destroyed. In the margin of his notebook he wrote the words "House of Usher." He even tried to include the idea of the "House of Usher" directly in the poem, using it in a few early versions as the name of one of the monuments along with the "Three Sisters." For example, he tried:

Hot pumice blew in one unending gust
Causing the 'House of Usher' and the 'Three Sisters' to shriek.

But he abandoned the idea rather early and did not return to it.

Psychodynamic Formulation

Both the first idea, consisting of the words and thought instigating this particular poem, and the inspirations occurring during the course of the writing, consisting of the thoughts that solve aesthetic problems and generate further activity, are indirect and figurative representations of the poet's unconscious preoccupations and conflicts. The initial thought of the horse looming up like Madeline Usher, the janusian thought of the horse as not-human and not-beast, and the homospatial thought of the riderless horse and the horse and rider occupying the same space are all embodiments and repesentations of unconscious material as well as elements directly contributing to the creation of the poem. With respect to the janusian thought of the horse as not-human and not-beast, I have already spelled out how that formulation figuratively represented the poet's unconscious preoccupation, his conflict between wanting to be free and independent and to be cared for by his mother. With respect to his homospatial thought, I have pointed out how it represented the poet's unconscious oedipal wish as well as a merging of his sexual and aggressive impulses. The initial ideas, inspirations, and metaphorical constructions incorporated into a poem are themselves indirect and figurative representations of unconscious material and, in the mirror-image process of creativity, they are way stations on the path to uncovering and revealing this material more directly. The poetic creative process facilitates the development of psychological insight, the rendering of the unconscious into consciousness, to a certain degree.[3]

The impending visit of the poet's friend Miriam was the preconscious and immediate stimulus for the writing of the poem. She stirred up feelings and thoughts about the incident at Monument Valley, an incident indirectly associated with her. But his first thoughts about the horse, the poetic thoughts and words beginning the poem, point to his deeper unconscious concern. In the light of all the information now derived about the poet's unconscious contents, it is possible to see that his first thoughts about the poem were figurative representations of his concern about his grandmother and his mother.

It is not necessary to trace the connections between Miriam and the poet's mother and grandmother. Such details would be unnecessarily revealing, and, for the present discussion, they would add little to understanding the relationship between the poem and the poet's psychological processes. But his thoughts of "The Fall of the House of Usher" and of the horse appearing on the scene like Madeline Usher looming up should certainly bring into bold relief the associations about his dead grandmother just described. Sitting by his grandmother in her bed, the first dead person he had ever seen, he imagined her to be still alive. The image of Madeline Usher, a literary prototype of the living dead (a female as well) was doubtless related to these remembrances about his grandmother. In the major dream of the night after starting the poem, his grandmother rose to meet him at the door much as Madeline Usher loomed up from the burning house.

In the earliest draft of the poem, the poet referred to a monument he called "The Three Sisters," and this reference, surviving all revisions, was incorporated into the final version of the poem. The phrase did not refer to an actual remembered name of a rock formation in Monument Valley. Like all of his other names for monuments in the poem, those of the final version as well as earlier drafts, he wasn't sure whether there was such a designated formation at the actual geographical site. There might have been one called "The Two Sisters," he said to me at one point, but he wasn't sure.[4] Why did he decide to refer to the "Three Sisters"? He said he was thinking of Chekhov's play of the same name, and there is no reason whatsoever to doubt such a conscious intent. The conscious intent, however, points also to a probable unconscious connection. In the light of the other data and associations about this poem, the idea of "three sisters," three closely related women together, refers also to the time of his life when he was the center of attention of three figurative sisters, his grandmother, his grandmother's sister, and his mother. Chekhov's play, in fact, concerns three mature women living together and takes place in the summertime, circumstances very similar to the ones in the poet's past that were so closely associated with this poem.

These initial thoughts of the poet about the poem are not the same as the previously described unearthed unconscious material, revealed later in the course of writing the poem as a result of the mirror-image process of creativity. For the poet, the connections between these initial thoughts and his unconscious concerns remained quite remote throughout the creative process. He seldom became aware of such connections while writing. Consequently, I have not been able to cite any spontaneous confirmations from the poet himself about the foregoing, but I have had to guess and presume on the basis of similarity to other material and evidence.[5] This situation is due to the nature of the material itself rather than any fault in data gathering. The initial thoughts of a poem are disguised representations of unconscious material analogous to the disguised symbols and images of dreams. At this phase of the process, censorship more than revelation guides the formation. I designate these initial ideas as figurative representations of unconscious material rather than as symbols because they appear in consciousness rather than in dreams and, unlike symbols, they bear a complicated structural relationship to the material they represent.[6] Both the thought of Madeline Usher and of the "Three Sisters" pertain to the poet's conflict about caring for an aged parent, the experiences of the grandmother's death, and of the constant summer contact.

Such representations characteristically instigate the creative process, not only in poetry but in diverse areas of creative activity. The creative person always becomes interested in an idea, an image, a life experience, or a scientific problem because it touches, in some way, on his unconscious concerns. The problem or idea and *how* he approaches it are always, in some respect, a figurative representation of the creator's personal conflicts and concerns. I emphasize manner of approach because often that is difficult to separate from the content of the problem or idea. For instance, it is hard to say whether the creator of "In Monument Valley" became interested in the horse incident because it immediately stirred up unconscious feelings at the site about his mother and grandmother, or whether the horse incident became an important vehicle for feelings and concerns primarily operating later at the time of writing, or whether both occurred. I think the distinction is not so important for our current purposes; in poetry, there is likely little distinction between these alternatives. With respect to this poem, all of these probably operated. When discussing a scientific creation (chaps. 5, 6, and 13 below), however, the distinction between the content of the idea and the manner of approach will be sharper and of greater significance.

To stipulate the overall psychodynamic development of the poem: the poet's thoughts at the time of the horse incident at Monument Valley and/or later thoughts about the incident touched aspects of his unconscious conflict about caring for an aged parent (or grandparent). Because of anxiety about the conflict (a factor that must be assumed) and the desire to create a poem, the poet became intrigued with the incident as an aesthetic problem. As he conceived of a poem, his first thoughts consisted of poetic phrases and ideas that were also figurative representations of his unconscious conflict. When he wrote them down and began constructing the specific poem, he simultaneously began a process of unearthing and uncovering his unconscious conflicts and concerns.

Following his writing a first version of the poem, the poet had dreams pertaining to the unconscious concerns represented in his poetic thoughts; the dreams bore a manifest structural resemblance to the poem and their latent content consisted of a wish to be cared for by his mother. The dream work continued the psychological process begun in the thoughts about the poem; in a disguised way, the dreams expressed the unconscious wish connected to the poetic ideas.

The poet had stopped working on the poem during that day at the point where he had formulated the line referring to the guiding idea of the horse as an emblematic beast of the age. Emblematic as an intermediary and a blend of species, the line was derived from the janusian formulation of the horse as simultaneously beast and human, not-human and not-beast. Following the dreams, the poet had a homospatial thought integrating the janusian conception of simultaneous antithesis.

The janusian and homospatial conceptions together functioned to bring the poet's unconscious wish closer to his awareness. When he returned to the poem, he thought of himself as being the horse's rider[7] and therefore put himself in the position of being physically supported and served by the horse rather than, as up to that point, only surprised, troubled, or emotionally burdened by it. He referred to a specific time in his life when the condition of being cared for by maternal figures came close to being realized. Although he ultimately changed the lines referring to the time before he "went off to study or to war," which suggested that period of his life, and gave a slightly different temporal reference,[8] the wish-fulfilling quality of his feelings associated with this period came to dominate the entire first two stanzas of the poem. The janusian thought and the homospatial thought, especially the latter because it more closely preceded the event, served to unearth a memory as well as a wish-fulfilling effect related to the initial idea of the poem.

As he continued to work on the poem, there was a further unearthing of unconscious material when he became conscious of some erotically tinged feelings while writing about the rider on the horse's back and then changed the horse's sex to female, designating the horse to be a "mare." This followed directly from his working on another janusian construction of simultaneous antithesis. Although the underlying connection of this poem to feelings about his mother was beginning to approach the poet's consciousness at that point, it had not yet come to awareness. The poet was primarily aware of thoughts about a poem he admired by a much respected colleague, Elizabeth Bishop.

After the several days' interruption of work on the poem, the unconscious connection to his mother was represented in a dream manifestly concerning Elizabeth Bishop herself as well as another important female poet, Marianne Moore. The manifest presence of Elizabeth Bishop in the dream indicates the close connections among the poet's previous conscious thoughts about her, the material in the first two stanzas of the poem, and the wishes for maternal care. She appears in the dream as a day residue connecting to thoughts about the poem.[9] His associations to that dream leave no doubt that the latent content concerns the wish for maternal care because they refer both to his grandmother and to the previous dreams. Although his associations did not relate directly to his mother, the feelings about his grandmother and his mother were essentially equivalent during this period of time. The dream representation of Marianne Moore married to a much younger man, though a disguise and a displacement, seems to indicate the interchangeability of his mother or grandmother. He (the much younger man) marries and possesses an esteemed and prized older woman, his mother and/or his grandmother.

On the day following this dream, the poet rewrote the poem again from the beginning, and, while working to bring it to completion, another homospatial process brought his mother even closer to awareness. Working on the homophonic relationship of the words "gate" and "gait" he formulated, "Hell's Gate," and although thinking of the Rodin doors in Paris, he surely thought fleetingly of his mother, since he had long been conscious of the connection between the word "hell" and his mother's name.

Another phrase connected to his mother was formulated during this phase of his writing, "Brief, polyphonic lives." Previously I mentioned that the phrase grew out of the poet's association to insect sounds but I did not describe the actual process leading to its production. The appearance of this phrase was facilitated by yet another form of homospatial thinking, one I have not previously mentioned. It is a mirror-image process of dreaming that involves the use of rhyme, assonance, alliteration, and other formal devices based on partial or total repetition of the sounds of words.[10] Similar to the homospatial superimposition of identities referring to disparate and distinct entities as described in the gait/gate example previously, creative rhyming and alliteration are the direct obverse and mirror image of the rhyming and alliteration in dreams.

Although it is somewhat of a digression from this exposition of the psychodynamics of the poem, I shall briefly describe and detail the operation of this other form of homospatial thinking. In dreams, rhyme and alliteration function as pathways for displacement, a displacement always onto the innocuous and irrelevant. Therefore, sound similarities among aspects of the manifest and latent content of a dream facilitate concealment of unconscious wishes, drives, and conflicts. In the creation of poetry and similar types of literary products, however, conceiving effective rhyme, alliteration, and other sound repetitions functions obversely. As used in secondary process and conscious thought, the formulation of sound repetitions helps to unearth and reveal unconscious preoccupations. Sound repetitions played just such a role in the poet's formulating the particular line, "Brief, polyphonic lives abounded everywhere." A choice of sound repetitions was involved in the sequence of versions leading finally to the line associated with a memory of his mother.

After having written the second stanza in the following form:

> Or outward from the buoyant sorrel mare
> Who moved as if not displeased by my weight upon her back.
> Her gait swung onto meadows heavy with out-of-sight lilac,

he thought of finding a rhyme for the word "mare" (the rhyme scheme is ABBA). Fond of "near rhymes" or "off rhymes" (words or phrases approximating each other in sound rather than rhyming exactly), he wrote the following words in the margin of his worksheet: "moor, paramour, mere, demure, immure, admire, more, nevermore." After writing this series, he thought of the phrase "Plaisir d'Amour," the name of a song suggesting, or providing an opportunity to introduce, the idea of a frog ("A frog unheeded sang 'Plaisir d'Amour' . . ."). After trying this idea, he substituted the insect "katydid," then tried "tree toads." Finally, he ended up with the construction pertaining to the word "ephemeral"—"Brief, polyphonic lives abounded everywhere" —the idea strongly associated with a pleasant experience with his mother. In the process of thinking of words he might use as rhymes for the word "mare," he had hit upon the word "amour," a word that led closer to his unconscious preoccupation rather than further away. There was a reversal of the displacement mechanism of dreams. Instead of using the sound series for displacing unconscious material onto the innocuous and irrelevant, the searching for rhyme words led to increasingly relevant associations.

Effective rhyming, alliteration, and other sound repetition devices function generally in the creation of poetry as mirror image of dreaming processes. This connection to unconscious material contributes to the emotional impact of the rhyme or repetition. As a general principle, the second word or sound conceived in an effectively rhymed or alliterative pair tends to be more closely connected to unconscious preoccupations because of the progressive process of unearthing. To find out which of the pair are such key words is impossible when looking at a final completed poem. A rhyme word at the end of a stanza in the final version of a poem may be a word the poet thought of early during creation, while a rhyme word at the end of the first line of the poem may actually have been conceived last. Poems are seldom written in the same sequence as we, the audience, read them. As my exposition here has I hope clearly shown, it is essential to have access to the poem in process to know something of the poet's mind.

This point about rhyme and other sound devices in poetic creation opens up a rich and fruitful area of exploration and investigation on its own. It surely requires more substantiation than I have given in these brief comments, but I must postpone further discussion until chapter 10 and return again to the psychodynamics of the writing of this poem.

When the poet finished what was essentially the final version of his work, he did not, in any specific way, think about an unconscious preoccupation underlying his creation. Certainly, he did not conceptualize that he had been conflicted about a wish to be cared for by his mother and a wish to be free and independent, nor would we expect him to do so. His purpose in writing was the creation of an aesthetic object, not, on a conscious level at least, the achievement of psychological insight. That many of the unconscious elements I have discussed here had reached his consciousness or become virtually conscious by the time he stopped is indisputable, in the light of our later discussions. In these discussions, held within a day or two of his writing the virtually final version, it was he who first proposed a connection of his dreams to parents. He suggested that his dreams on the night he started the poem were concerned with a theme of the burdens parents imposed on their children. In the light of all the other data I have discussed here, this first interpretation turns out to have been keenly appropriate.[11] It was he who realized that he had unconsciously used the word "mare" as a reference to his mother and he suggested many other unconscious connections as well. Therefore, he did succeed in unearthing unconscious material in a general way—engaging in the process of arousal I described earlier—in the course of creating the poem.

The psychodynamics of poetic creation in the general case are similar to the specific ones I have described here. The poet becomes intrigued by an initial idea[12] in the form of a thought, experience, word, or image having important unconscious meaning to him. He decides to write a poem because he is aware of some of the aesthetic potentialities, particularly the tension and conflict embodied in the idea, and also because he is moved to find out more about what the initial idea connotes. Although he does not think it consciously, he is moved to find out some of its unconscious determinants. He starts with a puzzle concomitantly aesthetic and psychological, and he tries to solve it or to disclose its elements. In trying to work out the puzzle, his thought has continuity on both unconscious and conscious levels, specifically, there are continuities and connections between a poet's waking thoughts about a poem and thoughts incorporated in his dreams, as has been amply demonstrated here. Both the dreams during this period of time and the unfolding creative process are concerned with similar underlying unconscious themes. The manner of handling the unconscious material in one of these spheres of psychological activity, dream or creative process, affects the way it is handled in the other. There is, in other words, a progression of psychological activity during the time of writing a poem, a progression leading to alteration in the specific underlying unconscious theme itself. As in the example presented here, the unconscious theme represented in the poet's earlier dreams developed into a later dream representing a disguised wish for marriage with his mother, partly because of the unearthing process concomitantly going on in the creation of the poem. As the unconscious material came closer to the surface in the poem, a (very likely) deeper wish was expressed in the dream. Although there may be a progressive continuity between dreaming and the creative process, and consequently a facilitation and a contribution, the particular functional relationship between the two forms of mental activity is still primarily an obverse one. The dream functions primarily to express unconscious preoccupation in disguised form, while the creative process functions progressively to reveal it. As the poem discussed here progressed, more and more direct connections to the poet's mother appeared while his dreams continued to present obscure or disguised representations. As both forms of mental activity occur in the same person, there is inevitably some mutual interaction. The revelation of unconscious material in the creative process may instigate dreams expressing deeper wishes and, vice versa, dream discharge can often influence the creative process.

By the time a poem is completed, or nearly so, poets are dimly aware of some of its personal significance to them. When this poem was nearly finished, the poet was aware of having tried to work out and assert something about his feelings about women in general as well as his feelings about independence, freedom, and going his own way. Later, he made direct connections between the poem and his mother.

Lest I be misunderstood, I do not mean to say that discovering the personal significance of an idea or an experience is the only function of the creative process or of writing poetry particularly. This poem makes a powerful statement about modern man's alienation from himself, conveys the emotional impact of the experience of significant encounter, and has philosophical and theological overtones. For example, there are implications of man's fall from grace or the expulsion from the Garden of Eden[13] and there are allusions to the relationship between soul and body in the structure and content of the poem. There are references to war and to Troy and a commentary in the poem on the devastation and terror of war from the time of antiquity. Making such statements and producing such effects are clearly among the functions of creating a poem. I am not deemphasizing the importance of this, the more conscious aspect of the creative process; nor do I presume, in these woefully brief comments about the aesthetic aspects of the poem, to do justice to its richness and, for me, its haunting evocation. These aspects of the poem are clearly very important to the poet as he writes and to ourselves as audience. But the less conscious functions of writing poetry, what I have earlier described as the psychological and biological functions of the creative process, are also clearly crucial and proceed in the manner I have described. These less conscious functions do not contradict the conscious aesthetic fabric of the poem. They are, in a large degree, responsible for it and enhance it.

Summation

I shall try to demonstrate the critical point I have just made within the complete context of the poem. First, I shall summarize and fill out what we now know about the psychodynamics and background of the specific parts of the poem, taking each stanza in order:

> One spring twilight, during a lull in the war,
> At Shoup's farm south of Troy, I last rode horseback.
> Stillnesses were swarming inward from the evening star
> Or outward from the buoyant sorrel mare

This stanza and the one following were written after the basic structure and content of the last three stanzas had been developed. The creation of these two stanzas was guided by the homospatial conception of the riderless horse and the horse and rider together, a conception generated by the poet's wish to be cared for by his mother. The first line of the stanza was derived from a formulation initially referring to times spent in the company of his mother, grandmother, and grandmother's sister. The allusion to war, originally constructed as a personal reference to a period prior to entry into the army, suggested Troy and the idea of the Trojan war and horse in the next line. There was also a real farm in Troy, New York, where the poet had ridden horseback. The last two lines of the stanza were based on the conception of simultaneous opposition between the words "inward" and "outward," a janusian process leading to the formulation of the horse as a "mare," the homophone for the French word for mother.

Who moved as if not displeased by the weight upon her.
Meadows received us, heady with unseen lilac.
Brief, polyphonic lives abounded everywhere.
With one accord we circled the small lake.

The first and second lines of this stanza were derived from the homospatial conception of the homophonic words "gate" and "gait," a conception involving the bringing together of the horse's stride (first line) and the idea of a door opening (second line). Both the original idea from which the phrase "heady with unseen lilac" was derived and the first line as finally formulated here have sexual overtones. This construction suggests the feelings of a woman during sexual intercourse, "not displeased by the weight upon her, "and the original idea, "bordered by thick hedges of invisible lilac," a vaginal orifice. The phrase, "brief, polyphonic lives" connects to the poet's memory of a pleasant and important interaction with his mother. The last line is an expression of the fusion in the horse/horse-rider homospatial conception.

Yet here I sit among the crazy shapes things take.
Wasp-waisted to a fault by long abrasion,
The 'Three Sisters' howl, 'Hell's Gate' yawns wide.
I'm eating something in the cool Hertz car

The idea of a rock formation called "Three Sisters" pertains to the summer experience with the three important and related women. This idea, one of the earliest ones in the poem, was an initially disguised representation of the poet's underlying preoccupation, a disguise later penetrated in part by the formulation and insertion in the same line of the phrase "Hell's Gate," a reference pertaining to the poet's mother.

When the shadow falls. There has come to my door
As to death's this creature stunted, cinder-eyed,
Tottering still half in trust, half in fear of man—
Dear god, a horse. I offer my apple-core

The idea of the horse appearing at the door and the reference to death in the first two lines were connected to the poet's thoughts about the looming up of the figure of Madeline Usher. It also involved a reference to his grandmother whom he had imagined as alive while dead, a person rising from death. The phrase "half in trust, half in fear of man" was derived from the janusian conception of horse as simultaneously not-beast and not-human as was the line referring to an ancient bond between the human and the horse in the last stanza.

> But she is past hunger, she lets it roll in the sand,
> And I, I raise the window and drive on.
> About the ancient bond between her kind and mine.
> Little more to speak of can be done.

These lines represent the conscious feelings—discouragement, noncommunication, the sense of an inability or unwillingness to return to the past—that stimulated the writing of the poem. They also represent the poet's conscious wish to be free and independent. The writing of the poem involved the poet's search both for an abstract meaning of these ideas and feelings and for their unconscious roots.

In the earliest version of the poem, the poet wrote lines presenting a fairly straightforward description of the circumstances of his experience at Monument Valley. He included the extreme sense of tension and discomfort he had felt at the scene and a fairly prosaic statement of the abstract and universal implications of the encounter with the horse: "A tradition in China as in modern verse / Gives to each age its emblematic beast." The janusian conception of the horse first formulated at this stage had not yet indicated an unearthing of unconscious material. These early lines stated the poet's personal anxiety and possessed some aesthetic tension but they did not yet possess the overall quality of dynamic movement and progression of the final poem.

How did it get better? How, to sharpen the question, did the poet mold these earlier lines into an excellent poem? A key factor was a change in structure. After his dreams concerning Miriam, his mother, and his grandmother, and after he arrived at the homospatial conception, he began thinking about a happy, wish-fulfilling connection. He thought of a personal memory and decided to develop it as the beginning of the poem, constructing stanzas to go *before* the original lines. Structurally, he was giving the Monument Valley experience a historical background and providing a temporal sequence in the poem. Psychodynamically, he was placing remembered emotions of gratification and wish fulfillment prior to tension and anxiety. Rather than resolving tension through gratification and fulfillment, he reversed the sequence; tension and anxiety follow wish fulfillment.

Such an emotional sequence is intrinsic to the structure of good art. Art that is primarily escapist and unimportant generally moves psychologically from expression and generation of tension to resolution in wish fulfillment. Happy or wish-fulfilling endings in literary works are mildly satisfying but are also quite dull and flat. Good art invariably leaves us stimulated and aroused. Always, there is some degree of psychological resolution along with tension at the end, as there is in this poem, but this resolution is not produced by wish fulfillment.[14] In this poem, some of the final resolution comes from the poet's act of moving on; he drives away and something decisive has occurred. There is a clear break of relationship, or a breakdown of communication, between himself and the horse species and what it represents. It is a sad and tense finale; something is resolved, but there is no sense of fulfillment.

The emotional power of the poem derives, I think—having invaded the realm of literary criticism against my vows, I now beg indulgence—from the sense of movement and development in this breaking of a relationship. Whatever the horse species represents, and it is clear that it poetically represents many things, the energy and dynamism comes from the sense of breaking a relationship with something in the past or with the past itself. Regardless of whether the horse is a metaphor for man's alienation, for death, for war, for sexuality, for womankind (including Miriam and the poet's mother)—and she is all of these—she is a thing of the past. At one time, the relationship with her was intensely gratifying, but a good deal changed; at the time of the encounter nothing more could be done with her or for her. Even an apple that was reminiscent of happier days of an Edenesque experience was only a core to be offered. Eden was lost. All that remained was to raise the window of the car and drive on, to renounce the relationship and move on to other things. Consequently, while there is a profound sense of loss in this poem, there is also a sense of progress. Both the poet and the horse have changed; the relationship is lost, but the poet at least can still move on.

The sense of progress and development results directly from placing the wish-fulfilling, gratifying stanzas at the beginning of the poem. The emotional sequence thereby moves away from wishful fantasy toward reality and captures the mixed feelings of loss and progress we all experience as we mature and grow up. And the decision to create the earlier stanzas was derived from homospatial and janusian thinking and the unearthing of unconscious material in mirror-image processes of creativity. The structuring of the poem was influenced by the poet's growing awareness as he proceeded.

The process of unearthing unconscious material during the writing of the poem functioned to unify disparate elements of the overt structure of the poem as well as its more covert emotional content. For one thing, the homospatial conception pertaining to the horse and rider served to give a formal and dynamic balance to the poem. It specifically generated the formal decision to have two lead-up stanzas before the description of the scene at Monument Valley, a decision which embued the poem with the quality of building up to a specific point and then receding. This formal buildup and recession complements the emotional theme of gratification and fulfillment followed by loss.

A second and important aspect of the homospatial conception was that it brought to the fore the poet's close relationship with his mother. The intense sense of closeness with the horse and the quality of happiness of the first two stanzas were dictated by the poet's almost-conscious touching on feelings related to his mother. The sense of closeness in these lines is coordinated with the sense of loss in the last lines because the feelings pertain to the same relationship. The basic loss felt is the loss that, at some point, leads to progress. Without his mother's care, the poet can achieve full freedom and independence. My point here is that the lines describing the loss would not, even if elaborated, have made a poem; it was necessary for the poet to unearth the source of his feeling of loss, to some degree, in order to be able to tell the story.

A third aspect of the emotional and formal unification produced by the operation of the homospatial and janusian processes pertains to specific words and ideas. The references to Troy and a war in the first stanza arouse ideas of the ancient world consonant with the reference to an "ancient bond" between the man and the horse at the end of the poem. Such linkages formally integrate the beginning and the end of the poem and suggest further levels of interpretation. The idea of an ancient bond between man and horse at the end of the poem was present in an early phase. Thoughts stimulated by or accompanying the homospatial conception—about the period of his life before the war and the ride on Shoup's farm near Troy—helped both to provide formal links and to suggest a concomitant personal and universal meaning to the idea of an ancient bond and of the past. Another example pertains to the homospatial process leading to the formulation of the line, "Meadows received us, heady with unseen lilac," and the phrase, "Hell's Gate." Both were derived from the homophonic gate/gait conception. The repetition of the idea of doors, gates, or meadows opening in these early lines and the reference to the horse at the poet's car door later also served as a structural-emotional integration of the beginning and end of the poem. Such repetition early and late in the poem also produces some stasis; it makes the poem somewhat atemporal and contrasts with a concomitant sense of progression. Doors appear both early and late, they are fixed aspects of life. Although there is the suggestion of an earlier opening onto heavenly meadows and a later shift to hell's gate, both are related to the final door of death. In an overall similar fashion, the poet's unconscious conflict both progressed and stood still during the writing of the poem. It was more conscious, but not changed too much.

Many emotional and structural congruencies can be developed from the specifics of the creation of this poem. But I think it is no longer necessary for me to stay in this realm of literary analysis to make my major point. My point is that the homospatial and janusian processes, processes which on the surface could seem to be merely aesthetic devices for connecting and integrating various aspects of the poem, have deep emotional roots and functions as well. The unearthing of unconscious material functions to make poetic form and content congruent with each other on an emotional level; surface and deep material are blended and unified.

I must finally mention something about the nature of the process of literary revision, a process I have been implicitly discussing throughout these chapters without explicitly analyzing. In a previous study of revisions[15] in the creation of a play by Eugene O'Neill, I demonstrated that the revision process functions to reveal unconscious material, but it is also used to remove psychological elements and content that are closest to the author's *immediate* conscious and preconscious concerns. In exception to the revelation in creativity I have so far strongly emphasized, there is some degree of suppression and deletion of elements pertaining to preoccupations close to the creator's consciousness. It is a form of psychological economizing and balancing. The creator deletes inadvertently overt and direct references to personal feelings and concerns, which he himself consciously recognizes as he proceeds. He removes superficial personal references, as it were, while he unearths deeper unconscious issues and meanings. Hence, he avoids and defends himself against minor anxieties attendant on immediate unacceptable ideas and feelings so that he becomes better able to tolerate the potentially major anxieties attendant on deeper unconscious concerns. He does not knowingly or purposely engage in such psychological balancing and trading, but follows the well-established aesthetic principles of using implication rather than direct reference and of orienting to universals rather than to particulars. Such principles or devices, as I have emphasized throughout, always serve important psychodynamic as well as aesthetic ends for the creator and also for the audience. In the case of deleting revelation of immediate personal concerns, the audience is spared the burden of an author's personal confession and of unnecessary involvement in the author's real life.

In the creation of "In Monument Valley," the poet deleted all references to immediate feelings and to the actual incidents he was thinking about by the time he arrived at the final version of the poem.

For example, he removed his earliest reference to being there with J.T. by changing all "we" references to "I" and he deleted references to the personal discomfort experienced during the picnic. After initially thinking about the time in his life when he spent his summers with his mother, grandmother, and grandmother's sister, he altered the time reference to have a more symbolic connection, "during a lull in the war," for the final version.[16] As O'Neill did in the creation of his play, the author of this poem deleted references to his more conscious and preconscious concerns and he also, like O'Neill, embodied his deeper, more unconscious preoccupations in the final product. The result is that the final product is far better than the initial formulation; it is an achievement of something new—not only a description of the author's actual experience[17]—and valuable. The process of revision shows us how this achievement came about.

I have now completed the analysis of a specific case. In spite of much detail and documentation, I have left much undone and unexplained about the creation of the poem. Such is, and may always be, the case with the splendor of creativity. But I cannot dwell on the specific case any longer because I must now proceed to more general considerations, applications, and evidence.

5

SCIENTIFIC CREATIVITY

Throughout the preceding exposition of the creation of a specific poem, I have continually asserted that I was presenting an illustrative example. The psychological processes I have described operate generally and universally in creativity and are not merely characteristic of this particular poet's functioning nor of the particular creation of this poem. I must now set about producing evidence for this assertion. To start, I shall shift the focus rather sharply and leap into an activity that seems very remote from the making of poetry. The subject matter is highly technical and impersonal and seems a far cry from the warm and vibrant, intensely personal material considered so far. My concerns here are the subjects of physical science and of the scientific enterprise.

This leap, extreme and hopefully creative in itself, could also turn out to be foolhardy. After all, not only is the subject matter of the physical sciences quite unlike that of the arts but scientific thinking has long been considered the sine qua non of the logical, the objective, and the rational mode. It might hardly seem likely that the emotionally perfused unusual thought processes I have so far described could play an important role in science. Furthermore, unlike the artist, the scientist presumably deals with external and consensually verifiable reality. His domain is not subjective or internal reality, nor are characteristically shifting standards of artistic preference and taste applicable to his productions. The scientist is said to *discover* laws that already existed, he does not himself create these laws. There are clear rules for evaluating the validity of scientific laws having nothing whatsoever to do with the scientist's personality, his way of working, nor with the personalities, biases, or tastes of his audience. The law exists in nature, he does not make it and place it there; unlike the artist, he makes nothing new but primarily sees and understands.

All of these distinctions between science and art engender serious reservations about whether identical psychological processes could possibly operate in the two endeavors. Indeed, I myself held such serious reservations for a very long time. Only slowly did I change my mind. Because of a serendipitous finding from my research, I virtually was driven to begin to acknowledge a similarity between artistic and scientific creativity. In a particular experiment designed to assess whether elements of janusian thinking were connected to creativity in a large group of college undergraduates, I divided the entire group into a creative subgroup and a noncreative control subgroup. My criteria for designating the members of the creative group, however, were derived solely on the basis of data I had obtained indicating creativity in the arts. Aside from further matching between the groups on the basis of sex, age, intelligence, and socioeconomic status, I paid no attention to any other information I had about characteristics of the subjects in the two groups. To my surprise, the results of the experiment were equivocal: there was no definite distinction between the subgroups with respect to the factors of janusian thinking tested. Only gradually did it dawn on me that, because of my own reservations about relating artistic and scientific creativity, I had neglected some important data. I had not paid any attention to subject characteristics pertaining to scientific creativity in distinguishing and designating the two subgroups.

After close inspection of information pertaining to such characteristics, I discovered that a large number of scientifically creative subjects had been placed in the "noncreative" control group! Only a few subjects who happened to be creative in science in addition to the arts had already been placed in the creative group. I shall present the details of this experiment later (chap. 7), but a striking discovery was that the results became completely unequivocal when all the data were reassessed and reevaluated after adding the scientific creators to the creative test group. The performance of the artistically and scientifically creative subjects on the experimental task was greatly similar and, statistically, was significantly different from all other subjects in the experiment to a very high degree.

After this influential experience, I began to search for a meaningful way of conceptualizing the creative process in science. It would not be appropriate to consider all accomplishments and discoveries in science to be the result of a creative process. A very large proportion of scientific work consists of the slow accumulation of facts through rigorous observation and experimentation; characteristically, there are carefully reasoned inferences and conclusions, and the application of universal and readily repeatable skills.[1] Little that is comparable to the dramatic bringing-forth-something-out-of-nothing quality characteristic of the creative arts appears. Only the most rudimentary definition of creation, that is, producing or making something of use, properly applies to such routine scientific activity. The same definition also applies to ordinary manufacturing and to successes in routine scientific work. While the word creativity often is applied in just this way—frequently it is used as an honorific term for carrying out a large number of successful experiments and publishing a large number of papers—we are charged with a more exacting definition here. We are interested in understanding a process that yields more than merely useful results and one that is comparable to creative activity in the arts.

I have discussed scientific creativity with numerous colleagues in the physical sciences and they have been virtually unanimous about the following considerations: meaningful criteria for scientific creativity cannot depend solely on the usefulness or potential usefulness of a discovery. Not only must there be more positive value such as an important usefulness or simply a general importance, there must be newness in some sense and, in analogy to artistic creativity, an element of individual accomplishment. Many useful scientific discoveries have come out of a cumulative process involving the collaboration of numerous investigators and the application of standard inductive and deductive procedures. Little comparable to the highly valued production of an individual artist has characteristically been involved. Among my scientific colleagues, the criteria for scientific creation generally considered most valid and most heuristically productive concern the nature of the discovery, its general importance, and the nature of the thought processes responsible for it.

From a philosophical point of view, the matter is highly complicated. One could take the position that all scientific discoveries are creations in the sense that they always result from an interaction between man and nature. Everything known about nature is processed by, and bears the stamp of, the human mind. Consequently, any discovery bears the impressions and the individual elements of the person who first described and formulated it, and of all the subsequent human minds that elaborated it and built upon it. The idea of left and right orientations of substances in the natural world, for example, is a projection onto nature of a human way of organizing and categorizing sides.

Although such a position may be quite feasible, it requires us to understand, as creative activity, virtually all of man's interaction with his environment. On the other hand, one may take the position I mentioned initially that scientific discoveries are not creations because they are in no sense new. Scientists only find and describe the absolute laws and features that were *always* there, always existing beforehand. But then our inquiry into scientific creativity must end before it starts. Finally, one may say that scientific discoveries that are very important, those that change life, society, or the physical environment in some significant way, are creations in that they *bring about* something new. While this last position raises questions about who really does the creating—society, the discoverer, God, or more mundanely the manufacturers and engineers who process and produce discoveries such as penicillin, nuclear energy, and the like—it is essentially the one I shall adopt here. It does not justify an interest in the scientist's thought processes, but neither do the other positions I have mentioned. The focus on thought processes is warranted on the basis of general interest, a general interest derived from certain known similarities between the scientific thinking involved in important discoveries and the thinking involved in artistic creation. So-called intuitive thinking and other types of leaps of thought analogous to what are commonly designated as artistic intuition and inspiration have played a definite role in scientific discovery.

According to my physical scientist colleagues, effective theory building fulfills their criteria and is the sine qua non of scientific creation. First, a theory can always be considered made or created because it never fully corresponds to anything discoverable in nature, at least such correspondence can never be proven. Second, effective theories by definition have far reaching and important consequences. Third, intuitive thought processes always, in some degree, play a role in the development of theories. Limiting scientific creativity only to effective theory building, however, would omit much of what we are looking for in scientific activity. Many scientific discoveries do not consist of general theories, they consist of the discovery of physical facts. As I shall illustrate presently, such facts are often discovered through leaps of thought that are directly analogous to types of thinking we characteristically associate with the creative arts. We must be interested not only in whether the scientist's product or discovery is technically and philosophically worthy of designation as a creation but also in whether he *functions* in a creative fashion in making it. Therefore, our interest is in scientific leaps of thought as well as the development of scientific theories.

Throughout the course of scientific history, leaps of thought and intuitions have been frequently connected to great discoveries. Some of the stories are virtually apocryphal such as the account of Newton's discovery of the law of gravitation while watching an apple fall in his mother's garden,[2] but the autobiographical statements of great scientists amply document the phenomenon. Darwin described his very important flash of intuition as follows:

> In October 1838, that is, fifteen months after I had begun my systematic enquiry, I happened to read for amusement Malthus on *Population*, and being well prepared to appreciate the struggle for existence which everywhere goes on from long continued observation of the habits of animals and plants, *it at once struck* me that under these circumstances favorable variations would tend to be preserved and unfavorable ones to be destroyed. The result of this would be the formation of a new species. *Here, then, I had at last got a theory by which to work.* [Italics added][3]

Darwin, as we well know, spent the remaining forty-four years of his life proving the hypothesis of natural selection, an hypothesis that came to him all at once as a leap of thought. Clearly, the thought did not emerge fully formed with no antecedent; Darwin stipulates that his previous experience and thought had prepared him well for this sudden understanding. But rather than a carefully reasoned, step-by-step inductive process of deriving inferences on the basis of specific observations and experiments, the idea came to him as a flash of intuition, a flash that waited on his further researches before it could be proven.

Another famous instance of an intuitive leap is described in the oft-quoted testimony of Henri Poincaré, the man responsible for some of the most important mathematical discoveries of the latter part of the nineteenth century. The following is his description of the events leading to one of his important discoveries or creations, the mathematical theory involving "Fuchsian functions," a special form of automorphic functions:

> For a fortnight I had been attempting to prove that there could not be any function analogous to what I have since called Fuchsian functions. I was at that time very ignorant. Every day I sat down at my table and spent an hour or two trying a great number of combinations, and I arrived at no result. One night I took some black coffee, contrary to my custom, and was unable to sleep. A host of ideas kept surging in my head; I could almost feel them jostling one another, until two of them coalesced, so to speak, to form a stable combination. When morning came, I had established the existence of one class of Fuchsian geometric series. I had only to verify the results, which only took a few hours.
>
> Then I wished to represent these functions by the quotient of two series. This idea was perfectly conscious and deliberate; I was guided by the analogy with elliptical functions. I asked myself what must be the properties of these series, if they existed, and I succeeded without difficulty in forming the series that I have called Theta-Fuchsian.
>
> At this moment I left Caen, where I was then living, to take part in a geological conference arranged by the School of Mines. The incidents of the journey made me forget my mathematical

> work. When we arrived at Coutances, we got into a break to go for a drive, and, just as I put my foot on the step, the idea came to me, though nothing in my former thoughts seemed to have prepared me for it, that the transformations I had used to define Fuchsian functions were identical with those of non-Euclidian geometry. I made no verification, and had no time to do so, since I took up the conversation again as soon as I had sat down in the break, but I felt absolute certainty at once. When I got back to Caen I verified the result at my leisure to satisfy my conscience.[4]

In the same speech before the *Société de Psychologie* in Paris, Poincaré went on to ascribe such discoveries, as I mentioned earlier, to the functioning of unconscious processes in scientific creation. Although this was not a completely revolutionary idea at the time, Poincaré's talk stimulated another famous mathematician, Jacques Hadamard, to collect and document instances of seemingly unconscious factors operating in his own work and the work of other important mathematical figures. Hadamard's specific description of what he called an "unconsciously" achieved discovery of his own, the discovery of the valuation of a determinant, was as follows:

> I see a schematic diagram: a square of whose sides only the verticals are drawn and inside of it, four points being the vertices of a rectangle and joined by (hardly apparent) diagonals. . . . It . . . seems to me that such was my visualization of the question in 1892 [when I made the discovery] as far as I can recollect.[5]

Many others have emphasized the importance of presumed unconscious factors in other types of scientific discoveries as well.[6] But, irrespective of the type of explanation, whether correctly attributed to unconscious factors or not, the major matter I want to emphasize now is that such leaps of thought or intuitions are highly characteristic of scientific discovery. Typically, as with Poincaré, a leap of thought occurs in the course of an investigation, often accompanied by a subjective sense of certainty, and subsequently it is submitted to verification through working out of equations, observation, or experimentation.

Many other testimonies of important scientific discoverers describe the leap of thought followed by verification. Helmholtz, the father of physiological optics and also a great mathematician and philosopher, talked about his discoveries as follows:

> In my papers and memoirs I have not, of course, given the reader an account of my wanderings, but have only described the beaten path along which one may reach the summit without trouble. . . . There are many people of narrow vision who admire themselves greatly if once they have had a good idea—or even think they have had one. An investigator or an artist who is

> continually having a great number of them is undoubtedly a privileged being and is recognized as a benefactor of humanity. But, who can count or measure such mental flashes? Who can follow the hidden paths by which ideas are connected? . . . As I have often found myself in the unpleasant position of having to wait for useful ideas, I have had some experience as to when and where they come to me which may perhaps be useful to others. They often steal into one's train of thought without their significance being at first understood; afterward some accidental circumstance shows how and under what conditions they originated. Sometimes they are present without or knowing whence they came. In other cases they occur suddenly, without effort, like an inspiration. As far as my experience goes they never come to a tired brain or at a desk.[7]

Other dramatic instances of leaps of thought abound in important scientific discoveries. Pasteur discovered immunology in a moment of sudden understanding; W. B. Cannon's biological theory of the flight-fight syndrome occurred to him during a sleepless night; Carl Friedrich Gauss, the physicist and mathematician, indicated the following in his memoirs: "The law of induction discovered January, 1835, at 7 A.M., before rising." Physicist Enrico Fermi arrived at his major discovery, the method for producing "slow" or "thermal" neutrons, as a result of an idea that came, as he said, "with no advanced warning, no conscious, prior reasoning."[8]

One of the most vivid descriptions of the thinking leading to an important discovery was given by August von Kekulé, the chemist who formulated the ring structure of the benzene molecule. Not only organic chemistry but biochemistry and the modern science of molecular biology are beneficiaries of his contribution. Kekulé arrived at the conception of a ring structure after a sudden visual experience in which a snake seized hold of its own tail. Although the story of this discovery has now become an apocryphal one in which Kekulé is represented as having been drunk or as dreaming at the time, in his original description he stipulated that he was in a state of halfsleep *(Halbschlaf)*. Prior to visualizing the snake, the active directed nature of his thinking was, as he described it, as follows: "My mind's eye, sharpened by repeated visions of similar art, distinguished now . . . structures of manifold form."[9]

These examples, some of which I shall discuss in greater detail, all indicate the importance of leaps of thought in scientific discovery. Although Poincaré expresses the feeling most explicitly, all of the descriptions indicate a sense of formulation achieved all at once, an idea lacking in clear antecedents and accompanied by a feeling of certainty. From the point of view of the subjective experience of the scientist, then, all of these thoughts are certainly creative. They are experienced as new and discontinuous with previous thoughts and they all have positive value. Initially valuable because sensed as correct and important, their value is verified by more ordinary types of deductive and inductive logical processes.

Unconscious Thought Processes and Scientific Creativity

Myriad examples of such leaps of thought in science are available. I have chosen to cite the particular ones above partly because they are connected to very important, far-reaching discoveries (or, as in the case of Helmholtz, because the person describing the thinking has made such discoveries) and partly because they are examples connected with rather varied subjective states of consciousness. Thus, Kekulé refers to a state of halfsleep; Cannon cites a state of sleeplessness in the middle of the night; Poincaré also refers to sleeplessness and, along with Helmholtz, he describes a state of relaxed wakefulness as well—the latter, in fact, insists that fatigue is antithetical to leaps of thought; Gauss describes a discovery right after awakening, a time when hypnopompic consciousness is often in full sway.[10] Darwin's and Pasteur's ideas, and presumably Hadamard's, occurred during full consciousness, Darwin while reading, Hadamard while working, and Pasteur while interpreting the results of an experiment.

Theories emphasizing the importance of unconscious factors in scientific creation have been largely influenced by the frequent descriptions of these sudden, subjectively mysterious leaps of thought. Such theories have proposed what seem equally mysterious explanations involving the idea of unconscious "work" going on in the mind of the creator, work that somehow sifts out the unnecessary aspects of his thinking and focuses him on the correct answer. For instance, Wallas's popular theory or description of creative thinking invokes an unclear analogy to physical and biological processes with the use of the word "incubation" to refer to a period of unconscious thinking or unconscious work occurring between preliminary stages of preparation and a stage of illumination or attainment of the correct idea.[11] Theorists unduly influenced by highly dramatic examples such as Kekulé's solution in a supposedly dreamlike state and by descriptions of solutions occurring early in the morning or late at night have assumed these constitute definite evidence for the importance of unconscious work in scientific creativity. The possibility of primary process thinking leading directly to scientific creations and discoveries arises.

The great variation and diversity of states of mind described in the previous examples, however, indicate that neither dreaming nor a markedly altered state of consciousness is necessary for scientific creativity. There is still no reason to postulate an upsurgence of primary process thinking in consciousness. Suddenness and a sharp shift of thinking are described by all and this must be explained, but the proper explanation pertains to the structure of thought processes leading to scientific creations rather than to primary process upsurgence or to the sole operation of a mysterious type of unconscious creative work. Unconscious processes do decidedly play a role in scientific creativity in a manner similar to the role of unconscious processes in art.[12] Janusian and homospatial thinking, the mirror image of dreaming types of thought that both represent and gradually unearth unconscious processes, also operate in scientific discovery.[13]

Two Momentous Scientific Discoveries of the Twentieth Century

I will illustrate the operation of one of the mirror-image processes, janusian thinking, in scientific creation by quoting extended descriptions of the key processes of thought involved in two of the most important scientific discoveries of this century: the discovery of the double helix structure of deoxyribonucleic acid (DNA) by James D. Watson and the formulation of the general theory of relativity by Albert Einstein.

The conception of the macromolecular structure of DNA as chains of smaller molecules (protein bases) oriented in double helical fashion was a momentous one. For some time before that, it had been known that DNA was the chemical substance responsible for the transmission of inherited capacities in living organisms, but the manner of carrying out the transmission was baffling. Many scientists had suspected that the answer to the problem of transmission, the so-called mechanism of genetic coding, lay in the structural qualities of DNA and a good deal of work had been done toward elucidating those qualities. Cumulative knowledge and scientific collaboration helped produce the solution. But the person who made the actual discovery, the person who conceived the specific double helical structure, was the young microbiologist, James D. Watson.[14] Fortunately, Watson has documented enough details about the discovery to make it possible to trace the thought processes involved. That he did not simply follow a step-by-step type of logical process but that the solution came as a leap of thought, fully comparable to the other creative leaps we have discussed, is clearly documented in his description.

In his book, *The Double Helix,* Dr. Watson describes a long period of evaluating various approaches and following hunches about the best way to proceed. Finally, he settled on collecting data provided by X-ray crystallography. Working on a wire model of the structure, he and Francis Crick carefully and logically assessed information from various sources and tried many alternative possibilities. While a good deal of careful logic, methodological judgment, and even luck played a role in his search, the key step of the discovery came as follows:

When I got to our still empty office the following morning, I quickly cleared away the papers from my desk top so that I would have a large flat surface on which to form pairs of bases held together by hydrogen bonds. Though I initially went back to my like-with-like [the bases adenine with adenine, guanine with guanine, thymine with thymine, cytosine with cytosine] prejudices, I saw all too well that they led nowhere. When Jerry [Donohue] came in I looked up, saw that it was not Francis [Crick], and began shifting the bases in and out of various other pairing possibilities. Suddenly I became aware that an adenine-thymine pair held together by two hydrogen bonds was identical in shape to a guanine-cytosine pair held together by at least two hydrogen bonds. All the hydrogen bonds seemed to form naturally; no fudging was required to make the two types of base pairs identical in shape. . . .

The hydrogen bonding requirement meant that adenine would always pair with thymine, while guanine could pair only with cytosine. Chargaff's rules [adenine equals thymine, guanine equals cytosine] then stood out as a consequence of a double-helical structure for DNA. *Even more exciting, this type of double helix suggested a replication scheme much more satisfactory than my briefly considered like-with-like pairing. Always pairing adenine with thymine and guanine with cytosine meant that the base sequences of the two intertwined chains were complementary to each other. Given the base sequence of one chain, that of its partner was automatically determined. Conceptually, it was thus very easy to visualize how a single chain could be the template for the synthesis of a chain with the complementary sequence.*

Upon his arrival Francis did not get more than halfway through the door before I let loose that the answer to everything was in our hands. Though as a matter of principle he maintained skepticism for a few moments, the similarly shaped A-T [adenine-thymine] and G-C [guanine-cytosine] pairs had their expected impact. His quickly pushing the bases together in a number of ways did not reveal any other way to satisfy Chargaff's rules. A few minutes later *he spotted the fact* that the two glycosidic bonds (joining base and sugar) of each base pair were systematically related by a diad axis perpendicular to the helical axis. *Thus, both pairs could be flipflopped over and still have their glysosidic bonds facing in the same direction. This had the important consequence that a given chain could contain both purines and pyrimidines at the same time, it strongly suggested that the backbones of the two chains must run in opposite directions.*

The question then became whether the A-T and G-C pairs would easily fit the backbone configuration devised during the previous two weeks. At first glance this looked like a good bet since I had left free in the center a large vacant area for the bases. However, we both knew that we would not be home until a com-

> plete model was built in which all the stereochemical contacts were satisfactory. There was also the obvious fact that the implications of its existence were far too important to risk crying wolf. Thus I felt slightly queasy when at lunch Francis winged into the Eagle [restaurant] to tell everyone within hearing distance that we had found the secret of life. [Italics added][15]

Compared to the descriptions of mental events connected with the creation of the poem in the earlier sections of this book, these passages are probably even more difficult to follow, especially if one is not familiar with the biochemical issues involved. Several points, however, emerge clearly from the description to give us an understanding of the nature of his thought processes. First, he had arrived at a conceptual formulation of a particular double helical structure all at once; much remained to be done to test his conception and establish its feasibility. Second, although he describes "shifting the bases in and out of various other pairing possibilities" in somewhat trial and error fashion, the conceptual formulation was not merely a proposal for pairing, it was not merely a conception of the means by which the chemicals were joined together in accordance with the previous findings by Chargaff. I have italicized the sentences (second paragraph here) indicating that the specific conception was of a complementary spatial structure rather than of a like-with-like pairing; he conceived of the structure of a double helix as explaining the mechanism of genetic replication. As his colleague Crick only later came to see, Watson's complete conceptual formulation (also in italics) of the double helix was of a spatial structure having two identical sequences of chemicals running in opposite directions. Watson says that Crick "spotted the fact," meaning that he, Watson, knew it already. His discovery, then, was due to a janusian thought: Watson *conceived that the chains were identical and opposite at the same time.* The structure of DNA, it may be said, existed in nature, but it required janusian thinking to recognize it.

The discovery of the very important mechanism of genetic replication, then, was the result of a leap of thought, a creative one, and the leap involved janusian thinking. Embedded as this discovery was in a process of collecting information from various sources, the primarily inductive process at most stages of the search, as well as the headlong race toward breaking the genetic code among many leading scientists of the time, it may seem hard in retrospect to see the creative leap and Watson's unique contribution. Wouldn't someone else have discovered this double helix if Watson hadn't (with Crick's important help)? Wasn't the discovery of the double helix only the uncovering of a fact of nature, a fact that could have been uncovered by other means? Could the structure have been discovered without conceiving the simultaneous opposition? All these questions may be posed and speculated about, but no speculation would alter the story of the actual discovery, Watson's arriving at the solution in just the manner he did. He shifted all at once from the idea of like-with-like pairing to the concept of simultaneous opposition.

Another enormously important twentieth-century discovery in the natural sciences also occurred by means of a leap of thought. This was the discovery, the formulation, to be more exact, of the general theory of relativity by Albert Einstein. For persons living in this day and age, I need hardly spell out, at any length, the significance of this particular theory for science and for the ethos of our time. As a new theory of gravitation, it embraced Newton's classic theory as a special case. Not only did nuclear explosives and power become possible because of this theory, but many of the major developments in modern physics, astronomy, and allied fields are a direct result of it. Our current knowledge of the nature of the physical universe depends significantly on it.

Virtually all scientific theories and discoveries are, as Helmholtz said in the quotation above, presented in a logical, sequential form when they are published. Seldom, if ever, does the scientist reveal the actual thoughts helping him to arrive at his solution (psychologists understandably do so more than others). Einstein was no exception; he presented the general theory of relativity in the manner best calculated to prove its efficacy and feasibility. Recently, however, Einstein's actual thoughts leading to the theory have come to light in an unpublished essay written by him in approximately 1919. The essay was discovered by Gerald Holton among other Einstein papers being collected for posthumous publication by Princeton University Press.[16]

Prior to the development of a general theory of relativity, Einstein had presented what is now called the special principle of relativity. While the special principle was the initial formulation, the later general theory, of course, had more widespread implications. The essay was written in Einstein's own hand, and entitled by him, "The Fundamental Idea of General Relativity in Its Original Form." Although some of it will again be difficult for the nontechnical reader, I will quote a large section of it and then return to discuss specific parts:

> In the development of special relativity theory, a thought—not previously mentioned—concerning Faraday's work on electromagnetic induction played for me a leading role.
>
> According to Faraday, when a magnet is in relative motion with respect to a conducting circuit, an electric current is induced in the latter. It is all the same whether the magnet moves or the

conductor; only the relative motion counts, according to the Maxwell-Lorentz theory. However, the theoretical interpretation of the phenomenon in these two cases is quite different:

If it is the magnet that moves, there exists in space a magnetic field that changes with time and which, according to Maxwell, generates closed lines of electric force—that is, a physically real electric field; this electric field sets in motion movable electric masses [that is, electrons] within the conductor.

However, if the magnet is at rest and the conducting circuit moves, no electric field is generated; the current arises in the conductor because the electric bodies being carried along with the conductor experience on electromotive force, as established hypothetically by Lorentz, on account of their (mechanically enforced) motion relative to the magnetic field.

The thought that one is dealing here with two fundamentally different cases was, for me, unbearable [*war mir unerträglich*]. The difference between these two cases could not be a real difference, but rather, in my conviction, could be only a difference in the choice of a reference point. Judged from the magnet there certainly were no electric fields; judged from the conducting circuit there certainly was one. The existence of an electric field was therefore a relative one, depending on the state of motion of the coordinate system being used, and a kind of objective reality could be granted only to the electric and magnetic field together, quite apart from the state of relative motion of the observer or the coordinate system. The phenomenon of the electromagnetic induction forced me to postulate the (special) relativity principle.

When, in the year 1907, I was working on a summary essay concerning the special theory of relativity for the *Yearbook for Radioactivity and Electronics* I tried to modify Newton's theory of gravitation in such a way that it would fit into the theory. Attempts in this direction showed the possibility of carrying out this enterprise, but they did not satisfy me because they had to be supported by hypotheses without physical basis. At that point there came to me the happiest thought of my life, in the following form:

Just as in the case where an electric field is produced by electromagnetic induction, the gravitational field similarly has only a relative existence. *Thus, for an observer in free fall from the roof of a house there exists, during his fall, no gravitational field* [italics Einstein's]—at least not in his immediate vicinity. If the observer releases any objects, they will remain, relative to him, in a state of rest, or in a state of uniform motion, independent of their particular chemical and physical nature. (In this consideration one must naturally neglect air resistance.) The observer is therefore justified in considering his state as one of "rest."

The extraordinarily curious, empirical law that all bodies in the same gravitational field fall with the same acceleration im-

> mediately took on, through this consideration, a deep physical meaning. . . . The fact, known from experience, that acceleration in free fall is independent of the material is therefore a mighty argument that the postulate of relativity is to be extended to coordinate systems that are moving non-uniformly relative to one another.[17]

These passages by Einstein are fascinating not only because they indicate that a janusian formulation of simultaneous antithesis, simultaneous motion and rest, played a key role in a generally unquestioned piece of scientific creation—both a leap of thought and the development of a theory—but because they help clarify the specific functioning of the mirror-image janusian process in scientific creativity. I will return to the essay as quoted to clarify the points I have just made.

In the first four paragraphs, Einstein spells out, in strictly logical terms, the specific theoretical problem initially attracting his attention. He shows his deep familiarity with the information and principles of the scientific area of his concern. In science, as in art, we must take for granted that the creative thinker has an excellent, if not exceptional, grasp of the technical aspects of his field.[18] As I stated previously with respect to Darwin and others, much preparation is required before creative leaps of thought occur. An additional factor is demonstrated in the material of these paragraphs; Einstein not only knows the field exceptionally well but he recognizes an important problem in it. Such recognition, some would say, is the crux of scientific creativity. To define crucial problems in a field, they assert, requires extraordinary ability; once a crucial problem is clearly and fully defined, methods can be found to solve it. While I would not disagree about the importance of recognizing crucial problems, I suspect that such overemphasis on this aspect of the process is based on an assumption that scientific problem solving is always logical in a straightforward and standard way. In view of what we have assessed so far, such an assumption clearly is not warranted.

Although I cannot at present provide an explanation for Einstein's recognition of the problem posed by the Faraday and Maxwell-Lorentz theories,[19] I draw attention to the phrase Einstein uses to describe his orientation to the problem: in the first sentence of the fifth paragraph, he says, "The thought that one is dealing here with two fundamentally different cases was, for me, unbearable." What have we here? This is hardly a cold, logical, objective approach to a scientific problem. Is it then Einstein's use of literary license? In other words, was he merely speaking figuratively and exaggerating for its dramatic effect?

In the light of other information we have about Einstein's position on scientific questions, notably his stormy rejection of quantum theory on the basis that he found it emotionally unsatisfactory,[20] it is unlikely that he was speaking figuratively. He is here expressing a strong emotional position about a scientific problem. Could we call this emotional position an aesthetic feeling? Surely. But to call it aesthetic should not, after the earlier discussion in this book, stop our search for other psychological factors in the emotion. The point I am leading to is that Einstein's strong statement of emotion at this juncture must be taken seriously. Why might he have felt so strongly about whether two fundamentally different cases were involved? Certainly in the absence of more detailed psychological information about Einstein—information about how and under what circumstances he bebecame acquainted with these theories, his associations about the sentence in question, and other material one would want for an adequate psychological assessment—we cannot precisely say what factors were involved. But we certainly should have reason to suspect that the conceptual problem involved particular emotional and unconscious concerns. On the basis of accumulated clinical knowledge from psychoanalysis and on the basis of recent trends in cognition research indicating strong connections between cognition and motivation, there is reason to believe that such emotional and unconscious correlates help to dictate a scientist's interest in a problem and even the particular way he initially defines and structures such a problem.[21]

Following the assertion of his strong emotional position on the matter, Einstein goes on to spell out the tight logic leading to his postulation of the first, special, relativity theory. Although he does not mention it here, Einstein's first presentation of his postulate in 1905 contained, of course, highly technical and elaborate extensions of this logic, a logic stated with great simplicity in this passage. As with the creative process in the arts, therefore, we see an emotionally laden idea subjected to rigorous unraveling and development, a development that depends on the requirements of the discipline. For Einstein, it is deductive logic and mathematical exegesis; for the poet, it is expressive verbalization, unification, metaphorization, etc. Because we lack data from this account about the specific unconscious factors in Einstein's emotionally charged position or about the actual cognitive steps he followed in the deductive and mathematical process, we should not assume that Einstein's unraveling and development was markedly different from the poet's. For instance, many leaps of thought and many types of affects may have accompanied the working out of the first special relativity principle.

My observations up to this juncture do not, of course, indicate the operation of a mirror image of dreaming process in Einstein's creativity. They merely lend plausibility to the possibility of such an emotion-driven operation. But now we come to the key aspect of the testimony—the leap of thought enabling him to extend the first relativity principle into the general theory of relativity. This is the idea Einstein called "the happiest thought of my life." We must now look at this aspect of the testimony very closely because the idea itself is quite complex.

The sixth paragraph begins with the connective phrase, "Just as in the case." This phrase is of interest because it indicates the introduction of an analogy. I bring this up, not because I am attempting to perform a close linguistic analysis here, but because analogy and so-called analogic thinking has been widely considered to be a hallmark of creative thought. And indeed, Einstein states directly, in the previous paragraph, that he was looking for an analogy in nature that would allow him to bring Newton's theory of gravitation into the theory of relativity, the step making it a general theory. There is no doubt, I think, that analogic thinking—the search for, and discovery of analogies—is a crucial part of creative thinking just as it is a crucial part of all effective thinking. Analogic thinking is a specific type of logical thinking and it can occur in stepwise fashion—careful and systematic consideration of one related analog after another—or it can occur within a creative leap of thought. In other words, although analogic thinking plays a role in creativity, sometimes a prominent one, it is not the determinant aspect of it.

Looking then at Einstein's arrival at the particular idea he called "the happiest thought" of his life, we see that he has discovered the particular analogy he sought. The *form* of the particular analogy, however, is distinctive: it is highly illogical and contradictory on the surface, but it contains a deep and important logic and rationality. He says, *"Thus, for an observer in free fall from the roof of a house, there exists, during his fall, no gravitational field."* This is the thought Einstein himself italicized. And what, on the surface, could be more antithetical and illogical? Imbued, as everyone was in the year 1907 and as nonphysicists still are today, to think of gravity and falling as motion—intense motion for that matter—how could there be both falling and no falling, the effects of gravity and no effects, and how could there be both motion and rest simultaneously? For Einstein emphatically indicates here that the "observer" in free fall is *both in motion and at rest at the same time.*

Immediately, Einstein tells us how. He explains the transcendent logic of the thought because he is fully aware of the apparent contradiction at the time he poses the complex solution. He explains how the fact of the observer both in motion and at rest simultaneously pertains to the larger principle of general relativity. Dramatically, this principle was confirmed through data collected during the solar eclipse of 1919. There is little doubt from the account recorded here that Einstein was fully rational and fully conscious at the moment that his "happiest thought" was formulated.

This concept of the observer in the opposite states of motion and at rest simultaneously is a definite instance of a janusian formulation, and the account indicates steps in the janusian process. Einstein's development of the general theory of relativity, as here described, resulted from a process that was the mirror image of dreaming. Both the presence of the janusian formulation and Einstein's statement of the emotional importance he attached to the problem outline a thought process in this creative sequence having direct analogies with the poetic creative sequence described earlier. Einstein, like the poet, seems to have been struggling with a problem having both intellectual and emotional roots, both conscious and unconscious aspects, and mirror-image-of-dreaming processes played a crucial role in the solution. What unconscious factors might have been incorporated in the janusian thought are totally a matter of speculation. The specification of someone falling from "the roof of a house" catches the psychologically speculative eye. Why such a definite image? What was in Einstein's Unconscious at the time?[22] All suggestive questions, to be sure, but forever speculations.[23]

Now, armed with this detailed specification of thought sequences by Watson and by Einstein and the documentation of the crucial role of janusian thinking in both these instances of scientific creation, I shall turn back to some of the important examples of supposedly unconsciously generated flashes of scientific intuition I cited earlier. A close examination of these examples will, I think, show the ubiquity of the mirror-image processes in diverse types of creation.

Mirror-Image Processes in Scientific Creation

Darwin's conception of the evolution of species and his formulation of the key notion of natural selection certainly ranks among the most important scientific achievements of all time. To be sure, Darwin's greatness does not inhere solely in the formulation itself but largely also in his intensive and extensive observation and documentation of supporting evidence. Let us look again at his description of the circumstances under which the specific leap of thought, the creative theoretical leap, occurred. After a long time of seaching for the appropriate formulation (at least four years according to his autobiography),[24] he states, "I happened to read for amusement Malthus on *Population,*" and then a few sentences later, "it at once struck me . . . ."

The fact that Darwin was reading Malthus when he finally hit on the idea of natural selection has always suggested something rather strange and paradoxical. The main point of Malthus's thesis is that untrammeled human population growth relative to a fixed environment would result in *extermination of the species* because of competition for existence. And yet we see Darwin postulating that this struggle for existence results in the enhancement and perfection of the species relative to its environment!

What does this tell us about Darwin's thinking? By no means am I the first to recognize this apparent contradiction in the momentous event. Several generations of scholars have noted it and, in passing, have concluded that Darwin completely misunderstood Malthus's point and took his own meaning from what he read. But is this conclusion really plausible? After reading all of Malthus's detailed descriptions of the negative effects of population growth, is it likely that a man of Darwin's enormous intellect would completely miss the point? It is seriously doubtful. Darwin nowhere disagreed with or contradicted Malthus's point. More plausible, therefore, is the postulate that Darwin's specific idea at that moment was a formulation of *the simultaneous operation of maladaptation and adaptation in the struggle for existence.* He accepted and understood Malthus's point that the struggle for existence could lead to devastating destruction of the species but thought that it also led to adaptive selection. As the Darwin scholar Gruber put it, in summing up the overall impact of the idea, "natural selection, although it might work against maladaptive variants, could also work in favor of occasional variants which were better adapted than their ancestors to the prevailing conditions under which they must survive."[25] Regardless of the particular content of the plausible exegesis of the idea, the structure of the conception is that of simultaneous antithesis, maladaptive together with adaptive, and a manifestation of janusian thinking.

Of additional interest is the fact that Malthus was also in the mind of A. R. Wallace at the time he formulated an idea of natural selection, independently and quite a bit after Darwin.[26] Wallace describes his thinking as follows: "in my case it was his [Malthus's] elaborate account of the action of 'preventive checks' in keeping down the population of savage races to a tolerably fixed but scanty number. This had strongly impressed me, and it suddenly flashed upon me that all animals are necessarily thus kept down—'the struggle for existence'—while *variations,* on which I was always thinking, must necessarily often be *beneficial,* and would then cause those varieties to increase while the injurious variations diminished."[27] Since Wallace patently did not misunderstand Malthus and since he also explicitly thought of the simultaneous oppositions of increase/diminution and beneficial/injurious, it seems clear that the discovery of natural selection required a janusian formulation in order to be made.

The testimonies by Poincaré and by Hadamard indicate the operation in creative scientific thought of homospatial thinking. Poincaré's account is rich and perhaps overly suggestive, but aside from emphasizing the spontaneous emergence of his thoughts, he provides us, in one place, with a specific description of their nature. He says "A host of ideas kept surging in my head; I could almost feel them *jostling one another, until two of them coalesced* [*s'accrochassent*], so to speak, to form a stable combination."[28] The phrase I italicize denotes a mental image of numerous discrete entities, the represented content of particular ideas, all occupying the same space. He speaks of ideas jostling one another and therefore being represented in some physical spatial form. He speaks of coalescing, and clearly suggests merging and superimposition (see fig. 3*A*).

Hadamard's discovery of the valuation of a determinant also demonstrates the operation of homospatial thinking, the active conception of two or more discrete entities occupying the same space. The schematic diagram he saw in his mind's eye consisted of a rectangle superimposed on, or occupying the same space as, a square. That the conception involved the same diffuse type of mental image as previously described for the poet's homospatial conception (the horse alone and the horse with a rider) is indicated by Hadamard's reference

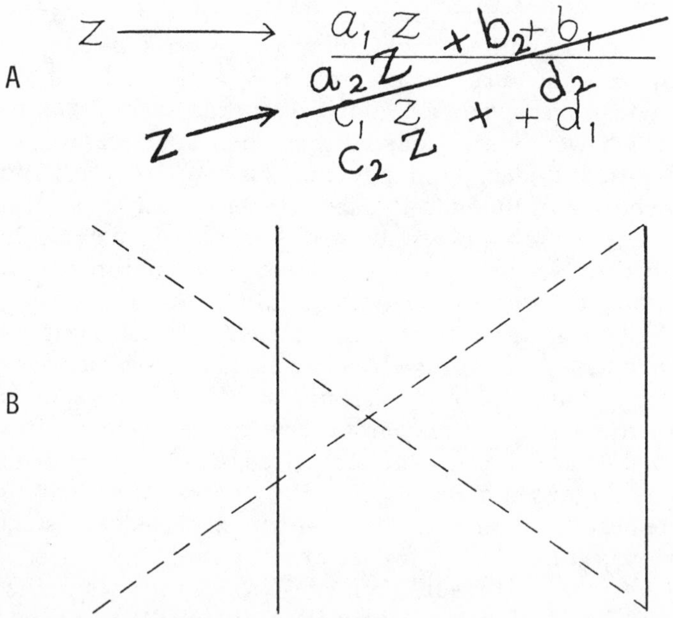

Fig. 3. Homospatial Conceptions. *A.* "Ideas . . . coalesce." Diagrammatic conception of Poincaré's description of his mental experiences leading to his creation of the Fuchsian functions. (Actual formulas used here pertain to the Fuchsian functions, but they are not intended to indicate the particular content of Poincaré's idea, a content he never specifies.) *B.* "A schematic diagram: a square of whose sides only the verticals are drawn and inside of it, four points being the vertices of a rectangle and joined by (hardly apparent) diagonals. . . ." Representation of Hadamard's conception leading to the creation of the valuation of a determinant. (Diagonals drawn to suggest an image that is impossible to present physically. The rectangle is superimposed upon the square; therefore, the mental image consists of diagonals within the area of the square, not, as drawn here, ending in an extrapolated spatial location.)

to "hardly apparent diagonals joining the four points of the rectangle." Conceiving a square, a rectangle, and diagonal lines all occupying the same space requires the type of diffuse image in which certain aspects are hardly apparent (see fig. 3*B*).

Other instances of homospatial and janusian thinking in scientific creation can be inferred from documented circumstances in which scientists have merely described the outcome of their leaps of thought and have not provided enough information about the content of their thinking to enable us to know for certain. Cannon's all-at-once formulation (during a sleepless night) of the flight-fight syndrome, an aroused physiological state of preparedness produced by secretion of the hormone adrenalin, connotes that he conceived the behavioral opposites of flight and fight at the same time. Fermi's spontaneous decision to place a piece of paraffin in the path of propelled neutrons produced slow neutrons which, to everyone's amazement, were more effective in bombarding an atomic nucleus than fast neutrons. As it had previously been assumed that fast neutrons had greater force, it is rather likely that, at the moment Fermi made his decision, he conceived of a neutron having simultaneously antithetical physical properties of having greater projectile power and moving at a diminished speed. In addition to these probable instances of janusian thinking in scientific discovery, the circumstances of James Watt's arriving at the key solution for the design of the steam engine suggests an instance of homospatial thinking. Watt describes the idea occurring on a Sunday walk through a green with an old washing house where Glasgow girls boiled and washed their clothes every day but Sunday, the Sabbath. It was a green near his home where he very frequently walked. His account is as follows: "I had gone to take a walk on a fine Sabbath afternoon. I had entered the Green by the gate at the foot of Charlotte Street—had passed the old washing house. *I was thinking upon the engine at the time,* and had gone as far as the Herd's-house, when the idea came into my mind, that as steam was an elastic body it would rush into a vacuum, and if communication was made between the cylinder and an exhausted vessel, it would rush into it, and might there be condensed without cooling the cylinder" [italics mine].[29] This idea of a separate cylinder was the basis of the condenser, the key step in Watt's development of the steam engine. Inasmuch as Watt made a point of mentioning the washing house, it is highly likely that he had an image of the familiar but absent washing girls in his mind's eye as he passed that point. Since the girls characteristically washed their clothes in steaming kail pots, standing both together and *separately,* it is also reasonable to assume that he had superimposed mental images of his steam engine apparatus ("I was thinking upon the engine at the time") onto images of the girls washing (see fig. 4). The articulation of the critical idea of steam in separate

Fig. 4. Artist's conception of the homospatial image leading to the creation of the steam condenser: Watt mentally visualized the girls doing laundry in their kail pots and, superimposing the cylinders upon them, he thought of steam in separate containers. Drawing by Robert C. Morris.

containers, then, followed when he arrived at the Herd's-house. This idea, obvious as it may seem in this day of complete familiarity with condensers and engines, was a culminating link in a general search for such uses of steam of at least a hundred years duration.[30]

A similar type of mental event led Eduard Benedictus, the French chemist, to the creation of shatterproof safety glass.[31] Benedictus describes having a flask in his laboratory drop ten feet to the floor without breaking or shattering. Noting only that the liquids inside had evaporated and that there was a layer of celluloid enamel inside, he thought no more about the incident until some time later. After dinner one evening, he was thinking about two recent automobile accidents in each of which a young girl had her throat cut and was killed by broken glass. Reflecting on these, he described visualizing the following: "the image of my flask appeared superimposed [*se superposa*], in the pale outline of an 'over-impression' upon the constantly changing backdrop of life." Following this image of the flask superimposed on images of the girls and of the accident scenes, he went to his laboratory where he worked until dawn on "a plan which I proceeded to execute, point by point. By evening of the following day, the first sheet of Triplex glass was created." The serendipitous event of a flask falling on the laboratory floor led to a very practical and valuable application through Benedictus's use of homospatial thinking and through further elaboration.

I will end this chapter by focusing on a scientific creator whose thinking characteristically shifted to opposite orientations, an overall pattern related to and generative of janusian thinking. Louis Pasteur, whose discoveries redounded to the everlasting benefit of mankind, approached both theoretical and experimental problems by adopting opposite conceptual orientations, either in fairly short succession or with a dogged persistence.[32] For instance, he devoted a large part of the final years of his life collecting experimental evidence for his cosmological theory that matter originally arose from life rather than, as scientists generally believe, life arose from matter.

Pasteur's first scientific triumph, the discovery of the stereochemical structure of the tartrates—a discovery he never tired of talking about—involved a janusian formulation at an early phase. Given his predilection for opposites, it is no surprise that he early chose a scientific area centrally involving polarity and mirror images. In a lecture delivered before the Société Chimique in Paris, he described his work on the crystalline structure of tartaric acid and of paratartaric acid and their salts as follows:

> I was a student at the Ecole Normale Supérieure, from 1843 to 1846. Chance made me read in the school library a note of the learned crystallographer, Mitscherlich, related to two salts: the tartrate and the paratartrate of sodium and ammonium. I meditated for a long time upon this note; it disturbed my schoolboy thoughts. I could not understand that two substances could be as similar as claimed by Mitscherlich, without being completely identical [Mitscherlich had discovered that the tartrates and paratartrates had the same chemical composition, the same crystal shape with the same angles, the same specific gravity, the same double refraction, but the solution of the tartrate rotated the plane of polarization, while the paratartrate was inactive]. . . . Hardly graduated from the Ecole Normale, I planned . . . studying . . . tartaric acid and its salts, as well as paratartaric acid. . . .
>
> I soon recognized that . . . tartaric acid and all its combinations

> exhibit asymmetric forms. Individually, each of these forms of tartaric acid gave a mirror image which was not superposable upon the substance itself. On the contrary, I could not find anything of the sort in paratartaric acid or its salts.
>
> Suddenly, I was seized by a great emotion. I had always kept in mind the profound surprise caused in me by Mitscherlich's note on the tartrate and paratartrate of sodium and ammonium. Despite the extreme thoroughness of their study, Mitscherlich, as well as M. de la Provostaye [a physicist who published an extensive crystallographic study of these substances], will have failed to notice that the tartrate is asymmetric, as it must be; nor will they have seen that the paratartrate is not asymmetric, which is also very likely. Immediately, and with a feverish ardor, I prepared . . . .[33]

Pasteur goes on in this account to describe first a disappointment in the outcome of his testing of the hypothesis and then a reassessment of the results by orienting the crystals with reference to a plane perdendicular to the observer; after some other interpretation and exploration, that reassessment provided the answer to the problem.

The ultimate solution to the problem was that paratartaric acid consisted of equal measures of *two opposite light-rotating forms of tartaric acid,* a solution requiring the janusian conception of opposites operating simultaneously. This janusian conception was presaged by Pasteur's earlier hunch which was also a janusian formulation. In attempting to explain Mitscherlich's observations, he had postulated that the reason the two acids shared so many chemical properties was that they were identical but opposite in structure with respect to asymmetry. This formulation, which first led him to an apparently negative result, ultimately produced the correct one and, in its broad outlines, was valid. Pasteur described the overall finding as follows: "the molecular arrangement of the two tartaric acids are asymmetric and, on the other hand, . . . these arrangements are absolutely identical, excepting that they exhibit asymmetry in opposite directions. . . . When this . . . molecular asymmetry appears in two opposed forms, then the chemical properties of the identical but optically opposite substances are exactly the same, from which it follows that this type of contrast and analogy does not interfere with the ordinary play of the chemical affinities."[34]

Although Pasteur and others subsequently found that the principle just propounded did not always hold absolutely true, his discovery had a great impact on crystallographic research and on the knowledge about levo and dextro rotation that is so taken for granted today. As we know, Pasteur went on from these early researches to make other very important discoveries. One of the most far-reaching of these was his discovery or creation of the science of immunology. Also the result of a leap of thought, the foundation for this discovery or creation was an immediate interpretation of a chance event. In view of Pasteur's famous aphorism, "La chance se favorée preparée" (chance favors the prepared mind), the account is of especial interest, because the circumstances illustrate the type of preparation and thinking involved.

In eighteenth-century England, Edward Jenner began the practice of using an injection of cowpox to protect human beings against virulent smallpox. Supposedly, he was led to this idea by a milkmaid patient who, he thought, was suffering from smallpox. When he told her his diagnosis, she said, "I cannot take the smallpox because I have had the cowpox." Jenner was impressed and began to study the phenomenon systematically; finally, he convinced himself that cowpox did prevent smallpox infection and he introduced the practice of using injections of the markedly milder infection throughout England and elsewhere in the world. Neither Jenner himself nor any of his enthusiastic followers, however, understood the mechanism of protection nor did they apply the idea to other diseases.

It was Louis Pasteur who discovered the mechanism and the wide applicability of the immunological principle connected to it. Here is the account of the circumstances of his discovery given by René Dubos:

> Pasteur had begun experiments on chicken cholera in the spring of 1879, but an unexpected difficulty interrupted the work after the summer vacation. The cultures of the chicken cholera bacillus that had been kept in the laboratory during the summer failed to produce disease when inoculated into chickens in the early autumn. A new virulent culture was obtained from a natural outbreak, and it was inoculated into new animals, as well as into the chickens which had resisted the old cultures. The new animals, just brought from the market, succumbed to the infection in the customary length of time, thus showing that the fresh culture was very active. But to everyone's astonishment, and the astonishment of Pasteur himself, almost all the other chickens survived the infection. According to the accounts left by one of his collaborators Pasteur remained silent for a minute, then exclaimed as if he had seen a vision, "Don't you see that these animals have been vaccinated!"[35]

Hence, in a flash, Pasteur coined a word which connected this event to Jenner's use of cowpox (Latin: *vacca,* "cow") and discovered the mechanism and the principle of immunization.

This story, like so many of the accounts of a creative scientist's leap of thought tends, on first reading, merely to emphasize the mysterious and presumably automatic nature of genius. Such an emphasis contributes to widely held beliefs, described earlier in this chapter, that unconscious factors are directly responsible for such creative leaps. After all, the circumstances suggest that the idea was not merely a matter of inductive thinking, carefully weighing alternatives and drawing logical inferences, nor merely a matter of being prepared to understand the astonishing event because of knowledge of the germ theory of disease. All of Pasteur's colleagues were witnesses to the same event, and it is known that several of them were excellent inductive thinkers and all certainly were thoroughly knowledgeable about the germ theory of the disease, but none of them could explain what happened nor did any formulate the general principle as Pasteur did. Some mysterious factor, "unconscious" work, would seem to have been involved. A careful analysis of the structure of the idea, however, reveals instead that it was an instance of janusian thinking. It appeared mysterious and astonishing partly because it involved the immediate conception of a simultaneous antithesis, a frequently surprising type of conception. It was not merely a matter of some undefined type of superior generalizing ability, nor of grasping remote analogies. In seeing the unexpected event of the chickens' survival as a manifestation of a principle, in seeing its connection to Jenner's practice of injecting cowpox to prevent smallpox, Pasteur needed to formulate the concept that the *surviving animals were both diseased and not-diseased at the same time.* His leap of thought consisted of realizing that the animals that had previously not shown any effects from the culture had nevertheless been affected and diseased in some way; this prior undetected infection had therefore kept them free from disease and protected them against further infection. Fully accepted now, the simultaneously antithetical idea that disease could function to prevent disease was the original basis for the science of immunology.

In spelling out the operation of the mirror-image processes in scientific creativity, I have done a good deal of reevaluating and reassessing many accounts of scientific discovery which do not necessarily reveal the processes on first inspection. Indeed, some of these accounts have been interpreted in totally different ways by previous investigators.[36] This should not be surprising nor, on that account, dismissable. If scientists or interpreters of scientific thinking paid attention to the aspects of thought we are considering here, the processes I am describing would have been discovered long ago. That the processes described are not merely hypothetical constructs without reference to creative scientific thinking today is dispelled by the following two accounts. (1) A Nobel-laureate microbiologist who was a research subject of mine arrived at a new idea about enzyme behavior in 1974 by *visualizing himself superimposed upon an atom in an enzyme molecule,* a homospatial conception. (2) Richard Feynman, the Nobel-laureate physicist, described the following janusian formulation to an interviewer: "*an electron and a positron are the same particle, reversed in time.*"[37]

6

THE CREATIVE PROCESS

We have, I think, just engaged in quite a dizzying leap. Although many people take for granted that creativity is a unitary phenomenon, that the same or similar factors operate in creative accomplishment in any field, my leap from poetry to science still has probably been a heady one. Horses represented as emblematic of the ethos of the time are strange companions with levo-tartrates, electrons, the Faraday and Maxwell-Lorentz laws, and genetic reduplication, despite the intrinsic similarities of the creator's thought. Moreover, much remains to be filled in and clarified about the nature and operation of the mirror-image processes. Before proceeding with more technical matters and data, therefore, I shall give an account of the overall nature of the creative process. In the course of this narrative I shall provide a picture of the subjective side of creative thinking and the manner in which the creative process, for both the artist and the scientist as well as other types of creators, is the mirror image of the dream.

The creative process begins in waking life. It begins in a state of awareness of external environment and physical circumstances, and a state of conscious intention as well. Regardless of the field in which the creator carries out his activities, he begins his task with the intention of creating something clearly in mind. No one creates anything without deliberately setting out to do so. While the creative intention of the artist is clear and well known without the need for special elaboration, the scientist's creative intention does require some clarification. Objectively it appears that the artist produces something new and valuable and he knowingly sets out to do so, while the scientist looks for and finds something not truly new but an entity previously existent in nature. From a subjective point of view, however, this distinction does not apply; the scientist in his quest for discovery is often interested in creating or producing something new and valuable in much the same way as the artist. Psychologically, the difference is primarily that a scientist does not think of producing something made by himself alone, but something which was, in essence, made by nature. Although constructing a theory imparts a greater sense of personal responsibility for the product than verifying an hypothesis by experiment, both types of scientific activity can involve a strong intent to find, or to produce, something strikingly valuable and new. From this subjective viewpoint, the creative process takes place in scientific activity whether the scientist is developing a theory or working primarily on experimental verification, or whether a discovery is made by means of serendipity. The serendipidous finding gets established because the scientist wants to make something new of information appearing by chance.

The intention to create must be both deliberate and very strong. Many factors deter creative achievement, factors involving both the limited and refractory nature of materials and the sometimes limited and refractory nature of social recognition. By and large, persons engaging in creative activity have this strong intention and motivation, for reasons derived from upbringing, heredity, group factors, and the complexities of the social ethos. The idea of automatic or unintentional creating is an impossibility. Even the seemingly automatic creations of so-called visionary poets Blake and Coleridge are no real exception, since they were conscious and strongly motivated poets before any visions or poetic lines appeared in their dreams. Surely their waking motivation to create pervaded their dream experience as well. Moreover, in the case of Coleridge's opium state and of Blake's dream, the resulting poems involved later extensions and later revisions and changes, respectively.[1] Despite the poets' public claims, conscious effort, intent, and creating entered into the stage of writing out the poems.

The creator begins with a high degree of knowledge of his field. The scientist has learned the technical knowledge available and he is capable of understanding complicated theories and laws. A creative scientist, in other words, must have a high level of what is usually designated as "intelligence" and he must have applied himself to obtaining as much of his field's information and knowledge as possible. Although scientific creations sometimes come from persons who switch from one scientific discipline to another, such persons usually are those who absorb a good deal of information in relatively short periods of time. The theories of certain historians of science such as that of Thomas Kuhn strongly suggest that scientific breakthroughs can often come from persons who shift between scientific fields.[2] Such shifting may provide the investigator or theorist with a specially broad perspective on a sister field because he learns it from the "top," so to speak, and doesn't get embroiled in technical complications and details. He may bring new models of thought and techniques to his new field. There may also be emotional factors. Depending on the circumstances of the shift, such factors as loss of previous position, disillusionment, or other crises may produce exceptionally strong motivation to create in the new field.[3] Nevertheless, he still must become highly knowledgeable about the models, data, and problems of his adopted field; there is no reason to believe that interdisciplinary shifting in itself confers magical powers.

Creation in the arts also requires a good deal of specialized knowledge. The type and degree of knowledge required vary a good deal, depending on the artistic field, and in some fields the type of intelligence required differs markedly from that ordinarily measured by IQ tests. Although the high degrees of technical knowledge needed for science may not be necessary in the arts, a certain minimal knowledge is mandatory. Despite the tendency of creative writers in particular to derogate the need for formal education and knowledge in their field, it is still necessary for good writers to attain considerable knowledge of word use, word nuances and meanings, and enough familiarity with common speech and with literature to produce something interesting and new. Good writing requires, at a minimum, the capacity to recognize cliché and banal phrases. There must also be a capacity to recognize banal and cliché literary themes, although some highly creative writers do seem to have been able to avoid repeating previous literary constructions without always knowing that they were doing so. Higher levels of literary sophistication and even formal education become necessary, depending on the nature of the literary creation and the intended audience. In music and the visual arts, the minimal requirements for successful creating involve rather high levels of technical knowledge. Knowledge of music theory and some degree of competence in performance has generally been necessary for musical creation; knowledge of art history, art materials, and technical matters of design, drawing, color, and visualization seems basic for creation in the visual arts. Primitives and idiot-savants, of course, have appeared in all artistic fields; it is possible that the great Shakespeare did not have very much literary education, although as an actor he surely had a good deal of familiarity with the theater. Successful creation with limited knowledge or with a limited technical background is, however, more the exception than the rule, even in artistic fields. Despite the appearance of the occasional so-called primitive, knowledge and creating are generally linked. Unusual capacities to perform without knowledge and education may be due to specific types of genetic factors, or to other unknowns, but these capacities lead more often only to successful performance or successful problem solving rather than creating.[4] Producing something new involves going beyond what is already known or accomplished and, although there are exceptions, creative persons have generally known when they have achieved this. They have, in other words, possessed enough information to recognize that they have produced creations.

Given a baseline of knowledge and technical competence, the creative process begins with the creator's interest in discovery, of which there are many types. The creative scientist is interested in discovering something about the nature of physical reality, but again—although he is generally not aware of this—he is interested in discovering something related to himself. Even a complicated technical problem has some particular psychological meaning: this can range from the symbolic significance of the behavior of enzymes and mold spores, molecular structure, a principle of falling bodies, or a discrepancy between the law of gravitation and the law of magnetic induction to the more general significance of finding that laws in nature conform to some regular order as an indirect means of reassuring oneself that one's seemingly chaotic internal psychological processes are also in order or are capable of being so. Symbolic meaning, it must be emphasized, is always complex in such cases and it never corresponds to simplistic formulations such as sublimated anal or oral impulses. The emotional need of finding order in nature is almost always important for a scientist, creative or not. Physical scientists tend to be intimidated by internal psychological experience; unlike the artist, the physical scientist tends to take the internal psychological world for granted and to turn for exploration to the physical world. In a deep emotional sense, physical scientists seem to doubt the reality of the external physical world and therefore to explore it in order to obtain reassurance about its regularities, principles, and ultimately its actuality. In creative scientists, this need for exploration and reassurance amounts to passion. The artist, on his side, tends to be intimidated by the external physical world. He takes its laws and regularities for granted, and tends to assume without question that the physical world will operate with little intervention from him. Sometimes he even may intellectually and philosophically doubt its reality, but he has little need to explore these doubts. His explorations concern the reality of the internal psychological world. He doubts the reality of this world and he is also less intimidated by it than the scientist. For the creative artist, the creative process is an attempt to discover the nature of his and other's internal psychological world including the following: the structure of emotional processes, the perceptual impact of external physical reality, the nature of interpersonal relationships, the roots and springs of language, the structure and impact of internal and external sound and rhythm, the structure and impact of imagery and visual forms, and the impact of social reality.

The creative process is motivated by the creator's interest in discovery. This interest in discovery begins the process and continues at every step of the way. Though the artistic creative process sometimes begins with an inspiration, that is, a dramatic idea or insight, such an inspiration is merely the stimulus for embarking on a process of discovering. Almost never does the creative artist know very much about the product he will eventually create. Not only are the details lacking at the start, but some of the most crucial elements—crucial both for him and for his audience—will be discovered during the course of the process of creating.[5] In art, the initial element or, to use Beardsley's term, "the incept,"[6] usually consists of a word or a phrase, a series of phrases, an overall structure or theme, an image or a visual form, a succession of sounds or rhythms, or an outline of a plot. These are far from completed ideas ready to be spelled out, but they are elements that the creator is interested in exploring. The creative process itself is the means and method of exploring these concepts.

As the artist begins to work out his initial idea, as he begins to execute the work of art, he discovers and develops the ramifications and the implications of the early ideas; then, new ideas occur along the way that instigate new quests for discovery in their own right. And the discoveries the artist makes are discoveries about the nature of experience and about the nature of the medium he is working with as well as discoveries about himself. A poet, for instance, may explore all the ramifications of a particular linguistic phrase and its connections to the things that it denotes. In the poetic creative process I have documented, the poet explored the idea of the horse with the horse's ramifications in mythology, in the modern ethos, and in the poet's own personal life. Concomitantly, he explored the implications and ramifications of certain words connected to horses, such as "gait," and discovered exciting integrations between words and experience.

During the course of this process of discovery, the creative person engages in a good deal of fantasy. This is so for both the scientist and the artist, although elaborate personal fantasy is more characteristic of, and more related to, the artistic creative process. The scientist's fantasies are often highly concrete and they suggest analogies and applications to abstract phenomena in science. When the creative leap occurs, these fantasies often enter into the homospatial process; elements of the fantasy become superimposed upon the mental images of natural phenomena. As I shall describe in chapter 10, the musician and the visual artist also often have fantasies involving concrete elements that are subjected to the homospatial process. Very likely, the literary creator's fantasies are the most personal of all. "His Majesty the Ego," as Freud put it,[7] or the creator himself may manifestly appear more often in the fantasy of literary creators because the literary art often devolves on stories having definite actors or agents. Freud was surely correct in suggesting that daydreaming or fantasy played an important role in creation, but he was incorrect in assuming that creative thinking consisted merely of disguising these fantasies in an acceptable form.[8] Creative fantasy, moreover, is quite different from ordinary fantasy and from the processes operating in dreams.

Creative persons have daydreams involving thought processes similar to nocturnal dreams just as anyone else does. But the thinking that goes on during the creative fantasy is not the same as that in dreams; it is the mirror image of dreaming. While engaged in creative fantasy or imagining, the creator uses abstract types of thinking a good deal. His thoughts may rove freely, but he is constantly alert and prepared to select and relate his thoughts to the creative task he is engaged in. He is oriented to discovery. Although he is not necessarily aware of doing so, he relates elements in his free-flowing thoughts to the dramatic themes, characters, situations, or to the visual forms, sound patterns, theoretical issues, and mathematical formulae he is struggling with. Even when he seems not to be thinking about the problem directly, the circumstance leading to the popular belief in the importance of the Unconscious in creativity, he does, at the moment of a creative conception, engage however briefly in focusing and in an act of will that consists in actively formulating by means of janusian or homospatial thinking as well as other abstract types of cognition. Moving away from thinking about a creative task, either resting or taking on some distracting activity, has many psychological functions but there is no reason to believe that it instigates unconscious work on the problem. When ideas arise suddenly in a rested or distracted state of mind, they do not arise fully formed from the Unconscious. Only the intention to solve the problem can be said to be unconscious at such moments; the creative thinking, however briefly it flashes, is conscious.[9] Unlike primary process or dreamlike manifestations of the Unconscious in waking life, such as the classically described jokes, slips of the tongue or pen, or other automatisms, there is neither condensation nor displacement in creative leaps of thought. Rather than disguising wishes and disrupting conscious thought, the mirror-image processes integrate unconscious wishes with solutions to a problem or task. The creative process moves in a direction opposite to that of the dream; abstract modes of cognition work toward unearthing and discovery rather than expression and gratification of wishes alone. Creating moves from free, wandering thinking to fixated solutions and constructions within a product. Unconscious processes do not push into and disrupt the creator's awareness; they are, in a sense, pulled by the mirror-image forms of cognition.

It would be a mistake to focus on creative fantasy as the only, or the major, mirror-image-of-dreaming manifestation in creation. Creation in any field does not consist of an isolated event or a single act, but it results from a long series of circumstances, sometimes occurring in an unbroken chain or sequence but often interrupted, reconstructed, and repeated over a period of time. The process of creation begins with the conscious selection of a task and a factor to be explored. Both janusian and homospatial thinking sometimes appear full-blown at this stage. The janusian process, usually occurring earlier than the homospatial one, may appear rapidly in the earliest phase of creation, the incept then consisting of an actively constructed simultaneous antithesis. In scientific creation, an initial problem may be formulated in just such terms. For instance, a scientist thinks the following: the law of electromagnetic induction and the law of gravitation, though appearing to be opposites, are really the same. Now, how can I go about proving this? When Einstein said that the idea of dealing with two different cases here was unbearable to him, it could indicate that at some point he consciously structured the initial problem in such a manner. In poetry, the idea that sexuality and violence are the same could be the incept instigating the task of creating a poem. With one of my subjects (see description of the circumstances in chap. 10), this particular janusian thought did in fact stimulate a poem about nude bodies on a beach and dead bodies in the gas ovens of Auschwitz. Janusian thinking thus frequently instigates a succession of thoughts and acts, and further janusian as well as homospatial conceptions occur along the way. Leaps of thought occur and unconscious material is revealed, particularly in art, but unlike the dream, consciousness or at times a sense of heightened consciousness is in full sway.

From a subjective point of view, the heightened sense of consciousness during the course of the creative process constitutes a distinct mirror image of dreaming. While terms such as "expansion of consciousness" are clearly figurative rather than literally descriptive of a psychological state, they convey the quality of intensity, the sense of increased comprehension, and the freedom from boundaries of time and space. I shall return to discuss the determinants of this state in a later chapter (chap. 12) but a further clarification of its subjective nature is warranted here. Intense concentration is characteristic of several phases in the creative process. Not unlike the type of concentration necessary for high levels of performance in any activity, from sports to strictly intellectual tasks, the intensity seems to be greater under conditions of exceptionally strong motivation such as that in the creative process. Every facet of a visual scene, every nuance of a musical tone or of a word or phrase, and every aspect of a scientific theory or experiment is explored and kept in focus at several particular stages of the creative process. Certain aspects of the heightened sense of consciousness and a subjective quality akin to dreaming arise from this factor of intense concentration. Just as dreaming occurs in a state where attention to external stimuli is suspended and there is intense concentration on internal psychological phenomena, creating also frequently involves intense fixation on mental images, thoughts, and constructs. Capacity for such intense concentration is a necessary factor in successful creating in any field. Although these states of intense concentration are similar to dreaming, they are also the obverse of dreaming. They are appropriately designated as heightened states of consciousness in opposition to the physical unconsciousness or sleep in which dreaming occurs. All the creator's conscious faculties are operating optimally and intensely, and there is the capacity to translate observations and thoughts immediately into action and tangible production. The heightened state of consciousness is highly pleasurable and it is both similar and opposite in form and function to dreaming, a reflection or a mirror-image state.

The specific mirror-image processes, janusian and homospatial thinking, tend to dominate a large portion of the creative process and to contribute to aspects of the heightened conscious state. Often, the steps in both processes are drawn out and extended. Motivated to discovery, the creator first senses or discerns some discrepancy, gap, or hiatus in the body of knowledge, beliefs, and practices pertaining to his field. Often in science, the creator gradually clarifies critical polarities, antitheses, and oppositions involved and later formulates an idea that they operate or exist simultaneously. Part of the scientific creative process consists of identifying the salient oppositions connected to a particular problem (see chap. 8) and many worthless ones are discarded along the way. Similarly, the creative artist discards many oppositions and equivalences among oppositions that are banal and cliché. While the creative artist may not formulate oppositions quite so gradually or specifically as the scientist, he, like the scientist, must have the previously mentioned technical knowledge and, more broadly, sufficient knowledge of human experience in order to know what technical matters and elements of experience are most widely held to be valid and true. In order to formulate that factors thought to be opposite or antithetical are actually simultaneously operative or true, the creative person must be deeply aware of what is generally known or believed. In the homospatial process, too, discrete elements often are chosen a considerable time before being actively superimposed or fused and conceived as occupying the same space. Such discrete elements may be identified and chosen because of their personal significance to the creator, because of an artistic or historical tradition, or because of their social, technical, philosophical, or political importance. Thus, the poet chose horses and riders both because of his personal preoccupations and because of the ageless human interest in the qualities of animals. The elements in Winston Churchill's political metaphor "iron curtain" must have derived from Churchill's long preoccupation with war and with iron as a metal of war. The curtain aspect may have been derived from his own, and the traditional English, interest in the theater, or in the curtain as a symbol of the home. The elements in the scientific metaphor "black holes in space" all derive from long-standing concerns with color, space, and emptiness in the field of physics, although the idea of "black holes" may have had some previous personal connection for the metaphor's creator, John Wheeler, with coal mines or with coal mining in the environment of his childhood and adolescence in Youngstown, Ohio. After choosing or becoming aware of the discrete elements—elements that linguists call the "ground" of the metaphor—there may be an immediate active fusion or superimposition, or a delayed one. Depending on the salience of the elements to the total context, since really effective metaphors seldom stand alone,[10] a new identity becomes articulated as the culmination of the homospatial process.

As the creative process continues to move from disguise and disorder to illumination and order, as it moves from personal preoccupation to generic and universal concerns, as it involves increasingly heightened states of consciousness and awareness rather than the restricted focus of the sleeping mind, it proceeds in a reverse direction from dreaming. And, as a mirror image, it bears resemblances to dreaming. There tends to be more sensory imagery than ordinary thought processes, more periods of seemingly undirected thought and suspension of awareness of physical surroundings, intense affectual experiences of heightened anxiety or heightened enjoyment and pleasure not often connected with ordinary waking thought, and a quality of vividness in the final product, in artistic creation especially, that is similar to the vividness in dreams. There are periods when the creator lets his thoughts run freely while he suspends critical judgment and there are periods of sheer playfulness. There are gratifications and fun in discharging impulses and feelings of all sorts: anger at an imagined oppressor, sexual fantasy involving imagined scenes and circumstances, fancied mastery of a difficult physical task. And there seems to be some form of pleasure associated directly with the use of sensory imagery itself. Some of these factors in the creative process arise from the same psychological needs and functions operating in dreams and many can be traced to the factor of unearthing unconscious processes as well as to other factors that I shall describe later (esp. chaps. 9, 11, 12).

Despite the overall similarities between the creative process and dreaming and some of the shared differences from ordinary waking thought, ordinary logical processes play a consistent and a crucial role. Deductive and inductive logic, analogic and dialectic thinking, and other rationalizing processes enter into the overall construction of the creation and play some role in crystallizing creations into tangible forms. Much of the creative process consists of elaboration, execution, and the attempt to differentiate and to clarify through language, symbols, and tangible constructions. Much of creation arises from hard systematic labor, the drive to perfect an entity roughly produced. This aspect of the creative process derives from the creator's intense motivation to persist, to master reality, and to discover. The constant shaping, differentiating, and clarifying for the purpose of communication to others yields new discoveries to the creator himself. Competition also plays a role. There is often competition with others who both previously and currently have persisted in a similar task. Vying with historical and contemporary colleagues, both for personal recognition and achievement and for the gratification of discovery itself, is a strong motive in creative people.[11] Again, as a reversal of dreaming, the creative process consists of highly motivated and directed behavior rather than involuntary thought processes passively received in sleep.

The directed push toward discovery and clarification persists to the culmination of the process. When a literary artist experiences discoveries about words and language as well as arrives at personal insights about himself and the characters and experiences he is writing about, he arrives at an end point. These discoveries, more than any other factor, dictate the judgment that a particular creation is finished and complete. Even though there may be doubts, the feeling or sense of discovery allows the artist enough gratification to stop. Usually, writers describe this sense as finding out what the poem, novel, short story, or play is "saying." Although visual artists and musicians do not generally use this term, their comparable goal might be expressed in such terms as finding out what the visual creation is "showing" and what the musical piece is "sounding," respectively. For the scientist, of course, the matter of discovery is more straightforward and clear: his goal is reached when he discovers a specific fact, law, or theoretical structure, and he is able to define the means for a consensus of his peers to recognize this discovery. It is not generally realized, however, that he also discovers many things along the way which give him some gratification but which he seldom, if ever, emphasizes. These discoveries include adventitious information about people and nature, improvement of personal technique and proficiency, as well as glimpses into the way his own mind and the minds of his colleagues operate. Discovery in conjunction with creation, regardless of how extensive or important, is gratifying for all types of creators.

After an artistic work is completed, or a scientific discovery attained, feelings and experiences continue. Further insights about the discovery or further insights into what the work is "saying," "sounding," or "showing" occur and these may lead to new preoccupations and ideas for further works. Although such insights about an artistic work are generally aesthetic in content, for instance an equilibrium between certain colors and forms, or between loss and gain, or between sound patterns in a sonority, they are sometimes explicit personal insights about such matters as struggles with self-defeating tendencies or particular personal emotional constellations. By and large, aesthetic and personal insights parallel and enrich each other. Although scientists do not generally experience personal insights following a discovery (except perhaps for social scientists), they do sometimes question themselves about their own motivations and personal investments in particular objective matters. As artistic works are more directly and fully connected with particular individuals than are scientific discoveries, however, artists tend to have more overt and extensive personal feelings about them. Some artists, writers especially, have described to me conscious feelings of sadness after the completion of every one of their works. Citing a manifest analogy between the production of a novel or other artistic work and the birth of a baby, they emphasize the feelings of transitory sadness connected with the simultaneous loss and achievement of bringing forth a creation.

Just as the creative process is the mirror image of dreaming, it is similarly a mirror image of certain types of psychopathological processes. Both dreams and psychopathological symptoms arise from primary process operations, but creations arise from secondary process ones. Symptoms function to keep unconscious processes and content out of awareness, but creative thinking by and large operates in a reverse direction. Also, because the creative process overall results in improved adaption to reality, it functions in reverse direction to psychopathological symptoms. Creating increases understanding of reality and overcomes impediments. Symptoms are always impediments and psychopathological functioning always consists of inability to cope with, and to change, external or internal reality. Symptoms are banal and static, creations are unique and dynamic. Creative people, in other words, need not, by any manner or means, be sick. Though creative thought patterns do seem to resemble some forms of pathological thinking, such as those in schizophrenia, they do so only in mirror-image fashion. Schizophrenic ambivalence, neologisms, splitting, and autistic timelessness and spacelessness are superficially similar but opposite both in function and contextual structure to the creative processes I have described. Shared in common between psychological illness and creativity is the factor of conflict, but, as I shall clarify in chapter 9, the relationship is complex.

Several famous creative people have been severely ill with a form of psychological disease, either neurosis, psychosis, or personality disorder. There is, as I stated in the introduction, a widespread belief that genius and insanity are very closely allied, but this generalization has arisen not from data but from dramatic cases. Creating does involve high degrees of anxiety and it can intensify psychological illness, because the unconscious material unearthed and the kind of insights achieved during the creative process are not of the sort to produce permanent relief of symptoms. But in the main, creating does not depend on psychological dysfunction or disease. As mirror-image processes, schizophrenic and creative thinking are more similar to each other than they are to ordinary forms of thinking; it may therefore be easier in some ways for a person suffering from schizophrenia to shift into using creative thought processes. This, however, can only occur at times when anxiety is reduced enough to use these processes, times when the schizophrenic person can tolerate the increased anxiety they produce. Creating is such a socially valued activity that persons suffering from schizophrenia may derive enough gratifying and protective reinforcement merely from engaging in such activity. Working at creation in the arts or in high level mathematics and science may provide enough social reinforcement so that anxiety is reduced and logical and adaptive thought is consistently possible. On the other hand, creation may only be attainable when anxiety is reduced as a direct result of psychological equilibrium produced by other factors in their lives. Or benefit may be derived merely from the structure imposed on their thinking by the stringencies of intellectual activity itself. Under all these conditions, healthy functioning may lead to creative activity.

In the arts, it appears that certain historical epochs and certain types of social factors have favored the incorporation into subject matter of the preoccupations of psychologically disturbed people. Art concerned with paranoid themes or with phantasmagoric content has been more popular at certain periods than at others. In times of extreme social upheaval, such as in the twentieth century, intense concerns about sexual identity, violence, rebellion to authority, and family interrelationships come more to the fore in art. Whether such concerns are matters of psychopathology is not for persons living in the current milieu to decide.

Knowledge, fantasy, drive for discovery, intense motivation and concentration, and pleasure and gratification characterize the creative process. The creator formulates his task or problem under the influence of his own unconscious interests and concerns. He suffers anxiety and unearths some of the unconscious content connected to the initial task. Psychopathology plays no causative role, except possibly in the choice of theme and subject matter. Essentially, psychopathology must be overcome for effective creating. Although differing mental states occur during the course of the creative process, which may in some cases evolve over years or decades, the creator is always under the influence of a deliberate desire to create. The creative process begins in waking life and ends in waking life. Some aspects of the phenomenon may occur in dreams and in sleep, and primary process thinking may play a role at certain points. It may help facilitate fantasy, sensory imagery, and childhood associations. Dream content and themes may develop and extend themes of waking thought and may often facilitate mastery of technical tasks through representations allowing for mental focusing, repetitive practice, and even for wish-fulfilling success. Such dream content and experiences may be directly influential on waking life. Theme progressions and developments such as the previously discussed representation of the mother carrying the grandmother in the poet subject's dream help promote creative work and transformations. However, despite traditional beliefs that dreams manifestly reveal important themes, and despite the practice of some artists to keep dream diaries and to use actual dream content in their work, dream material does not have an intrinsic or a direct function in creating. Starting from actual dreams or using dreams as subject matter has no special advantages. Abstract thinking predominates overall and two particular thought processes, janusian and homospatial thinking, which are the mirror images of such dream processes as making all opposites equivalent and transcending the ordinary boundaries of space, function in reverse direction from the dream. These processes serve to arouse the creator, and their results arouse those who perceive the creations as well. That art and creativity stimulate and awaken us is both literally and figuratively true.

7
JANUSIAN THINKING

Creativity is manifest in many and diverse types of human endeavor, including all varieties of art, religion, philosophy, engineering, business activities such as advertising and marketing, and, depending on the definition, in internal psychological states and in commonplace activities such as cooking, sports, and interpersonal interaction. If we keep the focus on activities leading to tangible products consensually considered to be both valuable and new, we can see that the type of thinking and activity involved in poetry and science are, in many ways, paradigms of the creative process. Poetic thinking and activity are paradigmatic of the thinking and activity in all forms of literary creation, and of creation in the other arts, in religion, and in philosophy. The type of thinking and activity involved in scientific creation is paradigmatic for a wide range of disciplines and pursuits concerned with the manipulation of physical reality and of so-called objective events. Therefore, from the evidence so far regarding janusian thinking in poetry and science, it could be assumed that this form of cognition plays a role in virtually all forms of tangible creation. Rather than let the matter rest with such a sweeping assumption, I shall now elucidate the particular operation of janusian thinking in diverse types of creations. I shall cite instances where janusian thinking is clearly manifest and instances where its presence can be strongly inferred. I shall then present, in some detail, experimental evidence regarding janusian thinking and creativity.

Religion, Philosophy, and Social Theory

Discussing creativity in the religious domain can be a sensitive, or even a confusing, matter. From the perspective of the adherent to a particular religion, the dogma or theology of that religion is usually considered to be revealed and absolute truth. Consequently, any suggestion that a particular religious conception is a creation of the mind of man might be considered overly relativistic or even sacrilegious. Though a responsible scientist cannot be deterred by such preconceptions, there is no necessity for assuming relativism in advance in a discussion of religious creative thought. As with discovery in science, our primary concern is not with whether the final product does or does not conform to objectively verifiable reality, intrinsic reality, or to any other metaphysical criteria for truth, but with the thought processes responsible for the creation of that product. In other words, creative thinking in the religious sphere could consist of processes responsible for the discovery of intrinsic or absolute reality. Such thinking could be considered to be the means by which man participates in revelation.

From a broad perspective on religious thought, therefore, it is notable that many major religions of the world contain core concepts involving opposing principles. In Taoism and Buddhism, the major religions of the oriental world,[1] there are the basic opposing principles of yin and yang, Nirvana and Samsara, respectively. In Zoroastrianism, the major religion of the massive Persian Empire, and a religion that still survives among the Parsees of India today, there are the opposing principles of the twin gods, Ahura Mazda (Ormuzd) and Angra Mainyu (Ahriman). According to the Zoroastrians, Ormuzd, the god of light and goodness, has continually confronted his twin, Ahriman, the god of darkness and evil, from the beginning of all things. And in the major religions of the Western world, Judaism and Christianity, there are the opposing principles of God and Satan or God and the Devil.

The mere presence of opposing principles in major religions does not, of course, indicate that janusian thinking played a role in their creation. Other types of thinking, such as the tendency to formulate two alternate principles—dualism—or the sequential consideration of a thesis and antithesis leading to a synthesis—dialectic thinking—or the attempt at reconciliation of oppositions—syncretism—certainly have been involved in much of the theological exegesis regarding these principles. The problem of good and evil has been a major concern of almost every religion, and reification or deification with respect to these factors is certainly another type of process involved. Furthermore, the conception of equal and opposite forces of good and evil, such as is contained in Zoroastrianism and its closely related offshoot Manichaeism, has long been considered heretical by Christian theology.

Nor would the conception of opposed but separated and sequential forces or principles be a direct manifestation of janusian thinking. In janusian thinking, opposing or antithetical ideas, images, or concepts

—sometimes two, but often more than two—are conceived as existing side by side and operating simultaneously. At the moment of conception, therefore,the opposing forces or principles are not separated in a temporal sequence. For example, first formulating an idea of God and later of the Devil would not be an instance of janusian thinking. The janusian formulation with its simultaneity is a way station toward integration of oppositions and antitheses into an overall theory or other type of creation. Knowledge about original religious conceptions is necessarily so uncertain and vague, because of their historical remoteness, that it is impossible to establish anything about their nature with any real authority.

Nevertheless, the repetitive appearance of opposite principles and forces in major religious formulations is striking. As core conceptions of their respective theologies, the oppositions may very well have been thought of early, formulated as operating simultaneously, and the formulation then instigated the subsequent elaboration of a total system. Many religions and religious reformations, as has been well documented,[2] can be traced to a single individual, a founder, prophet, or reformer. The core conceptions, therefore, may have been primarily that particular individual's creation. For instance, Zoroaster—the prophet of his religion—was unquestionably the originator of monotheism in ancient Persia and of the conceptions of the twin gods, Ormuzd and Ahriman. He may well have thought of both of these gods simultaneously, two antithetical forces within a single principle, and later elaborated them as particular gods with other characteristics. The idea of twins certainly indicates identity together with the antithesis and opposition.[3]

With a closer look at the oriental religions of Taoism and Buddhism, the inference of a janusian thought process leading to the core conceptions becomes compelling. The yin and yang conception of Taoism contains a distinctive janusian formulation. Conveyed most meaningful by a visual symbol called t'ai-chi tu rather than words (see fig. 5), yin and yang represent universal opposite forces or principles, loosely stipulated as female and male principles, respectively, functioning together as a single larger principle. As seen in the figure, the two forces of yin and yang are encompassed within the single circle—the circle denoting all of reality or all of the universe—and they are identical but opposed. As implied by their placement and interlocking or flowing form within the circle, they operate together and in dynamic accord. The single larger principle emerging from the interaction and simultaneous operation of yin and yang is, according to Taoism, responsible for all change in the universe. Yin and yang are the regulators of the four seasons and, by extension, all moral effects. In short, they are the major factors underlying everything. The initial

Fig. 5. The t'ai-chi tu, or the Chart of the Supreme Ultimate. This is the central symbol of the Taoist theology, depicting the two simultaneous and opposed forces of yin (dark side) and yang (light side).

janusian notion of simultaneous opposition or antithesis has been further elaborated into a religious creation, a highly complex and detailed theology extending beyond the core conception. Lao-tzu, the early Chinese mystic who supposedly composed the *Tao Tê Ching* or the Way of Life, the religious guide from which the name of the religion was derived, described the Tao or Way derived from these precepts as follows: "the Form of the Formless / The Image of the Imageless" (*Tao Tê Ching,* chap. 14).[4]

The Buddhist principle of Nirvana, considered to be the complete responsibility of Prince Siddhartha Gautama—the original Buddha—also contains a definite janusian construction. In the full theological formulation, Nirvana, the end of the cycle of rebirth, is opposed to the principle of Samsara, the endless series of incarnations and reincarnations to which living things are subject. As with Zoroastrianism and Judeo-Christianity, however, it is difficult to know whether these particular opposing principles were conceived simultaneously or whether each was formulated at different periods of time. Notwithstanding, the Nirvana principle alone, a principle conceived at a particular time in history by the particular Prince Gautama himself, definitely does manifest simultaneous opposition or antithesis. The definition of Nirvana, from its first formulation to the present day, is negative. But its negativity contains the property of incorporating antithesis simultaneously that we have seen in other janusian thoughts. Nirvana is a state of total peace of soul and indifference to all pleasure and pain because it is an escape from *eternal becoming* and *passing on.* It is neither life or becoming, nor is it death or passing on; *it is both non-life and non-death simultaneously.*[5] This formulation, reputedly achieved by Prince Gautama in a state of bliss, became the basis for the fully elaborated Buddhist theology, a theology adopted by a majority of persons in the Orient and also, in fact, a majority of the religious believers in the world. D. T. Suzuki, a leading modern teacher of the precepts of the Zen school of Buddhism, explained the formulation as follows: "So long as this world, as conceived by the human mind, is a realm of opposites, there is no way to escape from it and to enter into a world of emptiness where all opposites are supposed to merge . . . yet Buddhists all attempt to achieve it."[6]

Moving away from specific religious positions into the sphere of philosophy, a plethora of philosophers have given opposition a central position in their thought. Pre-Socratic philosophers were concerned with Being and Becoming as simultaneously present but opposite principles, and specific thinkers, such as Anaximander and Empedocles, developed complicated cosmologies concerning the creation and construction of the world based on the combination, antagonism and separation of opposites. Heraclitus postulated a unity of opposites in logus, the first principle of both knowledge and existence.[7] C. K. Ogden, in what must be considered a classic on linguistic opposition,[8] discusses other philosophers whose work focuses centrally on opposites and the relation of opposition. In addition to the philosophers named above, he includes these important ones: Aristotle, Kant, Hegel, Ludwig Fischer, and the social philosopher Tarde. To this list, Nietzsche and Sartre should surely be added, as the former formulated and focused throughout his work on the basic and opposing principles he called Dionysian and Apollonian and the latter constructed his existential philosophy on the opposition of Being and Nothingness.

Because philosophers have left little documentation regarding the thought processes and sequences of experiences and events leading to the construction of their creations, and because philosophy itself is always presented in highly elaborated logical exegesis, it is difficult to ascertain whether such emphasis on oppositions was derived from janusian thinking at an early or germinating phase. For instance, in the light of what we know about the elaborately constructed logical presentations of scientists, it could reasonably be presumed that Sartre initially conceived of Being and Nothingness operating simultaneously or existing side by side and, following that, sat down and arduously developed his dialectical analysis and synthesis of these states or factors. But, so far, nothing from Sartre affirms or denies this.

However, documented material from at least two philosophers provides evidence that janusian thinking played an early and germinating role in their philosophical creations. In his autobiographical account, *Ecce Homo,* Nietzsche describes the sequence of events leading to the creation of *Thus Spake Zarathustra,* the work many consider his major accomplishment and the one he called "the greatest gift that has ever been bestowed upon my fellow men."[9] That there was a specific germinating idea for the book is attested by his following account:

> During the . . . winter [1882–83], I was living not far from Genoa on that pleasant peaceful Gulf of Rapallo, which cuts in-

land between Chiavari and Cape Porto Fino. I was not in the best of health; the winter was cold and exceptionally rainy; and my small *albergo* was so close to shore that the noise of a rough sea rendered sleep impossible. These circumstances were the very reverse of favorable; and yet, despite them, and as if in proof of my theory that everything decisive arises as the result of opposition, it was during this very winter and amid these unfavorable circumstances that my *Zarathustra* was born. In the morning I used to start out in a southerly direction on the glorious road to Zoagli, which rises up through a forest of pines and gives one a view far out to sea. In the afternoon, whenever my health permitted, I would walk around the whole bay from Saint Margherita to beyond Porto Fino. . . . It was on these two roads that all *Zarathustra,* and particularly *Zarathustra* himself as a type, came to me—perhaps I should rather say—*invaded me.*"[10]

After this experience, Nietzsche wrote the first part of the book. In *Ecce Homo,* he explains that a key aspect of the "Zarathustra type" idea was what he called "great healthiness."[11] This "great healthiness" was intrinsic to his conception of the Superman, the conception he expounds throughout the *Zarathustra* book. But the actual germinating idea for the book was even more developed than "great healthiness"; it was a formulation of the complete "Zarathustra himself as a type." This complete "type" he presents as follows:

> The Zarathustra type . . . who to an unprecedented extent says no, and *acts* no, in reference to all to which man has hitherto said yes, nevertheless remain[s] the opposite of a no-saying spirit. . . . He who bears destiny's heaviest burden, whose life-task is a fatality, yet [is] the lightest and the most transcendental of spirits—for Zarathustra is a dancer. . . . He who has the hardest and most terrible insight into reality, and who has thought the most "abysmal thoughts" nevertheless find[s] in these things no objections to existence, or to its eternal recurrence. . . . On the contrary he finds reasons for being himself the everlasting Yea to all things, "the tremendous and unlimited saying of Yea and Amen."[12]

The formulation of the complete Zarathustra type, which Nietzsche describes as having "invaded" him all at once, was replete with simultaneous opposites of yes and no saying, heaviest and lightest, abysmal insights into reality together with affirmation of existence and eternal recurrence. Moreover, as Nietzsche continued to think about the *Zarathustra* book, the second part was also germinated from a janusian thought. The basis of this second part was an internally sounding refrain having, he said, the words, "dead through immortality."[13] After mentioning this conception, a conception of simultaneous opposition in that immortality is the antithesis of death, Nietzsche then immediately states in *Ecce Homo:* "In the summer, on my return to the sacred spot where the first thought of Zarathustra had flashed like lightning across my mind, I conceived the second part. Ten days sufficed."[14]

Another documented instance of janusian thinking as a germinating process in philosophy comes from the writings of Sören Kierkegaard. For Kierkegaard, the formulation "belief by virtue of the absurd" was central to his theological position and was developed throughout his works. As absurdity is synonymous with ridiculous, illogical, and untrue, this formulation is, on the surface, self-contradictory. The object of belief is the valid and the true, and therefore the formulation is an instance of a simultaneous antithesis. As a fully elaborated concept in Kierkegaard's work, however, we would have no definite way of knowing whether it was initially formulated as the simultaneous antithesis or whether it was developed in some other way, except that Kierkegaard himself wrote the following in his journals containing his preliminary ideas:

> Faith therefore hopes also for this life, but, be it noted, by virtue of the absurd, not by virtue of the human understanding; otherwise it is only practical wisdom, not faith. Faith is therefore what the Greeks called the divine madness. *This is not merely a witty remark but is a thought which can be clearly developed.* [Italics added][15]

This journal entry indicates that Kierkegaard conceived the simultaneous antithesis at an early phase of the creation of his philosophy. He clearly states that the particular idea would later be developed and elaborated. The entry also indicates that he was fully aware of the apparent contradiction in the formulation but saw it as germinating deeper truth and meaning.

Although primarily poets, the philosophically oriented Coleridge and Blake also formulated simultaneous antitheses as explanatory concepts. Coleridge stated that pleasure arising from art consisted of "the identity of two opposite elements, that is to say—sameness and variety."[16] Blake, in his treatise with the opposite juxtaposing title, *The Marriage of Heaven and Hell,* unequivocally asserted, "Without contraries is no progression."[17] From his further remarks, it is clear that Blake's meaning was that all factors of morality and substance spring from simultaneous opposition.

Related to some of Coleridge's ideas about artistic form ("form . . . is its self effected sphere of agency") is a striking example of a janusian formulation in the recent and popular work of the social theorist Marshall McLuhan. Though McLuhan's concepts about the intellectual impact of modern technology are not extensive enough to qualify as full-blown philosophical systems or even rigorously developed social theories, they have received a good deal of attention in recent years. His work has had an impact on the arts and on scores of young people in the United States. McLuhan's core concept, which he elaborated into a challenge to traditional and what he called "linear" modes of art and thinking, was formulated in the phrase "the medium is the message." This phrase is a clear example of simultaneous antithesis: taking the traditionally accepted phrase, "the content is the message," McLuhan substituted the opposite-meaning word "medium" for "content." Because the structure of the phrase still invokes the traditional idea, opposites are asserted simultaneously. McLuhan has it both ways.

Visual Arts

Modern art, especially surrealism, dadaism, and many forms of expressionism, is replete with images, forms, and symbols conveying simultaneous opposition and antithesis. Some outstanding examples are seen in the accompanying figures (figs. 6–12). In the painting *Nature Morte Vivante,* 1956 (fig. 6), Salvador Dali, one of the leading surrealists, depicts both rest and motion simultaneously. The fruit dish, for instance, is represented twice, one image is in twirling motion

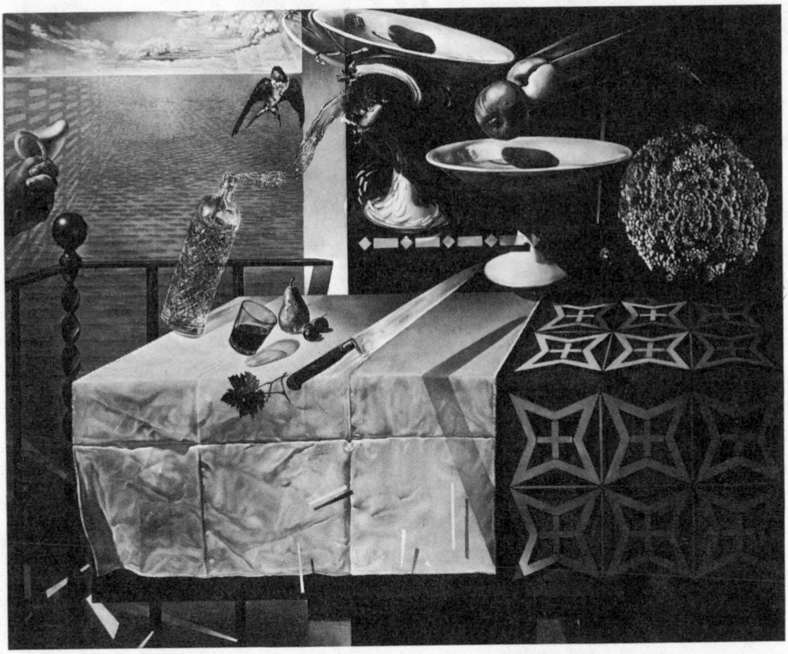

Fig. 6. Salvador Dali. *Nature Morte Vivante,* 1956. Motion and rest are depicted simultaneously: the apple is still and plummeting; the bird is motionless, while the objects move. Collection of Mr. and Mrs. A. Reynolds Morse, Salvador Dali Museum, Cleveland (Beachwood), Ohio.

Fig. 7. René Magritte. *Personal Values,* 1952. Numerous reversals of size are visualized simultaneously. Private collection, New York. © ADAGP, Paris, 1979.

and its twin is completely motionless. The apple is doubly represented as both plummeting and suspended totally motionless in air. Ordinary objects of a still life painting, the glass, the bottle, and the knife, are surprisingly represented as falling, while the ordinarily highly mobile meteor and even the bird are suspended in midair and motionless. The longer one looks at this painting, the more elements of simultaneous antithesis, as designated specifically in the painting's title, moving or living still life (literally from the French: "dead nature living"), are apparent. Magritte's painting *Personal Values,* 1952 (fig. 7), and Chagall's *Bouquet of the Lovers,* 1926 (fig. 8), both show numerous reversals of size indicating another type of simultaneous opposition. The smallest object, such as a plant or comb, is depicted as the largest and the largest, a house or room, is depicted as the smallest. In the Chagall painting, people are both too large and too small and in the Magritte painting a window is seen as both inside and outside a room simultaneously. Other types of oppositions of position, sex, and purpose are presented simultaneously in Max Ernst's *Aquis Submersus,* 1919 (fig. 9), Chagall's *I and the Village,* 1911 (fig. 10) and *Homage to Apollinaire,* 1911–13 (fig. 11), and Pierre Molinier's *The Paradise Flower* (fig. 12).

Fig. 8. Marc Chagall. *Bouquet of the Lovers,* 1926. Numerous size reversals: people larger than houses, flowers larger than people, violin larger than house. © ADAGP, Paris, 1979.

In addition to these striking examples, numerous other works of these artists and also of Marcel Duchamp, Man Ray, Yves Tanguy, Henri Rousseau, Edvard Munch, Joseph Cornell, and even Pablo Picasso show clear and frequent instances of simultaneous opposition and antithesis. Less manifest but nonetheless distinct implications of simultaneous opposition and antithesis abound in the dreamlike images and forms produced by these artists and by other moderns, notably the abstract expressionists, as well. As janusian thinking is a mirror-image process of dreaming, and as all these tacit and explicit

Fig. 9. Max Ernst. *Aquis Submersus,* 1919. Simultaneous oppositions and reversals of content and form are depicted. The Städelsches Kunstinstituts und Städtische Galerie, Frankfurt.

representations of simultaneous opposition and antithesis are surely intentionally produced, it can readily be assumed that janusian thinking plays a significant role in diverse types of modern art creation.

Modern artists have, of course, been interested in, and directly influenced by, psychoanalysis. Modern artists have also been particularly interested in analyzing, dissecting, and depicting the creative

Fig. 10. Marc Chagall. *I and the Village,* 1911. Oil on canvas, 6′3⅝″ x 59⅝″. Simultaneous oppositions of position (man and woman), and size (animals and people). Collection, the Museum of Modern Art, New York. Mrs. Simon Guggenheim Fund.

process itself. Many dada and surrealist artists, for instance, attempted to release themselves, to work completely spontaneously, and to capitalize on random events in order to represent unconscious life and material in their art. Others, such as Dali, have applied elements of psychoanalytic theory directly in attempting to portray and reconstruct the world of the dream. Such interests and practices do not,

Fig. 11. Marc Chagall. *Homage to Apollinaire,* 1911–13. Simultaneous sexual opposites and opposite spatial orientations. Van Abbemuseum, Eindhoven.

however, account for the effect of janusian thinking I have suggested. If merely expressing unconscious content were all there is to modern art, there would be little distinction between successful and unsuccessful art. Unconscious content always is essentially disorganized and chaotic rather than artistically formed. Because everyone shares the same general type of unconscious content, differences in different works would be based primarily on how much detail could be presented rather than on how they were done. Similarly, the simple following of a theoretical formula could not produce inventive art except for the first time it were tried; repetitiously following a theoretical

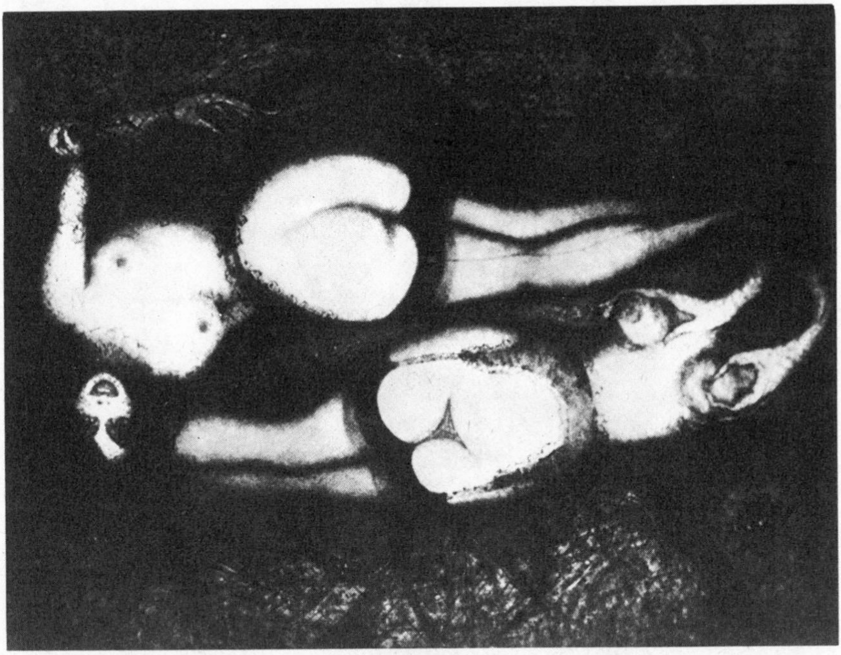

Fig. 12. Pierre Molinier. *The Paradise Flower.* A woman's body is seen from opposite sides simultaneously. Private collection.

formula for depicting dreams would produce uniform, uninteresting products. In short, janusian thinking is responsible for an organizing principle resulting in *successful* (new and valuable) created products from these schools of art. Regardless of whether the artist has approached his task through release or through applying a theoretical principle, the particular content and organization of a successful modern art creation results in part from janusian thinking. A brief illustration from the work of Dali should serve to clarify this point. His painting *Paranoiac Face,* 1934–35 (fig. 13), was derived from or inspired by the scene in the postcard shown in figure 14. Because Dali has called attention to the double image in this picture by reporting that he got the idea from the postcard and from Picasso's faces, some have considered it a "trick" painting. Its artistic success, however, does not depend on its being a trick image but on its expressive qualities. If this is understood, and acceptable, we can trace the steps in the development of this effect. Seeing the postcard picture of figure 14, Dali drew the sketch of figure 15 before doing the painting in figure 13. The overall painting consists of the hut turned into a wild half face conveying fear and suspicion, a strange and moving paranoiac face. How did Dali make this transformation? The sketch in figure 15 shows that Dali was interested in, and he reproduced, the tranquil qualities of the village scene on the postcard. By softening the lines of the picture,

Fig. 13. Salvador Dali. *Paranoiac Face,* 1934–35. © by ADAGP, Paris, 1979.

Fig. 14. Postcard photograph on which Dali based his painting, *Paranoiac Face.* Salvador Dali, "Objets surréalistes," *Le Surréalisme* [no. 5].

Fig. 15. Dali's preliminary sketch for *Paranoiac Face.* The drawing is almost identical to the postcard photograph, except that it is softer. Salvador Dali, "Objets surréalistes," *Le Surréalisme* [no. 5].

he actually intensified the sense of peace and tranquility. In order to conceive the final painting, therefore, it was necessary for him to formulate and/or to visualize both the wild face and the tranquil scene simultaneously. He also had to be able to conceptualize the hut shape both as horizontal in the original scene and as vertical in his ultimate plan. Although the final painting has various types of dreamlike or symbolic qualities, and the simultaneous antithesis I described are not immediately apparent, they intrinsically contribute to the expressive quality of the painting.

Max Ernst described his experience of using a similar organizing principle as follows:

> One day, in 1919, being in wet weather at a seaside inn, I was struck by . . . the pages of an illustrated catalogue. . . . It was a catalogue of objects for anthropological, microscopic, psychological, mineralogical and paleontological demonstration. I found here united elements such poles apart that the very incongruousness of the assembly started off a sudden intensification of my visionary faculties and a dreamlike succession of contradictory images—double, triple and multiple images coming one on top of the other with . . . persistence and rapidity. . . . These images . . . suggested new ways . . . to meet in a new unknown. . . . All I had to do was add, either by painting, or drawing, to the pages of the catalogue. And I had only to reproduce

obediently what made itself visible within me, a colour, a scrawl, a landscape strange to the objects gathered in it, a desert, a sky, a geological event, a floor, a single line drawn straight to represent the horizon, to get a fixed and faithful image . . . to transform what had been commonplaces of advertising into dramas revealing my most secret desires.[18]

Regardless of whether the subject matter of art is manifestly dreamlike, or focused on internal psychological states, or overtly oppositional such as in the movement known as anti-art, or more traditionally focused on naturalism, realism, and religious symbolism, there are general aspects of the creative process in the visual arts that involve janusian thinking. Throughout the ages, a major consideration for the visual artist has been the nature of what might be called "positive" and "negative" space. Whether he is drawing from nature, imagining a natural scene, or constructing a nonrepresentational work of art, this spatial factor always obtains. "Positive" space consists of the concrete tangible contents of a visual form and "negative" space consists of the undifferentiated area around it. Roughly, these types of visual phenomena correspond to what we commonly think of as "full" and "empty" spaces, respectively. Gestalt psychologists include these two types of perceived spaces under the more general rubric of distinction between a "figure" and a "ground," a distinction applying to all types of perception. According to the gestalt formulation, all percepts are organized in terms of a primary differentiated figure and a secondary undifferentiated ground. In viewing a scene or hearing a piece of music, certain forms or patterns such as a tree or a melodic theme come sharply into focus and predominantly occupy our attention while the remainder of the sights and sounds form a relatively diffuse background. This gestalt perceptual law operates even when a percept is initially vague and undifferentiated; attempts are made to organize the percept by focusing on some particular element or structure as a figure, even a somewhat vague one, and allowing the remainder to become the ground.

I shall have more to say later about the figure-ground law of perception in connection with homospatial thinking (chap. 10). The perception of positive or filled space and negative or empty space is a specific category within this general law and, with respect to visual art, it stands as a separate and particularly important subjective experience. Creation in the visual arts is, after all, especially a matter of filling empty spaces. The painter faces his empty canvas, the sculptor and graphic artist face the empty surface of the stone, wood, or metal block, and the architect looks at empty areas and empty ground. These are figurative descriptions, of course, but they emphasize that, in the visual arts, there is subjective reality to the idea of creation as a matter of bringing forth something out of nothing.[19] Objectively, that is, in a physical sense, none of these spaces are actually empty. Moreover, the creative artist characteristically pays attention to certain attributes of these spaces, such as the grain of the canvas or the wood, the texture of the metal or the stone, and the attributes guide him in the construction of his filled and developed creation. The creative artist does not, in other words, perceive empty space in the same way as people generally do. This, in a particular and specific way is where janusian thinking plays a wide and important role in creating in the visual arts.

In perceiving or constructing visual forms—by this I mean outline, colors, and composition as well as visual content—the creative visual artist pays special attention to negative or empty space. The attention he gives is not a matter merely of noticing this space, nor merely of bringing it into focus, nor is it only a matter of constantly comparing this empty space to spaces seen as filled or being filled, although such attention is a necessary part of ordinary construction in any of the visual art forms. In other words, a person who merely attempts to draw a tree must, in order to do so with any degree of competence, pay attention to the empty space around the tree, and to the spaces between the branches. While such visualizing is not characteristic of ordinary perception and needs to be learned, its main effect is to enhance the capacity to produce verisimilitude, thus enhancing craft rather than necessarily creative construction. A characteristic exercise in any elementary drawing class, for instance, is to practice drawing a form without first outlining the contours, but darkening surrounding areas to produce a white contoured shape. But the creative visual artist goes beyond this type of seeing and making: when visualizing a scene or constructing a visual form, *he sees negative space as having a content and shape of its own.* He sees empty space as filled, and what is ordinarily perceived as negative space he sees as both positive and negative at the same time. When viewing a forest of trees, for example, the creative artist is aware of the trees, the details of their shape and texture, and of their placement and pattern; he *simultaneously* visualizes the spaces between the trees as independent forms—he notices the shape and texture of these spaces as well as their patterning between the trees.

Such visualization also occurs with abstract forms or any form not directly manifest in nature. With virtually every visual image or form he constructs, and every space he fills, the creative artist gives active attention to the shape and content of the empty space around it. Does this include the modern artist who fills an entire canvas with a single unbroken color of paint? Yes. He also perceives positive and negative spaces simultaneously when, in choosing the shape and size of his canvas, he visualizes the shape of the empty space around it. Or, depending on his technique, he visualizes the highlights reflecting from his canvas as filled forms and the duller areas as unfilled forms which nevertheless have shape and texture of their own.

This visualization of positive and negative space simultaneously or, put more specifically, perceiving empty space as filled (N.B.: also filled space as homogeneous or empty of delineation) is an actively integrated aspect of visual art creation. Though we often speak of what the artist "sees" as though it were separate from what he does, such terminology does not reflect the actual psychological state of affairs. The creative artist does not merely see forms that others miss, nor does he only employ unusual perceptual modes which are then integrated conceptually and translated into tangible art through another type of mode or capacity such as manual manipulation and dexterity. Perceiving, conceiving, and executing are intricately and constantly interrelated. The janusian process of formulating, reversing, and equating positive and negative space is a continuing matter, operating during the early phases of mental conception of the work of art and guiding the creator's hand as he proceeds. In the course of producing visual forms, he produces other filled and empty spaces as he goes; these influence his perception and his perceptual formulations influence further execution. Merely to visualize differently is not sufficient.[20] Visualization, conception, and execution are integrated in an active ongoing process.

A comment by Michelangelo about the essentials of two art forms in which he excelled exemplifies a janusian formulation with respect to negative and positive space. In a letter to the consul of the Florentine Academy he discussed the relationships between painting and sculpture, and said: "By sculpture I understand that art which operates by taking away. That art which operates by laying on is similar to painting."[21] In case the janusian formulation here is not immediately apparent or, in the event that its impact has been dulled by frequent quoting in other contexts, I will elaborate: on first consideration, it would appear that this eminent creator is merely drawing a distinction between the two artistic modes on the basis of the physical operations involved in each. Hence, working primarily in marble as he did, he characteristically cut, chiseled, and chipped away at the hard, inert stone. Contrariwise, when painting he applied material to a surface and he therefore added pigments and other elements lying near at hand. So much for a literal interpretation of Michelangelo's remark. But, considering the conceptual nature of the artist's activity, the circumstance in both cases is quite the reverse. The sculptor gives contour and form to the inert and "empty" block of stone; though physically he takes away, he surely adds and fills the space in a conceptual and psychological sense. The painter, on the other hand, does not merely add to and thereby fill up the surface of a canvas or wall; he definitely organizes the surface space. In organizing, one of the primary operations of painting is to produce surface areas that appear empty, translucent, or even transparent by means of the very device of adding pigments and other elements. Michelangelo in fact never produced sculptured or contoured paintings such as those produced in recent times. Surely, then, this Renaissance master indicated a janusian conception of the general spatial relationships in his creative activity: taking away operated at the same time as forming in sculpture, and adding on operated while maintaining a flat surface in painting. For Michelangelo, space was both positive and negative simultaneously.

The modern painter Josef Albers described the simultaneous conception of positive and negative space even more directly in his following remarks in 1962 in an interview with Brian O'Doherty, then art critic for the *New York Times:*

> If I come to my own working . . . my sport is to see between two lines something happening. . . . There is one finger. And this is one finger. One finger and one finger are two fingers. But then I say this . . . width . . . in between is the same, and I can say [Interviewer: "Becomes a positive area."] one and one is three. And that's only permitted in art. . . . But I go further. In art, one and one is four. That's exciting.[22]

Albers's description of his visualization of the fingers themselves ("one and one . . . ," etc.) and of the spaces around them leaves no doubt that he sees and conceives both positive and negative space simultaneously.

In sculpture, the man considered by many to be the outstanding contemporary sculptor, the Englishman Henry Moore, indicated a similar orientation to positive and negative space as well as other janusian conceptions intrinsic to creating in the following statement:

> When the sculptor understands his material, has a knowledge of its possibilities and its constructive build, it is possible to keep within its limitations and yet turn an inert block into a composition which has a full form existence, with masses of varied size and section *conceived in their air-surrounded entirety,* stressing and straining, thrusting and opposing each other in spatial relationship—being static, in the sense that the center of gravity lies within the base (and does not seem to be falling over or moving off its base)—and yet having an alert dynamic tension between its parts. [Italics added][23]

In addition to the description of the "air-surrounded entirety" as a positive space, and the emphasis on simultaneous opposition between masses, spaces, and forms, Moore specifies a guiding janusian formulation which, as I will show in a moment, has also been emphasized by other visual artists and other creators: the production of static dynamisms or entities that are both moving and stationary at the same time. That Moore actively and consistently conceives simultaneous oppositions in creating his sculptures is evident from his following response to an interviewer who noted a spatial reversal in one of Moore's works:

> Things are like something else in that they're opposite. Opposites are like each other. I mean, pain and non-pain are connected. You only know what one is like if you know the other. Happiness and unhappiness are connected; everything has its opposite. And to know one thing you must know the opposite just as well, just as much, else you don't know that one thing. So that, quite often, one does the opposite as an expression of the positive.[24]

With respect to the conception of entities that are both moving and stationary at the same time, the Bauhaus artist Paul Klee used the term "dynamic repose" to describe an important guiding idea in his own work. Other artists, while not as explicit, often suggest that such a conception guides their work.[25] The term "dynamic repose" actually is a somewhat deceptive one. At first blush, it might not seem to convey the same degree of sharp antithesis as other janusian formulations cited here because of the ubiquitous experience of rest or repose generated by regular or constant motion. Note, however, that the form of the term does not indicate such restful motion but refers to rest as an active moving state. Moreover, as put into practice, Klee characteristically works with elements conveying a motion/rest antithesis (see fig. 16). Specific elements, such as forms, colors, and lines are, in the context of the painting, operating antithetically. As will become clearer in the next chapter of this book, such opposition or antithesis in context is characteristic of the janusian process, especially in art. Lines and forms, movement and rest, may not be oppositional or antithetical in all contexts, but they are antithetical for the artist himself and for the context in which he works. Motion can only be an abstract property of a painting on a canvas or of a fixed sculpture and therefore must always be conveyed by the context.

Another example of the operation of janusian thinking in the creative process in the visual arts also comes from Klee; he describes the interpenetration of general principles of "endotopic" and "exotopic" drawing and visual effect. Using the terms "endotopic" and "exotopic" to refer to internal and external shading as shown in the visual forms in figures 17*A* and 17*B*, Klee states: "These two principles of the positive-negative treatment of relief, applied to linear figures containing intersections. Rule: in handling boundary contrast, always stay on one side of the line."[26] In other words, these are principles of a visual antithesis. Klee's method of breaking this rule is through the janusian formulation, "interpenetration," or conceiving and visualiz-

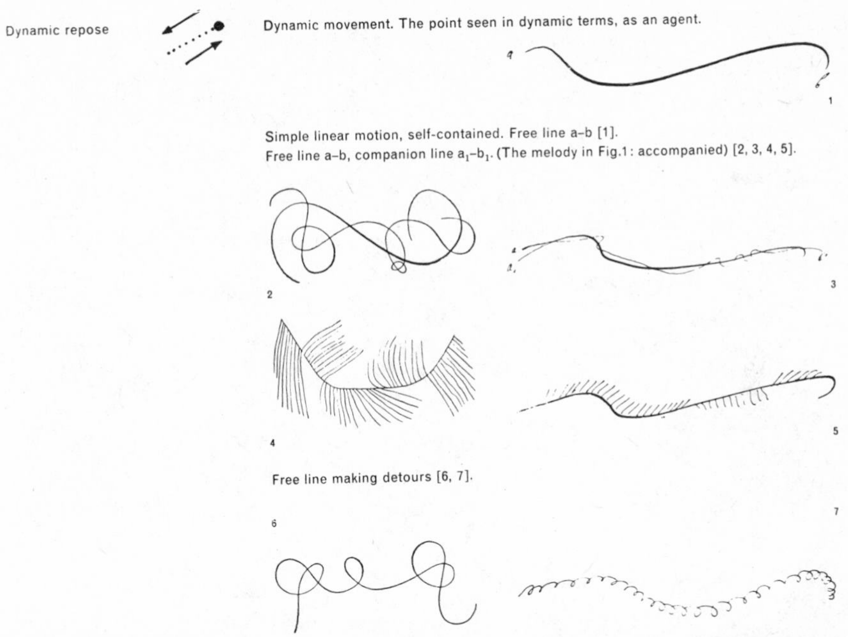

Fig. 16. From Paul Klee's textbook, *The Thinking Eye* (New York: Wittenborn Art Books, Inc., 1961) illustrating his conception of "dynamic repose."

ing both principles or forms together. Diagrammatic examples are seen in figure 18, and two of his finished paintings derived from this conception are seen in figures 19*A* and *B*. As general principles of forming boundary contrasts, alternative means of visualizing the endotopic and exotopic simultaneously are possible. About *Houses at Crossroads,* Klee said, "A conflict arises between endo- and exotopic. Then we have a sort of mesh of forms." Spiller, Klee's editor, called it "the simultaneous treatment of inside and outside points to the concept of simultaneity, i.e., of contacts between many dimensions."[27]

Dramatically similar to the types of visualizing so far described are the precepts and principles followed for centuries by Taoist artists. As Taoist painting and literature was always designed to express the overriding principles of t'ai-chi tu—the simultaneous operation of the opposites of yin and yang—and the effect on what was called the "life rhythm," the great Taoist artists focused on opposites such as: *hsü shih;* vacant space and solid; *kan shih,* dryness and wetness; *ming an,* darkness and light.[28] The following are taken from the commentaries of two Taoist painter-critics, one modern and one of the eighteenth century, respectively:

> . . . to draw trees or rocks the solid stroke is used; to draw clouds and mists the vacant stroke is used. Through that which

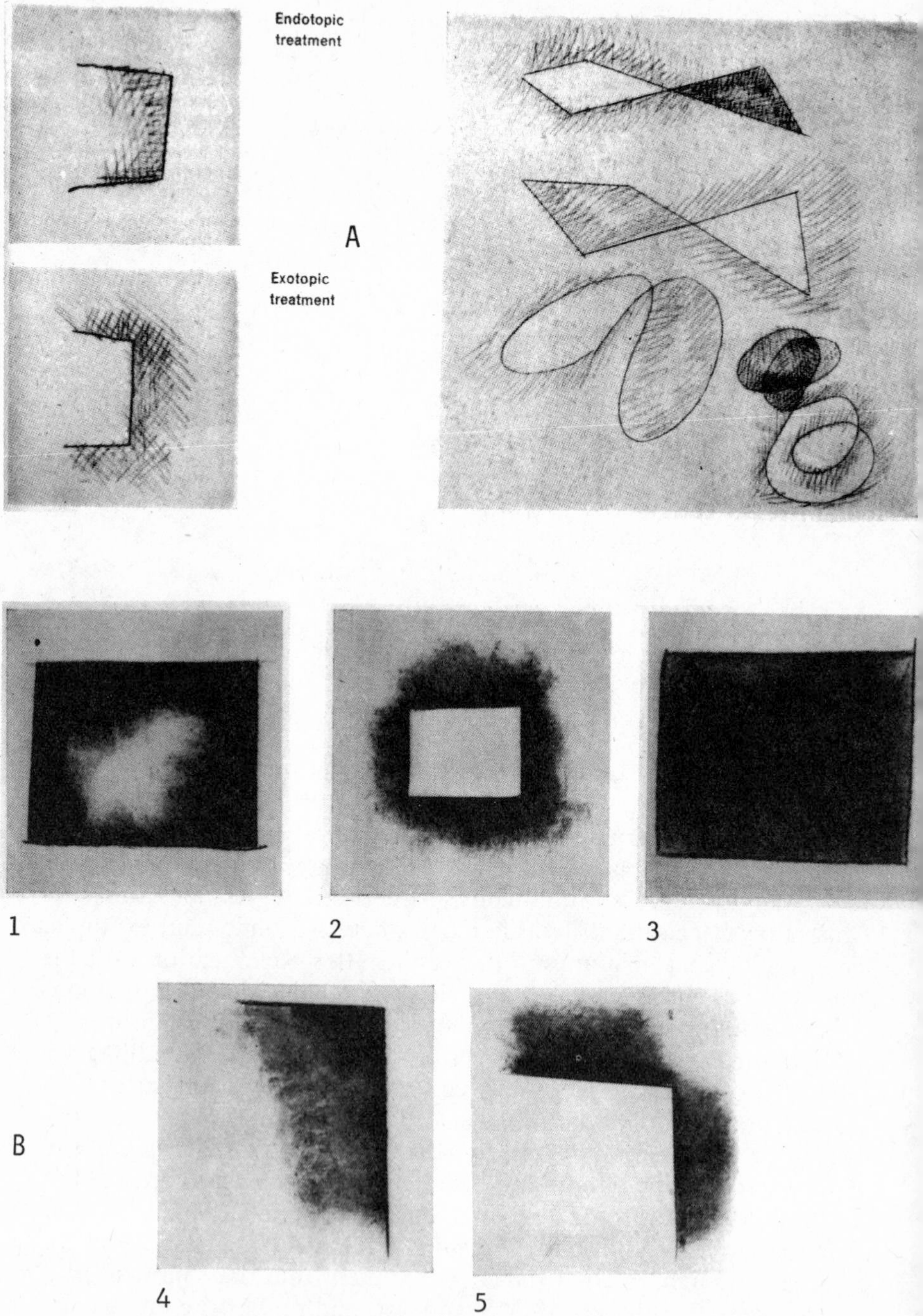

Fig. 17. Paul Klee's principles of endotopic and exotopic drawing. *A.* Linear figures with intersections. *B.* Squares and corners. 1, Square, endotopic treatment. 2, Square, exotopic treatment. 3, Square, treated as a body without reference to inside or outside. 4, Corner, endotopic treatment. 5, Corner, exotopic treatment. Wittenborn Art Books, Inc.

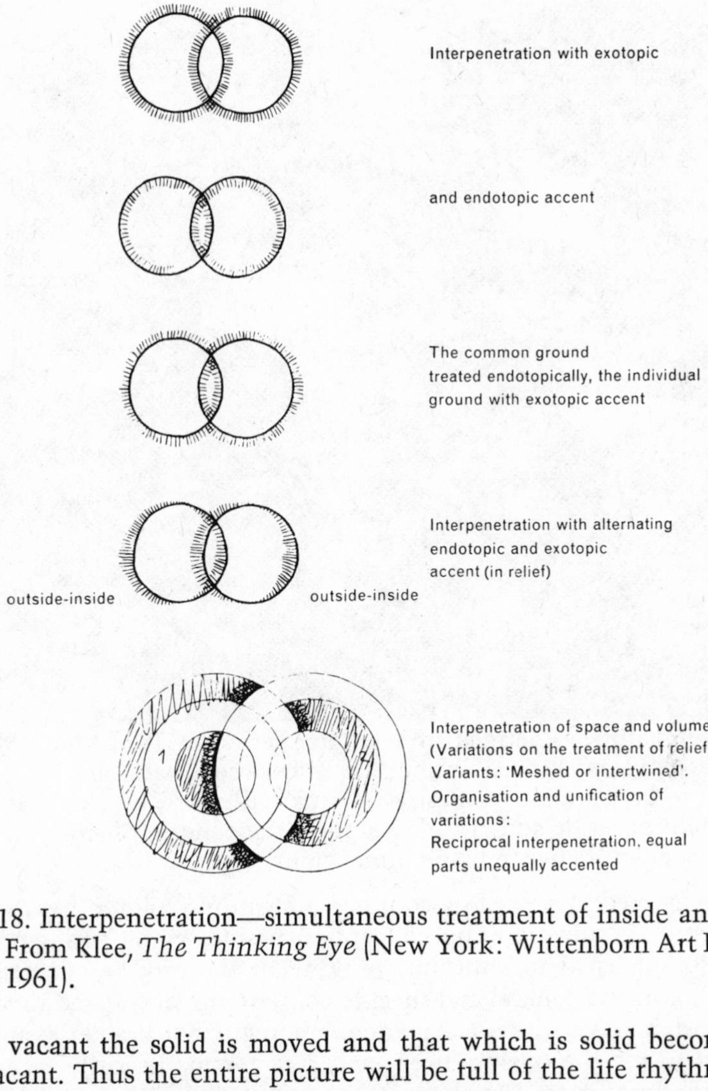

Fig. 18. Interpenetration—simultaneous treatment of inside and outside. From Klee, *The Thinking Eye* (New York: Wittenborn Art Books, Inc., 1961).

> is vacant the solid is moved and that which is solid becomes vacant. Thus the entire picture will be full of the life rhythm.[29]
>
> The color of a painting is not red, white, green or purple as ordinarily conceived. It is the shade seen between lightness and darkness. He who grasps this idea will reveal through his brush the Nature of things; the distance will be demarcated, the spirit will be set forth, and the scenery and the objects will be clear and beautiful. The reverberation of the life breath actually depends upon the proper manner of applying the ink-wash, which gives the picture great luminosity.[30]

Although it may be difficult to grasp the actual technical procedures indicated in both these commentaries, the conceptualization of simultaneously operating solidity and vacancy, or lightness and darkness, is clear and definite.

Fig. 19*A*. Paintings derived from interpenetration. Paul Klee. *Houses at Crossroads,* 1929. "A conflict arises between endo- and exotopic. Then we have a sort of mesh of forms" (Klee). "The simultaneous treatment of inside and outside points to the concept of simultaneity, i.e., of contacts between many dimensions" (Spiller, ed.).

As suggested by preceding comments regarding color, other aspects of artistic visualization and conception beside spatial configuration are also subjected to janusian thinking in the process of creating. Light, color, and general and specific content are formulated in terms of simultaneous antithesis. American photographer Walker Evans described to me the operation of such a factor in the early stages of pictorial conception. His photographs, as is well known, often depict scenes of poverty, isolation, and bleakness along with human beings somehow rising above their environment and circumstances. In choosing a particular subject to photograph, however, an early consideration was the nature of the light conditions in the scene. Acutely sensitive to the qualities of light and darkness in a locale, he photographed those images in which he saw both extreme light and extreme darkness at the same time. His visual conception blended with his orientation to the subject matter. Interested in depicting the stark and dreary but somehow vibrantly alive qualities of a bleak scene, perceiving aspects of extreme contrast or opposition of light and darkness simultaneously, he produced photographs bringing these extremes together.

Fig. 19*B*. Paintings derived from interpenetration. Paul Klee. *Landscapely-physiognomic,* 1923. From Klee, *The Thinking Eye* (New York: Wittenborn Art Books, Inc., 1961).

As for color, Albers, whose major artistic focus was on color, presented the following formulation of use of color in the creative process:

> With a middle mixture [of colors] all boundaries are equally soft or hard. As a consequence, a middle mixture appears frontal, as a color by itself. This is comparable to the reading of any symmetrical order and the middle mixture will behave unspatially, unless its own shape, or surrounding shapes, decides differently.
>
> Such a study, or a similar recognition, in my opinion led Cezanne to his unique and new articulation in painting. He was the first to develop color areas which produce both distinct and indistinct endings—areas connected and unconnected—areas with and without boundaries—as a means of plastic organization.[31]

In his own work, Albers described the process as follows in another portion of the previously cited interview:

> My associations contact me with former experiences. So I would say I start from experiences and read . . . always between

> polarities. It is between loud and not-loud. It is between young and old, between spring and winter or what you ever find as contrasts in life, . . . between polarities. . . . And the more tension there is between polarities—*if I can make black and white behave together* instead of shooting at each other only, you see, then I—I feel proud, let's say, instead of creative. I cannot say I am creative, that's others' job to say it.[32]

As a leader of the modern school of hard edge painting and the painter of an honored series of variations on the theme *Homage to the Square,*[33] others have certainly considered Albers highly creative indeed. There is evidence that creative artists before Albers also thought of color use in terms of simultaneous opposition, although in somewhat different terms. The postimpressionist Vincent van Gogh wrote the following to his brother Theo:

> . . . the study of colour. I am always in hope of making a discovery there, to express the love of two lovers by a marriage of two complementary colours, *their mingling and their opposition,* the mysterious vibration of kindred tones. To express the thought of a brow by the radiance of a light tone against a sombre background. [Italics added][34]

The conception of some antagonism between complementary colors, here suggested by van Gogh, pertains to another kind of visual effect. In 1839, Michel Eugene Chevreul, a professor of organic chemistry at the Museum of Natural History in Paris, discovered a complicated principle of color effect which he called "the law of simultaneous contrast."[35] Put simply, this law consists of the following: when two contrasting colors are juxtaposed, each will exaggerate its apparent difference in the direction of the other's complementary color. Complementaries placed side by side will not change, but, for example, when a gray is placed in a field with a positive color hue such as blue, the gray will take on some qualities of the complementary of blue, orange. The same gray will take on qualities of blue within an adjacent orange field (see fig. 20). This law or principle was well known to the impressionist painters and has been of interest to modern theorists and painters as well. However, my bringing it in here has more to do with the existence of such a physical principle in nature rather than with any painter's, or group of painters' specific knowledge of it. The art theorist J. F. A. Taylor has demonstrated instances in the paintings of both the medieval and nineteenth-century masters Giotto and Goya, respectively, in which important creative color effects were derived from an effective use of simultaneous contrast.[36] This factor is in fact so important in the effective use of color, it would seem that any creative colorist throughout the history of painting would, like Giotto and Goya, have needed to master the principle. In other

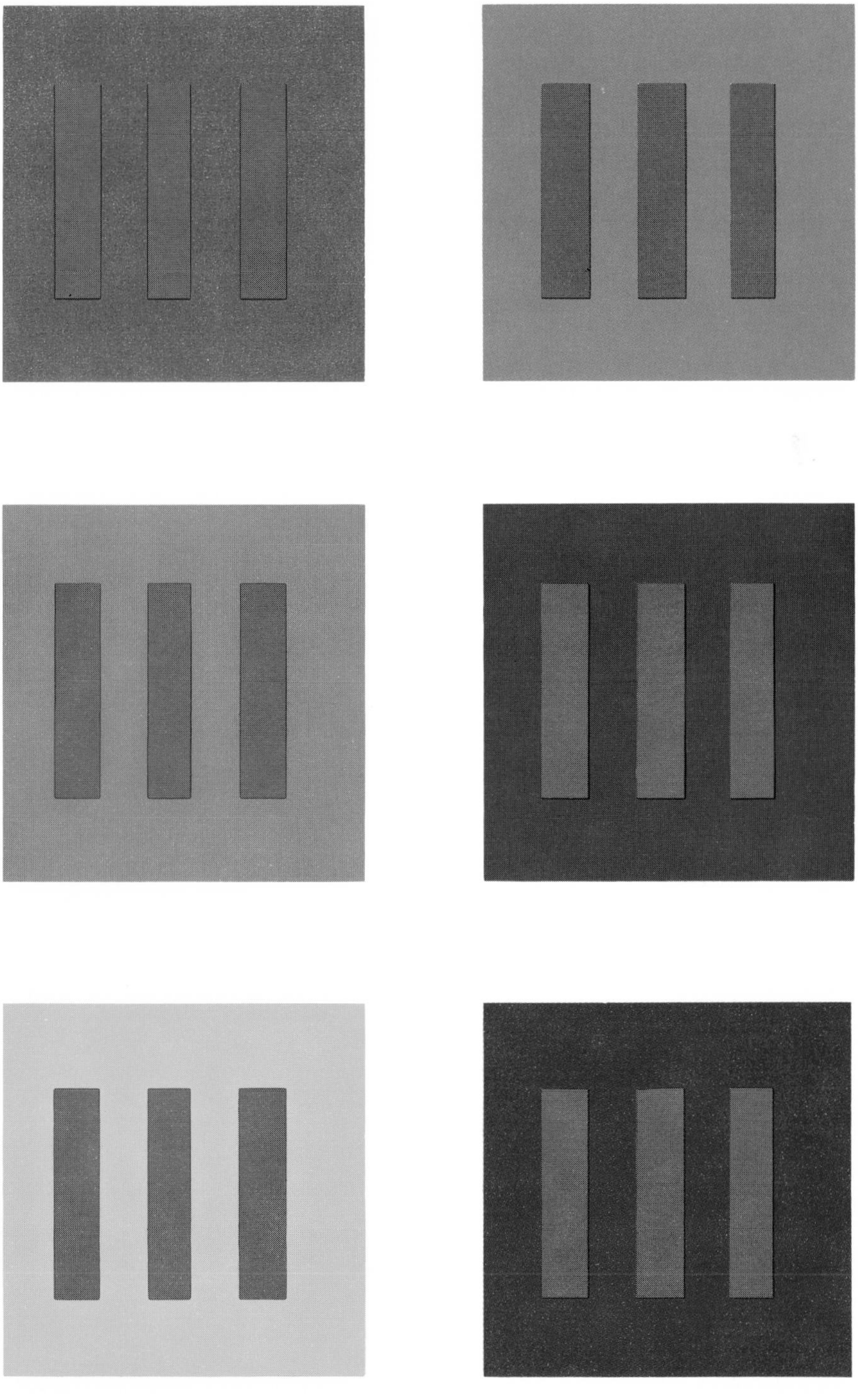

Fig. 20. The pigment is identical for all grays; the apparent differences depend on simultaneous contrast. From John F. A. Taylor, *Design and Expression in the Visual Arts* (New York: Dover Publications, 1964).

words, regardless of whether the early masters were intellectually aware of such a phenomenon, they would have needed somehow to be able to visualize such simultaneously contrasting or antagonistic color effects. When thinking of placing a gray hue in a blue field, they would have needed, as creative colorists, to be able to anticipate or otherwise handle the appearance of a subtle orange cast to the gray. This is also true for modern artists who are not specifically aware of the simultaneous contrast law.

As for janusian thinking with respect to content, artists of different types and from different periods have indicated such a process in varying ways. John Constable, the English naturalist landscape painter of the early nineteenth century, described his orientation to painting old mills and mill dams in a letter to his closest friend, Reverend Fisher, by emphasizing the following: "the sound of water escaping from . . . old rotten planks, slimy posts, and brickwork, I love such things. . . . As long as I do paint, I shall never cease to paint such places."[37]

That Constable was thinking of simultaneously opposing qualities of lively running water and decaying materials in such scenes is indicated by his referring to the sound rather than the sight of water stimulating his painting. The sound of water escaping surely suggests life, freshness, and activity in antithesis to stationary and decaying rot and slime. It is also supported by a comment relative to his perspective that he made in another context: "It is remarkable," he said in an 1836 talk to the Royal Institution, "how nearly, in all things, opposite extremes are allied."[38]

Odilon Redon, a postimpressionist symbolist painter of the late nineteenth century, described his orientation to his subject matter as follows: "My whole originality . . . consists in having made improbable beings live humanly according to the laws of the probable, by as far as possible putting the logic of the visible at the service of the invisible."[39]

One of the leading modern abstract expressionists, Piet Mondrian, stated a general aesthetic principle regarding subject matter conveying simultaneous antithesis in his following description of the artistic enterprise: "Disequilibrium means conflict, disorder. Conflict is also a part of life and of art, but it is not the whole of life or universal beauty. Real life is the *mutual interaction of two oppositions of the same value but of a different aspect and nature.* Its plastic expression is universal beauty."[40]

Albers's suggestion about the essence of Cezanne's unique breakthrough is at this point worth consideration from another aspect. As an indication of Albers's own janusian thinking with respect to color, it is vivid and highly illustrative, but as a scientific assessment of the nature of Cezanne's processes of visualizing, thinking and executing, it is, as Albers himself admits, a matter of opinion and speculation. Significantly, however, some other instances of general artistic innovations comparable to Cezanne's also suggest direct operation of broad types of janusian thinking in their production. Two recent examples are the apparently short-lived but distinctly influential and original modern movements called "op art" and "pop art." For the op school of art, the modus vivendi of the artistic work is to produce an effect in the observer of moving back and forth, or from side to side, while continuing to stand still and observe. To produce such works effectively, it surely seems crucial for the creators to conceive of simultaneously opposing or antithetical visual and dynamic orientations. The pop art conception, developed initially by Warhol, Lichtenstein, and Johns, also seems derived from a broad janusian formulation. In turning to the products of commercial art, these artists incorporated that traditional antithesis of serious art directly into the corpus of serious art itself. By focusing seriously on the modes and subject matter of popular art and experience, they juxtaposed two traditionally opposing orientations within a single frame of reference. Producing paintings of the labels on Campbell's soup cans or of scenes in comic strips, they instilled an effect of experiencing both the banal and the sublime at once. Seen as decorously and elegantly portrayed and enframed, the subject matter and the mode remained banal, but everyday experience became immortalized as art.

Modern art movements change so rapidly that shifting to extremes or conceiving simultaneous opposition could seem to be an aspect of the modern ethos. But, in addition to the already cited direct quotations and other evidence from artists in earlier historical periods, there is much in earlier masterpieces and the critical comment about them that suggests the ubiquitous operation of janusian thinking in visual art throughout history. The intense polarities of light and darkness in Rembrandt's great paintings, his extreme and virtually hallowed handling of chiaroscuro, surely suggests an operation of janusian thinking similar to that described by Walker Evans in photography. Is it not likely that Rembrandt conceived and visualized simultaneously the intensely dark browns and sharply light areas in his paintings? Moreover, is it not likely that he also conceived and visualized the antithetical effect of vibrant, glistening dark areas full of swirling motion along with intricately detailed unglistening though intensely lighted other ones? (See fig. 21.) Do not his paintings of dead persons and animals reveal a conception juxtaposing death with vibrant living forms and images? (See fig. 22.)

I call especial attention to another old master, Leonardo da Vinci. Not only are his writings replete with references to reversals, oppositions, and antitheses, in both his artistic and scientific formulations,[41] but it is of particular note that he adopted the procedure of carrying

A

Fig. 21. Rembrandt van Rijn's use of extremes of light and darkness is shown in these paintings. His famous *Night Watch* was not included here because, although it shows the same effect, some controversy exists about subsequent darkening of the oils. *A. The Man with the Golden Helmet,* 1652. Gemäldegalerie, Staatliche Museen Preussischer Kulturbesitz, Berlin (West). Photo Jörg P. Anders. *B. Jeremiah,* 1630. Rijksmuseum, Amsterdam.

B

out all his writings in mirror-image reversed script. For an interesting instance of manifest simultaneous opposition, note his drawing of pleasure and pain in figure 23 and compare it to Chagall's *Homage to Apollinaire* discussed earlier (fig. 11).[42] More particularly, however, I call attention to his painting *Mona Lisa* (fig. 24). Completed sometime between 1503 and 1505, this painting has been considered one

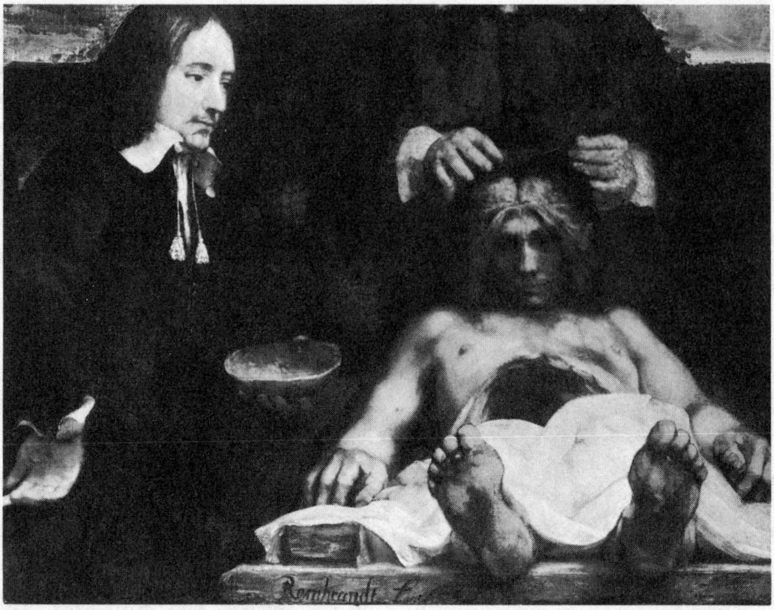

Fig. 22. This fragment from Rembrandt's *The Anatomical Lesson of Doctor Joan Deyman,* 1656, illustrates the simultaneous antithesis of death and life. Although Rembrandt was commissioned to do a portrait of the doctor, his graphic depiction of death was surely his own intentional conception. Rijksmuseum, Amsterdam.

of the great works in history. A cardinal feature of interest in it has been the enigmatic quality of the lady's smile. In a later chapter (chap. 10) I shall discuss some general features of the painting that contribute to this enigmatic quality. Here, I want to emphasize the particularly apt terms used by outstanding art critics to describe this smile: both "good and wicked," as well as both "cruel" and "compassionate;"[43] "smile of the Saints at Rheims" and "worldly, watchful and self satisfied;"[44] showing both "modesty and a secret sensuous joy."[45] Though there is surely disagreement about the particular attributes of the smile, there seems considerable agreement about its structural quality: simultaneous antithesis. Though enigmatic entities are often verbally described in terms emphasizing disparateness or incongruity, simultaneous antithesis is surely not their universal or intrinsic property.

As further suggestions of simultaneous antithesis operating in the conception of artistic masterpieces, there are the following commentaries about Michelangelo's painting (see fig. 25) of the prophet Jeremiah on the ceiling fresco of the Sistine Chapel (1508–10) and about Titian's painting (see fig. 26) entitled *Sacred and Profane Love* (1515–

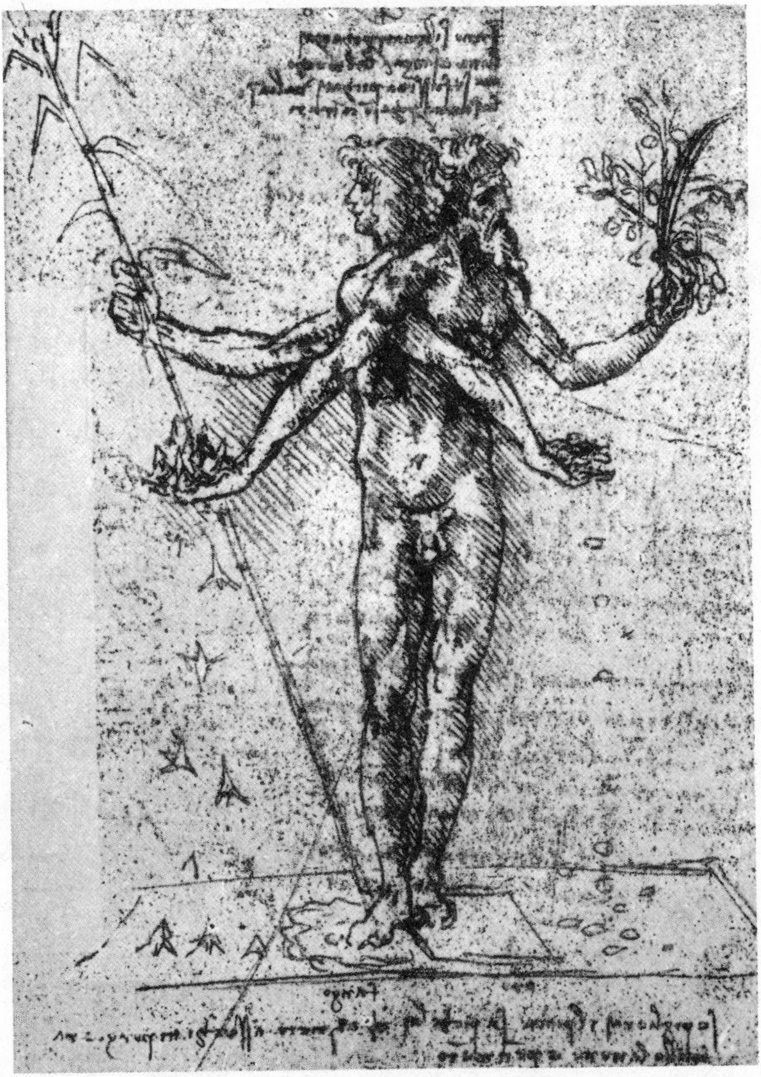

Fig. 23. Leonardo da Vinci, Sketch. A drawing of pleasure and pain as simultaneously opposed. The intermingling and reversals of the arms emphasize the simultaneous opposition. Oxford, Collection of the Governing Body of Christ Church.

16) by the art historians and critics Hiltgart Keller and Bodo Cichy, and William Gaunt, respectively:

> The sharpness of drawing in the architectural details, sills, pilasters, and consoles contrasts powerfully with the softness of

Fig. 24. Leonardo da Vinci. *Mona Lisa,* 1503. The smile demonstrates simultaneously antithetical qualities. Louvre, Paris. Photo Giraudon.

the figures, which, in the case of "Jeremiah" is almost pudgy and formless. But even more important than this contrast are the oppositions within the figures themselves. While head and limbs, and especially the powerful hands, suggest tremendous, superhuman energy and strength, the inward expression and deep

Fig. 25. Michelangelo Buonarroti. *Jeremiah* (from the ceiling fresco of the Sistine Chapel, Vatican), 1508–10. The figure shows oppositions of outer strength and inner control.

contemplation proclaim the strength of the soul that *keeps these energies from unfolding.* [Italics added][46]

Pictorially the two figures [representing the antithesis of sacred and profane love] provide quite simply a harmony of contrast. Contrast is emphasized by the different aspects of landscape in the background, hill and plain. . . . *Light forms are cunningly op-*

Fig. 26. Titian Vecellio. *Sacred and Profane Love* (Villa Borghese, Rome), 1515–16. Light forms are simultaneously opposed to dark.

> *posed to dark;* the dark bowl held by the nude against the sky, the rabbits behind the seated figure as a point of light against dark ground. [Italics added][47]

And, to include a well-known effect contributing to the powerful impact of another masterpiece, El Greco's *View of Toledo,* ca. 1610, there is the following phenomenon of a negative together with a fully realized positive image (fig. 27):

> The shock of irreality of that landscape . . . is realized by a transposition of values, which vision at once denounces and affirms. Edges appear as lights, planes as darks . . . [having the] aspect of a photographic negative, in which all values are transposed.[48]

These descriptions of simultaneous opposition in great masterpieces of the past, established as accurate, I believe, not merely on the authority of the particular critic but on the basis of a direct study of the painting itself, do not prove that janusian thinking operated during the creation of the particular work. However, they do suggest that diverse types of art works and artistic effects can result from this type of thinking, regardless of whether the style is naturalistic and representational, symbolic, romantic, impressionistic or expressionistic, or one of the particular modern modes. When simultaneous oppositions appear manifestly in completed works of art, they may sometimes engender a sense of balance and harmony as described in the Titian painting by Gaunt or they may engender a sense of tension and conflict, or both qualities may coexist. For the creator himself, formulating simultaneous opposition and antithesis early in the creative process, as is usually the case, there always is tension and contradiction in the initial conception.

I return now to direct examination of the creative process. A rarely obtainable complete documentation of the successive stages of de-

Fig. 27. El Greco. *View of Toledo,* ca. 1610. Light edges and dark planes are juxtaposed and produce the effect of a negative and a positive simultaneously. The Metropolitan Museum of Art, New York. Bequest of Mrs. H. O. Havemeyer, 1929. The H. O. Havemeyer Collection.

velopment of a great masterpiece by Pablo Picasso provides a striking illustration of the significant role of janusian thinking in artistic creation. It further clarifies how janusian thinking dictates both form and content during the creative process. Although Picasso himself insisted that important insights into the creative process could be gained from studying the "metamorphoses" of a painting,[49] he apparently preserved few of his planning and compositional sketches. Fortunately, most if not all of the sketches for one of his greatest works, *Guernica,* are available, and my illustration comes from these.[50]

Fig. 28. Pablo Picasso. *Guernica,* 1937. Oil on canvas, 11′5½″ x 25′ 5¾″. Collection, the Museum of Modern Art, New York.

Guernica, as is generally acknowledged, is one of the great masterpieces of modern times. A large mural pertaining to Hitler's bombing of the small Basque town of Guernica on May 1, 1937, it is a powerful antiwar statement and a visual triumph. The development of the complex and intricate composition of the completed mural, shown in figure 28, cannot be exhaustively traced merely by following sketches. Nor, in fact, is it possible to know what was in Picasso's mind beyond any of the particular preliminary sketches he drew. However, from Picasso's forty-five dated sketches and studies pertaining to the painting, it is possible to follow the broad evolution of the work from its earliest simpler stages to the more complex final one. And a janusian thought process appears in the very first sketch Picasso made, a sketch he entitled *Composition study* (fig. 29).

Fig. 29. Pablo Picasso. Composition study, 1937. Pencil on blue paper, 8¼″ x 10⅝″. Picasso's first sketch for the *Guernica* mural. Collection, the Museum of Modern Art, New York.

Comparing this very first sketch to the completed mural produces a very dramatic impact. The sketch is starkly simple; only a few basic elements are included, in contrast to the richly diverse elements of the final product. The structure is open and loose, in contrast to the final mural's tight, intricate, and crowded effect. But the essential rectangular orientation of the final painting is already set and four basic elements, all of which are retained at the end, appear in this earliest study. Indicating four basic positions, these four elements are the upright bull, the light bearer, the sprawling victim, and the inert base of destroyed bodies. The large circular curve embodies no specific element or position and appears designed to pull the vertical and horizontal dimensions together.[51]

In some ways, this earliest drawing appears quite conventional. At first glance, it could suggest a rather straightforward, almost realistic, scene containing animals and a single clearly drawn human being. We can discern the rather odd placement of a bird on the bull's back and, seeing the animal hoof in the air, we can sense something of the use of animals as symbols and the full-blown scene of carnage in the final painting. The human being holding the lamp is depicted with great dynamic energy even at this phase, and to a casual glance the figure seems to be in a rather conventional position of looking out of a window at the slightly unusual and slightly disturbing scene.

But now we must look closer. Careful examination of the drawing reveals an unusual disparity in the spatial configuration of this figure, and of the window, and of the wall. For one thing, the window is rather highly placed for the ground floor of the house and the positioning of the figure is almost impossible—at a minimum, excessively awkward—for standing and looking out. Furthermore, a careful examination of the lines drawn to represent the corner of the house near the figure reveals a decided duplexity in their deployment: they could either be seen as depicting an outside corner of a house or the inside corner of a room within a house, in the same location! In case these effects are thought to be accidental or unintentional, a quick comparison with the final painting, in figure 28, reveals that this same human being (a woman) holding the lamp is not only leaning *out* the window to view the animals and the remaining elements in the scene, but she also appears to be coming *in* through the same window from outside. She is looking *in at the scene* from a position ordinarily associated with looking *outside.* Widespread carnage and chaos ordinarily associated with an outside scene such as a street or battlefield are depicted as compressed within a room, according to this conception, and the woman at the window appears to be looking both inside and outside *simultaneously.*

Those who have not followed my exposition up to this point—for instance, those who immediately saw the human being looking into the room—may have been influenced by strong familiarity with the final painting. In other words, remembering the timbers in the ceiling and the sense of the person looking into a room in the final painting, one may not experience surprise about the placement appearing in the sketch. Nevertheless, the simultaneously antithetical spatial positions are clearly manifest in the spare scene depicted at that initial phase. That the initial conception of simultaneous antithesis guided

Picasso's further work and elaboration is seen in his also depicting the light in the center of the room in the completed mural as both a light bulb and a blazing sun at the same time. Also, the timbered ceiling of the inside of a room has the wide expansive quality of an outside sky. The resulting sense of massive carnage and chaos occurring inside a house or inside a room contributes to the mural's tremendous emotional power. And the simultaneous suggestion of carnage and chaos occurring in the more usual outside location under sun and sky further broadens the visual and emotional impact.

As with many other manifestations of janusian thinking described, Picasso's conception was formulated early in the creative process and was modified and elaborated in later stages. Some of his later composition sketches do not contain this figure at the window, and she appears in an altered shape in the final mural. More spiritual and ethereal there than in many of the sketches, the contradictory quality of her physical position became somewhat softened. Many other figures were also added along the way and alternative conceptions of these figures appear in several sketches. In successive formulations, overall composition and figure placement changed several times. Generally, however, the sense of choas in a confined space was increasingly enhanced and the janusian conception was integrated in various ways into the final product. The lines changing the center light to both bulb and sun simultaneously were, interestingly, only clearly added when the mural was virtually finished.[52]

Picasso's janusian conception of a scene of destruction and chaos occurring both inside and outside simultaneously led, in this instance, to a perfect blending of form and content. Formal aspects of this simultaneous contradiction embodied directly in the overall composition of the painting produced the type of visual tension and drama appropriate to the grand theme of the mural. The particular depiction of both inside and outside together in the same scene enhanced the quality of chaos and led to an emphasis on the universal and total destructiveness of war. Permeating all physical space, both inside and out, war also permeates our inner and outer being.

Two years before beginning this mural, Picasso said, "It would be very interesting to preserve photographically, not the stages, but the metamorphoses of a picture. Possibly one might then discover the path followed by the brain in materializing a dream. But there is one very odd thing to notice *that basically a picture doesn't change, that the first 'vision' remains almost intact, in spite of appearances.*"[53]

In view of the diverse manifestations of janusian thinking in a wide variety of visual modalities, it is reasonable to presume that it plays a role in creation of other forms of visual art beside sculpture and painting, such as graphics and weaving. A special word, however, is in order about architecture. Although many of the general principles of visual art creation apply directly to architecture, some particular considerations obtain because usefulness and aesthetics are blended together in architecture to a greater degree than in other visual arts.

When architects design structures, they pay attention to providing useful and psychologically comfortable space. To do this, architects may need to think about antithetical spatial effects simultaneously; janusian thinking then plays both an aesthetic and pragmatic role. When conceiving a very large building, for example, technical factors may require copious and bulky supports to be placed somewhere on the inside of the structure. Ordinarily, such supports impinge on and limit the inner contours and spaciousness of the building. The creative architect, however, is able to visualize both the inside and outside of the building simultaneously and to manipulate such spatial effects. He designs large buildings with a quality of unlimited inner space, and he may produce outer and inner convexities in the same portion of the building. Conversely, he may design sections of a building that appear concave from both these opposing spatial orientations at once. In recent times, some of our creative architects have adopted the procedure of putting enormous buildings on pedestals, an accomplishment derived from a conception of bringing the antithetical qualities of massiveness and lightness together. The famous early achievement of the Bauhaus architect Walter Gropius, "the curtain wall," was a wall allowing visualization of the area on either side. Consequently, it was both a separation and a continuity and the creator Gropius needed to conceive the effect of visualizing opposite sides of a wall simultaneously.

That janusian thinking pervades the creativity of architecture is nowhere better indicated than in the term used to describe his work by an unquestionably creative architect, Frank Lloyd Wright. In describing the form of architecture he introduced and developed into a high art, organic architecture, he called it an "affirmative negation," a development that simultaneously negated and affirmed architectural values. "The fruitful affirmative negation," he said, "[was] made by Organic Architecture in three dimensions."[54]

Music

Speaking of the possibility of composing music on the basis of timbre rather than on the traditional basis of pitch, Arnold Schoenberg said, "All this seems a fantasy of the future, which it probably is. Yet I am firmly convinced that it can be realized. I am convinced that [it] would dramatically increase the sensual, intellectual and soul pleasures which art is capable of rendering. I also believe that [it] would bring us closer to the realm which is mirrored for us in dreams."[55]

Though Schoenberg refers to a realm mirrored in dreams with particular respect to his interest in using timbre, it is clear he is describing what is for him a general principle of musical creation. As a composer whose influence on modern music has been wide sweeping and profound, and as a composer who has been unusually introspective about the nature of the creative process in music, Schoenberg's comment is of special interest. It leads us to expect that the mirror-image processes of dreaming might play a significant role in musical creativity. And Hans Mersmann, the German aesthetician, gives the suggestion greater weight and specificity with the following observation: "The possibility of expressing simultaneous opposition leads to the finest possibilities of expression, absolutely, leads to a place where music reaches far beyond the limits of the other arts. The significance of such tension grows when there are not only elements but formed forces which stand in opposition to each other."[56]

Mersmann's observation is not an isolated one; among others, music aestheticians Suzanne Langer and Gordon Epperson have cited it with approval and assent.[57] And Leonard Bernstein, the composer, conductor, and aesthetician, recently emphasized the importance of what he called ambiguity in music, an effect derived—according to his explanation—from simultaneous oppositions of factors such as diatonic and chromatic systems, tonality and atonality.[58]

Opposition and simultaneous opposition in music are both purer and more relative than in the other arts. As music has less definable and less referential content than literature or painting, polarities are delineated wholely by a particular musical context. The composer delineates oppositions as he composes, a counter theme is oppositional only in relation to another theme in the same piece.[59]In this way, musical form is replete with inversions, reversals, and mirror-image constructions of scalar, melodic, and harmonic elements. While elements in opposition to each other are not necessarily formulated simultaneously, there is reason to believe that such formulating is definitely important in creative composing. A case in point is Beethoven. Though documentation of instances of the creative process in music is particularly rare—composers more than other artists seem loath to give accounts of the creation of a specific work—it is fortunate indeed that Beethoven's notebooks, especially the extensive materials pertaining to the composition of his third ("Eroica") symphony, have been preserved. Moreover, unlike other composers such as Bach, whose notes and manuscripts are also available, Beethoven wrote out a good deal of his musical thought on paper.

Careful analysis and following of sequences in the Beethoven notebooks on the Eroica have led to a clear conclusion about his procedure: "the growth of one section is directly followed by increase in an adjoining section; the changing of one part involves that of another, and the later portions of the work develop out of the earlier."[60] And, as the musicologist Schmitz has shown, such changes

Fig. 30. Simultaneous antithesis of chromaticism and diatonicism in Wolfgang Amadeus Mozart's G Minor Symphony (as described by Leonard Bernstein). Reprinted by permission of the author and publishers from *The Unanswered Question* by Leonard Bernstein (Cambridge, Mass.: Harvard University Press). Copyright © 1976 by Leonard Bernstein.

and developments consistently involved *contrast,* a guiding principle he has called "contrasting derivation."[61] Hence, during the process of creating the Eroica, it appears that Beethoven constantly thought in terms of contrasts or oppositions.[62] As he almost invariably inserted a contrasting section somewhere in the piece whenever he made a change, it further appears that he formulated contrasts and oppositions *simultaneously* in reference to the entire piece.

Less-direct observations suggest a similar process of janusian thinking intrinsic to Mozart's compositional work. Bernstein illustrated his assertion about the importance of the simultaneous operation of the

[g]

[h]

[i]

[j]

[k]

[l]

[m]

[n]

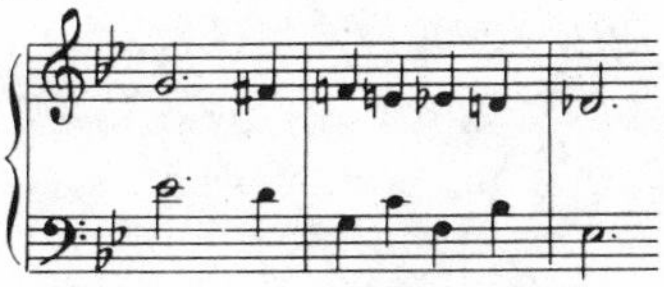

antithesis of chromaticism (key relationship) and diatonicism (tonic-dominant relationships involving seven tones in major and minor) in music by reference to a work of Mozart's, the G Minor Symphony, as follows (bracketed references are to fig. 30):

> . . . the opening of the first movement . . . [see fig. 30*a*]. Now this whole section moves quite easily and diatonically from its G-minor tonic to its first cadence, which is, naturally enough, on the dominant [see fig. 30*b*] and just as easily slips back into the tonic [see fig. 30*c*]. (You remember that this tonic-dominant relationship arises from the adjacency of the fundamental tone, in this case G [see fig. 30*d*], with its first overtone [see fig. 30*e*], that basic interval of a fifth.) From this point the music proceeds by

the circle of fifths in a downward progression [see fig. 30*f*], to its relative major, B flat, which is exactly where it's supposed to be (according to sonata-form principles), for the appearance of the second thematic section [see fig. 30g]. But notice that Mozart's new theme is already chromatically formed [see fig. 30*h*], and it gets more so as it goes on [see fig. 30*i*]; and even more so when it repeats [see fig. 30*j*]. What's this? A-flat major, a sudden new key, unrelated to either B flat or G minor. How did we get *here*? By the well known circle of fifths [see fig. 30*k*; here Bernstein is referring to a diatonic principle]. Do you hear those stable consecutive fifths striding inexorably from dominant to tonic in the bass? [See fig. 30*l*.] And each dominant leads to a tonic which instantly becomes itself a dominant, leading in turn to its tonic. *While above, the melodic line descends by chromatic half-steps into the nether regions of A-flat major!* [Italics added.] There's that classical balance we were talking about—chromatic wandering on top [see fig. 30*m*] but firmly supported by the inverted tonic-dominant structure underneath [see fig. 30*n*].

Do you see now what I mean by the beauty of ambiguity? It's the combination of those two contradictory forces, chromaticism and diatonicism, operating at the same time, that makes this passage so expressive.[63]

Bernstein's explanation, convincing as it is, merely indicates the operation of simultaneous antitheses in the completed work of art. That such broad and extensive oppositions as the chromatic and diatonic progressions Bernstein described *were conceived* simultaneously by Mozart during the process of composition is supported by Mozart's own famous description of his creative process. In response to a baron who made him a present of wine and inquired about his methods of composing, Mozart wrote:

When I am, as it were, completely myself, entirely alone, and of good cheer—say, travelling in a carriage, or walking after a good meal, or during the night when I cannot sleep; it is on such occasions that my ideas flow best and most abundantly. . . . This fires my soul and, provided I am not disturbed, my subject enlarges itself, becomes methodized and defined, and the whole, though it be long, stands almost complete and finished in my mind, so that I can survey it, like a fine picture or a beautiful statue, at a glance. Nor do I hear in my imagination the parts successively but I hear them, as it were, all at once [*gleich alles zusammen*]. What a delight this is I cannot tell! All this inventing, this producing, takes place in a pleasing lively dream. Still the actual hearing of the *tout ensemble* is after all the best.[64]

The experience Mozart describes of "actual" hearing of the entire musical piece all together (*tout ensemble*), or all at once, indicates that extensive oppositional sequences would surely have been heard simultaneously. Mozart's description is also suggestive of another type of janusian thinking in music creation: conceiving in opposite or antithetical temporal orientations simultaneously. Although such an experience may be difficult to imagine for someone who has never had it, it seems to be one of hearing what is to come concomitant both with what is unfolding and with what has already been heard, that is, hearing and/or conceiving in antithetical temporal progressions at the same time. And Mozart's use of the modifying phrase "as it were" indicates that he is not referring to a mystical experience, but is fully aware of the seemingly antithetical properties of the phenomenon. Coleridge gives an apt description of the successful musical effect which would result from such a type of thinking:

> . . . the present strain seems not only to recall, but almost to renew some past movement, another and yet the same! Each present movement bringing back, as it were, and embodying the spirit of some melody that has gone before, anticipates and seems to overtake something that is to come; and the musician has reached the summit of his art, when having thus modified the present by the past, he at the same time weds the past in the present to some prepared and corresponsive future. The auditor's thoughts and feelings move under the same influence, *retrospection blends with anticipation,* and hope, and memory, a female Janus, become one power with a double aspect. [Italics added][65]

Other composers, such as Paul Hindemith and Franz Schubert,[66] have also described similar comprehensive images of a musical composition though it is difficult to ascertain definitively whether opposing temporal orientations were involved. Yet, another type of manifestation of the creative cognition I am discussing, going back to an earlier time than Mozart, Hindemith, and Schubert, concerns the invention of a particular rhythmic style. The style, agitato, has today become highly standard in Western music and, as here professed by the inventor himself, it was produced by a single person rather than a group or a culture. In a book published in 1638, Monteverdi described his creation of the agitato style, as follows:

> I consider the principal passions or emotions of the soul to be three, namely anger, serenity and humility. The best philosophers affirm this; the very nature of our voice, with its high, low and middle ranges, show it; and the art of music clearly manifests it in these three terms: agitated, soft and moderate. I have not been able to find an example of the agitated style in the works of past composers, but I have discovered many of the soft and moderate types. . . .
>
> Considering that all the best philosophers maintain that the pyrrhic or fast tempo was used for agitated, warlike dances, and contrariwise, the slow spondaic tempo for their opposites, I thought about the semibreve [whole note] and proposed that each semibreve correspond to a spondee [slow unit]. Reducing this to sixteen semichromes [sixteenth notes], struck one after

> another and joined to words expressing anger and scorn, I could hear in this short example a resemblance to the emotion I was seeking, . . . the words did not follow the rapid beat of the instrument.
>
> To arrive at a better proof, I resorted to . . . [Tasso's] description of the combat between Jancred and Clorinda as theme for my music expressing the contrary passions aroused by war, prayer and death.
>
> In the year 1624 I had this work performed. . . . It was received with much applause and was highly praised.
>
> Having met with success in my method of depicting anger, I proceeded with even greater zeal in my investigations and wrote diverse compositions, both ecclesiastical and chamber works. These found such favor with other composers that they not only *spoke* their praise but to my great joy and honor, *wrote* it by imitating my work. Consequently, it has seemed wise to let it be known that the investigation and the first efforts in this style—so necessary to the art of music, and without which it can rightly be said that music has been imperfect up to now, having had but two styles, soft and moderate—originated with me.[67]

Monteverdi's analytic and controlled style of presentation differs sharply from the dramatic descriptions by other creators quoted here. From our vantage point of the twentieth century, it seems remarkable that such an important and now standard style was invented by a single individual in such a deliberate way. There is no reason to doubt Monteverdi's account, however, and it is clear that the crucial steps in this creative process consisted of first a specification of opposites, fast and slow tempo, and, then, the conception of presenting or performing them *simultaneously*. Of course, fast and slow tempos are considered such relative matters nowadays that it is difficult to conceive of them as opposites when played together. But there is little doubt from the account that Monteverdi, as well as his contemporaries, considered the tempos a matter of opposites, and the formulation therefore was of simultaneous antithesis or opposition. Opposition, as I have said, can be quite relative to a context, and janusian thinking may therefore only be identified on the basis of the creator's perspective, the particular stage of development of the art form or the level of knowledge in a field or discipline. Monteverdi, at that stage of Western music's development, formulated the agitato style by bringing opposite tempos together. His subsequent attempt to "prove" or work out his initial formulation through an application to Tasso's theme is an instance of what I have previously described as the characteristic elaborating and transforming of the janusian conception during the course of the creative process.

The type of analytic conceptualizing of opposites illustrated by Monteverdi's account is also found in the approaches of the modern masters, Schoenberg and Stravinsky. Schoenberg, throughout his writings on music,[68] is so directly concerned with inversions, reversals, retrograde inversions (his term), and mirror images that, taken in the context of his comment quoted at the beginning of this section, he almost seems manifestly aware of janusian thinking as a crucial factor in creating. Though he has left little record of the creation of specific pieces of music, his discussion of his revolutionary discovery of serial music, the twelve-tone scale, indicates a clear instance of his use of the thought process. Describing the historical evolution of the movement away from tonality in Western music during the hundred years prior to his own discoveries, Schoenberg termed the development "the emancipation of the dissonance." His use of this term, he explained, was intended to call attention to his own discovery of a factor that led to the final emancipation. He was the first, he said, to point out the essential *equivalence between consonance and dissonance,* specifically that dissonances were merely "more remote consonances." As he further described it: "The term *emancipation of the dissonance* refers to its comprehensibility; which is considered equivalent to the consonance's comprehensibility. A style based on this premise treats dissonances like consonances and renounces a tonal center."[69]

Here is another instance of the development of a musical style based on janusian thinking. As can be recognized by now, the type of thinking indicated by Schoenberg means that the creator is having things both ways: he thinks of dissonances as being like consonances and he therefore uses dissonant elements to produce new sonorities, or sound entities, that initially retain qualities both of dissonances and consonances at once. Serial music, with its manifest atonality, was based, at least in part, on this type of thinking. Though Western music, at least from the time of Wagner, seems in retrospect to have been clearly moving toward atonality, Schoenberg's development of that particular form and style was his own individual creation.[70]

Stravinsky was influenced by Schoenberg in varying ways, but independently he had always emphasized opposition in musical form throughout his writings on music.[71] His following discussion of the compositional importance of the principle of atonality, excerpted from a longer treatise but preserving the overall conception, contains a clear emphasis on the use of a broad form of janusian thinking:

> So our chief concern is not so much what is known as tonality as what one might term the polar attraction of sound, of an interval, or even of a complex of tones. The sounding tone constitutes in a way the essential axis of music. Musical form would be unimaginable in the absence of elements of attraction which make up every musical organism and which are bound up with its psychology. . . .

> In view of the fact that our poles of attraction are no longer within the closed system which was the diatonic system, *we can bring the poles together* without being compelled to conform to the exigencies of tonality. For we no longer believe in the absolute value of the major-minor system based on the entity which musicologists call the c-scale. [Italics added][72]

Abstract and theoretical as the above passage seems, Stravinsky must surely have derived these formulations from his own felt experience of bringing poles or opposites together in the creative process. This experience, as Stravinsky's first paragraph here suggests, does not itself depend on overthrowing the diatonic system, as poles of attraction always exist in music. For Stravinsky, at that point at least, the overthrow of tonality was a vehicle for formulating opposites simultaneously.

An exceptionally rare discussion of specific details of the creation of a particular musical work was presented somewhat in passing by the American composer Roger Sessions in a series of lectures presented in 1949 at the Juilliard School of Music, in New York City. To illustrate growth and change in creation of music, he described the initial phases of conceiving his own First Piano Sonata. As the documentation is rare and, as it both illustrates a good deal about the musical creative process and a complicated manifestation of janusian thinking, I shall present it at some length. I shall start with a truncated version of the composer's words, omitting the musical notation to which they refer so that the overall sequence of events and the composer's own point about the material will be easier to follow. All the omitted phrases are designated by letter in the quotation and are produced in their entirety with the corresponding letter and musical notation indicated in the accompanying figure on the facing page (fig. 31). The complete text, therefore, can be readily reconstructed by reposing the phrases into their original context.

> Let me give a brief example from my own work. The first idea that came to me for my First Piano Sonata, begun in 1927, was in the form of a complex chord . . . [fig. 31*a*]. This chord rang through my ear almost obsessively one day as I was walking in Pisa, Italy. The next day, or, in other words, when I sat down to work on the piece, I wrote the first phrase of the Allegro; . . . [fig. 31*b*]. Later it became clear to me that the motif must be preceded by an introduction, and the melody . . . [fig. 31*c*] with which the Sonata begins, immediately suggested itself, quite without conscious thought on my part. A few days later the original complex chord came back to my ear, again almost obsessively; I found myself continuing it in my mind, and only then made the discovery . . . [fig. 31*d*] that the germ of the key relationship on

(a) 

"[a complex chord] preceded by a sharp but heavy upbeat."

(b) 

meas. 27–32

"[Allegro;] as you see, the chord had become simpler—a C minor triad, in fact, and its complex sonority had given way to a motif of very syncopated rhythmic character."

(c) 

meas. 234–244
(*Allegro*)

"[the melody] in B minor."

(d) 

meas. 1–2

"[I made the discovery] that the two lower notes of the chord, F# and E, formed the minor seventh of the dominant of the key of B minor, and that the continuation I had been hearing led me back to B."

Fig. 31. Roger Sessions's creation of his First Piano Sonata. Reprinted by permission of Princeton University Press from *The Musical Experience of Composer, Performer, Listener*, by Roger Sessions (copyright 1950 by Princeton University Press, Princeton Paperback, 1971). Copyright © 1931 by B. Schott's Söhne, Mainz. Copyright renewed. All rights for the U.S.A. and Mexico controlled by European American Music Distributors Corporation. Used by permission.

> which the first two movements of the Sonata were based were already implicit in the chordal idea with which the musical train of thought—which eventually took shape in the completed Sonata—had started.
>
> I point out these things in order to throw some light on some of the ways in which a composer's mind, his creative musical mind, that is, works; and more especially to illustrate the nature of the musical idea as I have defined it. Once more, I am not implying that the so-called principle "themes" of a given piece of music are not musical ideas or, in most cases, the most important formative ideas of the work. It is obvious that they frequently are. I have been trying to show, rather, that a composer's relation to his work is an organic one; that the conception and the composition of a piece of music are not a matter of set procedure but a living process of growth.[73]

The main reason I have truncated the quotation should now be clear. Here, in Sessions's description, is the familiar sequence of a germinal idea, followed by some elaboration, and then a return to the original idea frequently encountered in the creative process. It is also a familiar description of the creator's finding further possibilities on returning to his original idea. Illustrated again is the importance of a single idea, an idea that is not necessarily the very first one, nor is it necessarily directly manifest in the completed work. As Sessions says, the important idea may or may not be the major theme or other fully developed motif in the work.

Let us then look closely at the particular germinal musical idea described here; see fig. 31*a*. Carefully comparing the composer's verbal description of "a complex chord preceded by a sharp but heavy upbeat" with the actual musical notation recorded reveals an important musical discrepancy and an apparent contradiction. Although the composer verbally says that the upbeat precedes the complex chord, his notation indicates that the chord in fact sounds *at the same time as the upbeat.* Since the chord continues to sound in the downbeat of the next measure, the structure is of an upbeat *simultaneous* with a downbeat, a simultaneous opposition or antithesis. It must be emphasized that this is no typesetter's error nor a mistake in transcription on Sessions's part. Though he does not point it out explicitly,[74] the complex sonority he had in mind contained antithetical rhythmic factors. That this self-contradictory rhythmic aspect was a known and critical aspect of the idea and that it stimulated further creation and elaboration is borne out by the composer's comment on the next phase of his work on the piece. In figure 31*b* he says, "its complex sonority had given way to a motif of very syncopated rhythmic character." Hence, the particular form of syncopation in this piece—that is, the complex sounding of upbeats together with downbeats—was already implicit in the original idea and it unfolded in a successive rhythmic motif as he worked the idea out.

Also included in the illustration are other factors implicit in Sessions's original idea (the tonic factors in fig. 31*c* and *d*) which, together with the rhythmic aspect of the initial thought, played a significant role in the overall sequence. Simultaneous opposition was a critical aspect of the initial idea and, I want to emphasize, the opposition or antithesis is more specific and perhaps more basic than in previous musical cases I have cited. Upbeat and downbeat are virtually unreconcilable stresses; they cannot acoustically be identified simultaneously.

Underlying musical creation, in all modes and throughout history, is an orientation to auditory phenomena and a form of janusian cognition that is similar to janusian cognition in visual art creation. Just as the creative visual artist perceives and conceptualizes positive and negative spaces simultaneously, the creative composer has a similar cognitive orientation with respect to both sound and rhythm. Corresponding to the empty or negative space confronting the visual artist are both the noise or random sound and the random stresses and sequences confronting the composer. Noise and randomness are intrinsic components of all auditory and kinesthetic perception, the latter being the principal mode of rhythmic experience. Corresponding to the positive space of visual experience are the formed elements of sound and motion: melodic and harmonic patterns, definable qualities of timbre, repetitions of sequences, and, concretely, bird calls, voices, heart beats, or tapping feet.

Unlike negative visual space, negative sound consisting of noise or random emission is a constant constituent of auditory experience. Although voluntary elimination of visual sensations by closing the eyes is possible, analogous elimination of sound during consciousness is not possible; we cannot stop hearing or close our ears. A readily available proof of this is that in order to "shut off" hearing completely, it has always been necessary, in psychological experiments and elsewhere, to apply a constant invariant source of sound (usually called "white noise") rather than to attempt the virtually impossible task of producing a soundless environment. Because total silence is consciously unknown to us, therefore, we characteristically treat random sound or noise as though it were soundlessness; we do not attend to the myriad unformed random sounds in our environment although they are constantly with us.

The creative composer pays significant attention to this, the "negative" aspect of auditory experience. This does not mean that he necessarily listens to or brings noise into focus during the process of composing, though many composers have been known to derive inspiration from listening to apparently random sounds in their environment. For example, Beethoven supposedly got his initial ideas for the Pastoral Symphony while listening to the sounds of a brook;[75] Weber composed music while listening to the wheels of his carriage;[76] the dadaist composers, as is well known, attempted to base their music on the sounds of cities and machines. Listening to the negative aspect specifically means that creative composers are aware, in their mental "inner ears," of the random sounds related to or accompanying the formed elements they are constructing. This is not merely an organizing of random sounds. Composers are aware of random or negative elements at the same time as they conceive and hear the formed elements. This is borne out by the presence of a constant structural element in great music demonstrated fairly conclusively by the musicologist Leonard Meyer.[77] Meyer has shown that an invariable factor in such music, in all cultures and periods in history, has been the presence of elements producing unexpected effects. These elements "weaken" the shape or expected progression of a musical sequence, and they produce a momentary sense bordering on chaos and on attendant conflict and tension. It is not necessary to subscribe to Meyer's aesthetic position, nor even to explain this process in terms of the particular theory (information theory) he uses, in order to apply his discovery to the musical creative process as follows: In order to produce deviations of sound bordering on chaos, the composer would need to attend to the random negative qualities of the sounds at the same time as he follows principles of constructing and hearing formed qualities. Consequently, the composer conceives and formulates in positive and negative aspects of auditory experience simultaneously.

Just as random sound and noise are the negative aspect of the auditory sphere, random motion is the negative aspect of rhythm. In the deviations and weakenings of musical shape, momentary tendencies toward chaos and the appearance of unexpected elements, traditional patterns, and sequences of movement constitute the formed positive aspects of rhythm. These latter positive aspects conflict with negative aspects of random motion. In the creation of musical rhythm as well as in the creation of dance rhythms and sequences, both aspects must be attended simultaneously.[78]

A comment about the musical style called random music should help clarify this further. Though proponents of the style such as the composer John Cage may disagree, I would suggest, as others have, that the appeal of such music depends on a creative form of listening by the audience. Here, the point I have made about the composer attending to both positive and negative—formed and random—aspects simultaneously operates in the reverse direction. Confronted with random sound from an electronic or other source, the listener brings formed patterns, timbres, etc., into mind which he conceives and hears in his mental inner ear at the same time as he hears the random sounds. Though he may at times impose a form or organization onto the random sounds, just as obversely the creative composer imposes random elements onto formed sequences, the overall sense of the experience is one of hearing random and formed elements separately and simultaneously. Sometimes a sense of unification occurs.

The listening experience is, however, not fully analogous to the experience of the creative composer. The composer both elaborates and transforms these janusian perceptions and cognitions within his musical work, but the listener to random music must, unless he has the capacity for inner elaboration (unless he is himself a creative composer), be restricted to solely having the experience of simultaneous antithesis. This type of janusian cognition is a portion but not the whole of the musical creation process.

Literature

That paradox, opposition, and antithesis are intrinsic to literary structure and to literary value and appeal has been postulated, argued, and reemphasized by leading thinkers and critics throughout the ages. In the *Poetics,* Aristotle discussed both paradox and reversal as important elements in complex or high tragedy. Later, Coleridge proposed that poetry consisted of a balance or reconciliation of opposite or discordant qualities, a position that echoed the previously mentioned dictum by Blake regarding the importance of contraries. Modern literary critics such as I. A. Richards, William Empson, Allen Tate, John Crowe Ransom, Robert Penn Warren, and Cleanth Brooks have all emphasized the bipolar, ambiguous, and antithetical elements in poetry and literature, Brooks particularly arguing in a famous essay that paradox is "the language appropriate and inevitable to poetry." And Kenneth Burke, a modern critic whose general perspective differs from the ones mentioned, related incongruity and incongruous relationships to literary metaphor.[79]

Robert Graves, the English classicist poet, described one source of poetry as "the unforeseen fusion in [the poet's] . . . mind of apparently contradictory ideas." And a very suggestive and influential analysis of literary metaphor in line with the previous assertions, has been presented by the noted aesthetician, Monroe Beardsley. Following Max Black's proposition that the effect of a metaphor derives from the interaction among its elements, Beardsley proposed that a critical aspect of literary metaphor was a relationship of verbal opposition. Calling this effect, "the metaphorical twist," Beardsley insisted that contradiction, which he equated with opposition, must be present in order for verbal elements to be recognizable as metaphors. Because of this oppositional and logically incompatible aspect, verbal metaphors always generated a quality of conflict and tension. Hausman, in a more extensive analysis of the contradictory aspects of metaphor, strongly emphasized this conflictual quality.[80]

Conflict, tragedy, and metaphor are intrinsic factors in all serious literature. As these factors are derived in large measure from relationships of opposition and antithesis, we can infer that janusian thinking plays an extensive role in literary creation. I have already documented in some detail the operation of janusian thinking in the creation of a poem and indicated widespread applications to the creation of poetry in general. Therefore, I shall shift to the genesis of novels and plays and to descriptions of the thought process in operation there.

In the preface to his novel *Nostromo,* Joseph Conrad described his interest in the story of a robbery by an "unmitigated rascal" of a large quantity of silver somewhere on the seaboard of South America during a revolution. He thought he might write about it, but hesitated as he designated in the following: "I did not see anything at first in the mere story. A rascal steals a large parcel of a valuable commodity —so people say. It's either true or untrue; and in any case it has no value in itself. To invent a circumstantial account of the robbery did not appeal to me."

After this indecision, the key idea for the novel, as Conrad reported it, came at the following point: "when it dawned upon me that the purloiner of the treasure need not necessarily be a confirmed rogue, that he could be even a man of character." The turning point idea of the criminal as rascal or rogue and man of character together led to a specific elaboration of a "twilight" land of good and evil simultaneously and the drive to write the novel:

> . . . it was only then that I had the first vision of a twilight country which was to become the province of Sulaco, with its high, shadowy Sierra and its misty campo for mute witnesses of events flowing from the passions of men short-sighted in good and evil.
>
> Such are in very truth the obscure origins of *Nostromo*—the book. From that moment, I suppose it had to be.[81]

In his *Autobiography,* Anthony Trollope, the eminent English novelist of the nineteenth century, described the background of his novel *The Warden,* the first of a series of novels about English clergy set in the area called Barchester. Though considered a master depiction of the clergy of the time, Trollope confessed the following: "But my first idea had no reference to clergy in general. I had been struck by two opposite evils . . . and . . . I thought I might be able to expose them, or rather to describe them, both in one and the same tale." He went on to elaborate the content of his janusian conception regarding the two opposites, as follows:

> The first evil was the possession by the Church of certain funds and endowments which had been intended for charitable purposes, but which had been allowed to become incomes for idle Church dignitaries. . . . The second evil was its very opposite. . . . I had . . . often been angered by the undeserved severity of the newspapers toward the recipients of such incomes, who could hardly be considered to be the chief sinners in the matter.[82]

His idea, then, was to be condemnatory and noncondemnatory (or justifying) at the same time. Despite some doubts about whether this approach would be successful, he remarked, "Nevertheless, I thought much about it, and on the 29th July 1852,—having been then two years without having made any literary effort,—I began *The Warden*, at Tenbury in Herefordshire."[83]

A somewhat more complex instance of a janusian formulation germinating a novel, from a complex novelist, is the following description taken from the diary of Virginia Woolf:

> Now about this book, *The Moths*. How am I to begin it? And what is it to be? . . . a mind thinking. They might be islands of light—islands in the stream that I am trying to convey; life itself going on. The current of moths flying strongly this way. A lamp and a flower pot in the centre. . . . I shall have the two different currents—the moths flying along; the flower upright in the centre; a *perpetual crumbling and renewing of the plant*. In its leaves she might see things happen. [Italics added.][84]

The novel Woolf struggled with here eventually became *The Waves*, and a central image of the simultaneous dying and renewal of the plant, reflected through and by the thinking mind and the stream of consciousness of the leading character, was conceived at this very early stage.

In the creation of plays, the American playwright Arthur Miller told me that he developed his initial idea for the drama *Incident at Vichy* while he was traveling in Germany. He thought of writing a play expressing the beauty and growth of modern Germany and of Hitler's destructiveness simultaneously. This led him to think of a story he had heard about a noble sacrifice in the waiting room of a Nazi official, a sacrifice he later incorporated into the play. Also, Eugene O'Neill's writing of *The Iceman Cometh* developed from a conception that a friend's suicide was motivated by simultaneously antithetical feelings about a wife's infidelity. O'Neill realized that the friend had both wanted and not wanted his wife to be unfaithful and to sleep with another man.[85]

Federico Garcia Lorca, the Spanish playwright whose poetic plays are full of manifest paradoxes and ironies, stated the following about the genesis of the play, *The Shoemaker's Prodigious Wife*: "In my Shoemaker's Wife I sought to express . . . the struggle of reality with fantasy that exists within every human being. (By fantasy I mean everything that is unrealizable.)[86]

Lorca's parenthetical definition of fantasy in this context makes clear that he was thinking of a simultaneous antithesis of the unrealizable and the realized, rather than of the common comparison of fantasy and reality as two modes of experience. And the absurdist playwright, Eugene Ionesco, whose plays are sometimes thought to be spontaneous unconscious automatisms, described the following genesis of his play, *The Chairs:*

> when I wrote *The Chairs,* I first had the image of chairs, then that of a person bringing chairs as fast as possible on to an empty stage. . . . The play itself consisted of empty chairs, and more chairs arriving, a whirlwind of them being brought on and taking over the whole stage as if a massive, all-invading void were settling in. . . . It was both multiplication and absence, proliferation and nothingness.[87]

Clearly, Ionesco was actively and intentionally—*not* unconsciously—formulating simultaneous antitheses to express the idea he thought was implicit in his image of someone bringing empty chairs onto an empty stage—the idea of filling empty space with emptiness.

Some other instances of janusian thinking in literary creation, derived from careful retracing with my own writer research subjects of the steps in producing a particular work, are the following:

> Early in the process of conceiving the plot of a novel, a novelist formulated the idea of a revolutionary hero responsible for the death of hundreds of people, who only killed one person with his own hand. The person he murdered was someone who had been kind to him and whom he had loved.
>
> A novelist conceived a phrase stating that love and hate were the same; this phrase was the initial idea and the basis for an ensuing novel.
>
> A poet, walking on a beach, picked up some rocks and thought they felt like human skin. They were, for him, both weapons and sensual objects at the same time. This led to a conception of the simultaneous operation of sex and violence in the world, and he wrote a poem elaborating this theme.
>
> This same poet thought of writing a poem about marathon racing; a line connoting rest simultaneous with running and with motion instigated the poem.

Experimental Studies

Shifting away from evidence derived from research interviews and published documents, I shall outline some results of controlled experimentation which I have reported in some detail elsewhere.[88] Although the following experiments were performed with creative students and businessmen, preliminary experiments with the highly creative writers and scientists in my interview studies, carried out in a manner similar to that described here, have yielded similar results.

In the following experiments I used a word association testing procedure to assess a tendency toward janusian thinking in creative subjects. Two major considerations were involved. First, as I will clarify further in the chapter to follow, verbal opposition tends to be clearer and more specific than opposition in any other mode. Opposition between or among words is easier to define and to assess than other types of oppositional relationship. On classical word association tests, opposite word responses have traditionally been recognized and have regularly been scored and calculated as a separate category. Second, in an important word association study, focused primarily on psycholinguistic questions, the psychologists Carroll, Kjeldegaard, and Carton had developed findings that seemed to have applications to janusian thinking. By means of a systematic quantitative analysis of their own and others' word association results, these investigators definitively established a specific opposite responding tendency, a tendency among certain experimental subjects to give opposite word associations or responses to test word stimuli.[89] Unlike other subjects who responded in numerous and diverse ways to the single word stimuli on the test (when asked to give the first word that came to mind, others tended to respond more with synonyms of the test words or with other types of related and unrelated words) these subjects showed a definite and self-consistent tendency to reply with opposites.[90] The findings had important repercussions for word association research but no conclusions could be drawn from that study about the psychological basis of this response tendency. For one thing, the researchers had made no attempt to collect any other identifying information about subjects manifesting the tendency. They were interested in explaining and clarifying some confounding and contradictory results that had been obtained in others' word association experiments and they succeeded. Assessing the study, however, I wondered whether this tendency to opposite responding on word association tests might be connected to janusian thinking and to creative capacities and interests, and I set out to repeat their experiment with some modifications and additions, especially adding a method of collecting identifying information about experimental subjects.

Subjects for the experiment were Yale undergraduates enrolled in an introductory psychology course; a request for volunteers was posted and 115 students signed up for the experiment simply entitled, "Aesthetic Preference and Cognition." Direct reference to creativity was purposely avoided in order to reduce as much as possible preconceptions affecting response tendencies. Most people have definite preconceptions about creativity and when they believe they are being tested for creative capacity, they respond according to their preconceptions rather than in a natural spontaneous manner. All of the 115 volunteers were included in the experiment although two subjects had to be eliminated in the tabulation of results because of language difficulty in one case and because of a technical experimental error related to the other.

In the experimental procedure, a word association test was administered individually to each subject.[91] Ninety-nine words from the standard Kent-Rosanoff word association list were used as test stimuli.[92] These words appear in the column labelled "Stimulus Word" on table 1. After a brief discussion with the subject about his previous experience with word association tests, a discussion serving to clear up any misconceptions he might have had about the procedure and helping to reduce pretest anxiety, the tester instructed the subject to respond to the individually presented word stimuli with the "first word that came to mind." The importance of complying with these instructions was emphasized at the beginning and throughout the ensuing test procedure. Word stimuli were presented and the time required for each of the subject's responses was obtained. The entire procedure was tape recorded.[93] After completing all of the word association test, the subject was asked to answer a questionnaire, in the presence of the experimenter, a questionnaire designed to elicit specific types of information related to the subject's creativity.

I have presented the procedure in some detail in order to clarify the nature of the psychological process assessed. Free spontaneous responses to word stimuli are fairly good indicators of associational patterns of thought. Although early use of the word association procedure had been overly ambitious in attempting to identify "complexes," and although subsequent diagnostic uses have turned out to be overly inferential and unreliable, there is little reason to shift to the extreme limitation of restricting use to descriptive or purely linguistic analysis. Psycholinguistic analysis often approaches word association responses solely as manifestations of linguistic habits or of conscious response strategies. While such analysis has value for psycholinguistic studies, it is quite important to bear in mind that word association responses also reflect other types of cognitive processes. Under the individually administered testing conditions I have described, the subject was actively encouraged to give the first word response that came to his mind and, by and large, all subjects did. A tendency to respond with opposite words, therefore, would directly reflect a tendency to associate opposites in thought. Moreover, precise timing of word association response provided an opportunity to compare the speed of opposite responding to other types of response. Giving opposite word responses rapidly, more rapidly than other types of responses, therefore, would reflect a tendency to rapid opposite associates in thinking.

As rapid associating of opposites would be expected to be a factor in janusian thinking, the experimental hypothesis was that subjects who were more creative would manifest a greater tendency toward rapid opposite response than less creative ones. Responses to the questionnaire served to distinguish two subject groups: one that was high in creative potential or accomplishment and another that was low. Evidence of independent initiative and early success in the creative arts or in science (included later as a criterion) classified a subject as a high creative and absence of such evidence led to classification as low creative. In previous research, this means of classifying subjects on the basis of responses to this questionnaire showed a significant correlation with independent creativity ratings by teachers and peers as well as subjects' ratings of their own creativity.[94] Specific evidence that the discriminating factor was creativity rather than scholastic aptitude was derived from assessing scores on the College Entrance Examination Aptitude Test. The two subject groups identified as high and low creative did not differ significantly on intelligence and aptitude as measured by that test ($t = 0.34$, $df = 111$).

All word association responses of all subjects were scored according to whether they were opposites on the basis of criteria for opposite response derived by the original experimenters, Carroll et al. Using an empirical consensual approach to classification, these investigators identified a list of words classified as opposite responses by four out of five experimenters and forty-two other judges. This list of responses classified as opposites appears in the column labelled "Opposite" on table 1.

Another type of scoring of responses was also necessary because of a special type of problem with the word stimuli from the standard Kent-Rosanoff list. As might be obvious, even to someone unfamiliar with word association, Kent-Rosanoff words are simple commonly used ones and opposite responses to these word stimuli are themselves also simple common words. Subjects might respond with opposites merely because their vocabulary is limited or because the words are frequently connected in common discourse. In order, therefore, to distinguish opposite responding from a tendency to give common or popular responses, it was necessary to score, as did Carroll and his collaborators, subjects' responses that correspond to those most commonly given on standard word association norms—that is, the "primary" or most common responses to standard word association stimuli. Word responses falling in this primary category are shown in the column labelled "Primary" on table 1. The table shows that a number of opposite responses—for example, "hot" as a response to "cold," "fast" as a response to "slow"—are also primary responses. In

Table 1. Stimulus Words and Opposite and Primary Responses

Stimulus Word	*Opposite*	*Primary*	*Stimulus Word*	*Opposite*	*Primary*	*Stimulus Word*	*Opposite*	*Primary*
table	. . .	chair*	foot	. . .	shoe*	hungry	full	food*
dark	light	light	spider	. . .	web*	priest	. . .	church*
music	. . .	sound*	needle	. . .	thread*	ocean	. . .	water*
sickness	health	health	red	. . .	white*	head	. . .	hair*
man	woman	woman	sleep	. . .	bed*	stove	. . .	heat*
deep	shallow	shallow	anger	. . .	mad*	long	short	short
soft	hard	hard	carpet	. . .	rug*	religion	. . .	God*
eating	. . .	food*	girl	boy	boy	whiskey	. . .	drink*
mountain	valley	hill*	high	low	low	child	. . .	baby*
house	. . .	home*	working	loafing	hard*	bitter	sweet	sweet
black	white	white	sour	sweet	sweet	hammer	. . .	nail*
mutton	. . .	sheep*	earth	. . .	dirt*	thirsty	. . .	water*
comfort	. . .	chair*	trouble	. . .	bad*	city	. . .	town*
hand	. . .	foot*	soldier	. . .	man*	square	round circle	round
short	long tall	tall	cabbage	. . .	vegetable*			
			hard	soft	soft	butter	. . .	bread*
fruit	. . .	apple*	eagle	. . .	bird*	doctor	. . .	nurse*
butterfly	. . .	moth*	stomach	. . .	food*	loud	soft	soft

smooth	rough	rough	stem	. . .	flower*	thief	. . .	steal*
command	. . .	order*	lamp	. . .	light*	lion	. . .	tiger*
sweet	sour / bitter	sour	dream	. . .	sleep*	joy	sorrow	happy*
			yellow	. . .	color*	bed	. . .	sleep*
whistle	. . .	train*	bread	. . .	butter*	heavy	light	light
woman	man	man	justice	injustice	law*	tobacco	. . .	smoke*
cold	hot / warm	hot	boy	girl	girl	baby	. . .	cry*
						moon	. . .	star*
			light	dark / heavy	dark	scissors	. . .	cut*
slow	fast / rapid	fast	health	sickness	sickness	quiet	noisy	loud*
wish	. . .	want*	bible	. . .	God*	green	. . .	grass*
river	. . .	water*	memory	. . .	mind*	salt	. . .	pepper*
white	black	black	sheep	. . .	wool*	street	. . .	road*
beautiful	ugly	girl*	bath	. . .	clean*	king	. . .	queen*
window	. . .	glass*	cottage	. . .	house*	cheese	. . .	mouse*
rough	smooth	smooth	swift	slow	fast*	blossom	. . .	flowers*
citizen	. . .	man*	blue	. . .	sky*	afraid	. . .	scared*

NOTE: Although several stimuli have clear opposite responses not given—e.g., comfort-discomfort; citizen-alien; sleep-wake; afraid-courageous—only the empirically determined opposites above (Carroll et al.) were scored.

* Nonopposite primaries.

the calculation of final results, therefore, still another response category was separated out, primaries that were not opposites or "nonopposite primary responses," in order to compare with and assess the tendency to give popular primary responses. Word responses in this category are shown by asterisk in the "Primary" column of table 1.[95]

Results are shown in tables 2 and 3. The mean percentage of opposite responses (to words considered to be opposite evoking) given by high creative subjects was considerably greater than the mean percentage of this type of responses by the low creative subjects (table 2). Statistically, this difference is significant at a probability of less than .0005 ($t = 6.46$, $df = 33$). Also, the mean percentage of opposite responses by the creative subjects was considerably greater than their mean percentage of nonopposite primary responses; they had a much greater tendency to give opposite responses than they did to give popular responses. The less-creative subjects also gave more opposite responses than nonopposite primaries, but the difference between the mean percentage of these two types of responses was considerably smaller than in the creative group. In fact, the less-creative group gave almost the same mean percentage of nonopposite primaries as the creative group. As the mean percentage of opposite responses was already significantly higher in the more creative group, the more creative subjects' tendency to respond with opposites rather than with primaries was also significantly greater than the same tendency in the less creative subjects. As there was little to no difference between the two types with respect to giving popular responses, the significant difference with respect to opposite responding shows a decisive comparison. Interestingly also, the creative subjects gave the larger percentage of opposite responses despite the fact that many opposites are very popular responses.

Table 2. Mean Percentages and Standard Deviations for Opposite and Nonopposite Primary Responses in the High-Creative and Low-Creative Groups

		High (n = 63)		*Low (n = 50)*	
Type of Score	*No. of Stimuli*	*M%*	*SD*	*M%*	*SD*
Opposites	34	50.77	26.80	40.77	23.66
Nonopposite primaries	65	25.75	18.83	26.57	19.27

NOTE: M% = mean percentage; n = number of subjects; SD = standard deviation.

Average time of response with respect to opposite and nonopposite primary response was also sharply different for the two types of subject as seen in table 3. More-creative subjects gave opposite responses more rapidly on the average than less-creative ones, a difference that was statistically significant at a probability of less than .0005 ($t = 5.25$, $df = 33$). Again, there was no significant difference between the two

Table 3. Means of Average Response Times and Standard Deviations for Opposite and Nonopposite Primary Responses in High-Creative and Low-Creative Groups

		High (n = 63)		Low (n = 50)	
Type of Score	*No. of Stimuli*	*M avg. Response Time (sec)*	*SD*	*M avg. Response Time (sec)*	*SD*
Opposites	34	1.24	.28	1.41	.37
Nonopposite primaries	65	1.53	.39	1.62	.48

NOTE: M avg. Response Time (sec) = mean of average times of response in seconds.

types of subjects in their rapidity of response with nonopposite primaries.[96] The tendency to respond faster with opposites than with nonopposite primaries was significantly greater for the more-creative subjects than for the less-creative ones. And the more-creative subjects' *average* time of response when giving opposites was so rapid, 1.24 seconds, it is probable that these words came generally into their minds immediately, or almost immediately, upon hearing the word stimuli.

In this experiment, then, rapid opposite response was clearly a characteristic of those subjects identified as more creative. If we had not been testing the janusian thinking construct, this result would in many ways be quite surprising. Opposite responding to several word stimuli on the standard Kent-Rosanoff word list is rather common and, as will be seen in the next chapter, several psycholinguists have developed explanations for this, explanations emphasizing a presumed simplicitly and ingrained nature of this type of response. As creative people put a very high premium on the uncommon and complex—at least so it generally seems—how could creativity be connected with a common and possibly simple type of response? The answer to this question is important for proper evaluation of this result. In the first place, I must emphasize a point that might have been missed in the description of the experiment. Many subjects give opposite responses to certain stimuli on the word association test, but, as Carroll and his colleagues first showed, certain subjects give opposite responses frequently and *characteristically.* In the Carroll et al. experiment, this type of characteristic opposite responding—this opposite responding tendency—was also connected to a tendency to give contrast responses, a category of response related to, but not identical with, opposite response. The tendency for subjects in the more-creative group of the current experiment to give contrast responses was extremely marked. The difference with respect to this response category between the more-creative subjects and the less-creative ones was even more statistically significant than the difference in opposite responding. Thus, there is a general and consistent tendency to a certain type of responding involving opposites and the related category of contrasts among more creative subjects. Creative subjects respond with common and even, in certain instances, simple opposites because of this strong and overriding tendency.

Actually, the use of common popular words is not, in itself, surprising in connection with creativity. Creative persons, even creative literary persons with extensive vocabularies, use common ordinary words quite frequently in their works, and they use them in new ways. Poets, for example, are often interested in converting banal phrases, clichés, and dead metaphors to new uses and new meanings. Creative literature does not at all require unusual words or even unusual subject matter but it requires a special ability to mold and structure words and subject matter, whether common or extraordinary. Giving common words and responses in this experiment resulted from the subjects' showing both the *oppositional structure* and the sometimes somewhat ordinary *content* of their thinking. Some degree of aversion to the common and popular does, of course, prevail among creative people, and these subjects were no exception. During the experiment, several subjects expressed dismay at their own tendencies to give plain and inelegant opposites as responses. Nevertheless these responses reflected the subjects' thinking tendency; every effort had been made to discourage and eliminate any distorting or biasing factors. The testers obscured the purpose of the experiment, allayed the subjects' anxieties, corrected misconceptions, and emphasized the importance of responding with the very first word that came to mind. Paper and pencil word association tests group-administered by psycholinguists do not provide for such safeguards and controls and therefore the connection between opposite responding and creativity would have been obscured with such techniques.

The result most pertinent to janusian thinking is that the findings involved not merely the tendency to respond with opposites but also the speed of opposite response. Janusian thinking is not merely a matter of conceiving opposites, opposite words, or opposite and antithetical ideas; it is the *simultaneous* conception of any or all of these. The more creative subjects gave opposite responses considerably more rapidly than the less creative ones even though the two groups were equal in intelligence and aptitude, factors which might have affected speed of response. And the creative subjects' speed of response was rapid enough to indicate the possibility of simultaneous conception of opposites in thought. Here, some obstacle or a reverse result might actually have been expected. Given a reluctance of creative people to respond in popular ways, some subjects might have hesitated before reporting some of their popular opposite responses.[97]

As some internal guarding and aversion to giving opposites must have occurred despite our safeguards and techniques, the emergence of the rapid opposite response pattern is rather influential evidence for the connection between janusian thinking and creativity. Although word association response is primarily indicative of associational rather than directed patterns of thought—word association is not a creative task and not a manifestation of the directed thought processes involved in producing a creation—the strong associational pathways, demonstrated in this experiment, very likely serve to set the stage for the active positing of simultaneous opposition or antithesis in the creative process. As the more creative subjects characteristically gave rapid opposite responses to the standard word association list, even though there may have been some aversion to do so, the association patterns would seem to be rather powerful and persistent. Rather than responding rapidly with opposites because several are simple, popular words (N.B.: all of the nonopposite primaries are simple and popular), of course, the more creative subjects respond in this fashion because of the pattern of their thought processes.

In another experiment carried out in an essentially similar manner, subjects were a group of thirty-four successful business executives. Engaged in managing two different institutions, a bank and a silver manufacturing corporation, these executives performed a wide range of functions, including designing, marketing, and sales, as well as personnel administration. Degree of creativity was again assessed on the basis of information about independent initiative and successful performance in creative areas, and a modified form of the special questionnaire used in the previous experiment was administered.

In order to carry out a more specific assessment of the relationship between rapid opposite response and creativity than in the previous experiment, results on the word association test were analyzed somewhat differently. Rather than calculating opposite, nonopposite primary response and response times for the subjects as a group, these scores were calculated for each individual. Tendency to rapid opposite response was independently defined and the presence or absence of such a tendency was determined for the individual subject. Presence of the rapid opposite response tendency was designated on the basis of two combined criteria: (1) an opposite responding score consisting of an absolute number of opposite responses larger than the absolute number of nonopposite primaries; (2) a rapid opposite measurement consisting of an average speed of opposite response at least 0.05 seconds faster than the average speed of nonopposite primary response.[98] Any other combinations, such as a rapid opposite measurement without an opposite responding score and vice versa, were designated as an absence of the rapid opposite response tendency.

Results of this experiment were in the same direction as the previous. There was a statistically significant association (chi-square = 8.76, $p < 0.05$) between the presence of the rapid opposite response tendency and questionnaire-measured high degrees of creativity. Among successful business executives, the tendency to rapid opposite response, and assumedly therefore to janusian thinking, is associated with creativity.

A side product of these experiments was the development of a method for identifying persons with creative potential. One of the practical values of the scoring method used with business executives is that it determines a tendency in individuals to rapid opposite responding, and by extension, to janusian thinking. Applied to the easily administered Kent-Rosanoff test, the scoring method is relatively easy. Also, the widely used test can be administered along with a battery of other tests without the subject being at all aware of its function as a measure of creativity.[99] More word association experiments are required, however, in order to extend the results I have reported and to establish the best testing procedure for identifying creative potential. While the Kent-Rosanoff stimuli evoke word responses that are clearly recognized as opposites, such opposites are rather superficial and easily conceived. Essentially, creative thinking involves complex and recondite, rather than superficial, opposition. A more clear-cut means of identifying creative potential, and a more specific experiment regarding janusian thinking, would therefore involve the use of word stimuli that evoke opposites which are not primary responses, that is, nonprimary or nonpopular opposites. With such stimuli, it would not be necessary to compute both opposite and nonopposite primary scores, but opposite scores alone would suffice. I have carried out pretesting of a list (see chap. 8) evoking such nonpopular opposites and other types of responses.

I have alluded repeatedly to the subtleties and complexities of the factor of opposition; it is now time to explore them and clarify them in greater detail. Moreover, I have said little about the nature of janusian thinking as a psychological process that is both distinct from and related to other psychological processes. Exploring these aspects—opposition, and the psychological nature of janusian thinking—will lead us through psycholinguistics, philosophy, and diverse aspects of psychological theory.

8

OPPOSITION AND CREATIVITY

A story: It is a rainy day, a mother and her eighteen-month-old child are caught in the house all day. In order to amuse her child, the mother puts him in his playpen and surrounds him with toys. Almost immediately, the child begins to cry, wanting to get out. The mother then puts him on the living room floor and decides to let him follow her while she vacuums the rug, an activity he usually enjoys. At first, it works; happily, the child toddles and crawls after her. A few minutes later, however, he is crying again. Now, she finds him on the outside of the playpen, alternately trying to reach one of the toys inside or attempting to climb back in. She puts him inside and the cycle is repeated. At lunchtime, she serves him his favorite sandwich, peanut butter and jelly. He hardly touches it and, not wanting to make a fuss about his eating, she clears the table and lets him get down from his chair. Twenty minutes later, he complains of hunger and asks for his sandwich. Further into the afternoon, he responds to his mother's toilet training program and agrees to go to the potty when she asks him. Nothing happens there and ten minutes later he has soiled his diaper. Alternating cycles with food and play are repeated. Finally, at the end of the day when the father comes home, the first words out of the mother's mouth are: "I don't know what to do with our child; whatever I want him to do, he does the *opposite.*"

Another story: A seven-year-old child in an open classroom setting containing school children of various ages and levels is sitting with his group using Cuisinere rods for learning arithmetic. After a fairly concentrated period of working alone, his interest declines somewhat and he spies a child in the group on the other side of the room making a model with a piece of shiny tinfoil. He gets up and starts over to the other group. When the teacher asks him where he's going, he says, "I'm going to the *opposite* side of the room."

The last: Ten-year-old children are doing a review assignment during their English period in school. They are asked to write the antonyms of a series of words in blank spaces next to the words. The words are: slow, tall, fat, hard, sharp, smooth, white, fair, always. They have previously been told what the antonyms to these words were and all but a few students do the assignment easily and rapidly. The dictionary definition of an antonym is: a word *opposite* in meaning to another.

All of the stories, of course, contain a reference to opposition and each story pertains to a different period of childhood development. Are the types of opposition couched in these examples related to the opposition intrinsic to janusian thinking? Or, put more dramatically, is it possible that these homely experiences pertaining to opposition in childhood have anything to do with creativity, the exalted and hallowed capacity of man? Let us see.

On first approach, opposition might seem to be a rather simple and straightforward entity, so simple and straightforward that—as my own examples might suggest—"even a child can understand it." The opposites of words such as slow, tall, and fat are clearly and unequivocally fast, short, and thin, and the seven-year-old child uses the word "opposite" correctly with respect to a side of the room. Psycholinguists have recently been impressed by the frequent and facile use of verbal opposition by experimental subjects carrying out verbal learning and association tasks, and by the universality of opposition or binary contrasts in all languages. Viewed from the perspective of the features or linguistic characteristics of words, some psycholinguists have alleged an apparently minimal difference between antonyms or opposite words consisting only of a change of sign from positive to negative or vice versa.[1] But I must now emphatically point out that the simplicity of opposition is more apparent than real. For one thing, there is an important difference between linguistic opposition and conceptual or logical opposition.

Linguistic and Logical Opposition

Linguistic opposition is a fairly easy category to identify by empirical means. Certain words are readily considered to be the opposite of other words on the basis of ingrained and constant association. Thus, when one asks for the opposite of "low," the response will almost invariably be "high," although "elevated," "lofty," and "soaring" might also be acceptable on logical grounds. "High" is given as a response not necessarily because it is the logically perfect opposite but because the two words "low" and "high" are commonly associated with each other in speech and writing. Nevertheless, this linguistic pairing between "low" and "high" produces no conceptual complexities; high *is* logically opposite to low. Difficulties arise when considering a pair such as man and woman, or, better still, king and queen. For, when experimental subjects are asked for the opposites of man and king, the responses are almost invariably woman and queen, respectively.

Such responses must give us pause because they invite a consideration of the logical grounds for the pairing. After all, leaving aside formal dictionary definitions for the moment, we always think of opposition as consisting of some sense of sharp or radical difference. Positing that queen is the opposite of king is somewhat logically jarring because the king-queen pairing seems to conjure up more similarities than differences. Kings and queens are nobility, they share more in common with each other than they share with any of us, etc. Their only difference is their gender and, in the ultimate scheme of things—aside from the unisex obliteration of gender difference in current times—this seems too minor to warrant the clear designation of queen as true opposite to king. Some would argue that commoner or slave are better opposites to king, but there are problems with those solutions as well. So, too, the prior opposition between man and woman—prior in the sense that it enters into the king-queen pairing—is subject to question. We are aware of the so-called opposition in sex between man and woman but are equally aware of their shared similarities, such as humanness and maturity.

One of the factors involved in the logical discrepancies I have just cited is the matter of logical context, whether or not man or king is viewed in one or in several contexts. But before I get into this thorny issue, and the related one of the knowledge or sophistication of the person making judgments of opposites, I must stick with the difference between linguistic and conceptual opposition. The root meaning of the word "oppose," the basic term from which our words opposite and opposition derive, is simply "to put against." Without recourse to a lengthy and in this case essentially digressive account of dictionary definitions, I think few would disagree that current usage of the term falls into the following two broad and related categories: (1) "oppose" as being against or as providing resistance to an idea, act, command, etc.; (2) "oppose" as being contrary or radically different. Thus opposition means either resistance or conflict or being situated in a contrary or a radically different mode. There are implied issues of similarity, too, but I will come to that in a moment.

The term antonym, as I have said, refers to opposition of words. A cursory familiarity with some of the attempts to establish an adequate definition of this term for classification purposes—I now am referring to definitions in synonym-antonym dictionaries—illustrates the point I am making about the difference between linguistic and conceptual opposition. Webster's provides the best example. After a lengthy discussion of the complications and nuances regarding various definitions of an antonym, the editors of Webster's finally opt for the most restrictive and logically consistent definition possible: "a word so opposed in meaning to another word, its equal in breadth or range of application, that it negates or nullifies every single one of its implications."[2] Examples of such antonyms are perfect-imperfect, black-white, and admit-reject. In order to use this definition in the word classification scheme within the dictionary, a task covering *normative* as well as *common* ordinary word use, the editors find it necessary to stipulate other types of word categories related to antonyms such as complementaries, relatives, and contrasts. This highly precise and reliable dictionary, in other words, recognizes a sharp discrepancy between the logical definition of antonyms and ordinary linguistic usage. In order to represent both aspects, the editors use a special classification scheme.

Linguistic opposition consists of all categories of verbal relationships commonly used to denote antonyms or opposites. Categories designated by Webster's both as relative terms, terms that appear in pairs and suggest one another such as husband and wife, and as complementary terms, pair terms that are incomplete without each other such as question and answer, are forms of linguistic opposition. In these categories, linguistic experience—that is, frequent association in speech and writing—dictates the designation of opposition more than strictly applied logical or conceptual criteria.

One of the reasons that opposition is sometimes thought to be simple and straightforward is that linguistic opposition is often not distinguished from conceptual opposition. Terms such as man and woman, husband and wife, and question and answer seem to differ only in one aspect or merely by having positive and negative qualities. But when more restrictive logical criteria are applied, such as Webster's nullification of "every single one of its implications," opposition becomes a far more complicated matter. With regard to the examples I cited earlier pertaining to opposition with respect to childhood experiences, the matter is more complicated still.

Opposition as a Concept

To clarify the import of my childhood examples, I will shift away from opposition between words, antonym classification, to the concept of opposition itself. While the distinction between linguistic and logical opposition continues to be borne in mind, I shall return to the two broad categories I mentioned before, resistance and being contrary or radically different. As I suggested in passing above, these categories are not sufficient alone for an adequate definition of opposition; some issue of similarity is implied and must be incorporated. Opposites must be similar to each other in some particular respect in order to be considered opposed; they must, that is, be *specifically* resistant to each other or *specifically* different. Mere negation or absence of a quality or qualities does not produce opposition, it only produces nonspecific difference. Thus, not-tall is not a proper opposite of tall because not-tall could simply indicate regular or medium or even gigantic in size. Short is the proper opposite of tall, and short is a designation with definite properties of its own, properties which are specifically different from tallness.[3] Because the properties relate to each other in this way, both short and tall are placed in the same conceptual category—they are both dimensions within the category of height. Absence of resistance does not constitute opposition; in an argument, points of view must pertain to the same category in order to be considered opposed. There is a reciprocity in all opposition; applying the term "tall" to a particular person or a particular measurement intrinsically determines the general range of short, and vice versa for applying the term "short." Such categorical relatedness and reciprocity is a feature of all opposition, and therefore the proper definition should include "resistant or radically different as well as reciprocal within the same category."

In saying this, it is immediately necessary to add a caution: because opposites invariably belong to the same category, one cannot therefore say that essentially opposites are the same, as some have suggested.[4] To do so not only begs the logic of the matter, but requires extensive assumptions about the nature of reality.

With this more precise definition of opposition, let us return to the first of the childhood examples. The mother, confronting the highly common type of behavior in an eighteen-month-old child, describes it to her husband as doing the opposite. In using the term, she is not, of course, concerned with definitions or with the weighty considerations just outlined, but she is saying what most people would, and have, said about this phase of childhood: eighteen month olds tend to be negativistic and oppositional. The question I want to consider, however, is whether this term is appropriately used, not for semantic reasons but in order to assess the status of opposition as a concept or behavioral mode at this level of development. Is it correct to describe the child's behavior as oppositional and, if so, is the child aware of opposing?

Our best understanding of the child's behavior and thought at this level is that he is in the early throes of identity formation, more precisely, that he is beginning to individuate. Following the long period of extensive dependency, during which the child gradually develops a sense of differentiation from his parents and from his environment, there is a rather sharp spurt of activity at this age, activity that seems to function to help the child differentiate himself further and to gain some sense of himself as an individual. Such activity, however, is not clear and consistent; the child does not adopt a pattern of asserting his own will or his desires in a constant way, he is quite willy-nilly about it. Characteristically, in fact, he seems to be indecisive, going back and forth over the same ground or reversing previous behavior. Toilet training can, of course, be a particular focus—possibly an instigating factor—in the spurt of individuating behavior at this age level. Toilet training usually involves a fairly consistent attempt, on the parents' part, to impose their wishes upon the child while offering little compensation, gratification, or reward outside of verbal encouragement or praise. By that I mean that verbal encouragement is less palpable than the food gratification associated with learning to eat on schedule earlier. In any event, the child is beginning to explore, with a vengeance, his own wants and needs now, and sometimes he tries things for their own sake and sometimes he does something because it is merely different from what the parent wants. From the parents' point of view, however, there are few clues to any distinctions between various aspects of the child's behavior. For the mother, it seems as though everything the child does is in direct resistance to her, or in defiance of her needs and wishes; the child appears to be *opposing* her.

Precious little about the child's behavior is really oppositional, however, and, as a corollary, there is little justification for believing that the child knows what opposition is, either as an experienced mode of behavior or as a concept. He probably knows the word, "opposite," and some of its referents by now—if not, he has just heard his mother use it to describe his behavior to his father—but such a small part of his behavior is directed against his mother, and he feels so minimally differentiated as a person that there is little basis for cognitive and/or affective appreciation of the meaning of the word.[5]

So far, I assume, there is no quibble with the argument I have proposed. The child himself does not use the word "opposite" and he is so young that most would be willing intuitively to acknowledge the lack of comprehension I describe. But now we come to the more complicated example of the seven-year-old child who actually uses the word to indicate the place he is going, the "opposite" side of the room. And here I would insist that there is still no comprehension of the meaning of opposition, merely the use of a word that the child has *learned,* through repeated association, to apply to that position in space. Furthermore, in order to reveal the full dimensions of this point I am making, I will quickly add that, in my final example of children performing an antonym task, there is also no way of being sure whether each of them understands the meaning of opposition, even when the child performs the task successfully.

I have chosen these examples of opposition at various stages of childhood in order to clarify a potential source of confusion. In considering the development status of a concept or an intellectual operation, it is important to make a distinction between comprehension or a meaningful grasp, and use on the basis of learned association. In other words, when I raise the question about whether children understand opposition, whether there is comprehension of the concept of opposition or of its operational usage, many will immediately respond, "Why, of course, they understand, they use the word quite early (as shown in the example)." Word use and comprehension are not equivalent, however. When the child says that he is going to the opposite side of the room, it is not certain whether he is merely using the word "opposite" as a synonym for the word "other," the other side of the room, because he has frequently heard the words "opposite" and "other" used interchangeably, such as in "cross to the other side of the street," or "cross to the opposite side of the street."

In the case of the children performing the antonym task, it is not certain whether most give the correct answers because they have previously been told which words were called antonyms or whether they actually grasp the intellectual operation involved in identifying such antonyms. And it remains unclear even when they are able to supply the definition of an antonym; many or most may not understand the idea of opposite in the antonym definition, they may be repeating from memory.

It is easy to check what is going on in an individual case, of course. The child using the word opposite to refer to a side of the room or to "other" will eventually make tell-tale mistakes in usage, and the children supplying the antonym answers from memory will be unable to supply antonyms on an unrehearsed list. Those who take the trouble to make the assessment find that such errors and failings frequently do occur at both the seven- and ten-year-old levels. Use of the word "opposite" is not evidence for comprehension of the concept of opposition in childhood. In an experiment carried out with 100 high intellectual and social status level children ranging in age from five to seven and a half years, Kreezer and Dallenbach discovered that the children would often say that they understood the meaning of the word or idea "opposite," but, when asked to give opposites to an unrehearsed series of words, they could not do so. Few children in the group gave evidence that they understood the opposition relation despite saying they understood the meaning. None below the age of six and a half understood it at all and only seven out of twenty of the seven and a half year olds showed any grasp of it.[6]

Though opposition applies to concrete and spatial phenomena, as a relation it is a purely abstract, and for a child, therefore, a difficult concept. Unlike symmetry or sameness, which derive fairly readily from perceived repetitions in the concrete world, nothing in nature is opposite unless we define it so. Opposition is relative, it depends on establishing a reference point and relating other points to it: "this side is opposite to that," "that side is opposite this." Not even left and right, which are also relative and notoriously difficult for a child to keep straight, are as complicated as opposition. One side is designated as left and the other as right, but then, as the child learns, the right side can never be left side nor vice versa. Fixed are the terms and their concrete referents and therefore the relationship eventually is grasped. Depending on the circumstances, however, either or both left and right can be labeled as opposites, and that is confusing.

Two further research findings, one focused on cognitive development and the other on language acquisition, tend to support the thesis that opposition is grasped fairly late in childhood. Piaget and Inhelder, whose extensive and outstanding research on the development of logic in childhood can only be touched on here, present findings about the acquisition of the notion of complementarity, negation, and duality which bear on the issue. While they have much to say about these concepts in general, I will, for the moment, focus on their work on the "null class." I will quote their posing of the question about this classification because their particular manner of presentation is of interest. For those not familiar with Piagetian terminology, the term "formal operations" in the following quotation roughly coincides with abstract or logical thinking and "concrete operations" is a type of thinking characteristic of a prelogical phase of development.

> There is . . . [a] question relevant to the dividing line between concrete and formal operations: the question of the null or empty class. "Elementary groupings" of classes imply this notion, for if $A = B - A'$, then $B - A - A' = 0$ (or, more simply, $A - A = 0$). Also, $A \cap A' = 0$. In other words, a class becomes empty when subtracted from itself, and the intersection of two disjoint classes is empty. From a strictly operational point of view, the child of 7–8 years may be said to understand the operation $+ A - A = 0$, insofar as he knows that adding A, and then taking it away, is equivalent to doing nothing, i.e. $+ 0$. But, since concrete operations apply to objects and the empty class has no objects, we may well ask whether a child is likely to think of it as being on a par with other classes? This is not at all a question of operational manipulation. We know that zero was the last number discovered in arithmetic and that it was long after the invention of addition and subtraction (from which it results by virtue of the equation $n - n = 0$) that it was recognized as a true number. We might therefore follow up our study of complementarity and negation by finding out how children at different levels, will deal with a situation where a complementary class exists, as a class, but contains no objects and is therefore the null class.[7]

This presentation of the question is of interest because, aside from its valuable and clear specification of the nature of the null class, the reference to the historical background of the acquisition of the concept of zero in arithmetic introduces a pertinent analogy. Inhelder and Piaget suggest that the difficulty of developing an intellectual operation in childhood is paralleled in the culture; the more difficult the concept in childhood, the later and more difficult has it been to acquire or use in the historical development of knowledge. To return, however, to their findings, findings that are based on presentation of classification tasks to several children, I will again quote directly:

> "a class without any elements is . . . incompatible with the logic of "concrete" operations, i.e. operations in which form is inseparably bound up with content. That is why the null class is rejected right up to the time when the structure of inclusion relations [differentiating "some" and "all"] begins to be separated from their concrete content, at 10–11 years.[8]

These findings of the late development of comprehension of negation are further supported by a host of cognitive and linguistic experiments by others indicating difficulty in dealing with negative information and negative statements in adulthood as well.[9]

I have said that negation, or nullity in the Piaget and Inhelder research, is not the same as opposition. More must be included in the definition of opposition than negation alone and that is a specific contrariness or resistance and, hence, a factor of similarity. Nevertheless, with respect to the task of identifying classes, I think it is reasonable to assume that the capacity to form negative or null classes is intrinsic to the capacity to comprehend and to use the opposition relation. To return to the example of students giving antonyms in class: if the child were asked to give the antonym to an unrehearsed word, say "light," and he knew both the words "dim" and "dark," it would be necessary for him to be able to conceive the class of total absence of light before he could decide that "dark" is the proper term. As another instance, for the antonym of "hot," he requires facility with the null class to decide between "cool" and "cold." The task becomes even more difficult when picking antonym pairs among "crooked," "circular," and "straight."

With respect to the matter of similarity in the opposition relation, this further complicates the concept for the child. I did not mean to suggest just now that the antonym task is approached by children, or anyone else for that matter, in some stepwise fashion such as thinking of the null class first and then picking a word related to the one presented. Nor is the solution found specifically by thinking of similar words and then deciding which belong closest to the null class. Words also similar to light are: bright, daytime, shiny, radiant, and glowing; and it is highly doubtful that such a diversity of associations is evoked in performing an antonym task. Grasp of opposition involves the capacity to use nullity, negation, and similarity in varying ways, all together and/or in sequence. The comprehension of similarity required to understand opposition, moreover, is not merely of the type involved in concrete operations, the recognition of similarity between objects. Understanding similarity with respect to opposition, and applying this understanding to the recognition and production of antonyms or other opposites, requires what Piaget has called the idea of the principle of conservation (what logicians call the "logic of relations").[10] The child must have mastered this idea in order to be able to comprehend that the specific features of two given opposites do not change despite their apparent differences. Horizontal and vertical, for instance, retain a common feature called direction despite differences in name and sharp differences in information, feeling, and effects. Characteristically, according to Piaget, understanding of this principle of conservation only begins at about nine years of age. Added then to the difficulty of understanding the null case is the ten-year-old child's only rudimentary appreciation of the stable feature of similarity in the opposition relation.

From linguistic studies of word association patterns of young children comes further evidence pertinent to opposition and development. Administering word association tests to 1,140 urban students at prekindergarten, kindergarten, first-grade, third-grade, and fifth-grade levels in Baltimore County, Maryland, Entwisle found that a very small percentage of responses to opposite evoking stimulus words by kindergarten and first-grade children consisted of opposites.[11] On the third-grade or nine-year-old level, however, percentage of opposite responses was markedly higher than at the earlier levels and, in the case of some stimulus words, the percentage of opposite responses was four times greater in the older group.[12] Such results, marked as they are, cannot be considered direct evidence for comprehension of opposition at the older levels because of the independence between conceptualization and word use or so-called linguistic habits in childhood. The upsurge of opposite word associations does, however, suggest an increased tendency toward connecting opposite words at the age of nine and later, a tendency that very likely sets the stage for the understanding of the opposition relation that develops during the Piagetian phase of formal operations. Children often use words in an exploratory way, prior to the full comprehension of the referents of the words and as a means of achieving fuller comprehension. A conclusive finding, however, is the markedly low percentage of opposite associations at younger ages. At the kindergarten and first-grade level, the average percentage of opposite response to opposite evoking stimuli was 6.8 and 16.2, respectively as compared with 45–50 percent averages characteristic of college age adults.[13] Surely there is no reason to assume that six and seven year olds have less general exposure than do older children to such common opposite combinations as are elicited by the standard word association test, nor are particular words such as hot, cold, long, or black missing from their vocabularies. The virtual absence of opposite associations, therefore, is strong evidence for a corollary lack of perceived connectedness between words denoting opposites and a lack of comprehension of the opposition relations at these earlier age levels.

Sharply distinct from the lack of conceptual comprehension of opposition is the well-known tendency of children to think in simple dualisms, many of which have oppositional content. Terms such as good and bad, big and small, childish and grown-up, are among children's earliest verbal acquisitions and they constantly classify their experiences into these categories throughout childhood. This tendency to formulate simple dualisms does not end abruptly with the arrival at adolescence or the exalted state of adulthood. In an extensive investigation carried out at Harvard University, a group of investigators documented the large-scale persistence of dualistic thinking in adolescence and early adulthood. These investigators went on to propose, moreover, that the transition away from dualistic thinking to an appreciation of pluralism and more advanced types of conceptualization was the hallmark of mature intellectual and ethical development.[14] For the purposes of our discussion here, it is unnecessary to go into a lengthy digression at this point about the nature of dualistic thinking in childhood and the parents' role in instigating and encouraging it, nor is it necessary to trace manifestations of dualistic thinking in adulthood and evaluate the effects. For that matter, dualistic conceptions of the nature of the world, of the relationship of mind and body, and dualistic theories about virtually every aspect of human experience have been formulated throughout the history of intellectual thought. I want merely to emphasize that thinking in opposites, such as forming dichotomies between good and bad, may relate more to dualistic types of thinking than it does to the grasp of opposition I have discussed. As for the general topic of thinking in opposites, dualistic or not, and related matters of unification and flow of opposites, all of which have interested philosophers and other thinkers, I shall return to these shortly.

The distinction between dualism and grasp of opposition brings us to the heart of the complexities, and incidentally the power, of opposition as a concept. Comparing dualism and opposition, we must immediately realize that opposites are not merely dual or binary but that there are also multiple opposites; binary opposition, therefore, is only one of the forms. Given that important clarification, I want to consider some other distinctions pertaining to opposition, many of which are analogous: binary and polar opposition; "scale" and "cut" opposition;[15] qualitative and quantitative opposition; opposites and contraries, contrasts, and contradictions. Considering these differentiations, the abstract nature of opposites and of the opposition relation becomes strikingly apparent.

Of all the types of opposition, binary opposition is usually the most frequently thought of, and most readily applied, in tasks requiring strictly logical application of the concept. This should be no surprise because binary opposition derives more closely than other types from tangible and irreducible spatial experience. The simplest way of forming a binary opposition is first to produce a dichotomy and then to define both parts as opposite to each other. This is exemplified spatially through a demarcation on the ground or on a surface produced by a fence or more sharply by a chasm. The chasm example is probably the most vivid one, and it led C. K. Ogden to formulate the term "cut" for this type of opposition. "Cut" refers to opposition produced when two areas, factors, or classes are related or compared to each other. The left side of the chasm or cut is thus always opposite the right side, the near side is always opposite the far side and vice versa, and so on. Important to note is that this type of opposition involves complete contradictions; the cut produces complete separation of the two sides. In distinction to the opposition of cut, Ogden proposed the term "scale" to refer to the oppositional relationship of the extremes of a series. Thus, hot and cold, darkness and light, and empty and full are oppositions of scale, while enemy and friend, citizen and alien, and here and there are oppositions of cut. This distinction essentially coincides with a distinction between oppositions designated as either binary or polar, either qualitative or quantitative, as well as a distinction between contradiction and contrariness. Although scalar or polar opposites such as darkness and light could also be compared to each other in an either-or cut or binary fashion, they are more appropriately considered the extremes or poles of a series or scale. In addition, though the difference between hot and cold could be considered qualitative, that is, sharply distinct or cut apart on the basis of contradictory sensory qualities, just as citizen and alien are distinct on the basis of a quality or attribute of belonging or not belonging to a group or country, hot is more knowledgeably distinguished from cold in a quantitative way, that is, as a matter of degree. So, too, contradiction and contrariness tend to be distinguished in terms of quantity and matters of degree.

We cannot progress very far in a discussion such as this before exceptions are raised and assertions are challenged—because opposition is such an abstract concept. Moreover, it is a concept which, in its application to the world of things and ideas, admits of much relativity. The sharp critic, therefore, who is constantly on the lookout for lapses of logic and of definition, will immediately challenge my equating of binary, cut, and qualitative opposition. After all, he will say, when you compare darkness and light or hot and cold with each other, you only consider two elements each time. Yet you forswear calling that binary opposition and opt for the polar type. Also, you said earlier that there were multiple oppositions as well as binary ones and therefore you disclaimed dualism, but don't multiple oppositions of cut merely consist of repetitions of the very aspect you disclaim, namely dualisms over and over again? And one more point: I noticed you used the terms "knowledgeably" and "appropriately" distinguished to justify your examples of differentiations between scale, cut, qualitative, and quantitative, but who decides about such knowledge and appropriateness? Is the physicist talking about degrees of illumination or the electrician measuring the wattage of a bulb using the terms darkness and light more appropriately and more knowledgeably than the writer who describes scenes and sensations? For that matter, why aren't the designations zero and peak luminosity more appropriate scalar oppositions than darkness and light, respectively?

Yes, these criticisms and questions are all relevant, though not, I believe, fatal, because the answer in each case is the same: opposition is always a matter of context. When darkness and light or hot and cold are used in a context that highlights or specifies their sensory differences, then they are related according to qualitative, binary, or cut opposition; when they are taken out of that context and related directly to each other, the implied opposition is usually scalar, polar, or quantitative. So, too, most oppositions of scale can be transformed into oppositions of cut and vice versa, depending on the context. As scientific and other knowledge increases, the extremes of previously determined scales are changed.

Multiple opposition also depends on context. A simple example is the opposition arising from the multiple meanings of certain words: light is the opposite of dark or darkness and also of heavy. Another example comes from shifts of reference points on certain scales: shallow and elevated are, from one perspective or context, opposites, but shallow is also the opposite of deep or profound when the context is reversed. Many forms of multiple opposition, particularly those appearing in art, are far more complex than that, moreover. In art, different contexts of meaning, word nuance, and metaphorical use are employed to produce multiple oppositions. Depending on context, death is opposed to life, birth, or resurrection, but it is also more remotely opposed to spring, growth, sexuality, procreation, and bright colors. While many of these oppositions are derived from a dichotomy and are therefore examples of the binary or cut type, others are clearly derived from a context where some form of scale is implied.

The importance of context in defining and understanding instances of opposition helps clarify the confusing state of affairs pertaining to linguistic and logical opposition. Because context is crucial to all opposition, there should be no critical difference between these two types. Linguistic oppositions are appropriately considered to be opposed according to rules of logic, but such logic pertains strongly to the realities of the linguistic context. Linguistic oppositions differ from purely logical or conceptual ones in that the former are linked together by habitual association. Language patterns, in other words, take primacy over advances in knowledge, ideological shifts, and other factors playing a role in establishing logical contexts.

Returning now to our earlier controversial example of man opposed to woman, we see the following take place: man and woman are two classifications within the category of sex. If we admit into this category intermediate forms such as hermaphrodite, then we are liable to consider man and woman as scalar, polar, or quantitative opposites. If we do not admit intermediates, we have formed a dichotomous category in which man and woman are binary, cut, or qualitative opposites. For both alternatives, there is a defined and accepted designation of opposition, an opposition that pervades linguistic usage in all languages and is incorporated as a grammatical principle in some, and an opposition that has been adopted into the systems of philosophers, theologians, scientists as well as electricians. But then logic intervenes. By logic here I do not mean strict attention to the adequacy of the gender category and its classifications; questions could be raised about that at the start. I mean logic as influenced by increases in knowledge and changes in ideology. Informed by scientific knowledge of intersexuality in anatomy and physiology, as well as in psychological makeup, and influenced by humanism, women's liberation, or some other ideological shift of context, logic declares that man and woman are, by no means, opposite. There is far more in common than not. If we compare men and women to rocks and trees, there is absolutely no doubt about it.

Linguistic opposition is not supravened by such logic, ideology or what-have-you. Most people, despite highly ingrained convictions or extensive scientific knowledge will, when asked to state the opposite of "man," reflexly say "woman," and the term "opposite sex" will probably never die. There is no real reason that it should, moreover. Not only are linguistic oppositions perfectly respectable, given an understanding of their contexts, but they have considerable psychological importance. And now, to introduce one more term at the possible risk of alienating my readers: "psychological opposition" is, after all, the matter which most concerns us here. Psychological opposition includes both the linguistic and logical forms.

Psychological Opposition

The factors of contradiction, contrariness, and contrast provide a useful means for discussing the common ground between linguistic and logical opposition. Although contradiction and contrariness are both primarily negative operations, and therefore not actually opposition types, they enter into the opposition relation as well as the more inclusive relation of contrast. Far less stringent a relation than opposition, contrast depends less on a particular context, or an extreme difference. Defined either through contradiction or contrariness, or both together, no full dichotomy nor scale need be involved. Most linguistic oppositions, because they have lost connection with their initial oppositional context through intervening logic, information, and ideology, probably belong within this more general category of contrast.

Like opposition, contrast requires similarity as well as difference. While neither point for point contradiction nor a scale of contrariness is necessary between elements in a contrast, there is relatedness and specificity. Circles and squares, for instance, are contrasts in that they are both geometric forms but are specifically different in overall shape; circles and spheres or circles and trees are not contrasts, however, because they are either too similar or too nonspecifically different, respectively. The line between contrast and mere difference is, in many cases, hard to draw. While contrast does not require as much specificity of context as does opposition, some designation of context is necessary to distinguish contrasting factors from merely different ones. With respect to colors, for example, red and brown of the same value are merely different unless we refer to contrasting brightness. Even red and yellow are not considered contrasts by everyone. Factors such as hue, tint, and lighting must be considered and defined before designating color contrasts. To say, "today's weather is a welcome contrast to yesterday's" indicates more than difference because a dimension or context is specified; today's weather differs in that it is *better* than yesterday's.

The designation of "extreme" contrast is, on logical grounds, equivalent to opposition, as such a designation indicates a polar relation having both similarity and specific difference. The term "contrast" alone is quite general, however, and both logical and linguistic oppositions are often subsumed within it. The use of the term and the idea of contrast, therefore, is an instance of psychologically defined opposition. Many people designate contrasts as equivalent to opposites because the two categories are psychologically experienced as similar.

Opposition and Intellectual Thought

In his impressive book on opposition mentioned earlier, Ogden pays a good deal of attention to Aristotle, whom he describes as "obsessed by the problem of opposition." Claiming that Aristotle regards everything as proceeding from contraries, he also cites this philosopher's considerations of Unity and Multiplicity as well as Being and Not-Being in the *Metaphysics,* the deliberations on the causal aspect of opposition and on the Dense and the Rare, the Full and the Empty, the High and the Low in the *Physics,* and he suggests that Aristotelian ethics is based on a theory of contraries in which virtue is a mean between extremes. Ogden also discusses the key importance of opposition in the philosophies of the pre-Socratic thinkers Heraclitus, Xenophanes, and Parmenides, and later in the works of Saint Thomas Aquinas (Material and Subsistent forms), Nicholas of Cusa, Boehme, Kant, and Hegel. For the last mentioned, of course, opposition explicitly dominated his entire philosophical system, and Ogden argues that Kant's expositors have often missed the general importance of opposition—that is, Inner-Outer, Unity-Multiplicity, Activity-Passivity, Spontaneity-Receptivity, and Understanding-Sense—in that great thinker's deliberations and conclusions.[16] Continuing an historical account, Ogden cites in the nineteenth century the works of Schopenhauer, Hartmann, Rehmke, and Spencer as focused in a large degree on opposites and opposition. Ludwig Fischer, also of the nineteenth century, gave the topic systematic philosophical consideration. Finally, there was the late-nineteenth-century social philosopher Tarde, whose extensive exploration and classification contained in *L'Opposition Universale* was the first application to an understanding of social forces.

To extend Ogden's account of the emphasis on opposition in intellectual history, another important pre-Socratic philosopher, Anaximander, conceived that the construction of the world consisted of the separating out of elemental opposites, such as fire and water, from a primitive togetherness, the "boundless." These opposites were then in constant conflict with each other, an undeniable fact of nature according to Anaximander, and from this conflict and the equilibrium between the opposites, all understanding of the universe arose. Empedocles, Pythagoras, and Heraclitus as well conceived of the world as composed of opposites. Heraclitus emphasized the unity of opposites or their constant equality in the face of conflict; he used the term "enantiodromia," opposites flowing into each other, to describe an overall principle or law. Empedocles specified four sensible opposites, the hot, the cold, the wet, and the dry as making up the entire "Sphere of Being." Pythagoras and his followers specified particular opposites, probably ten ascribed to them by Aristotle[17] (limit-unlimited; odd-even; one-many; right-left; male-female; rest-motion; straight-curved; light-dark; good-bad; square-oblong), as the major categories through which they understood the world. Although Ogden's extensive listing includes Plato's basing his theory of ideas on contradictions between this world and the eternal as unchangeable and perfect, it does not include Socrates' famous argument for immortality in the *Phaedo* which is based on the assertion that opposites generate each other.

In addition to this early and extensive emphasis on opposition in Western intellectual thought, recent history bears witness to a rather massive adoption of Hegelian concepts regarding opposition by a highly influential intellectual movement, that is, the Marxist philosophy of dialectical materialism with its emphasis on the "negation of the negation" and other cyclical opposition. Furthermore, religious movements, some of which I have already mentioned, have frequently established opposition as an important principle of theological understanding. A couple of decades ago, in fact, a theist philosopher attempted to present a systematic case for the overriding significance of thinking in opposites for attaining religious knowledge and faith.[18] Aside from the sphere of Western intellectual thought, moreover, opposition has played an exceptionally prominent role in Eastern philosophy, religion, and intellectual thought from early times of the already ancient Eastern civilizations. A major focus and pervasive interest in opposites has characterized the Eastern philosophies of Taoism, Confucianism, Buddhism, and some forms of Hinduism, from their beginnings up to the present. In these philosophies, there are constant allusions to the merging of opposites, expression of opposites, unity of opposites, succession of opposites, as well as formulations of questions in terms of irreconcilable opposites or paradoxes. It is probably a fair generalization to say, in fact, that much of what is referred to as Eastern mysticism turns on opposition as a basic issue, both as a problem and a solution.

In the previous chapter, I mentioned and quoted some of the specific oppositions involved in the thinking of Buddha and Lao-tzu and in the Zen formulations, and I do not intend here to produce a cataloging of the extensive focusing on opposition in Eastern thought.[19] I do, however, want to emphasize that, despite the large quantity of references to opposites and opposition in Eastern philosophy, it would not be appropriate to assert that opposition *characterizes* Eastern intellectual thought more than Western. There is little in Eastern philosophy, for example, to compare with Hegel's great system based on opposition, a system which was influenced by and, in turn, influenced many philosophers. Hegelian philosophy and its impact alone bears testimony to the pervasive importance of opposition in the West.

I have had several purposes in tracing opposition throughout the history of intellectual thought, East and West. For one, I have intended to continue the discourse, begun in the early part of this chapter, about the highly abstract and complicated nature of opposition as a conceptual tool. Though not a direct and incontrovertible piece of evidence, the major role of opposition and particular opposites in the highly complicated and abstract formulations of great thinkers emphasizes complexity. There is more to opposition than is grasped in naming operations and references to concrete phenomena, and there is more to thinking about opposites and opposition than following patterns of learned verbal association. Also, I have dwelt on the importance of opposition in intellectual history in order to introduce the suggestion that there are intrinsic reasons for the significance of opposition in creative thought. Not only does opposition, and by implication janusian thinking, play a role in the development of great intellectual formulations and other creations, but it is also likely that these great intellectual formulations point to something basic about the nature of reality. Opposition and factors derived from opposition may in fact be a crucial factor in the structure of reality, at least as it is grasped by and interacts with human understanding. More of this later (chap. 13). Now, I shall clarify the cognitive structure of opposition further by considering some linguistic studies and analyses, including my own.

Linguistic Opposition

The psycholinguistic interest in opposition is, to some extent, a result of an historical accident having to do with the development of the word association test, the test described in the previous chapter. Invented by Sir Francis Galton in the nineteenth century, this test was relatively neglected by psychologists and other scientists until Carl Gustav Jung took it up in the early part of the current century. While Galton's interest in the test was based on his concepts of associational mental functioning, Jung used it as a diagnostic procedure aimed at identifying specific psychological blocks or "complexes" in connection with particular types of words. Then, influenced by Jung but diverging somewhat from him, the two psychiatrists Kent and Rosanoff began to apply a form of the word association test in the diagnosis of "insanity" or psychosis; this became the standard form of the test that is still in use today. In order to provide an easily administered, unambiguous, and repeatable procedure, one that produced responses regardless of education level, illness, and other circumstances, they settled on 100 relatively simple and common stimulus words after extensive sampling and experimentation. A host of administrations and the collection of an enormous body of data by clinicians and others followed in subsequent years. Because of the large amount of data, the ease of administration, and the obvious linguistic pertinence of the testing procedure, psycholinguists adopted the Kent-Rosanoff word association test as a major experimental tool. Turning away from the psychological and diagnostic interpretations of the clinicians and back to Galton's original concepts, psycholinguists attempted to explore patterns of verbal learning and verbal usage by means of this test or minor variations of it.

Now, it happens that several of the common, simple words on the Kent-Rosanoff list have elicited responses which, in the view of psycholinguists carrying out their explorations, seemed readily classifiable as opposites to the stimulus words. Another list of stimulus words would not in fact have done so, but the presence of this interesting finding has given rise to some extensive speculation on opposition. I stress this somewhat accidental nature of the finding about opposites because it bears on the discussion to follow.

I have already presented some of my own findings regarding opposite responding on the Kent-Rosanoff word association test. In discussing the investigations and analyses of others, as well as the phenomenon I have described as linguistic opposition, I can perhaps put those findings into perspective as well as clarify opposition further. Several aspects of the opposite response to stimuli on the word association test have been studied and assessed. Already mentioned here was the landmark study of Carroll, Kjeldegaard, and Carton, on which my own experiment was based. Interested not at all in creativity but in the nature of popular or common responses to the test, the so-called commonality of response category, these investigators were able to identify a partly overlapping but independent tendency they called "opposite responding."[20] Another group, led by R. D. Wynne,[21] attempted to explore the reasons for such a tendency by carrying out experiments designed to reveal a particular response set in subjects taking the test. Wynne and his associates believed that subjects responding to a word association test adopted strategies of response in accordance with their understanding of the tester's implicit instructions. They pointed out that several so-called opposite-evoking words, such as dark, sickness, man, soft, and black, appeared quite early in the standard test stimulus sequence. Accordingly, they reasoned, some subjects responded with opposites throughout because, after responding to the early part of the test, they perceived an implicit instruction to give opposites. By altering the sequence of stimuli presentation, Wynne and his group achieved results that seemed to support their hypothesis: different orders of presentation modified the total number of opposites elicited.

While this finding of a modification of opposite response depending on word sequence is of some interest, the interpretation of the finding is based on a series of assumptions that must be seriously questioned. First, these investigators assume that the early opposite-evoking words on the list automatically produce opposite responses, an assumption that is totally unwarranted in view of the large number of subjects who do not give any opposite associations to these words. Second, they make several implicit assumptions about the nature of the testing situation, particularly the unsupported idea that subjects are so compliant they will search for and always respond to an implicit instruction of the tester. Third, they seem to believe that subjects always consciously adopt a particular response strategy.[22]

Although it is possible that conscious strategies of response are developed under the conditions of paper and pencil administration of the test used by these and other psycholinguistic investigators, my own experience with timed oral testing contravenes such an assumption. Subjects' oral associations under any type of time pressure tend to be too automatic to result from any conscious and consistent strategies. On the contrary, many of my subjects were surprised or distressed when they became consciously aware of their own particular tendency to favor opposites, simple common words, or other patterns of response. Even under paper and pencil test conditions, testers give explicit instructions to respond with the first word that comes to mind and time pressure is involved. Consequently, although subjects may not have done so in the Wynne et al. study, they usually reply automatically, in all probability, rather than in accord with a conscious response strategy. The possibility of an unconscious response strategy affecting spontaneous response is another matter, but such an unconscious strategy would not likely result from the rather overwhelming degree of unrewarded and implicit compliance motivation suggested by Wynne et al. In view of the fact that many subjects hardly give any opposite responses at all, a particular unconscious opposite responding strategy is actually likely. Rather than a matter of test compliance, however, the difference among subjects and the tendency to respond in opposites indicate a particular pattern of thinking.

Other psycholinguistic investigators have been interested in opposite responding as a factor illuminating linguistic meaning, the acquisition of language, and the structure of associational process. Deese, carrying out an extensive factor analytical study of word association responses derived from large samples of subjects, developed patterns of organization of associations involving different types of English form classes such as nouns, adverbs, and adjectives.[23] The structure of associations to common adjectives, he concluded, was based on opposition or, as he called it, contrast. Explaining this association structure on the basis of the "contextual pattern of underlying sentences," or the relationship of these common adjectives to events in the natural world, he criticized classical formulations of associational laws that merely emphasized the effect of word frequency and contiguity, that is, either direct contiguity in speech and writing or contiguity mediated by another associated word.

Another psycholinguist, McNeill, using the previously mentioned argument that opposite word association responses consist of words having all features but one identical with the stimulus word, also emphasized contrast rather than contiguity as an explanation of another word association phenomenon. McNeill suggested that a characteristic change in children's patterns of response to word association tests at a certain age was due to the factor of contrast and not to contiguity.[24]

Pollio and his associates, interested in assessing the challenge to classical association theory posed by the previous two investigators, carried out a series of experiments testing the assumption or hypothesis of identical attributes or features between pairs of opposite words.[25] In one experiment, judges were asked to rate pairs of opposite words on a semantic differential scale, a scale allowing for judgments of various attributes of a concept or a set of words. In another experiment involving subjects learning a series of nonsense words, interference in learning due to the use of the opposite words "hot" and "cold" was compared to the interference produced between similar words such as "hot" and "warm," "cold" and "cool." Both experiments showed little support for the hypothesis that opposites were markedly similar as proposed. In the first, judges designated many differences in attributes between opposing pairs. In the second experiment, subjects demonstrated less confusion and consequently less learning error in connection with "hot" and "cold" than in connection with the similar pairs. The authors conclude that opposites are predominantly divergent rather than similar and they propose a "law of oppositional word pairs" that reaffirms the associational principle of contiguity. They suggest that, in the course of language acquisition, oppositional word pairs are brought together on the basis of "conceptual convenience," which they define as follows: "For purposes of conception and communication, it becomes extremely convenient to refer to a dimension in terms of contrasting pairs, with the understanding that if more precise distinctions are required these can always be provided by specifying the appropriate intermediary positions."[26] After oppositional pairs are brought into contiguity on the basis of conceptual convenience, the Pollio group argue, they undergo repeated concurrences and therefore mutual evocation becomes increasingly likely. In other words, "Frequency and contiguity *follow* rather than precede association."[27]

Psycholinguists' discussions of opposition tend to make little distinction between contrast and opposition; rather, both terms are used interchangeably and the designations "polar" and "reciprocal" relationships between word pairs are used to denote the more restrictive logical opposition I have discussed. Moreover, the concepts of "minimal contrast" and "conceptual convenience" arising from linguistic analyses are oriented to resolving a controversy about associational laws of language and thought, as I have indicated, and they also pertain to controversies about the linguistic approaches proposed by Noam Chomsky.[28] For example, Chomsky's system of syntactical signs is the basis for the mentioned proposals, especially H. H. Clark's, that opposite words involve only a sign change from positive to negative or vice versa.[29] Using these signs to denote several syntactical features of oppositional word pairs, such as commonness, abstractness, form class (noun, verb, etc.), Clark emphasizes a similarity between opposites rather than divergence.

I do not intend here to enter into a discussion of Chomsky's important and productive linguistic theories and systems, nor do I propose to evaluate the controversy about associational principles and laws. In order to clarify further the distinctions I have made between linguistic, logical, and psychological oppositions, however, I want to emphasize an aspect of Deese's findings that has escaped general attention. Deese's data on opposite responding to the adjective form class, data derived from tables of standard word association norms as well as from his own experiments, unequivocally apply only to *common* adjectives and not at all to so-called rare ones. Common adjectives are defined as those that occur with a frequency of fifty instances per million words on the Thorndike-Lorge norms of word frequency, a table compiled of word counts from extensive samples of written language.[30] Other adjectives, designated by Deese as "rare," *do not* generally stimulate opposite responses but often produce responses of a different kind.

Deese's explanation for this finding is that rare adjectives are qualitatively different from common ones, because rare adjectives derive their meanings from the meaning of underlying roots borrowed from other form classes, primarily nouns. The rare adjective "continental," for instance, is derived from the noun "continent." Although such an explanation has superficial plausibility and therefore some immediate appeal, it hardly stands up to a more rigorous consideration. Included among rare adjectives are scores of words underived from nouns such as "banal," "effete," "viscous," and "teeny," while, on the other hand, common adjectives include numerous noun derivatives such as "national" and "natural." My point here is that linguistic postulates about opposition such as Deese's, which emphasize association connections between adjectives as well as contrast or opposition, are derived solely from analyses of common responses and common adjectives, not at all on analyses of rare ones. This is partly due to the historical accident I mentioned earlier: linguists initially became interested in opposition because the Kent-Rosanoff list contained numerous common words that elicited common opposite responses. Also, it is due to linguists's proper concern with overall trends in linguistic patterns and usage and their interest in developing general laws. Focusing exclusively on common responses, however, is misleading and inadequate for assessing the word association response of creative persons, as has already been indicated in my own experimental studies reported in the previous chapter. In those studies, I discriminated the creative subject's tendency to respond with opposites (N.B.: to both adjective and other form class stimuli) and the tendency to give common popular responses. But, aside from these issues about opposite responding and creativity, the linguistic approach to opposition does not in itself do justice to the psychological complexity of the matter.

Two studies of my own serve to illustrate some of this complexity. In one study, I asked a group of raters to make judgments about a series of word pairs derived from stimuli and responses on my previous word association studies.[31] Raters consisted of forty-three females and eighteen males ranging in age from twenty to sixty-four years and ranging in educational background from high school graduates to persons with doctoral degrees. Presented to these raters were a series of eighty-six randomly ordered word pairs consisting of the following: twenty-nine that my co-investigator and I considered in some sense to be opposites; twenty-five that were made up of a stimulus word and the primary (most popular on word association norms) response; thirty-two designated as "chaff" that we chose as having either little relationship or else a good deal of similarity to each other. They were asked to rate which pairs they considered to be opposites according to the following definition: "Two words are in opposition to each other if together they denote a continuum in which they are at different poles. For example: cold and hot are opposites because they are at different poles of a temperature continuum."[32] Table 4 shows the number of opposite judgments for each of the word pairs used. The results are organized in accordance with the investigators' grouping of the pairs as opposites, primaries (stimulus with primary response), or chaff. The randomized order of presentation of word pairs is indicated by the accompanying numbers to the left of each.

The results are of interest, not because they demonstrate high correlations or unanimity of agreement, but for precisely the reverse reason: there was a good deal of divergence of opinion in the raters' response. For one thing, several raters judged primary pairs and similars to be opposites. Although there was 50 percent or better agreement about twenty-four opposite word pairs, 100 percent agreement occurred only with the pairs "fair-unfair" and "comfort-discomfort;" 90 percent or better agreement includes four other pairs (hard-easy, quiet-loud, sleep-awake, soft-loud), six pairs in all.

The results of this rating task reveal the difficulties of applying linguistic concepts of conceptual convenience and minimal contrast to behavior pertaining to opposition. Although there was 100 percent agreement on the opposition between comfort and discomfort, and both words have all syntactical features in common, "discomfort" is a very rare response to the stimulus word "comfort" on the Kent-Rosanoff list or on any type of word association response norm. Furthermore, the minimal contrast principle alone cannot account for the 90 percent or better agreement on the six word pairs. All con-

Table 4. Ratings of Opposition in Different Types of Word Pairs

Opposites	*No. of Opposite Ratings*	*Primaries*	*No. of Opposite Ratings*	*Chaff*	*No. of Opposite Ratings*
6. hard–easy	58	1. table–chair	22	3. deep–soft	15
8. short–high	52	2. stomach–food	13	5. house–place to live	4
9. anger–smoothing it over	35	4. eating–food	7	7. hand–glove	9
13. fair–unfair	61	12. foot–shoe	9	10. carpet–fluffy	7
17. eagle–St. Bernard	32	14. citizen–man	8	11. smooth–gentle	7
25. white–dark	47	15. wish–want	8	16. table–food	11
26. command–obey	42	18. whistle–sound	5	21. needle–sharp	6
29. beautiful–horrible	49	19. cabbage–vegetable	4	24. fruit–tree	11
30. music–noise	24	20. mutton–sheep	8	27. sour–not sweet	9
32. wish–command	34	22. earth–dirt	8	31. stomach–hunger	9
34. comfort–discomfort	61	23. river–water	5	38. fair–light	8
35. soldier–civilian	50	28. spider–web	11	39. mutton–stew	6
36. quiet–loud	59	33. mountain–hill	13	42. girl–hair	10
37. sleep–awake	58	41. window–glass	5	47. whistle–wolf	13

40. high–bottom	39	44. eagle–bird	5	49. hand–warmth	7
43. man–child	35	46. house–home	8	50. short–low	10
45. soft–loud	57	51. beautiful–girl	6	55. river–boat	12
48. butterfly–egg	21	54. trouble–bad	8	56. music–horn	9
52. working–sleeping	41	59. soldier–man	11	58. spider–black	7
53. citizen–king	33	61. comfort–chair	6	62. red–bright	7
57. deep–high	44	63. fruit–apple	3	67. foot–walk	6
60. smooth–harsh	54	65. anger–mad	5	69. high–windy	9
64. girl–man	41	77. sleep–bed	4	70. man–male	2
66. sour–beautiful	22	82. command–order	5	71. hard–ice	3
68. eating–hunger	19	84. working–hard	7	72. soft–fluffy	6
73. trouble–ease	51			74. cabbage–leaf	6
76. earth–water	39			75. needle–syringe	6
78. carpet–high	12			79. white–light	8
83. mountain–molehill	48			80. butterfly–collecting	10
				81. window–sill	8
				85. quiet–rest	5
				86. red–color	8

NOTE: There were 61 raters.

sist of words in the form class of adjectives and all are contrasting, but these two attributes were not at all limited to the six pairs. Several pairs of words with both of these attributes received less than 50 percent of the positive opposite judgments. Strikingly, also, only 40 percent of the raters judged the music-noise pair to be opposites. These words share the syntactical features of being nonabstract nouns referring to inanimate entities and they are contrasting with respect to a particular attribute. According to the definition of opposition specified in the instructions to the raters, these words in fact do define a continuum with polar extremes. Comparing the music-noise pair to the pairs receiving 100 percent agreement indicates that the raters opted for the characteristic of total contradiction in agreeing on the latter pairs. Fair and unfair totally and completely contradict and negate each other, as do comfort and discomfort. This is the quality they both have specifically in common. Of the six pairs rated opposites by 90 percent or more, five are totally contradictory: hard-easy, fair-unfair, comfort-discomfort, quiet-loud, sleep-awake. Only soft-loud could be considered to have some overlapping content and, like music-noise, to have a positive attribute of being types of sound. According to these results, the psychological sense of opposition is not one of minimal contrast, but of extreme difference. Syntactical features, in a direct rating of opposites, do not play a primary or major role. While contrast or polarity may seem to be a single attribute of word pairs for a linguist concerned with word relationships, it is, as the diversity of results on this task shows, a difficult attribute to determine. Moreover, the psychological structure of opposition consists primarily of the sense of reversing all of a word's attributes rather than only a single one. Discomfort, for example, is the reverse of comfort in every one of the contexts in which the word can be used.

On the other hand, the results also show the influence of linguistic factors on the concept of opposition. How else can the surprisingly large number of judgments of opposition (20 percent or more) for the pairs deep-soft, table-chair, mountain-hill, stomach-food, whistle-wolf, be explained? Logically, it is very difficult to conceive of the context in which these word pairs could denote opposition. Tables and chairs could possibly be considered opposite in terms of use: one neither sits on tables nor eats from chairs; stomach and food could be conceived of as being located at opposite ends of the esophagus while a person is chewing or else dichotomously opposite in function or action; mountain and hill could be considered to be to some degree opposite in size. But deep and soft could only be opposite if the hard rocks or the hard earth of a deep chasm or pit are brought to mind. Wolf and whistle would not in the ordinary colloquial use of "wolf whistle" be opposites but, in the context of sound, a wolf's baying and a whistle could seem to be opposed. And trying to establish the context for the few opposite judgments on other primary or chaff pairs would be extremely difficult indeed.[33] Remote logical contexts are in fact highly improbable; it is far more likely that some linguistic quality of these word pairs dictated the opposite judgment. Minimal contrast is a possibility—the five pairs from the primary and chaff list having 20 percent or better opposite ratings could be considered to have more of a quality of difference than others on those lists.

I believe there is another even more pervasive linguistic factor. When pairs of words are presented together, they form a binary and potentially dichotomous linguistic entity. This is especially so for the popular associated primaries on the list. Dichotomy, as I stated earlier, is an intrinsic aspect of one type of opposition, and binary entities therefore readily lend themselves to being structured as opposites. The mere presentation of word pairs in series, as done here, produces a linguistic context in which mere difference is overstressed and is therefore perceived as divergence or dichotomous opposition.[34]

In separating the roles of logic and language in relation to these rating results, I hardly mean to suggest that thought and language are independent of each other. I brought up the matter of logical context here because a particular feature of any rating or appreciation of opposition often involves somewhat remote logical, or linguistic, contexts. In our own initial choosing of the "eagle-St. Bernard" pair as opposites, for instance, we were thinking of the context of the aggressive predatory qualities of the eagle as opposed to the gentle savior stereotype of the dog. That most raters considered this to be a non-salient context, or merely did not think of it at all, is evidenced by the small number of opposite ratings for this pair. On the other hand, a very large number of raters agreed on the opposition in the pair "smooth-harsh," despite the more common oppositional contexts of "smooth" with "rough" as well as "soft" with "harsh."

Besides linguistic factors and logical context, other matters such as experience, sophistication, and point of view also play an important role in judgments of opposition. Because, for instance, few of the raters were musicians, the "music-noise" pair was not highly frequently rated as opposites; it is hard to imagine that a musician would ignore that pair. Also, unlike the relatively small number from this group of American—non-royalty oriented—raters, one would, with English or European raters, expect a large number of opposite judgments for the pair "citizen-king." On the other hand, a rater who was a king, or a guerrilla sniper, might not see much opposition between "soldier" and "civilian," while quite a large number of the raters here did. And biologists would surely rate "butterfly" and "egg" as opposites far more frequently than the few times here.

Another problem in linguistic discussions of opposition has been an exclusive focus on binary word pairs, dictated in part historically by the interest in simple word association. In another investigation, I have attempted to assess the effects of using multiple stimulus words in a word association task. In constructing the task, a series of single words and short phrases of multiple words were selected, all of which were determined beforehand to have clear opposites. As the purpose of the experiment was to determine the effect of multiple word stimuli on opposite responding, care was taken to use only low-frequency single words (according to the Thorndike-Lorge tables) but compound phrases containing words with higher frequency. On the basis of Deese's finding mentioned earlier that high-frequency adjectives stimulated opposite word associations, an attempt was made to stack the cards in favor of getting opposite responses to multiple word phrases. In order to use both structures of opposite word and opposite phrase pairs, two test protocols were made up. One of an opposite pair, either a single word or a compound phrase, was relegated to one test protocol or the other in order to avoid any suggestion effects. Sequence of presentation of single words and multiple word phrases was randomized on both protocols. Administered orally to thirty-eight student subjects, table 5 shows the two sets of test stimuli used. Twenty subjects received test 1 and eighteen received test 2. The number of opposite responses for each stimulus was computed and is shown on the table.

Total opposite response on both tests was 15 percent. This amount is considerably below the usual student percentage of approximately 30–35 percent opposite response on the standard Kent-Rosanoff test and it indicates that using rare adjectives and multiple words, as might be expected, reduces the opposite responding tendency overall. But comparing the opposite response to the two types of stimuli on both test protocols yields a striking result. As seen on the table, the 24 single stimulus words evoked 102 opposite responses while the compound or multiple word stimuli evoked 70 opposite responses. This degree of association of a larger number of opposite responses with single stimuli and a smaller number of responses with compound stimuli is significant at the $p < .001$ level (chi-square = 33.59, $df = 1$). When these results are broken down for each type of test administered, test 2 shows a somewhat stronger tendency in this direction but neither is alone responsible for the result. For test 1, chi-square equals 7.08 (significant at $p < .01$); for test 2, chi-square equals 32.82 (significant at $p < .001$).

Multiple word stimuli do not tend, in other words, to evoke opposite responses in a word association task to the degree that single word

Table 5. Opposite Responses to Single and Multiple Word Stimuli

Single Word Stimuli	*No. of Opposite Responses*	*Multiple Word Stimuli*	*No. of Opposite Responses*
	Test 1 ($n = 20$)		
Careless	6	Death is long	8
Repel	3	Come down	7
Lucky	2	Fall apart	2
Inside	10	Hang loose	1
Forbid	1	Wake up	4
Hindsight	8	Hot and light	1
Exclude	3	Daylight breaks	1
Output	8	Speed up	6
Mobile	0	First breath	0
Hopeless	1	Soft and wet	2
Past	5	Dark night	1
Cowardly	4	Tear down	5
		Small time loser	2
		Dirty wash	0
		Give in	0
		Count me out	4
		New joys	2
		Hurry up	1
Subtotal	51	Subtotal	47
	Test 2 ($n = 18$)		
Careful	1	Life is short	1
Attract	3	Get high	1
Unlucky	3	Pull together	2
Outside	8	Up tight	0
Allow	2	Sack out	0
Foresight	3	Cold and dark	0
Include	6	Night falls	0
Input	13	Slow down	4
Immobile	5	Last gasp	1
Hopeful	0	Hard and dry	1
Future	7	Bright day	0
Bold	0	Build up	3
		Big time winner	1
		Clean laundry	2
		Hold out	1
		Count me in	2
		Old sorrows	2
		Go to sleep	0
		Go up	2
Subtotal	51	Subtotal	23
Total	102	Total	70

NOTE: n = number of subjects

stimuli do. This finding lends strong support to my previous suggestion that the use of tasks involving binary word pairs has strongly influenced the results and conclusions pertaining to opposition in linguistic investigations. Single word stimuli call for single word responses; most word association test procedures include an instruction for subjects to respond with a single word but such an instruction is generally unnecessary. In the investigation I just reported, single word stimuli evoked single word responses in 100 percent of the cases even though, because of the inclusion of multiple word stimuli, no such instruction was given. Multiple word stimuli, on the other hand, generally evoked multiple word responses. Presenting a single word stimulus does, therefore, produce what can properly be considered a response set, a set to respond with a single word and to produce *a binary word pair.* Such binary pairs seem to suggest dichotomies, and dichotomies, as I pointed out, are connected or related to opposition. Consequently, single word stimuli seem to stimulate subjects to respond with opposites or else, as the high level of relativity of the previous rating experiment suggests, data presented in binary pairs may influence experimenters who score subject responses as having contrasting or oppositional qualities between stimulus and response.

The paucity of opposite responses to multiple word stimuli also bears on the hypotheses both of "conceptual convenience" with respect to opposites and of conscious opposite responding strategies on the word association test. If opposite responding were only a matter of conceptual convenience there would be every reason to expect that the common compound phrases included in these tests would have been strongly connected to opposites just as much as single words. But such was not the case at all. Instead, it appears that thinking of the opposite to a multiple word phrase required some conceptual effort rather than ease or convenience. Not only were there fewer opposites on multiple word phrases, but there was also another pattern shown on the test response: several partial opposites were given as responses, such as "old joys" to "new joys" and "soft and dry" to "soft and wet," indicating a not-quite-but-almost attempt to give an opposite response. If opposition or opposite responding were a matter of conceptual convenience alone, why wouldn't "new joys" and "old sorrows" be strongly associated with each other and therefore be a preferred response?

Opposite responses to multiple word stimuli surely should betray an intentional opposite responding strategy as well, if one existed in the ordinary case. As seen in the partial type of opposite response just mentioned, multiple word stimuli on this task generally contained at least two reference points with regard to the formation of opposite responses, such as "new" and "joy," respectively, for "old" and "sorrow," or "soft" and "wet" for "hard" and "dry," and so on.

Forming an opposite to such stimuli, giving a complete opposite response involving both reference points, would surely indicate a responder's intent or strategy. In distinction to the ambiguity with respect to an individual word stimulus with one reference point, responses such as "big time winner" to the stimulus "small time loser" definitely indicate an intentional conceiving of the opposite. That relatively few such complete opposite responses occurred on these tests suggests that intentional opposite responding strategies are the exception rather than the rule.

Despite some limitations of linguistic studies pertaining to opposition, contributions such as Deese's suggestion that opposition has something to do with the structure of common adjectives as a form class are noteworthy and important. The connection between adjectives and opposition pertains to issues I shall pursue for the remainder of this chapter. Adjectives belong to a linguistic form class denoting abstract entities; adjectives are words for the qualities of things, and qualities always consist of abstractions. To determine qualities, features that appear salient to the human mind are abstracted from the concrete world. To some extent, opposition is intrinsic to the structure and definition of adjectives of all sorts because opposition pertains to abstractions. An opposite relationship exists on an abstract level only, and conceiving of opposition requires the abstracting mental capacity. Because opposition is an abstraction and because it is quite complex are two of the reasons opposition is important in creativity.

Opposition and Creativity

One of the baffling aspects of creativity has been the startling leaps of thought, the penetration into the unknown and the unfamiliar, and the sometimes dazzling and highly complex formulations in art, science, and other areas. New ideas, new discoveries, new forms, new metaphors, new styles, these are the hallmarks of creativity and, though classically we have difficulty understanding and accepting this newness—sometimes we even reject it—we eventually come to appreciate it. We eventually accord the creator the accolades he so richly deserves. In chapter 12, I shall take up some of the complicated psychological and philosophical matters pertaining to the newness (novelty) of creativity. Now, I shall relate some aspects of opposition to these dazzling and complex products of creativity, a task I have been leading up to all along.

While creations in art, science, and other fields invariably appear to be new and unfamiliar, they cannot ever be completely so. Such creations are products of a human mind, understood by other human minds. Hence, they cannot be totally disconnected from the previous experience of either the creator himself, or of his audience, or of other types of recipients. This much seems obvious: the creator does not, at any given moment in time, use totally new thought processes or develop a totally new language to convey them; nor does he produce theories, inventions, or works of art completely devoid of relationship to previous human experience. Were he to do so, there probably would be no way of understanding his creation. Labeled idiosyncratic or otherwise incomprehensible, it would be relegated to the dustbins of history—if even it received that much attention—until some future creator came along, perhaps to create its meaning or use. This does not merely apply to creations that are highly abstract or very difficult to understand: Einstein's theories of relatively when first proposed, or quantum theory, for instance. Though a theory be highly abstract, with little in the way of concrete referents that aid understanding, the abstract elements nevertheless can and do relate to other abstractions previously known. Someone with a particular type of knowledge does understand it. Modern conceptions in physics of atomic or subatomic structure or of black holes in space are difficult to grasp in visual or concrete terms but, as abstractions, they are comprehensible and useful. In music, early experiments with electronically produced and randomized sound seemed totally meaningless and incomprehensible to some, but many musicians found something in it related to their previous experience. They hailed it as a new form.

The comprehensibility of creations does not arise merely from some minor factor such as that literature must be conveyed in existing language or physical theories are transmitted in generally accepted mathematical terms, or music consists of recognizable and preexisting physical sounds. These are surely aspects of the matter, but more is involved. For comprehension to occur, elements relating to shared experience must to some degree be present in the substance of the creation. I realize, in saying this, that I am skirting on the edge of controversy with respect to modern art forms such as random music. But rather than pursue somewhat digressionary particular issues about whether the listener completely imposes patterns on the sounds, and about what the composer does, I want to push my point further and assert that, in artistic creation, familiarity allowing for comprehension along with unfamiliarity and newness are crucial for the development of an aesthetic experience.

It is easier with art than with science and other fields to emphasize the importance of the familiar together with the unfamiliar because everyone has experienced the pleasures of hearing and rehearing the same piece of music or of seeing and reseeing the same Shakespearean play.[35] Everyone knows the powerful alternation and balance between familiarity and unfamiliarity or strangeness in art: the hearing of new sounds in familiar music and of new meanings in old soliloquies, and the reverse experience of an immediate feeling of recognition when confronting new metaphors in a poem. I particularly mean to emphasize this latter intuition of familiarity with respect to new metaphors, an intuition that imparts the sense of comprehensibility.[36]

Scientific and other intellectual creations do require some balance between familiarity and strangeness but this balance is not always so apparent in a scientific discovery or a scientific theory. After all, for a scientific creation particularly to be believed or accepted, the scientist must go to great lengths to render it familiar—in science, this means logically comprehensible—despite its newness and strangeness. Tightly knit logic, experimentation, indeed a major portion of the scientific enterprise is devoted to accomplishing familiarity and producing widespread and general acceptability and agreement. With scientific creations, the balance between familiarity and strangeness appears less in the result or product and more in the thinking that goes into the development and discovery of theory or fact. Because of the need for comprehensibility and agreement, the essence of such exciting thinking must be hidden or submerged in scientific presentations; witness the necessarily dry but rigorous articles that abound in scientific journals. Yet seldom does the process of scientific discovery occur along the well-trod familiar paths such as journal articles would seem to indicate; neither does it involve totally new experiences or totally strange and unfamiliar territory at every step of the way. The creative scientist dips into the unknown with firm footing in the known.

The balance between the familiar and the strange both in artistic and scientific creation especially points to the widespread importance of opposition as a conceptual tool. As an abstract operation, conceiving the opposite provides a means for moving as far into the unknown as possible while still retaining a reference point in the known. A pertinent illustration comes from the physicist Dirac's revolutionary theory of the existence of antimatter. Confronting a whole series of physical phenomena in which the behavior of elementary particles could not be explained, Dirac postulated the existence of particles that were completely opposite in electric charge to all particles then known. These oppositely charged but otherwise identical particles he called collectively "antimatter." Both electrons and positrons had corresponding antielectrons and antipositrons in the universe. Now, for anyone reading my intentionally sketchy account of this theory and confronting the idea for the first time, I am sure there is an experience of strangeness, a "mind-bending" quality in attempting to comprehend this "antimatter." And that quality, of course, is due to the highly abstract nature of such a concept. Here, I hope I have made a difficult point: rather than reconceptualizing the whole of particle physics and, for instance, proposing to explain the data with a new concept of matter that encompassed both types or classes of particles he was postulating—I personally have no idea how or whether anything such as that could possibly be done—he developed a strange and new abstraction. There was another type of entity, he said, that was exactly opposite to the known entity of matter; therefore, all laws pertaining to the known entity also applied to the hitherto unknown one. Thus, he was able to understand and to describe the strange and unknown in terms of the familiar.

In art, conceiving opposites also serves to help the artist move from the familiar to the strange. As I briefly mentioned in the previous chapter, styles in the visual arts especially have undergone many oppositional shifts in the last century, some gradual and some more rapid. There was a major shift from representational art to abstract art, the dadaist's reversal of traditional artistic conventions in what was called "antiart," and the rise of the pop art movement as another type of reversal both of traditional art and of antiart as well. Others could be mentioned, but suffice it to cite the development of the op art movement, a movement producing yet another type of reversal by definitively shifting the locus of aesthetic creation to the eye of the observer. Although other artists and art movements had been interested in optical effects, the op movement produced objects with optical qualities that required the onlooker to integrate the perceptual experience in his mind rather than to admire separated qualities of an external art object. Op art could not, for instance, be reproduced in photographs. In modern literature also, there has been a shift from naturalism to absurdism as well as the emergence of the antihero as the major modern literary entity. And in music, the development of random, or, as John Cage calls it, antiteleological music, the supposed opposite of traditional goal-oriented composition, has already been mentioned. More basically, however, oppositions intrinsic to metaphor, comedy, and tragedy in all artistic forms play a critical role in producing a balance, and a shift, between the familiar and the strange. I shall specifically discuss these more basic oppositions in the final chapter of this book.

To return to science, opposition also plays a basic and general role in the development of scientific creations. As the broad and erudite historian of science, Gerald Holton, points out, scientific knowledge itself is often structured in terms of antithesis. I shall quote him extensively and directly:

> Not far below the surface, there have coexisted in science, in almost every period since Thales and Pythagoras, sets of two or more antithetical systems or attitudes, for example, one reductionistic and the other holistic, or one mechanistic and the other vitalistic, or one positivistic and the other teleological. In addition, there has always existed another set of antitheses or polarities, even though, to be sure, one or the other was at a given time

> more prominent—namely, between the Galilean (or, more properly, Archimedean) attempt at precision and measurement that purged public, "objective" science of those qualitative elements that interfere with reaching reasonable "objective" agreement among fellow investigators, and, on the other hand, the intuitions, glimpses, daydreams, and *a priori* commitments that make up half the world of science in the form of a personal, private, "subjective" activity.
>
> Science has always been propelled and buffeted by such contrary or antithetical forces. Like vessels with draught deep enough to catch more than merely the surface current, scientists of genius are those who are doomed, or privileged to experience these deeper currents in their complexity. It is precisely their special sensitivity to contraries that has made it possible for them to do so, and it is an inner necessity that has made them demand nothing less from themselves.[37]

Cited also by Holton are specific and crucial conceptual antitheses in physical science as follows: matter and energy; space and time; the gravitational and electromagnetic field; and what he calls "the great themata" of continuum versus the discrete, of classically causal law versus statistical law, of the mechanistic versus the theistic world interpretation. All of these themata have, he says, "haunted" great scientists such as Newton, Bohr, and Einstein. Holton's view, then, points to opposition as a concern and a central preoccupation of creative scientists. His further developed description of progress in science as both moving calmly in one direction in a monolithic way and being buffeted by contrary or antithetical forces also coincides with Kuhn's.[38]

While Holton's description of the great scientists' preoccupation with antitheses or opposites strongly emphasizes the importance of opposition in creative scientific thought, further clarification is necessary. Of key significance for understanding the role of opposition in scientific and other types of creative thought are two matters I have discussed here: (1) opposition is an abstract relation; (2) designation of specific opposites is always relative, dependent on context, and a matter of sophistication and point of view. The abstract nature of opposition has already been emphasized; the relativity and point of view have only been touched on.

A clear and commonplace example of the relativity of opposition comes from the elementary art class. When a student is learning to paint or color, he is very early exposed to the dictum of three primary colors: blue, red, and yellow. Because these colors are elemental and do not reduce to other colors, it is easy to think of them as extremes—not merely as broadly contrasting colors but as opposites. When in the course of painting, however, the student thinks of putting in opposite color effects, as often happens, he will, if he is using primaries, invariably choose either blue and yellow or red and yellow, never blue and red. The example need not be confined to the use of primary colors, of course, and most students—and accomplished artists as well—will also think of red and green, or perhaps purple and yellow, or orange and green, as opposites, depending on the context and their own color experiences and associations. And, taking into consideration factors of tone and value, I believe all artists would agree that such thinking is perfectly valid and artistically meaningful.[39] From the point of view of optical physics, however, there is less room for variation in the judgment of color opposites: blue and red are clearly at opposite ends of the physical optical spectrum and they are therefore *the* opposites.

I don't intend to make these points of view appear antagonistic to each other because the differences between colors as part of the wave spectrum and colors of the palette produced by reflected light are well known; artists and scientists function very comfortably with both perspectives. Also, it should be clear from my previous discussion that two types of opposition, binary and scalar, are involved. To move on to other examples, however: cold and hot are, everyone would agree, clear opposites. If a ruthless examiner, interested in opposites, raised his eyebrows and pushed on to question this judgment, most people would come up with "freezing" and "boiling" as better designations. And surely they would be right. A person standing outside on a winter day, shiveringly viewing ice-covered ponds and lakes, would need little convincing that he is experiencing the end point of an extreme and would readily acknowledge that the boiling water for his tea or coffee waiting on the stove inside was at the other end of the scale. The physical behavior of water has served as a fairly adequate standard for the temperature scale and, despite our possession of thermometers registering well below 32° Fahrenheit or 0° Celsius, we still use the term "freezing" to describe the lower end of the temperature scale. As we enter the domain of the physical scientist, however, water disappears as a standard, and judgment of opposites of temperature depends on the freezing point of substances such as nitrogen at minus 273° Celsius or, with increasing knowledge, on the range of temperatures actually measured in the physical world. The physical scientist, in fact, brings in a notion of temperature as a virtually limitless scale on which opposite points are totally determined by the particular standard employed or by the knowledge then available.

One more example, from my own field: in my early days of word association testing and working with judgments of opposition in word pairs, I was constantly struck by the large number of people who made the judgment that the opposite of "anger" was "happiness," or its equivalent. Because I happened to be particularly interested in anger,[40] both clinically and theoretically, I was quite taken by this response because it seemed to reveal an important psychological and, perhaps, a sociological problem. The judgment that anger and happiness were opposites seemed to mean that many people viewed the total absence of anger as necessary to a state of being happy. I should say that I was struck but not really surprised by this implication, as it coincided with what I and numerous other clinicians have constantly observed to be a dominant point of view both of society in general and of our patients in particular, that is, the conviction that anger is a noxious emotion that should be denied and suppressed. On the contrary, however, a considered view of healthy psychological functioning—not experimentally proven but consistently derived from clinical observation—holds that anger is not at all antithetical to happiness. Expression of anger or, more important, recognition of one's anger, is important to psychological health and, consequently, to happiness as well. Notice I have not said that expression or recognition of anger does away with anger; expression and recognition of anger may facilitate happiness, and happiness and anger may often therefore coexist. Psychologically, an appropriate opposite of anger is "smoothing it over" (as in the rating task described). Thus, again, sophistication and viewpoint play a role in choice of appropriate opposites.

These examples should sharpen the position about opposition in science Professor Holton has taken. I do not intend to suggest that a scientific designation of opposites is invariably more true, in some absolute sense, than is an ordinary, unsophisticated choice of particular opposites. Creative artists, in fact, deal with opposites and opposition in a manner closer to common ordinary usage and understanding and, surely, they arrive at deep understandings or, if you will, truths. The examples serve to illustrate that opposites and opposition are relative. Close consideration of some of the antitheses Holton cites would lead to challenges from various quarters about whether a given pair were truly antithetical or whether a particular antithesis adequately described a system or attitude. What, for example, is really antithetical about space and time? Isn't time experienced as a result of movement through space? Or, from the point of view of existential philosophy, is there really an antithesis between subjective and objective? Such challenges, which can be raised about virtually any designated opposites, are potentially productive of more refined definitions and better ideas.

Opposition is relative but formulating oppositions in science, in art, and in other intellectual pursuits as well, serves as an aid to thought, conceptualization, and progress. Sophistication is important because increases in knowledge lead to the formulation of oppositions which more and more adequately characterize the materials and the understandings required within a particular context. While the ordinary man, out on a cold blustery winter's day, need have no more complex standard of temperature than the behavior of water, the scientist must go beyond this. And, in going beyond, he formulates new polarities and oppositions of temperature that aid him to tackle problems about physical reality. The conceptual antithesis between matter and energy cited by Holton is a cardinal case in point. Einstein's interest in this seemingly rockbound antithesis led him to overthrow it as an antithesis by showing that matter and energy were interchangeable or the same. In so doing, he increased sophistication to the point that new antitheses were conceived. As another instance, waves and particles have for many years been considered antithetical or else, in some way, similar. When the particular formulation is developed that renders them simultaneously operative, another set of antitheses will appear. Science does indeed progress because of the presence of antithesis. But these antitheses are products of the mind of man interacting with the world of nature. It is also necessary for man to formulate antitheses in order to move from the known to the unknown. Working with antitheses or oppositions in art, in science, and in other intellectual areas does not require that such antitheses or oppositions be absolute, or applicable to every context, only that they be meaningful and applicable in the context in which they are considered.

Creators formulate antitheses and oppositions in order to gain conceptual clarity. In distinction to contrasts and differences, oppositions and antitheses are crucial for scientific and intellectual creative thought because they are *specific* and *clear.* Entities in opposition have distinct, definite and reciprocal relationships to each other and, as in the Dirac example of antimatter, the characteristics of one side of the opposition also apply to the other. Sophistication in science and other fields allows for greater and greater specification of meaningful and appropriate opposites. As old opposites are overthrown, new ones arise in a never ending spiral of self-generation paralleling the spiral of increasing knowledge.

An important aspect of scientific discovery, acknowledged by most creativity researchers and by outstanding creative scientists who have been my research subjects as well, is the initial formulation of the problem to be solved. It is at this stage of the process of discovery that formulating oppositions can play a crucial role. Just as it is necessary for the scientist, both ordinary and creative, to deal with red and blue as opposites in optics, it is necessary for the creative scientist also to go beyond everyday scientific matters and to abstract other oppositions from the body of scientific knowledge or from the activities of the scientific enterprise. The antitheses proposed by Holton are examples of abstractions that seem to have contributed to the formulation of scientific problems and to the progress of science. A careful reading of the historical account by Kuhn provides a good deal of evidence that formulating such large-scale antitheses and oppositions, and resolving them, has been a cardinal characteristic of scientific advance.[41] Increases in knowledge do not, in themselves, lead to the formulation of new opposites and antitheses, but scientists—especially creative ones—tend to organize new knowledge in terms of antitheses and opposites in order to facilitate conceptualization. This is done not merely out of "conceptual convenience," incidentally, even though antitheses are clearer and more specific than difference and contrast. Formulating appropriate and meaningful antitheses is conceptually difficult and the results are perplexing and challenging. Making such difficulties for oneself is, as I have said earlier, a particular characteristic of the creative process. Formulating antitheses and opposites is helpful and facilitative, but it is not easy.

In addition to specificity and clarity, opposition involves either or both dichotomies and scales. Consequently, formulating opposites provides a means for structuring information and concepts in a useful way. Known dichotomies and scales can be organized to facilitate abstract manipulation. To use a mundane illustration, ice is cold and therefore at the opposite pole from entities that are hot, but ice formed from carbon dioxide, "dry ice," belongs to two different scales. It feels hot when touched but, on the temperature scale, it is quite cold. Conceptualizing the circumstances in these terms facilitates an understanding of the nature of sensation as a form of interpretation of physical events. Moreover, formulating oppositions provides a means for dichotomizing or scaling information that might otherwise appear totally haphazard. Another everyday example: calling men and women opposites served for many centuries to aid the—now rejected—dichotomization of work tasks in human society. A more contemporary view maintained the notion of opposition but, instead of the man-woman dichotomy, emphasized scalar features of maleness and femaleness with many intervening degrees. That the most modern position on the relationship between men and women is geared toward overthrowing the opposition completely should not suggest that the previous conceptualizations had no purpose. On the contrary, one of the most telling approaches of the modern women's liberation movement is to ask for examination of the basis for the notion of opposition between sexes in order to facilitate understanding of the impact of this long held idea on both men's and women's characteristic ways of thinking and behaving. Another illustration of the conceptual usefulness and significance of formulating oppositions in order to organize otherwise haphazard data into dichotomies and scales comes from a very influential modern movement in linguistics and anthropology, the structuralism of Roman Jakobson and Claude Lévi-Strauss. Jakobson, whose work was antecedent, developed a point of view—now known as structural linguistics—which virtually revolutionized the modern field of linguistics. A cardinal feature of Jakobson's approach was identifying binary oppositions in complicated linguistic forms. Lévi-Strauss, whose work in anthropology stimulated the adoption of structuralism by numerous intellectual disciplines—literature, art, psychology, natural science—was able to develop extensive understanding of primitive cultures on the basis of a highly perceptive identification of binary oppositions in rituals and myths.[42]

Opposition and Artistic Creativity

So far, I have drawn most of my illustrations of the role of opposition in the creative process from the realm of science. Formulating oppositions in the arts is intrinsic to creative thinking for some of the same reasons as already discussed. While it is difficult to speak of art as a body of knowledge analogous to the body of scientific knowledge, there surely are traditional canons in art and referential features pertaining to knowledge outside of the artistic realm. I have already alluded to the tendency of modern artists to overthrow old styles and traditions within the artistic canon by developing opposite styles and principles. Such a tendency is, in modern times, only more extreme and obvious than in the past. Artists characteristically have adopted opposite styles and movements, both with respect to artistic canons and with respect to knowledge outside of the artistic realm. Artists frequently formulate opposites of what is generally accepted and believed, whether derived from science, politics, philosophy, or from everyday experience, and such opposites are intricately interwoven into the fabric of their art. Moreover, sophistication with respect to opposites also plays a critical role. If a previous artist has used a particular pair or multiplicity of opposites in his work, a later artist often attempts to develop the issue further by going beyond, superceding, or providing different and hopefully more knowledgeable or penetrating terms. Opposition between death and life may be superceded or enlarged to include opposition between inanimate and animate in the universe; James Joyce retold the Odyssey of Homer and, rather than focusing on the opposition between man and the gods, he emphasized the opposition between man's will and forces within himself.

Artists find the clarity, specificity, dichotomizing, and scaling factors involved in opposition quite as useful and facilitating as creative scientists do, and for artists, the relativistic and reciprocal aspects of opposition seem to play an even larger role. Insofar as art deals with the entire realm of human experience, it confronts issues and areas where truth seems almost entirely relative, or at least a far lesser degree of absolute than sometimes appears in science. In the face of such large-scale relativism, the relativism of opposition serves the artist well in his attempts to organize and integrate experience of all types. For opposition, while pertinent only within particular contexts, also has another feature that has particular value for the artist. Opposites are, by definition, *limits.* The opposite ends of a scale are reciprocal and the same as the limits of that scale, and binary opposition defines the limits of a class. Man and woman, again, are only opposites if no other entity is included in the same class, such as a third sex or an animal, and male or female are the end limits of a sexual attribute scale. Such limits are immovable, totally restrictive, and absolute; one could not change these limits without redefining the opposites involved. This limit-setting aspect of formulating oppositions is one of its most salient and intrinsic features and one that is extremely valuable for the artist. In seeking stability, coherence, and oftentimes a perspective on human experience that yields a sense of the absolute, in some cases possibly absolute truth itself, the artist formulates oppositions and defines clear limits. Though opposition is essentially relative, for the artist it may not be necessarily so. He hopes to find basic and even absolute truths, if such exist, behind and beyond the surface of things. Thus, he formulates and uses opposites. The artist uses the relativistic device of opposition to find limits and absolutes in an apparently relativistic world.

Artists, art critics, and scholars constantly allude to opposition and elements of opposition in artistic works. Indeed, I anticipate little criticism from those quarters about what I say here about the importance of opposition in art. Despite the wide agreement about the salience of opposition, however, it is another matter to identify particular opposites with certainty. In many art fields, the relativistic aspect of opposition is quite apparent when the matter is subjected to careful scrutiny. In the visual arts, for instance, where it might be expected that the originally spatial basis of the idea of opposition—putting against or establishing sides—would make for easy and consistent use and identification of opposites, agreement in any particular case can be quite hard to attain. Only the familiar and definite spatial orientations of left and right, up and down, and also perhaps inner and outer, concave and convex, foreground and background, provide a clear and incontrovertible basis for designating particular oppositions in visual form. Now, I don't mean to say that thinking about these orientations in connection with varying and unlimited types of content does not provide a virtual infinitude of possible oppositions; as a matter of fact, such possibility exists. But the visual artist is often interested in highly subtle and complex forms of opposition in his works and it is therefore difficult to identify and obtain definite agreement about various oppositions of tone and value as well as in-context oppositions between the form of lines or geometric shapes, such as squares, rectangles, circles, triangles, or spheres, and the highly relative oppositions of dark and light or short and long. When visual art is representational, of course, agreement about particular opposites can be easier to attain. In representational art, such familiar categories as man and woman, sacred and profane, rich and poor, downtrodden and uplifted, saint and sinner, or gaiety and sadness are unequivocally manifest and doubts and questions are stilled. Hence, when specificity and increasingly abstract categories are possible, the chances of wide agreement about opposition are increased.

From these considerations, it would appear that literature is the art form *par excellence* for producing and identifying definite oppositions. Literature depends on language and, in comparison to other media, language provides the possibility of the highest degree of specificity.[43] And, in practice, such is the case: opposition in literature is rather easily described and discussions of particular opposites in a literary work need little exegesis or justification in the majority of instances. But this circumstance reflects a more general issue with respect to the analysis of art. The more there is a focus on the non-specific, so-called formal aspects of art, the more difficult it is to achieve widespread consensus and agreement. As opposition is often a quality of artistic form, its presence and function are often controversial. Music, the type of art that stimulates a focus on form more persistently than others, provides a clear instance of the difficulty. Musicians, including composers, constantly refer to oppositions in music: opposite themes, rhythms, keys, tempos, symphonic movements; inversions, counterpoints, opposite ends of the scale, retrogrades future and retrogrades past; and dissonance opposed to consonance. But close inspection of any particular allegation of opposition invariably raises an issue of relativism along with diverging points of view because music has few stable or specific reference points to support a particular claim. Many proponents of opposition of themes in various composer's music, for instance, find themselves referring to so-called extramusical experiences or the description of particular emotional states, to try to make their case.[44] Appreciation and understanding of music need not involve such extramusical elements, yet a strict or logical analysis of incontrovertible opposition in music requires that only physically antagonistic elements and complete antitheses be considered. Thus, only upbeats and downbeats, silence and sound, extremes of sound, or possibly antithetical motions required to produce different sounds or rhythms on a particular instrument, are clearly and uncontestably opposites.

Are musicians, and other artists not using language as a medium, wrong, then, when they talk about oppositions in their thinking and their art products? Surely this could not be so, because particular pieces of music, painting, sculptures, dances, and works of architecture constantly generate a sense of opposition about which sophisticated persons, and the not-sophisticated as well, can often agree. The answer to the dilemma resides in the limit-setting aspect of opposition, the defining and construction of particular contexts involved clearly both in the production and in the appreciation of works of art. The artist defines opposition by the limits of the particular context in which he is working as follows: a painting dull overall in tone may have striking opposition of dark and light within that particular tone range or context; a melodic sequence once stated in a piece of music is opposite to another sequence in which the tones are reversed; fast and slow tempos are oppositional in a particular work; square and round may appear as opposites in a particular building and the same architect may build another building in which square and round appear similar; finally, the dancer may produce a dance in which moving forward and backward are sharply emphasized despite their occurring in a rather narrow range of space.

Setting limits is a crucial aspect of the focus on opposition in art and, although not superficially apparent, setting limits is an aspect of the formulation of opposites in science as well. When the creative scientist pays attention to the alleged opposition between holism and reductionism, space and time, or electromagnetic versus gravitational field, he too is circumscribing and setting limits on his area of inquiry. In formulating such oppositions, or taking them seriously, he must ignore much blurring or subtlety that make it very difficult to specify such categories clearly. Usually aware of these subtleties at the time he formulates the opposition, he may even return to use them later in arriving at the solution of a given problem he poses. The stage of formulating oppositions and limits is, however, a critical aid to his thought.

Although formulating oppositions involves limit setting and specificity, that by no means interferes with the subtlety and complexity of creative thought. For one thing, oppositions themselves frequently involve highly complex interrelationships and domains of knowledge. Although many of the examples I have used here consist of rather simple oppositions, these should certainly not necessarily be considered to be the particular oppositions in creative thinking. Most oppositions involved in intellectual creations cannot be designated by single words or phases. Though we talk about an opposition between a wave and a particle, for instance, we refer to a highly complex series of antithetical relationships. Moreover, much of the opposition in creative thinking consists of multiple rather than binary elements. Again, while many examples here have referred merely to binaries such as hot and cold, darkness and light, and so on, opposition in creative thinking involves the great complexity and subtlety of concatenations of ideas denoting such multiplicities as formed and formless, human and animal, sacred and profane, adult and child, ideal and natural. Such multiplicities enter into the multilevel nature of art and of other types of creation as well.

In discussing the various features of opposition such as limit setting, dichotomizing, scaling, clarity, specificity, and relativity, I trust it has also been clear that I have not meant to suggest that any one of these features in itself dictates a particular choice of opposites by the artist or scientist. Nor have I meant to indicate a defined and invariant sequence of events involved in thinking of opposites. The scientist does not formulate a particular opposition in order to dichotomize data, set limits, etc., nor does he first dichotomize data, clarify it, etc., before formulating a particular opposition. He, as well as the artist, formulates particular opposites because for both it seems that these opposites are *there,* that is, a specific and reciprocal difference exists between the electromagnetic and gravitational field, between space and time, between red and green, and so on. And, in developing a work of art especially, an artist may perceive an oppositional context that others cannot immediately perceive. Creative people do not use opposition consciously to accomplish any set purpose, but they are drawn to opposition and they tend to formulate opposites because such a procedure is useful, and often critical, for making discoveries and producing artistic creations.

Opposition and Janusian Thinking

At this stage of the exploration of the creative process, it should be readily apparent that everything pertaining to the role of opposition in creative thinking also pertains to janusian thinking. The complexity, abstractness, limit-setting, structuring, and specifying qualities of opposition are all features of janusian thoughts. Opposition is intrinsically related to janusian thinking in that it is necessary for particular opposites to be formulated in order for them to be conceived as operating simultaneously. But again, no set sequences are involved. In the process of janusian thinking, formulating particular opposites does not necessarily occur at a separate, or distinctly prior, point of time. Often, the complete conception of particular opposites operating simultaneously occurs all at once. The process, in such cases, consists of recognition and identification of an opposition (or merely a tension) together with the conception or realization that particular opposites are operating simultaneously in a particular context. Such thinking frequently appears in artistic creation, as artistic metaphors expressing simultaneous oppositions emerge commonly fully formed. Sometimes, the artist himself may dimly sense rather than be explicitly aware of the particular oppositions he has formulated; he does not at all pause to analyze their logical interrelationships but is interested in their aesthetic impact and appeal.

The janusian process, although it may occur dimly and in a moment of time, consists of interest in opposites, formulating opposites, recognizing the salience or impact of particular opposites with respect to a particular problem, task, or field, and conceiving or postulating the opposites simultaneously. The creative person, in other words, engages in all these aspects of the process without systematically or explicitly knowing he is doing so. Though both formulating opposites and thinking about opposites are vital aspects of the janusian process, they also can be entirely independent activities. Formulating opposites, for instance, may play a role in any type of task, manual, intellectual, or creative. Important to the distinction between formulating opposites and janusian thinking is the factor of temporal sequence. In ordinary thinking, and some specialized types I shall discuss in the following chapter, opposites are formed or developed and considered sequentially or successively in time; in janusian thinking they are formed or developed and considered simultaneously. With this distinction firmly in mind, we can turn more fully to the nature of janusian thinking as a psychological process.

9

JANUSIAN THINKING AS A PSYCHOLOGICAL PROCESS

Throughout this book, I have emphasized the psychological status of janusian thinking as a conscious, intentional process and as a special type of secondary process cognition. This emphasis has been necessary because, in Freud's description of the more primitive form of thought, primary process thinking, equivalence of opposites was a definite feature.[1] Freud's own recognition of this feature of primary process thinking, this creative leap on his part, was a product, I would now suggest, of janusian thinking.[2] While there is no reason to doubt the validity of Freud's specific formulation,[3] psychoanalytic theorists and practitioners have unthinkingly tended to relegate all psychological references to opposition to the primary process realm. Freud himself made this error in his small but enthusiastic work, "The Antithetical Meaning of Primal Words,"[4] written ten years after his monumental work on dreams. Finding what he thought were numerous instances of words having bimodally antithetical meanings—for example, "cleave," meaning both to separate and to join, "altus," meaning both high and low—in primitive or historically older languages, he believed he had discovered additional evidence for equivalence of opposites in primitive or primary process thought. Not only were his conclusions incorrect from the point of view of linguistics and etymology (i.e., words such as "cleave" and "altus" were not initially bimodal in meaning, such words had homographic homophones—identical in both spelling and sound—with different etymological roots), but he was also unaware of the rather adaptive and sophisticated nature of the linguistic categories used by so-called primitive peoples. The latter has since been impressively demonstrated by modern anthropologists such as Lévi-Strauss.[5]

Freud's errors can certainly be excused on the basis of incautious zeal in a great first explorer, and buttressed by our understanding of the complexities and abstractions involved in the conceptualization and manipulation of opposition, it should now be easier to see how conceptualization of simultaneous opposites belongs in the realm of high level secondary process thinking. But more clarification is still needed. Other types of psychological phenomena, including modes of cognition, affects, psychological structures, and dynamisms, bear some resemblance to janusian thinking and, in order to establish the psychological dimensions of the thought process distinctly, it is necessary to consider several of them. In this chapter, I shall discuss the following: Jungian psychology, dialectical thinking, dualistic thinking, conflict, and ambivalence. In order to avoid extensive digression, my discussion will be, in some cases, cursory and brief. I shall, however, show some outstanding points of dissimilarity and similarity or contact with the janusian process.

Jung and Opposites

So prominent is opposition in the psychological theory propounded by Jung that his work should properly be cited, along with that of the philosophers in the last chapter, as a major instance of Western intellectual thought emphasizing opposites.[6] Though initially a follower of Freud, Jung eventually developed a related but alternate psychological theory that has wide influence today. As an attempt at scientific psychology, Jung's theory properly belongs in the realm of Western intellectual thought, but it also shows the strong influence of Eastern philosophy and mysticism. And, to a certain extent, it is from Eastern thought that Jung derived his emphasis on opposites.

A basic tenet of Jungian psychology is the psychic struggle to achieve reconciliation of opposites. Many aspects of human psychological structure are, according to Jung, in opposition to each other and reconciling opposites is a major motivating force for behavior. In opposition are the attitudes he called introversion and extroversion, functions he distinguished as thinking and feeling, intuition and sensation, the principles of Logos and Eros, archetypes of anima and animus, and inner and outer worlds. While each of the two attitudes of introversion and extroversion as well as the four psychological functions often characterize or define particular "psychological types" such as the introvert, the extrovert, or the feeling type, a cardinal point in Jungian psychology is that no person is ever completely of one defined type. The introvert has an extroverted side, for instance, and vice versa, and between these sides there is an interplay and a struggle for reconciliation.

Emphasis on opposites in Jungian theory is most fully realized in the formulations about the anima and animus archetypes. Anima is the male soul image and animus the female one. Not only are these images or archetypes considered unequivocally opposite to each other, but Jung intentionally inverted the usual Latin endings for male ("us") and female ("a") in applying these terms in order to make clear that the anima was the female aspect of the male psyche and the animus the male aspect of the female psyche. The female soul image represents unconscious forces, such as tendencies toward close interpersonal relationships (unconscious Eros), that were often opposed to and in conflict with conscious forces (conscious Logos) in the male. Conversely, the male soul image represented unconscious forces that were often in opposition to conscious female strivings.

The notion of an interplay between the anima and animus archetypes was the basis for a good deal of Jung's theorizing about the relationship between the individual and the culture. He became quite interested in the Taoist symbol of the t'ai-chi tu, the symbol discussed earlier (fig. 5) which represents the mystical relationship of male and female forces in the universe and is the central Taoist symbol of the nature of all things. This symbol pictorially represents both the opposition and the close affinity—with an almost fluid interaction—between the male and female principles or forces. For Jung, also, there was often a close affinity between these and other opposites. Another symbol depicting a relationship between opposites and dating back in origin as far as paleolithic times, is the mandala or magic circle. Mandalas generally represent the transformation of opposites into a third term or uniting symbol, the phenomenon called *coincidentia oppositorum.* Jung often used the mandala as a specific representation for his construct of the Self, and it commanded his interest so much and in so many different ways that he and others have sometimes considered it a symbol for his entire psychology.

Janusian thinking and the pervasive opposition in psychic nature emphasized by Jung are not the same. Janusian thinking is a distinct cognitive function operating particularly in the creative process. It is not involved in other types of processes, nor does it depend on, and necessarily arise from, human psychic structure as composed of opposites. Surely there is some compatibility between the construct of janusian thinking and the Jungian theoretical formulations. If, for example, Jung were correct that psychic life is perfused with various types of opposites, janusian thinking would have specially extensive penetration and power, particularly when its effects are overtly manifest in a completed work of art. Simultaneous oppositions directly presented in artistic works would embody many of the salient elements of psychic life, and give an appearance, though not necessarily a realization, of the reconciliation of opposites.[7]

Janusian thinking does not, however, arise from a general force motivating everyone toward reconciliation of opposites. Janusian thinking is a particular characteristic of the creative process and therefore is a function of the psychological structure of creative persons. As there is no reason to assume that all persons have the capacity to use this type of thought or, at least, there is no evidence that ordinarily they do use it, the thinking does not arise directly from a general force present in everyone. Moreover, janusian thinking is not motivated by a need to reconcile opposites, nor do janusian constructs and formulations represent *realized reconciliations* of opposites. Janusian thinking posits temporal and functional *coexistence* of opposites within a single framework or context and the possibility of *simultaneous validity* of antithetical entities or constructs, but as a form of cognition it does not reconcile these antitheses or oppositions. Janusian thinking may provide a basis for reconciliation surely, a step toward reconciliation more exactly, but actual reconciliation is carried out by other thought processes such as induction and logic. These statements will gain strength and clarity when the precise meaning of reconciliation is considered in connection with the dialectic presently.

Jung's interest in the t'ai-chi tu and the mandala, and his recognition of similarities, confluences, and interrelationships among oppositions great and small are related to factors in the janusian process. As a creative theorist, many of his concepts pertaining to opposition, and to other factors also, may have arisen from his own janusian thoughts and constructs. However, although psychic life, even cosmic forces, might conceivably operate as Jung suggests through the confluence and antagonism of opposites, that alone would not account for janusian thinking as a creative form of cognition, though it might account for some of its power.

Dialectical Thinking

The greatest source of confusion about janusian thinking concerns its relationship to dialectics. Many of the finest philosophers, theorists, scientists, and other outstanding thinkers characteristically have applied a dialectic approach to some of the most difficult conceptual problems, and the value of such an approach has been demonstrated over and over throughout the history of thought. Moreover, the dialectic approach, as a style of writing or of presenting arguments, is a notably effective one: criticisms and counter arguments are considered before they are raised by a reader or by an opponent, polarities are appraised, and this mode of presentation is often emotionally stimulating and dramatic.

Though the term "dialectic" has been used in different senses and in different ways by different philosophers, it is, in its lexical sense, merely the word for logical discourse or argument. I am here, however, specifically referring to a type of thinking that has long been recognized and used in intellectual circles, and was first systematically described and used by Hegel.[8] According to Hegel, this type of thinking proceeds by means of a sequence of steps: an assertion of a thesis or statement of a position, point of view, problem, or series of facts; followed by the statement and discussion of the antithesis, the contrary or opposite position or point of view, or the denial of the thesis; followed by the synthesis, the combination of the partial truths of the thesis and antithesis into a higher stage of truths. Once arrived at, of course, the synthesis can serve—according to Hegel, it always serves—as a thesis for further progressions.

Now, janusian thinking differs from this type of progression in two major ways: (1) it does not involve a synthesis; (2) it does involve simultaneity of opposites or antitheses rather than sequence. The Hegelian formulation of synthesis is quite specific and clear: elements of the thesis and antithesis are *combined* to form another, presumably more valid, position. Such a combination brings about a reconciliation of opposites because, as the word reconciliation implies, opposing positions are brought into harmony with each other and conflicting aspects are resolved. Characteristically, the synthesis is achieved in one or more of several different ways as follows: showing that all of the elements in the conflicting positions are not and never were truly antithetical; demonstrating that many of the conflicting elements can be logically combined with each other; or, by taking advantage of the contextual relativism of oppositions discussed in the last chapter, showing how opposites may not be antithetical in another, presumably higher, context. Synthesis and reconciliation of opposites are strongly related and interconnected; synthesis produces reconciliation of opposites and such reconciliation is, in turn, an aspect of the wider synthesizing function.

But janusian thinking is not the same as reconciling or as synthesizing opposites; if it were, it would hardly be a new discovery. The assertion that a pair or group of antitheses while being in conflict are yet all valid at the same time does not obliterate or compromise the identity or the integrity of the component antitheses. No combination or reconciliation is indicated. In many cases, the assertion can and does lead, by means of logical processes, to the formulation of a synthesis or reconciliation, but the janusian construct is not the same as that synthesis or reconciliation. The construct may stimulate and facilitate synthesis, sometimes in a crucial way, but it is not itself a synthesis. As a facilitating factor, janusian thinking may enter into a dialectic sequence and procedure, particularly a creative one. But synthesis, and especially combination of antithetical elements, is not a necessary outcome of janusian thinking; the janusian thought may consist of positing a paradox which is *intrinsically* unresolvable, unreconciliable, and unsusceptible to synthesis.

It may be further helpful to consider in some detail the difference between the factors of combination and integration. Combination involves the bringing together of entities, or parts of entities, to form another entity in which the original entities no longer retain their individual properties. Thus, in the classically described case, atoms such as hydrogen and oxygen are brought together to form water, a compound having none of the properties of the original atoms. Integration, on the other hand, involves the formation of an entity different from its components in which the properties of the original components are still *manifest* or *operative.* A characteristic example of an integration is shown by a poetic metaphor such as Sylvia Plath's "How long can my hands be a bandage to his hurt?"[9] This metaphor is a total entity conveying an overall meaning and impact while the properties of the individual elements are neither obliterated, nor compromised, nor submerged. All aspects, whole and part, contribute to the effect and sense. The idea of the protection and the dependency of another person stimulates numerous associations and thoughts and the specific elements of hands, bandage, and hurt all arouse specific associations as well. "Hurt" suggests psychological suffering as well as physical injury; "hands" are gripping, or supplicating as well as protective; "bandage" is a covering, not a cure. Furthermore, there is interaction between, and mutual modification of elements: the hands take on some of the soft, swathing and encircling qualities of the bandage, and the bandage takes on the strength and adherence of the hands. Rather than combination of a hand and a bandage, we experience an active integration of these elements with the overall sense. Both overall meaning and individual components operate to produce the integrated entity, here, the metaphor. Janusian thinking is more intrinsically related to such an integration than it is to combination and synthesis. In janusian constructs, opposites retain their antithetical qualities while being simultaneously valid or operative; they thereby readily form the basis for an integrated product.[10]

I shall not draw hard and fast distinctions between the synthesis aspect of the dialectic and janusian thinking because products of the latter can and do lead to syntheses, especially in science, and dialectic syntheses can be elaborated into integrations. Distinct from the factors involved in janusian thinking, however, are the combination or reconciliation effect and the highly generic principles of the dialectic. When janusian constructs enter into the dialectic process, they may, once they are formulated and proposed, be subjected to and elaborated by a dialectic analysis, but the analysis does not generate them.

An even more critical distinction between the dialectic and the janusian process involves the temporal factors of sequence and simultaneity. In the former, opposites or antitheses are treated sequentially and in the latter, simultaneously. Because the dialectic is a logical discursive process, it requires the sequential weighing and analysis of antithetical or conflicting propositions, points of view, or facts. Only when each of the opposing positions are carefully and separately considered is it possible to propose a synthesis or, viewed more impressionistically, only then does a meaningful synthesis become immanent or apparent. But janusian thinking is, if you will, significantly more impatient; opposites and antitheses are proposed as being *simultaneously* valid. While the initiator of the janusian thought is also aware of the logical possibilities of the proposition, they are neither fully in his mind nor has he worked them out beforehand. At different points, janusian thinking involves the positing of a problem and the finding of a solution. Again, Sartre may very well have realized, in a single moment, that both Being and Nothingness were essential and were irreducible in a meaningful ontology and, following that, turned to a long and brilliant dialectical process to work out his previously arrived at solution. So, too, a scientist may interpret his data in terms of simultaneous opposition, say, proposing that entities behave simultaneously as particles and waves. For him this is an early formulation of a problem. After a laborious series of procedures—involving observations and experiments as well as dialectic and other types of analysis—he discovers how particles and waves operate simultaneously. This is not tautological; the solution and the problem are both janusian formulations but a good deal of exegesis lies between.

In a given dialectical account, it is always difficult to know whether the thinker developed either or both his problems and solutions in the manner as presented to "the world," so to speak. Frequently it is difficult for the thinker himself to remember the exact steps and sequences and he cannot report about this. Simultaneous antitheses and oppositions especially are difficult to keep in mind and simultaneity soon gives way to sequences and to the demands of logic, factors that begin the dialectic process. Positing for instance that sex and death are the same, or that they coexist simultaneously in the same process, leads rather quickly to a separate consideration of the attributes of various aspects of sexuality followed by a separate consideration of the attributes of death.[11] Sexual intercourse involves spasmodic bodily movements, a sense of release, a loss of individuality or a self annihilation, and a profound relaxation. Death involves release, an annihilation of self, and dying can involve spasmodic movements and total relaxation. With further contemplation, aspects of one are compared to aspects of the other in a continuing sequence. The requirements of writing something out and putting it on a page inevitably produce a sequence, for that matter. Initially simultaneous conceptions are made sequential, straightened out, or otherwise submerged. Only careful retracing of steps, requiring careful and sometimes dogged questioning or analysis, will reveal the original structure of the thought.

Certain types of sequences occur in the janusian process, but sequential analysis of the nature of the oppositions is not one of them; that is part of the dialectic. One type is a sequence starting with general interest in and attraction to antitheses and oppositions, then recognition and specification of particular opposites, then formulation of simultaneous opposites. Another type is careful preparation for and development of a task, extensive assessment and data gathering, and formulation of hypotheses, all carried out without any attention to opposition until, at the final moment in the sequence, opposites are specified and conceptualized simultaneously.

Janusian constructs are way stations toward integration of opposites and antitheses. Although conceptualization of simultaneous antitheses or opposites is not the same as integration of these entities, it sets the stage or provides the basis for a subsequent integration. Usually, homospatial thinking functions to produce such integrations, but dialectic thinking or analysis can serve in some fashion also. Although characteristically oriented toward synthesis and combination, dialectic thinking can facilitate integration of opposites and antitheses, especially in science and philosophy. Dialectic analyses and syntheses of the elements in a janusian construct could function as steps toward integration and they could function to integrate janusian formulations into larger theories or analyses. Examples of the latter might be Freud's or Sartre's use of dialectic thinking to integrate Conscious/Unconscious or sex/aggression and Being and Nothingness, respectively, into comprehensive systems. As some persons who employ janusian thinking also tend otherwise to think in dialectical terms, there surely are some close relationships between the two forms of thought despite the separation and distinctiveness of their functions with respect to creativity. While janusian thinking is intrinsic to the creative process, effective dialectical thinking, like any other form of effective thinking, sometimes plays a role. Cardinally shared by both janusian and dialectical thinking is a concern with opposition and antithesis, and future exploration may reveal other interesting and important connections.

Dualistic Thinking

Because janusian thinking is a step toward integration of antitheses and opposites, there is really little reason to confuse it with dualistic thinking, the tendency to formulate concepts or systems in terms of two exhaustive categories. However, confusion could arise because of common elements between janusian and dialectical thinking. Dialecticians are particularly prone to formulating dualisms and, in assessing a particular dialectic system of thought, it is often hard to judge whether fondness for duality or the saliency of the dialectic method has been primary. To this day, there is still much controversy about the presence of dualistic thinking in the works of such influential giants as Plato, Descartes, Kant, Hegel, Leibniz, Marx, Nietzsche, and Freud. Are they, for instance, limited by such dualisms as real and ideal, matter and mind, mind and body, reason and faith, material and spiritual, and so forth? Are two alternatives or factors emphasized and considered on the basis of economy, symmetry, or merely simplistic and limited conceptualizing? And, from a more profound point of view, philosophers and theologians often wonder about a metaphysical basis for dualistic versus trinitarian religions and systems of thought.[12]

Although the dialectic method is often associated with dualistic formulations, there is no necessary reason that it must be so. Moreover, janusian thinking, which occurs in conjunction with many other types of thinking beside the dialectic one, need hardly share any guilt by association. Nevertheless, both janusian thinking and dialectics are based in part on opposition, and opposition, it will be remembered, is often conceived in binary or dichotomous terms. Binary oppositions such as sex and aggression or material and spiritual are surely dualisms. How does dualism actually fit in? In no intrinsic or direct fashion. In the first place, dualisms only logically enter the picture when certain types of opposites are formulated; scalar or polar opposites (based on continuities) do not lend themselves to dualistic descriptions because no two exhaustive categories are formed. It would be totally inappropriate, for instance, to propose that all color is based on a dualism of black and white because it is clearly necessary to take account of the scale of various grades of gray. Indeed, attempting to make a dualism out of black and white has figuratively come to represent poor thinking and perception; "seeing things in black and white" is the exemplar of a pejorative reference to dualism.

Second, and especially pertinent to janusian thinking, there is no intrinsic reason for any opposites, whether dichotomous (cut) or scalar, to be considered as dualistic pairs. When real and ideal are considered as opposites, many other oppositions are possible as well: real and unreal, real and supernatural, real and fantastic; also, there is ideal and flawed, ideal and low, ideal and ordinary, and so on. For sex and aggression, there are virtually unlimited possibilities: aggression and docility, aggression and peace, aggression and conciliation, sex and chastity, sex and death, sex and abstinence, sex and religion, and many, many others depending on which of the manifold aspects of these concepts are considered. Multiple oppositions of this sort are characteristically involved in janusian thinking and, for that matter, they are often involved in other advanced types of thinking about opposites, in science and in dialectic thinking as well. But the sine qua non of janusian thinking is multiplicity and multiple opposition involving the multiple and varied nuances of words, concepts, and sensory phenomena. Therefore, no intrinsic dualism could be at all involved in the janusian process. To say that multiple opposition could be ultimately reduced to a dualism—that is, multiples of two are binary or dualistic in basic structure, multiples of three are treble in structure—is begging the question because multiple oppositions are rich and complex and not systematically related to each other.

Conflict

While dualism, dialectic thinking, and the Jungian structure of the psyche have no intrinsic or direct relationship to janusian thinking, conflict is connected to this process in a major way. Conflict instigates and generates the process of janusian thinking, and conflict is manifest, or at least influential, in the products and results. Both scientific and artistic creations retain an element of conflict—psychological, aesthetic, and/or intellectual—in their substance and structure. The impulse to create arises from psychological conflict, conflict that is necessary for the antithetical structure of janusian thinking. One of the reasons janusian thinking plays such a large role in creations is that it helps produce the sense that we treasure so highly in art of both tension and conflict together with balance and harmony. In science, it produces both intellectual discovery and resolution together with a sense of discrepancy, an intellectual tension and conflict that propels the creative scientist to search further. Although conflict is necessary for janusian thinking, it is not sufficient to produce the process. The janusian process is not merely a direct or an indirect manifestation of psychological conflict.

Psychological conflict is universal and ubiquitous in human experience. To say that psychological conflict is necessary for janusian thinking and for both the artistic and scientific creative processes is not to connect psychopathology with creativity. Psychological conflict is not intrinsically pathological or inevitably connected to illness. Indeed, such conflict is so ubiquitous and, in some ways, such an appropriate response to the complexity and flux of human experience that it is objectively best described only as a state of being. This state of being is not much different for the creative person than it is for the rest of us: it is experienced both consciously and unconsciously as a sense of particular inner forces in opposition with each other, an opposition that sometimes abates, or is shunted away, or is resolved, or is replaced, or continues throughout the course of life. What may be different about the creative person is his capacity to embody this inner psychological conflict in janusian constructs and formulations. For, in structure, such constructs and formulations are either or both the expression of conflict or the wished-for resolution of conflict. Formulating two or more specific opposites or antitheses coexisting simultaneously embodies and expresses conflict. As the coexistence and cooperation obviates total and intolerable contradiction or, at the very least, mutual annihilation, a sense of resolution is also expressed. In short, the janusian thought is emotionally coordinate with the idea of having one's cake and eating it, too.

If janusian thinking were merely an expression of the emotional wish to have one's cake and eat it too, if it were only the hoped-for magical resolution of conflict, it would be a direct manifestation of primary process thinking. Such, however, is not the case. Powered and motivated by emotional conflict and unconscious wishes, janusian thinking is a form of conscious abstract formulating and conceptualizing that produces creations. It is, again, a form of secondary, not primary, process cognition. Although the elements of an unconscious conflict may appear in the context of a janusian construct, the defense mechanism of negation is operating rather than either primary process thinking or an eruption of unconscious conflict into consciousness. For the creative person, negation and janusian thinking are special ways of dealing with unconscious conflict. Conscious conflicts also are at times involved. Seldom, however, does the janusian process function to resolve conscious or unconscious conflicts directly, but such conflicts may be resolved as a result of their externalization in the creative process and the concomitant operation of other types of cognitive and emotional factors, creative and otherwise.

In producing creations, janusian thinking brings conflictual elements—intellectual, aesthetic, and emotional—together and into juxtaposition with one another. This in itself helps reduce certain types of conflict maintained by lack of comprehension and understanding; in other cases, juxtaposed elements are rendered more susceptible to comparision and integration as well as resolution. Despite its potential for integration and harmony, however, the janusian construct and concatenation of opposites and antitheses is itself always fraught with a sense of discord and tension. The thoughts and ideas are subjectively uncomfortable to formulate and they produce an intense quality of what Festinger called cognitive dissonance,[13] or a feeling of cognitive conflict.

Ambivalence

The relationship between ambivalence and janusian thinking is highly complex. Consideration of this relationship leads to the labyrinthian realm of topics such as creativity and schizophrenia, and creativity and general psychopathology. I shall not attempt here to pursue the latter issue to the extent it deserves, but instead I shall touch on some highlights pending a fuller discussion in the future.

The term "ambivalence" was first applied to psychological phenomena by Eugen Bleuler in 1919. Derived from chemical terminology, the root, valence, denotes the "value" or combining power of an atom. By "ambi-valence," Bleuler intended to designate the tendency of his schizophrenic patients to "endow the most diverse psychisms with both a positive and negative indicator,"[14] and he distinguished three types: affective ambivalence, ambivalence of will, and intellectual ambivalence. Although he provided rich and detailed descriptions of apparent instances of the three types in schizophrenia, Freud and other clinicians restricted the use of the term to one type, affective ambivalence, and proving more useful and precise, such restricted use has persisted in contemporary psychiatric practice.

Affective ambivalence consists of the tendency of persons suffering from schizophrenia—and, as we now know, a wide range of other types of illness are also included, notably the obsessive compulsive neurosis—to possess strong contradictory feelings, such as love and hate, toward a single person or object. With respect to janusian thinking, an immediate and sharp distinction obtains. Janusian thinking involves simultaneous and conscious cognitions, and it is the nature of affects that they can neither be experienced definitively and precisely nor simultaneously on a conscious level. Affective ambivalence is always inferred from a person's behavior by an observer; the person himself does not consciously experience defined contradictory affects simultaneously, he feels only a general sense of uncertainty and indecisiveness. For an observer, the uncertainty is manifest in the person's actions, and affective ambivalence is assumed to be the cause. Eventually, concrete feelings such as love and hate may come alternately into the ambivalent person's awareness, and he then may come to understand the roots of such uncertainty. It is at that point described in conceptual terms, such as, "I have mixed feelings," or "I think I both love and hate my mother." In Bleuler's original description of affective ambivalence, he cites the example of a patient referring to her lover in the following way: "You devil, you angel, you devil, you angel."[15] Sequential feelings oscillating between opposite poles are represented. If the patient were able to say, "I feel you are both a devil and an angel," or even, "I both love and hate you," she would be making abstract inferences from her own concrete feelings and behavior.

This is not a hair-splitting distinction: it is based on an important difference between affects and cognitions and helps to specify a probable connection between affective ambivalence and janusian thought. Affective ambivalence, like conflict, is very likely one of the motivating forces leading to janusian thoughts. This should not be surprising, because ambivalence and conflict are highly interrelated with one another: ambivalence leads to conflict and conflict produces various types of ambivalences. Thus, ambivalent feelings may instigate the janusian process, but particular janusian constructs do not themselves consist of feelings or concrete experiences, they consist of abstract conceptualizations. Experience with creative people does indicate that they are in fact often highly ambivalent in many areas of their lives.[16] But, although ambivalent feelings may instigate the janusian process, such feelings, unlike the more general factor of conflict, are not continually involved.

But what of the other types of ambivalence described by Bleuler, ambivalence of will and intellectual ambivalence? As an example of ambivalence of will, Bleuler describes a patient who clamors for release from the institution and then violently and abusively resists when informed that he is about to be discharged. Here, again, there is a sequential oscillation informing an observer that contradictory tendencies exist. To draw a meaningful distinction between this type of ambivalence and the previous affective type is actually quite difficult. Will, in the sense described, is quite close to affect; we could easily say, for example, that the patient *feels* ambivalent about going home. Bleuler himself realized this similarity between the types. Because the types are similar, ambivalence both of will and of affect are essentially distinct from janusian thinking in a similar way. Bleuler's ambivalence of will should more appropriately be considered to be a form of conflict which, in modern terms, would be designated as a conflict of motives. In that case, it would have the same relationship to janusian thinking as other forms of conflict.

Seldom is the term ambivalence applied nowadays to the type of behavior exemplifying Bleuler's third type: intellectual ambivalence. Here, the patient says, "I am a human being like yourself even though I am not a human being."[17] But regardless of what it is called, such behavior is still found in schizophrenic patients and it requires careful analysis because in form it is close to the conceptualization of simultaneous antithesis of janusian thinking.

The patient's statement, "I am a human being like yourself even though I am not a human being," taken by itself appears to have all the features of a janusian formulation. As an assertion of simultaneous antithesis, it seems pregnant with meaning and somewhat poetic. Taken figuratively, it suggests many levels of meaning: the patient knows that he is human, but he doesn't feel human; he is at war within himself, a human aspect clashing with what he considers to be a nonhuman aspect; you, the other person, do not treat him as a human being; something about him is lacking; you and the patient both belong to some mystical or superordinate category where humanness is beside the point. As a psychotherapist working with this patient, all of these figurative meanings of his statement should be taken as potentially relevant. Presenting one or more in the form of an interpretation of what the patient is really "saying" can lead to an engagement, an inroad into the patient's emotional life that produces further clarification and exploration. But is it correct to say that the patient had all these meanings consciously in mind when he made the statement? In answering this, I do not mean to presume that I know exactly what goes on, at any given moment, in a schizophrenic patient's mind. Nevertheless, I believe I can answer it on the basis of what is currently known about schizophrenia from various types of clinical observations. No, it is highly unlikely that the patient has these meanings consciously in mind when he makes the statement because that would require a conscious intention for the remark to be taken *figuratively.* In order for the patient to intend figurative meaning, it is necessary that he be aware of the contradictory elements in the statement.[18] He must know (and believe) that he is expressing a literal impossibility because such impossibility alone denotes figurative intent (for the person speaking as well as the person spoken to). But, there is little reason to believe that the schizophrenic person making such a remark is aware of the impossibility and contradiction. In fact, quite the reverse applies: the patient believes in the literal truth of the statement that he is both a human being and not a human being at the same time. This type of equivalence of opopposites is a criterion attribute of primary process thinking; such literal equivalence characterizes schizophrenic thought. The patient in this instance has not formulated a janusian thought at all; he cannot use the thought for creative production because it is conceptually meaningless and idiosyncratic, rather than profound. Referring to my discussion of opposition in the previous chapter, it appears that the patient thinks only of the similarities rather than the contradictions in opposites.

Some factors operating with this patient can perhaps be made clearer in terms of Lidz's recent and salient formulations about the nature of schizophrenic thinking. Tracing the origin of cognitive deficit in schizophrenia to childhood egocentricity (as the term is used by Piaget), Lidz describes a resulting difficulty in conceptual category formation as the hallmark of the illness. "Categories," he says, "are formed by selecting common attributes of things or events to bestow some degree of equivalence to experiences that can never be identical."[19] Necessary to such category formation is the capacity to discern and define boundaries between elements of experience and to distinguish the essential from the nonessential. Category formation, therefore, is the basis for abstract thinking. Typically, Lidz points out, the schizophrenic has difficulty forming such categories, both in language and in thought, and becomes preoccupied with what Lidz terms, "the intercategorical realm."[20] This realm consists of fantasies about fusion of the self and the mother, intersexuality, and other matters lying between the ordinary boundaries of experience and thought.

Consistent with this view, a difficulty in forming categories involves a fluidity and a lack of distinction among opposites and contradictions. Essential to forming categories is the capacity to separate both elements that belong together and those that do *not* belong. Therefore, recognition of contradiction is a crucial factor. Persons suffering from schizophrenia, however, have enormous difficulty in just this area; they cannot eliminate contradictory elements and they include inessentials (overinclusion)[21] in the categories they form. Opposites and antitheses are therefore often considered equivalent or identical because of superficial resemblances. Such superficial resemblances usually have some egocentric relevance, and when we explore the basis for equating a particular pair or group of opposites, we often learn a good deal about the patient's preoccupations and concerns.

The basis, then, of statements by schizophrenic persons demonstrating what Bleuler called intellectual ambivalence is this significant difficulty in recognizing contradictions and in forming appropriate categories, along with egocentric preoccupations and concerns. This is a far cry from janusian thinking, where the creative person is acutely and sharply aware of the contradictory elements between a particular pair or among a series of opposites or antitheses and he nevertheless posits that they are equivalently valid or simultaneously operative for the purpose of attaining aesthetic effects and higher truths.

With respect to affective ambivalence and ambivalence of will, lack of contradiction also plays a role. When the schizophrenic patient utters a series of remarks suggesting affective ambivalence or when he first asks to leave the hospital and then resists discharge the next day, he is also *not* aware of the contradictory nature of his behavior. This is not to say that the patient lacks an experience of conflict; quite the contrary. A constant and recurrent feeling of conflict without awareness of the nature of the conflict is particularly marked in schizophrenia. But the patient does seem unable to understand and to formulate conceptually at that moment that he has said something contradictory or behaved in a contradictory fashion. When he becomes able to say, "I have mixed feelings" about someone or something, this usually means that he has come to acknowledge and/or recognize contradiction. As therapists, we acknowledge this achievement by saying that the patient has attained insight.

Though I have devoted the major part of this discussion to a consideration of ambivalence in the schizophrenic condition, severe and persistent ambivalent feelings also occur in a large number of clinical conditions. Furthermore, ambivalent feelings are involved, though less severely and persistently, in a wide variety of interpersonal relationships; they occur in the healthy as well as the sick. In none of these cases are such feelings necessarily connected with janusian thinking. As feelings, they are neither experienced simultaneously nor do they necessarily become translated into the special conceptual configurations, nor become applied to the special contexts, of the creative process. When Bleuler's type of intellectual ambivalence becomes manifest in schizophrenia or in other conditions such as the obsessive compulsive neurosis, it is a product of primary process rather than janusian thinking. When a person with an obsessive compulsive neurosis believes that he can both decide and not decide, or can leave his wife and not leave her, we have little trouble recognizing the inability to acknowledge contradiction and the emergence of primary process thought. Sometimes, such ambivalent feelings could provide a basis for a janusian formulation, even constructed by the obsessive compulsive or schizophrenic, but in such cases a specific recognition of logical contradiction—the intervention of abstract thinking and insight—has invariably occurred.

In sum, janusian thinking is a cognitive process involving high degrees of abstraction. Not based on or derived from an oppositionally structured psyche or a type of dialectic discourse or method, it is a special type of secondary process thinking. Arising always from psychological and intellectual conflict, janusian thinking embodies and presents conflicts and provides a means to their resolution. Sometimes the janusian process is associated with ambivalence, but it always involves strong appreciation of the contradictory nature of opposites and antitheses. As a process, janusian thinking involves specification of opposites or antitheses, presentation or postulation of opposites or antitheses existing or operating simultaneously, application in a creative context with elaboration, and frequently some type of later transformation. Experientially, the process is often truncated and a janusian formulation arises as a leap of thought that overcomes apparent contradictions and both initiates and facilitates the construction and development of creations.

10

HOMOSPATIAL THINKING

Given a grasp of what is so far known about janusian thinking, it is possible to explore and to clarify further the role in creativity of homospatial thinking. One function of the homospatial process is to operate in conjunction with the janusian process in order to produce integrated aesthetic entities, and scientific discoveries and formulations. I have already emphasized a preliminary or preparatory aspect of the latter process: the tendency to operate in early stages of the creative process with a later alteration or transformation into completed creations. I have pointed out that other types of cognition operate in conjunction with this one to produce various types of overt effects in the substance of a final created product. In science, philosophy, and other types of rationalistic discourse, logical, dialectical, or technically oriented forms of thinking may operate to render janusian formulations into formats necessary for communication, consensus, or experimentation. Such formats may consist of resolutions, combinations, reconciliations, and syntheses of the particular simultaneous antitheses and oppositions in a janusian construct. In art, such operations and effects may function to produce plausible representation, moral and logical consistency, or effective communication. But both in science and in art, janusian formulations are overtly, and with little alteration, frequently incorporated directly into integrations, unities in which the elements retain their individual qualities rather than combine.

Either at the very moment of formulation or at some later time, homospatial thinking operates in conjunction with janusian thinking to produce integrated entities such as artistic and scientific metaphors or more fully developed paradigms and models. By means of homospatial thinking, opposites and antitheses in a janusian construct are superimposed or otherwise fused in space and integrations are produced. Earlier, we saw an example of this effect in the poetic creative process when the janusian formulation of the horse as simultaneously human and beastly was followed by the fusion of these opposites in the visual conception of the riderless horse together with the horse and rider, and then by integrated presentation of horse and rider in the poem. In the scientific creative process, Einstein's initial conception leading to the general theory of relativity, the janusian construct of falling and being at rest at the same time, was couched in an arresting spatial image—"a man falling from the roof of a house"—that suggests the concomitant operation of the homospatial process. As janusian formulations usually lead to an integration of antitheses and opposites—simultaneous operation or existence is not the same as unification or effective representation[1]—homospatial thinking is frequently conjointly operative. Moreover, janusian constructs are intrinsically abstract; oppositions and antitheses are by themselves abstract, and simultaneous opposites and antitheses are even more so. Homospatial thinking and other cognitive processes are required to render janusian constructs into apprehensible, concrete, or even comprehensible entities.

Aside from this function in conjunction with the janusian process, homospatial thinking operates independently and extensively in the creative process. The homospatial process is directly responsible for the creation of all types of effective metaphors and it has a considerable and wide effect. Earlier, I cited several instances of this form of thinking in the achievement of important scientific discoveries. Since effective metaphors, both narrow and highly extensive ones, have a far-reaching function in all creative intellectual accomplishments, homospatial thinking can be assumed to have operated in religious and philosophical creations as well. But, in order now to provide some further documented evidence of the creative function of the homospatial process and to clarify its diverse types of operation and various effects, I shall turn to the areas of the visual arts and music. Following that, I shall return to poetry and literature, where there are yet some striking manifestations and extensions to describe.[2]

Visual Arts

Because homospatial thinking often involves visual imagery, we might expect to find it widely operating in the visual arts, namely, painting, sculpture, architecture, and related forms. This is indeed the case. In order to explain the particular manner in which homospatial thinking operates in these arts, however, I must first clarify some aesthetic and psychological matters. For the person not accustomed to think in visual terms, there is the need for "seeing" a particular constant factor in visual works of art, and for the psychologist accustomed to the traditional terminology of perceptual psychology—particularly gestalt psychology—there is a need to go beyond those terms. Postponing a direct focus on the creative process in the visual arts, we shall consider a factor in the completed work.

The constant factor in the visual arts to which I refer is the *visual metaphor*, a factor defined and described by the aesthetician Virgil Aldrich. Although others, including Picasso, have used similar terms or have at least recognized aspects of the phenomenon, Aldrich explicated it rather fully in two seminal papers.[3] A particular example of such a visual metaphor discussed by Aldrich should clarify the meaning of the term. In a landscape painting called *Courmayeur* (or *Courmayeur et les dents des géants;* see fig. 32), by the expressionist Kokoschka, Aldrich calls attention to the particular area where the roofs of the houses of this Alpine village are in direct juxtaposition with the mountains in the background, and he says:

> Look . . . at the roof-mountain area of the picture. . . . The similarity of the colours and shapes . . . draws the part of the mountain . . . forward and tends to recess the house similarly qualified until they appear in the same plane in the picture. The result of this sort of fusion is *partly* a denaturing of house and mountain . . . a structuring [of] picture-space without the influence of representation. But only partly. One does not get entirely away from seeing the pictorial elements as a roof and part of a mountain. But . . . the *represented* distance between them [is overcome] by placement in the same plane, there is fusion of house and mountain natures. Thus is a part of the mountain domesticated, and the house (domicile) takes on a mountainous character. If "organic" unity has ever meant anything as applied to a work of visual art, it means interanimation or fusion in this latter sense, where different sorts of things with separate natures in routine life are transformed into a single (though complex) nature. Such transfiguration by metaphor is accurately reported in linguistic metaphors, such as "the roof *is* a part of the mountain" or the other way around; though . . . unifications of elements within the content of the picture are not usually verbally reported but are more an affair of what is visually sensed.[4]

Central to the concept of visual metaphor is an integration of elements into a whole or a unity, an integration with its own identity and also with individual elements that are recognizable and retain discrete characteristics. As I pointed out in the previous chapter, such integration is the essence of linguistic metaphors, such as "How long can my hands be a bandage to his hurt?" and Aldrich aptly alludes to a direct analogy between the visual and linguistic types. Moreover, Aldrich points out that seeing the visual metaphor involves fusion and the visualization of the elements of house and mountain *in the same plane* in the picture.

Fig. 32. Oskar Kokoschka. *Courmayeur et les dents des géants,* 1927. The roofs of the houses and the mountains interact with each other to produce a visual metaphor; the mountain is "domesticated" and the house aggrandized. The Phillips Collection, Washington, D.C.

Let us turn now to the sculpture by Henry Moore entitled *Helmet Head No. 5,* shown in figure 33. I chose this particular sculpture for discussion partly because it will readily be perceived, by both the naive and sophisticated observer (psychoanalytic or not), as a rather blatant example of sexual symbolism. The inner solid structure has definite phallic features and the outer encapsulating portion is clearly reminiscent of the female womb. We can properly assume that Moore himself definitely had this aspect in mind as either a satirical or serious aspect of the piece. But the visual metaphor does not consist of such symbolic representation, the visual metaphors in this sculpture serve, as other types of metaphors do, to integrate form and content.

Both the symbolic sexual content and the military content referred to in the title of the work are integrated with form and shape. Note first the massive nature of the solid aspects of this piece: the elongated structure with the phallic features and the concave outer structure. Next, focus on the geometric aspects: the elongated inner solid is rather linear, sharp, and pointed, while the outer structure is round and partly spherical as well as partly cylindrical with a suggestion in the crossing band of a somewhat helical shape. So far, we have paid attention only to qualities of the separate elements; much more could be said about these. But now I would venture to say that,

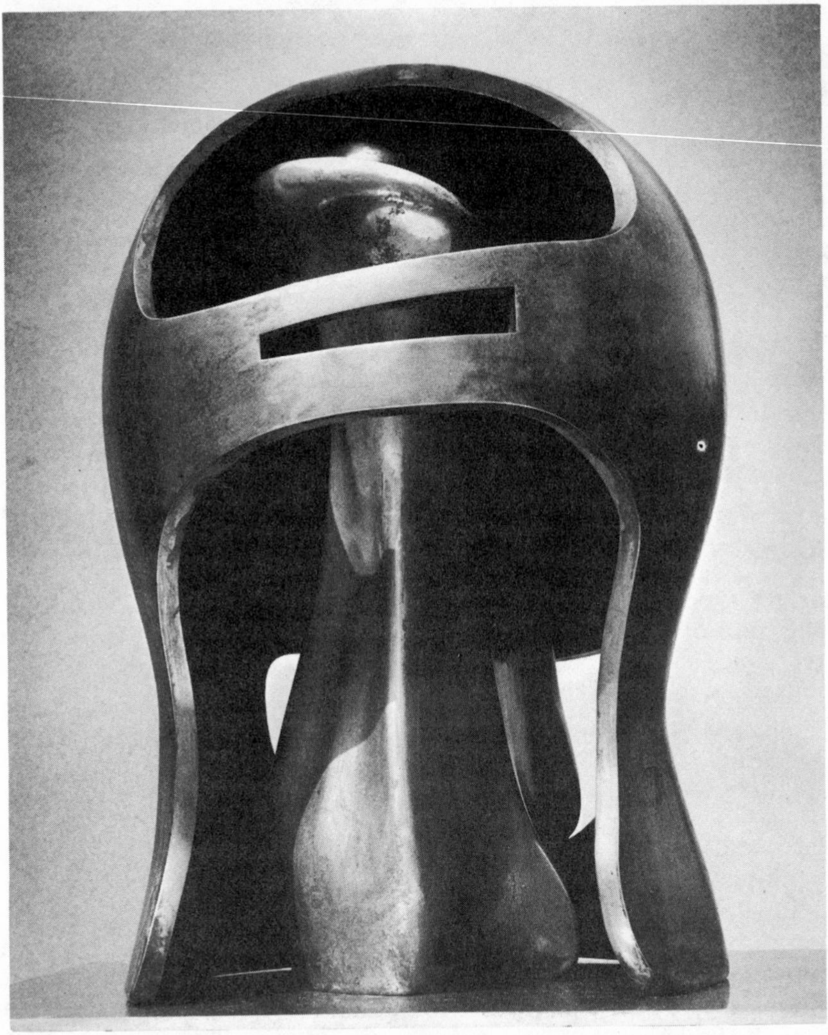

Fig. 33. Henry Moore. *Helmet Head No. 5,* sculpture. Private collection.

after looking at the piece for a short time, it is rather difficult to continue to visualize the particular elements separately;[5] the juxtaposition of the elongated and concave structure and the spherical, cylindrical, helical and linear shapes produce such a powerful impact that we begin to see effects based on the relationships among the various elements, we see the shapes and forms operating together as well as separately. At the moment of such a perception, we begin to be aware of, and to appreciate, the visual metaphor. There is a dynamic effect: viewing the inner phallic structure together with the outer, the former has an unmistakable quality of upward thrust while the latter appears just as unmistakably to be heavily rooted and moving downward toward the base or ground. This effect, it can be stated categorically, does not arise either from the inner structure or from the outer considered separately. If the viewer performs a visual trick of alternately imagining the inner structure and then the outer structure standing isolated somewhere and separate, he could then see the inner structure as heavy and rooted to the ground despite the tendency of upright linear forms to seem to move upward. On the other hand, when visualizing the outer structure or shell standing free and alone, the rather delicate curves at the base impart a sense of lightness and upward movement to this heavy form. All these complexities of the forms, taken both separately and together, surely add to the richness and complexity of the visual metaphor, but the major point to consider is that the sense of upward and downward movement together is derived from a perception oriented toward interaction or even fusion of forms, a way of seeing that begins to bring forms together toward a common location in the same space. The structures are seen both separately and potentially overlapping; the quality of potential movement mentioned first is abstracted from their overall appearance and they interact in the "mind's eye." Such a sense of dynamic interaction activates and animates both the sexual and military content to produce an overall integration of content with shape and form.

Continue to visualize the discrete forms interacting and bring even more elements and aspects into the same spatial location. Particularly, bring the upper metal shell into the same visual plane as the empty area beneath it. Transpose and superimpose the shell, in your mind's eye, onto the area occupied by the inner empty space. This produces another visual metaphor that is perhaps even more telling than the dynamic one. When the entire inner empty area is viewed as being approximately on the same visual plane and occupying the same spatial location as the solid structure, it is seen not merely as a diffuse opening surrounding the inner elongated structure or enclosed by the outer shell, but as a shape and structure in its own right. When such a mental visualization is achieved, the inner empty area appears more extensive, larger, and more imposing than the solid structures. In metaphorical terms, the empty space is then stronger and more powerful than the solid stone. Noting that, I believe we experience more intensely the psychological and aesthetic impact of this fascinating piece of art. On one level, there is the ominous war helmet with its powerful and faceless inner aspect; on another level, there is the thrust of the phallus into the female structure, the equal and downward force of the latter, and a merging of the two aspects across the "empty" space. Many will see more and more in all of this. The actual sculpture rather than the photograph yields other and deeper visual metaphors, the further merging of form and content characteristic of a perfect work of art.

The gestalt psychology description of the visual field in terms of a significant and discrete "figure" and a less significant, more diffuse "ground" does not provide an adequate basis for understanding the visual metaphor. The gestalt perceptual laws require that each aspect of the sculpture be seen in terms of a particular discrete and defined figure, say the phallic structure here, while the remainder is *at that moment* perceived as the more amorphous ground. As one continued to look at this sculpture, different aspects would accordingly be perceived successively as figures while other portions successively became the ground. Thus the womblike helmet would alternately become a figure and the empty space or even the phallic structure would become the ground. When an element previously seen as a figure, such as the phallic structure, becomes the ground, gestalt psychologists speak of figure-ground reversal. For gestalt psychology, the rather immediate integrative effects I just described would not occur because the visualizing operations would consist of successive figure-ground reversals. Major aspects of the visual field could never be perceived in the same spatial plane, and they could certainly not be perceived as occupying the same spatial location.

The rather oversimplified instance of the case of Rubin's double profiles (fig. 34) can clarify and sharpen this distinction from gestalt formulations further.[6] In order to recognize the outlines of the profiles, it may at first be helpful to focus on each in alternation. According to the gestalt formulation, this is the necessary condition: each face would need to become a figure, however rapidly, while the other receded into the ground or even disappeared. However, if the faces are thought of as both being on the same plane, it should be possible to see both of them together, interacting with one another. It is this sense of interaction, whether it be purely the visual interaction of shapes and forms or a slightly unfocused sense of two persons talking or kissing, that constitutes the visual metaphor, an integrated perception continuing to manifest discrete elements and identities.

Visual metaphor is derived not only from shapes, forms, and referential content, such as houses and mountains, but also from color. Albers, whose janusian thinking in artistic creation was described earlier, also gave some salient testimony with regard to color interaction and visual metaphor. In his color instruction course described in the book *Interaction of Color,* Albers indicates many conditions involving visual metaphor. Though not using that particular term, the stated purpose of the book and course is to increase the student's appreciation and perception of colors interrelating, modifying, and reinforcing each other. Task after task is designed to orient the student to look at a color field both as a unity and with discrete color

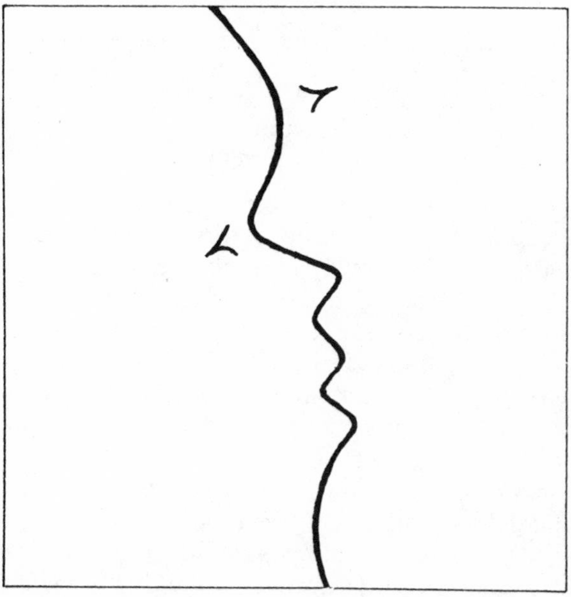

Fig. 34. Rubin's double profiles. According to gestalt principles, the two faces in this drawing can only be seen successively. The homospatial perception involves seeing both on the same visual plane, and interacting with one another.

elements operating together. The tasks constantly emphasize the interactions among colors and the interaction between colors and shapes. His verbal designations, though necessarily far less eloquent than the visual tasks themselves, give some of the flavor of his presentation:

On the relationship between discrete colors and the whole:

> when we see opaque color as transparent or perceive opacity as translucence, then the optical reception in our eye has changed in our mind to something different. The same is true when we see three colors as four or as two, or four colors as three, when we see flat, even colors as intersecting colors and their fluting effect, or when we see distinct one-contour boundaries doubled or vibrating or just vanishing.[7]

And on the purpose of the course:

> The purpose of most of our color studies is to prove that color is the most relative medium in art, that we almost never perceive what color is physically. The mutual influencing of colors we call—interaction. Seen from the opposite viewpoint, it is—interdependence.[8]

And, finally, using a "theatrical parallel" to explain a particular task:

> Although they remain unchanged in hue and light, in "character," and appear in an unchanging outer frame, the "stage," they are to produce 4 different "scenes" or "plays," each to be so different that one and the same set of colors will be seen as 4 different sets, presented by 4 different casts.[9]

Albers's focus on the interaction between colors, the seeing of colors as discrete yet interrelating to form wholes and unities in the same place such as in the "stage" example, emphasizes the visual metaphor with respect to color. I think it is legitimate to assume that the visual orientation Albers teaches derives from his own creative processes. In the book, he himself indicates that in the following prefatory remark: "This book . . . does not follow an academic conception of 'theory and practice.' It reverses this order and places practice before theory."

Before pursuing further connections between the visual metaphor in the completed work of art and factors in the artistic creative process, I shall give one more specific example of visual metaphor. While examples so far described have covered varying aspects of the visual arts including sculpture, general considerations about use of color, and factors relating to an expressionist but virtually representational painting (*Courmayeur* by Kokaschka), the artists themselves have been all fairly contemporary. Therefore, I shall once again move further back in history to the work of Leonardo da Vinci, particularly the painting *Mona Lisa.* So widely acclaimed, the outstanding qualities of this painting hardly need extensive recounting. There are the muted but living colors, the sense of movement, the soft and penetrating gaze and, as I discussed earlier (chap. 6), the famous Gioconda smile. The many and diverse adjective combinations used to describe the qualities of that barely perceptible smile emphasize its antithetical quality, a quality that has, for centuries, been an important factor in the painting's appeal. But where, I ask now, does this antithetical quality in the completed painting come from? Previously, I suggested that Leonardo's early conception must have consisted of a janusian construct, a smile having simultaneous antithetical properties. Now, I want to consider how this construct was rendered and integrated into the completed image on the canvas. Does the quality of simultaneous antithesis arise from the particular shape given to the mouth, or its color, or the shadows in the corners, or, to shift to a more general focus, because of the expression in the lady's eyes? Surely all these factors play a role, but a careful viewing of the entire painting (see fig. 24) in accordance with the perceptual principles outlined here shows some other particular and crucial factors at work as well. If the so-called background of the painting[10] is viewed on the same visual plane as the woman, if, in other words, the foreground and background are considered superimposed upon one another, neither being dominant nor secondary but both occupying the same space, much of the effect of the painting can be understood and intensified. The two sides of the landscape are seen as sharply in contrast with each other: the left side consists of a rather gentle undulating road amidst somewhat rounded softened forms while the right side consists of a rough, tumbling river amidst sharp, angular rocks; the road on the left seems to move upward while the river goes down; the scene on the left is set in a much warmer season than the one suggested by the whitened peaks of the mountains on the right.

It could seem that, in comparing the attributes of the two sides of the landscape, one's eye is moving back and forth and one therefore is not experiencing a superimposition. If, however, the superimposition properly includes many different planes at once, that is, left and right, horizontal and vertical, foreground and background, such a reservation can be dispelled. Superimposing the left and right sides of the landscape especially should show most of the contrasts described. Such sharp contrasts, seen in direct *juxtaposition* with the lady's face, certainly contribute strongly to the antithetical qualities perceived in her smile. Also, and perhaps more important, the features of this landscape in juxtaposition with, or in apposition to, the face and figure impact a dreamy overall quality to the picture. Landscape such as this is unreal: no such sharp terrestrial contrasts can exist as close together as depicted here. Moreover, the road on the left side seems to go off into a dimly imagined terrain or else to nowhere, while the river on the other side moves sharply forward toward the viewer and, ultimately, it too moves off the painting. Other unreal and contrasting qualities are present. The overall effect is that—viewed on the same plane as the face and figure—the landscape appears to depict something in the lady's mind, something seen with her inner eye rather than only as a scene behind her. In this, I believe, resides one of the most powerful and metaphorical aspects of the painting: the lady appears to be looking both inwardly and outside of herself at once, she looks out beyond the painting and inwardly into her thoughts. Through the particular qualities of the landscape scene interacting with the qualities of the head and face, we are drawn both into her inner world and into the receding dimensions of the painting as well. In short, while Leonardo mastered the art of perspective to present a lifelike and representational portrait of a woman, he also enhanced the metaphorical qualities, the visual metaphorical qualities, of the art of painting.

That superimposition and fusion of visual images, planes, and locations were factors in Leonardo's thinking and working is evident from many of his preliminary and final productions. In figure 35, the preliminary drawing or cartoon for the famous painting *St. Anne with Virgin* (fig. 35*A*) shows two bodies superimposed and fused to the

Fig. 35*A*. Leonardo da Vinci. *Cartoon for St. Anne.* The bodies are superimposed or fused to the point that there appears to be one body with two heads. Reproduced by courtesy of the Trustees, The National Gallery, London.

extent that there appears one body with two heads.[11] In the final painting (fig. 35*B*), the effect is continued and the child is included so that the three figures of Mary, Anne, and Jesus appear to form a single unit. Figure 36 shows two drawings. One is the widely known anatomical illustration of the proportions of the human body (fig.

Fig. 35*B*. Leonardo da Vinci. *St. Anne with Virgin*, ca. 1498–99. The figures of Saint Anne and Mary are virtually fused in this final painting. Louvre, Paris. Photo Giraudon.

36*A*), which Leonardo based on the writings of the first-century B.C. Roman architect Vitruvius. In attempting to idealize the proportions of the body as conforming to a square (span of arms equal to height)

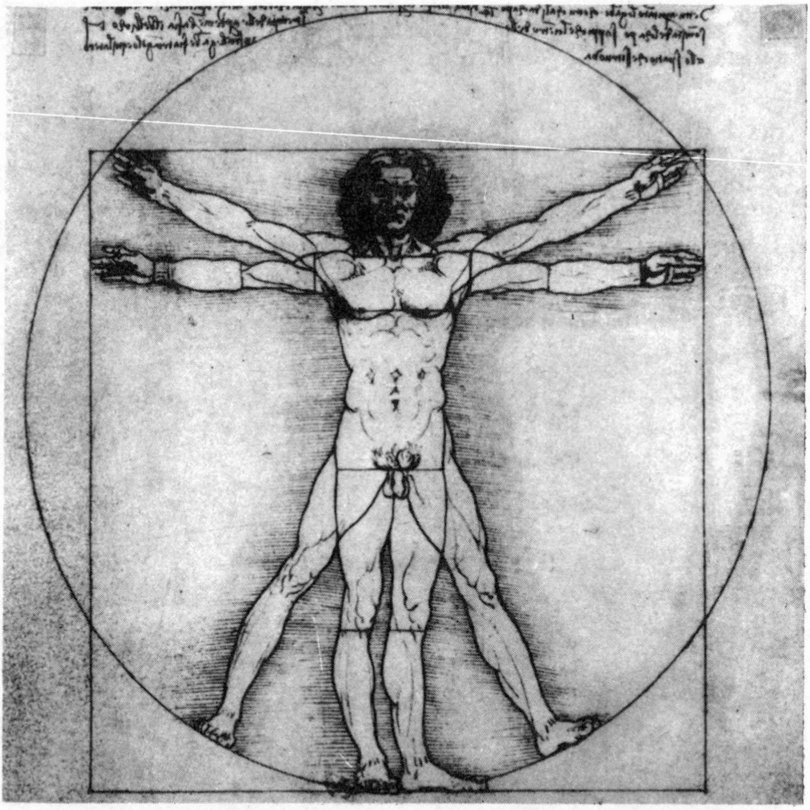

A

B

Fig. 36. Leonardo da Vinci. Superimpositions and fusions. *A*. Leonardo's famous drawing illustrating the proportions of the human figure shows two men superimposed on each other. Accademia di Belle Arti, Venice. *B*. "Beastly madness"—horse, lion, and man's head in successive fusions of each with the others. Royal Library, Windsor Castle, copyright reserved.

and a circle (center at the navel) and an equilateral triangle (position of spread legs), he superimposed two figures and these geometrical patterns upon one another. The other is a sketch for the cartoon of *The Battle of Anghiari* consisting of a series of heads—a lion's, a horse's, and a human—each fused in sequence with one another which, according to Leonardo scholar Brizio, represents Leonardo's view of war as "beastly madness" (fig. 36*b*).[12] Consequently, it is a reasonable assumption that the visual metaphorical effect I have described in connection with a completed painting was a direct result of Leonardo's use of homospatial thinking during the course of the creative process. To produce the visual metaphor of the Gioconda smile, and of the figure looking both outside and within simultaneously, Leonardo transformed and integrated janusian conceptions by means of the spatial superimpositions and fusions of the homospatial process.

Now, let us go on to some evidence pertaining directly to the creative process. Visualizing or seeing the visual metaphors I have described requires the viewer to construct a mental image in which discrete elements occupy the same plane, spatial location, or area of space. That such metaphors as I have identified in completed works are derived from superimpositions and fusions on the creator's part during the process of creation is strongly suggested by the personal testimony of diverse types of artists. Here is an indication from the creator of the visual metaphor in sculpture I discussed, Henry Moore:

> This is what the sculptor must do. He must strive continually to think of, and use, form in its full spatial completeness. He gets the solid shape, as it were, inside his head—he thinks of it, whatever its size, as if he were holding it completely enclosed in the hollow of his hand. He mentally visualizes a complex form *from all round itself;* he knows while he looks at one side what the other side is like. [Italics added][13]

As Moore describes it, the sculptor has a mental image involving the multiple aspects of a form and of masses "completely enclosed" in a single spatial area, the figurative "hollow of his hand," a clear instance of homospatial thinking. Unlike ordinary perception involving a general sensing of other (nonvisualized) sides of a form, he indicates the bringing together of complex and detailed features into a single image. Though we lack exact data linking this thought process to any one of Moore's particular works, such as systematic observations gathered during the creative process, Moore's description of his conscious creative thinking can be readily related to those effects stipulated for *Helmet Head No. 5.* Kokoschka, with whose painting Aldrich explicated the visual metaphor effect, also made comments indicating conscious awareness of visual metaphor effects and of the experience of discrete entities occupying the same space. The following are remarks taken from a letter by Kokoschka to his friend, Hans Tietze, about his painting in progress, *Gamblers:*

> It represents my friends playing cards. Each terrifyingly naked in his passions, and all submerged by a color which binds them together just as light raises an object and its reflection into a higher category by revealing something of reality and something of its reflection, and therefore more of both.[14]

Other artists of different types and periods have provided other descriptions of and evidence for the homospatial process in visual art creation. Auguste Rodin, the French sculptor of the nineteenth century, said it as follows:

> to make a bust does not consist in executing the different surfaces and their details one after another, successively making the forehead, the cheeks, the chin and then the eyes, nose and mouth. On the contrary, from the first sitting the whole mass must be conceived and constructed in its varying circumferences; that is to say, in each of its profiles.[15]

Michelangelo wrote some lines in a poem which, if they represented his own creative thinking, indicated a homospatial process. The lines are the following: "The best of artists hath no thought to show / Which the rough stone in superfluous shell doth not include." The suggestion is that the sculptor has already seen something in the stone when he starts to work, a superimposition therefore of a mental image onto the material. In another poem, a madrigal, it is even more explicit: "Lady, in hard and craggy stone·the mere removal of the surface gives being to a figure, which ever grows the more the stone is hewn away."[16]

Claes Oldenburg, the modern pop art sculptor and originator of "soft" sculpture, documented a manifest and distinct form of the thought process in his notebooks of preliminary drawings and sketches representing ideas for his works. Figures 37–39 show drawings involving fusion and superimposition of discrete entities and forms. The drawing labeled *Typewriter-Pie* (fig. 37) shows a fusion of an old typewriter with a pie shape; both entities are integrated into a visual metaphor that Oldenburg designates as relating to an aircraft carrier.[17] For *Circus Girl on a Big Ball* (fig. 38), Oldenburg documented the following: "Sketch done after attending the circus. The interesting element here is the fusion of ball and body."[18] And for *Material and Scissors* (fig. 39), he wrote: "A sketch for a sculpture not yet executed. The conception here is that material and scissors are unified."[19]

As Oldenburg is sometimes considered not to be serious, and therefore is a difficult creative artist to evaluate, it will be of interest to focus on evidence gleaned from the creative work of Klee. Klee, cited

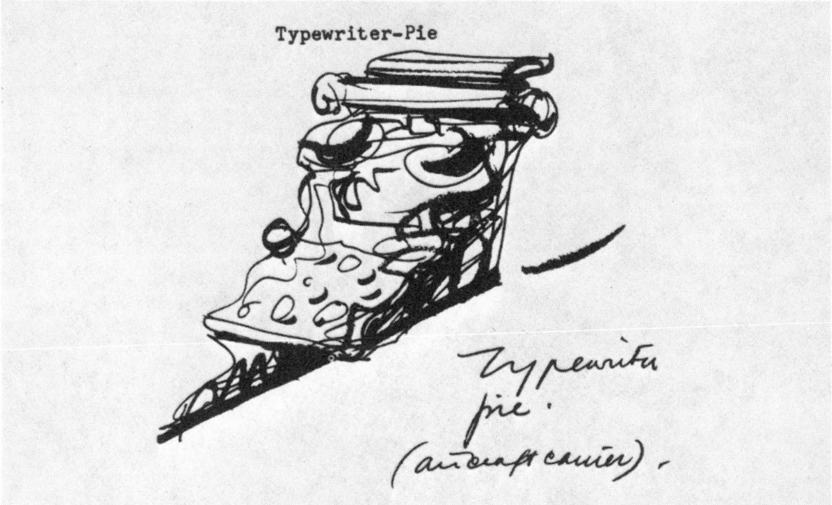

Fig. 37. Claes Oldenburg. *Typewriter-Pie.* A typewriter superimposed onto a pie. From Claes Oldenburg, *Notes in Hand* (London: Petersburg Press, 1972).

earlier in connection with endotopic and exotopic perception (chap. 7), provides a stepwise account of the nature of the homospatial process (see fig. 40)[20]—though he does not call it that—involved in his creation of the watercolor entitled *Physiognomic Lightning* (and other works). As the material comes from his notes for teaching art students, the conception is presented in sequence and alternatives are discussed analytically. He first presents the problem of how to fuse a circle and a line. Then he differentiates between combination (fig. 40*a*), repetition (fig. 40*b*), transposition (fig. 40*c*), compromise or "evasion" (fig. 40*d*), and the active striking of the middle (fig. 40*e*) that is the solution of the problem and the fusion of homospatial thinking. As this is a didactic format, there is little reason to believe that Klee himself developed the conception for the painting in the plodding, stepwise fashion described. On the contrary, it appears to be Klee's retrospective explanation of his own more spontaneous cognition.

Another leading German expressionist painter, Max Beckmann, less analytic and didactic than Klee, described a rather global bringing together of discrete entities into the same space in his creative work: "What helps me most in this task is the penetration of space. Height, width, depth are three phenomena which I must transfer into one place to form the abstract surface of the picture."[21]

Two further instances come from completely different types of painters. These painters, the English satirist of the eighteenth century, William Hogarth, and the unclassifiable French original of the

Fig. 38. Claes Oldenburg. *Circus Girl on a Big Ball,* 1958. Ball and body are fused. From Claes Oldenburg, *Drawings and Prints* (London: Chelsea House Publishers, 1969, p. 25).

twentieth century, Henri Matisse, advocate an emphasis on visual integration in creation and, by implication, homospatial thinking. First, Matisse. He discusses his experience with the art movements of divisionism and fauvism to which he had belonged:

> These rebellions led me to study each element of construction separately—drawing, color, values, composition; to explore how

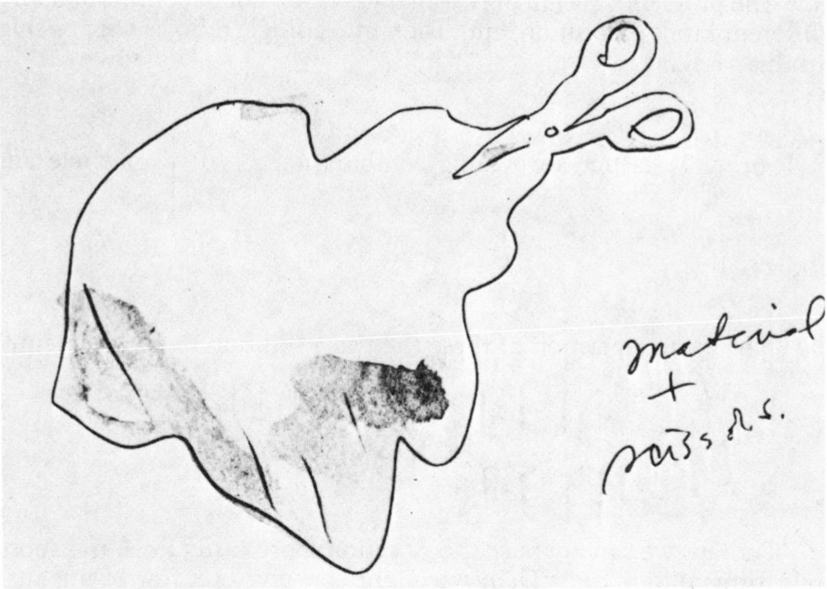

Fig. 39. Claes Oldenburg. *Material and Scissors,* 1963. The material and the scissors are fused. From Claes Oldenburg, *Drawings and Prints* (London: Chelsea House Publishers, 1969, p. 127).

> these elements could be combined into a synthesis without diminishing the eloquence of any one of them by the presence of the others and to construct with these elements, *combining them without reducing their intrinsic quality;* in other words, to respect the purity of the means. [Italics added][22]

As I discussed earlier, combining *without reducing* intrinsic quality is the essence of integration. In integration, elements retain their identity within a whole. Hogarth advocated a similar approach in his discussion of the creative use of color in his classical treatise on art: "By the beauty of coloring, the painters mean that disposition of colors on objects, together with their proper shades, which appear at the same time both distinctly varied and artfully united, in compositions of any kind." And also, "the utmost beauty of coloring depends on the great principle of varying by all the means of varying, and on the proper and artful union of that variety."[23]

Homospatial thinking in the visual arts is not connected to particular styles, time periods, schools, or movements; it is intrinsic to the creation of art. Neither is this type of thinking limited to visual imagery or mental seeing. Although visual imagery is frequently a major ingredient of homospatial thinking in the visual arts, as I stated earlier, all sensory modalities and all types of sensory imagery are also involved. Discrete kinesthetic, tactile, gustatory, olfactory, audi-

a. "The problem: 'Fusion of two characters' no doubt permits of many different kinds of solution, but fusion into a single thing is not possible in this case, for

 or  is not an organic combination  of circle and straight line!"

b. "Nor is the repetition of these themes a solution to our problem."

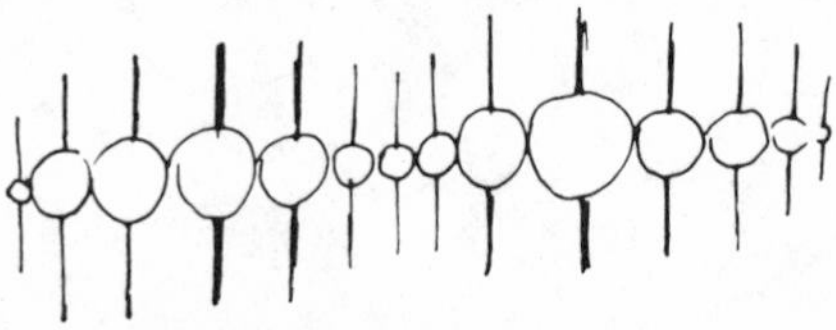

c. "Perhaps we can appraise the situation more easily if we transpose our forms into matter. Then we might conceive of a row of unequal sticks, a bit like piano keys, each with the top of a tin lying over it.

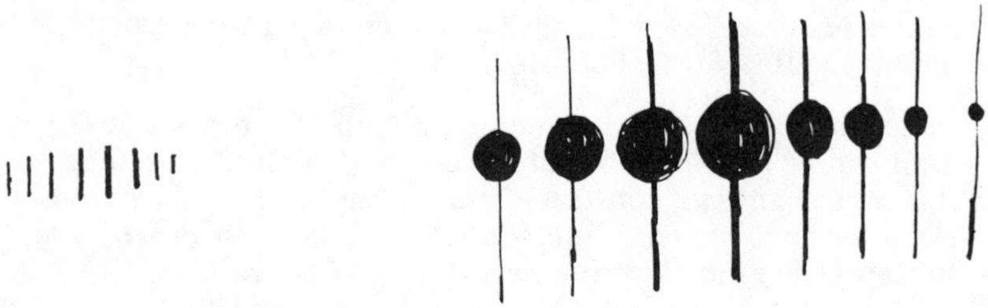

In this case we no longer have unified objects but rather two material items without visible relation between them, just one on top of the other, quite meaningless."

Fig. 40. Paul Klee's steps toward the creation of the painting *Physiognomic Lightning,* from Klee's *The Thinking Eye* (New York: Wittenborn Art Books, 1961).

tory as well as visual sensations are also conceived as fused, superimposed, and occupying the same space. Kinesthetic sensations of moving both frontways and sideways in the same space, tactile sensations of smoothness together with lumpiness or sharp together with round, influence and direct the artist's creation. In sum, homospatial thinking may involve all sensory modalities at once and, in a related way, the artist may conceive of *himself* as occupying the space of the work or of the materials of which it is to be constructed. The cubist painters Gleizes and Metzinger described such a phenomenon as follows: "To establish pictorial space, we must have recourse to tactile and motor sensations, indeed to all our faculties. It is our whole

d. "Adaptation by evasion; in the first case they go round on one side [1], in the other they split and go round on both sides [2]. Or the circle avoids the battle by adapting itself to the straight line and becoming an elipse [3]."

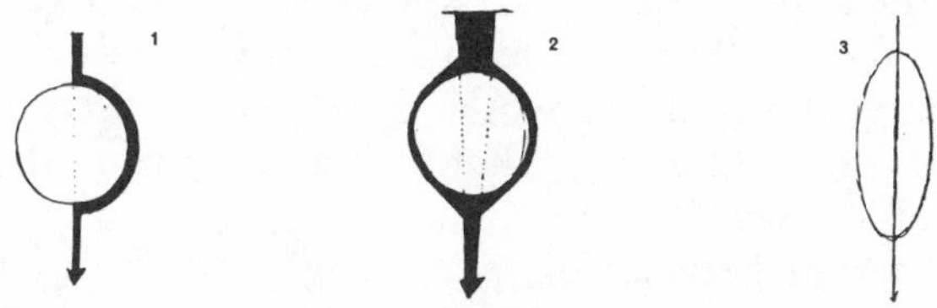

e. Paul Klee. *Physiognomic Lightning,* 1927. Klee says: "The middle realm is actively struck. Two heterogeneous elements enter into relation with one another. . . ."

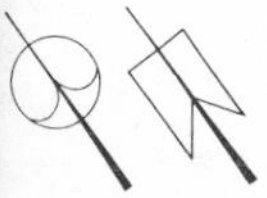

Middle is actively struck.

personality which, contracting or expanding, transforms the plane of the picture."[24]

Moore even more pointedly describes the superimposition of an image of the self onto the object: "he [the sculptor] identifies himself with its [the solid shape's] center of gravity, its mass, its weight; he realizes its volume as the space that the shape displaces in the air."[25] And is it not likely that he "identifies" with its hardness as well? In another place, Moore indicated the intrinsic nature of the superimposition of material and mental image, and the factor of psychological interaction, as follows: "Every material has its own individual qualities. It is only when the sculptor works direct, when there is an active relationship with his material, that the material can take its part in the shaping of an idea."[26]

Such interaction between mental image and the materials with which the artist works is crucial in every type of visual art. The painter visualizes lines, colors, and shapes all occupying the same space or spatial location as the textured canvas itself, and he allows visualized images and texture to interact, mutually modifying and influencing each other. The creative artist brings into a single mental percept the qualities of his material together with his conception; his work develops from the intense unbridled co-mingling of image and object and results in an integration of qualities of line, color, and texture. The paintings of Rembrandt, where the striking sense of emergent soft light results from both dark and lighter pigments mixing with the finely textured but flat surface of the underlying canvas, surely suggest that such conceptions are necessary. In another type of fusion of image and material, the heavy swirls of paint characteristic of van Gogh must have derived from a mental conception in which the qualities of paint and brush were as distinct and prominent as the subjects and scenes they depicted. Indeed, numerous artists after van Gogh have intentionally focused on just this particular fusion and this type of visual interaction. Covering large canvases with a single color or with a simple arrangement of lines and colors, they celebrate the interaction of these colors and lines with the texture and shape of the canvas, the qualities of the paint, and the action of a brush or other implement.

Graphic artists, especially, approach their task by superimposing visual conception with tangible material at every step of the way. Working with wood, metal, glass, or stone, they are constantly mindful of grains and surfaces and they capitalize on the nuances of shape and shadow produced by every cut or scratch they make. Every aspect of the material—smoothness, hardness, blemishes, and lines—provides continual sensory impressions and feedback that intermingle and interact with the artist's mental image. Totally immersed in his material, the graphic artist continually touches, looks, and smells wood, rose paper, or rice paper as he goes along. At times, he even seems to have a sense of the material's taste.

Interaction with the object, spatial fusion or superimposition of mental percepts of the work in process with mental images and conceptualizations, is a crucial aspect of the creative process in other areas beside the visual arts. But before leaving the visual arts to discuss other art forms, I will again consider architecture, the complicated enterprise that defies strict categorization as a type of art. Even a cursory reflection on architecture should, in the light of what I have shown so far, suggest that homospatial thinking is very important there. Architects are preeminently concerned with space and they conceptualize in spatial terms. Functional considerations of developing "multiuse space"[27] and artistic considerations of keeping in mind multiple spatial aspects—similar to conditions of sculptural creation—all suggest the operation of homospatial thinking. Just as in valued sculpture, empty space is an object to be manipulated by creative architects. But, in addition to considering its perceptual interaction with solid massive areas, the architect must manipulate empty space for functional use.

A striking example of homospatial thinking in architectural creation comes from the work of the American architect Louis Kahn. Although it was never built, the design by Kahn for the "Palazzo dei Congressi," the Congress Hall in Venice, was honored in a Single Building Exhibition in 1968, Kahn's last exhibition during his lifetime. In creating the design for this civic theatre, Kahn reported that he was from the first confronted with the problem of providing for the assemblage of a large crowd of people in a building to be constructed on a narrow and extended lot. The solution to this problem, he said, was represented in a diagrammatic drawing shown in figure 41 (left). His comments about this drawing, in response to a question from an interviewer, were as follows:

> I don't know how one identifies the first idea, but for me it is usually the sense of the building in its core, its full meaning, its nature, *not* its shape. Its nature was that of involvement, of participation. A simple shape which only emphasizes a direction [meaning the narrow parallel lines] doesn't have the nature of participation in it. It is, on the contrary, analogous to watching or hearing, not participation. The circle, to me, was participation. The fact that I could adjust to a site which was narrow has to require that one side looked to the other. But the shape should not be adjusted to that narrow site in such a way that it becomes purely directional, because there would be no participation. . . .
>
> In the center of this is the organizational position, and this center was the dimension I had to include to make sure that people saw people. It was a confrontation of people with people.[28]

The final ground plan Kahn developed is shown in figure 41 (right) and it details his idea of a circular center merging with longer areas to allow for participation. In addition to its salience as an example of homospatial thinking, the sequence Kahn describes provides a particularly full account of the rapidly occurring steps in the process.

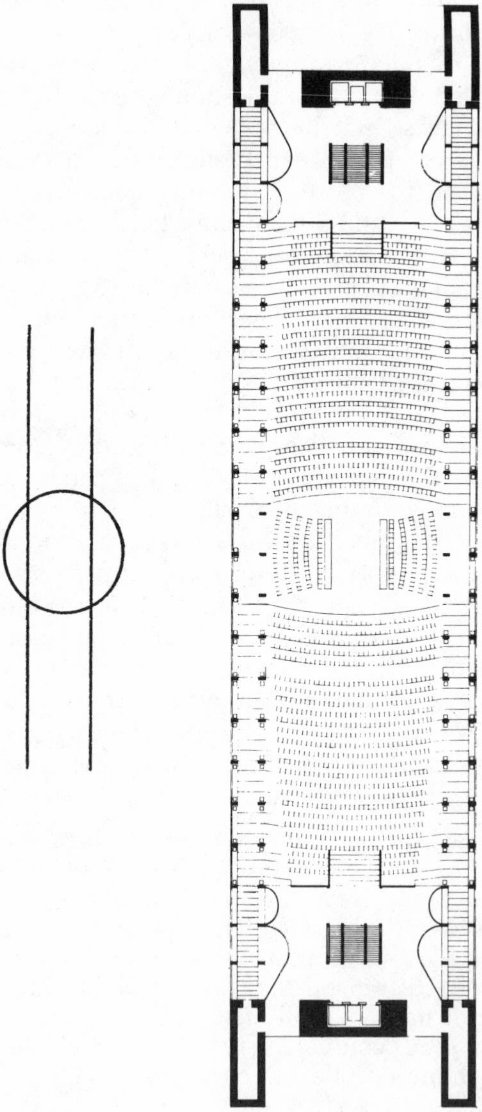

Fig. 41. Louis Kahn's development of a design: diagrammatic representation of his first conception of the Congress Hall in Venice *(left)* and Congress Hall, ground plan *(right)*. The superimposition of a circle onto parallel lines resulted in the design allowing for participation. From *Conversations with Architects* by John W. Cook and Heinrich Klotz. Copyright © 1973 John W. Cook and Heinrich Klotz. Praeger Publishers, Inc. Reprinted by permission of Praeger Publishers, Inc., a division of Holt, Rinehart and Winston.

Kahn emphasizes that his first idea was a particular formulation or conception: he was aware of the narrow building lot but he wanted to produce a sense of involvement and participation in that space. This sense of involvement he thought of in terms of a particular shape, the circle. He then superimposed the circle upon the narrow lines representing the dimension and shape of the building lot. He conceived of the discrete shapes as occupying the same space because he felt they *ought* to do so. Then, he used this image as the basis for the actual ground plan he designed.

Fusing and superimposing because discrete entities *ought* to be together is a cardinal feature of the homospatial process. The creator does not bring them together because of accidental or random association, nor merely because of learned similarities or contiguities. He *willfully* and *intentionally* brings them together for aesthetic, practical, scientific, emotional, or philosophical reasons. He wants, for instance, to provide for a particular function in a particular space or to explore the visual qualities of particular forms, or to relate emotionally charged objects or colors, or to plumb the meaning of a personal or universal experience. There are often similarities between aspects of the discrete entities brought together in this way but such similarities *do not dictate* the superimposition and fusion, they merely facilitate it to some degree. Commonly, unexpected similarities are discovered after the specific homospatial conception: a woman's face superimposed on a white marble block may suggest a particular milky pallor to be emphasized. With literary metaphors, as I shall shortly describe, this is usually the case. For Kahn, the flat sides in the center of the narrow lot became similar to a circular form when he saw that people could be placed to look across at each other in varying ways. As he so vividly described, his visual conception of a circle superimposed upon the elongated straight lines enabled him to develop that particular design.

All homospatial thinking in the visual arts proceeds in the manner Kahn has indicated. The sculptor, painter, graphic artist, and the architect begin with a vague thought or intention. The thought may consist of a functional idea such as the need for assemblage or it may be primarily a visual or sensory one, such as contemplating a possible painting based on a scene, on several colors, or shapes or lines. At some point in the process, discrete entities are conceived as occupying the same space and a visual metaphor or, in conjunction with other processes, a more elaborated visual creation is produced.

Music

Because music is an auditory and temporal art, consisting of sounds occurring in time, it is difficult to discuss in terms of spatial experience. Primarily, this is because we tend to think of space as consisting only of visually perceived phenomena. While there is a fascinating and continuing philosophical controversy about the spatial attributes of music as well as about the nature of space itself, I shall for the moment bypass those issues.[29] With respect to psychological experience, we characteristically perceive distinctly differentiated relationships within music, designated as high and low and as foreground and background. Such designations are, at the very least, appropriately used to refer to a psychological experience of space in music. Auditory patterns with foreground and background features and directional features of high and low are subjectively experienced as real attributes. In all likelihood, the directional features are based on the portions of the human body involved in the physical production of sound. Rapid sound waves associated with high-pitched sound are produced by the upper or higher portions of the human vocal apparatus and slower waves associated with lower-pitched sound are produced lower down. Because, moreover, all sound is derived from waves occurring in a physical space generally perceived as distinct from our own spatial location, we organize it in terms of patterns having spatial characteristics. These factors form the basis for the considerable importance of homospatial thinking in the creation of music.

Just as there is visual metaphor in painting and the other visual arts, there is auditory or sound metaphor in music. Auditory metaphor is just as essential to music as is visual metaphor to the visual arts. Because music may depend more on so-called formal qualities than does visual art, metaphor as a formal integration may in fact be more important for music. By auditory metaphor, I am referring to an experience or a structure that is familiar to sophisticated music listeners: a sound unity in which variety continues to be discernible, an integration of multiple elements—be they melodies, harmonies, rhythms, or types of instruments—in which the discrete elements are heard.[30] All good music contains such integration throughout and all good music listening discerns and appreciates it. Successful polyphonic music is a clear instance; such music consists of many voices or types of sounds heard both as effectively unified and effectively separate, a broad type of auditory metaphor. And music based on traditional harmonies, on tonality or atonality, and even on electronic sources contains it. In harmonic music, for instance, one of the effects of thematic progression and development is to emphasize various harmonic elements accompanying the melody, an emphasis that stimulates and intensifies the hearing of interactions between melody and harmony. Such interaction, the sine qua non of metaphor, is produced on hearing the musical work itself; it is not derived from "extramusical" sources such as visual or even emotional associations of the sounds, although these latter factors may also play a role. It is an auditory experience of unity with diversity, a sense of polyphony within homophony, and of homophony within polyphony. Its presence is a criterion of excellence throughout all forms and types of music.

To produce such metaphors, the composer uses homospatial thinking. Just as the visual artist brings foreground and background into the same visual plane, superimposing and fusing the images in his mind, so too the composer superimposes auditory patterns and images. Such a process is described by Beethoven in a description of his creative experience:

> I carry my thoughts about with me for a long time, often for a very long time, before writing them down. I can rely on my memory for this and can be sure that once I have grasped a theme, I shall not forget it even years later. I change many things, discard others, and try again and again until I am satisfied; then, in my head, I begin to elaborate the work in its breadth, its narrowness, its height, its depth and, since I am aware of what I want to do, the underlying idea never deserts me. It rises, it grows, *I hear and see the image in front of me from every angle, as if it had been cast,* and only the labor of writing it down remains. [Italics added][31]

In referring to the casting of an image, the great composer draws a direct analogy with sculpture and this description of his creative thinking is strikingly reminiscent of the previous description by Henry Moore. Every angle of the image is seen within the same space. For Beethoven, auditory images already formed are spatially manipulated and superimposed; for another composer, Robert Schumann, there are diffuse spatial superimpositions and fusions of sounds and shapes even earlier in the creative process, at the point of attaining his initial musical ideas:

> People err when they suppose that composers prepare pens and paper with the predetermination of sketching, painting, expressing this or that. Yet we must not estimate outward influences too lightly. Involuntarily an idea sometimes develops itself simultaneously with the musical fancy; the eye is awake as well as the ear, and this ever-busy organ sometimes holds fast *to certain outlines amid all the sounds and tones, which, keeping pace with the music, form and condense into clear shapes.* The more elements congenially related to music which the thought or picture created in tones contains within it, the more poetic and plastic will be the expressiveness of the composition, and in proportion to the imaginativeness and keenness of the musican in receiving these impressions will be the elevating and touching power of the work. [Italics added][32]

Both Schumann and Beethoven allude to visual images in these experiences during the creative process, but there is no reason to assume that purely auditory factors could not be handled in a similar manner. The composer conceives a thematic pattern in which high and low sounds define a vertical auditory dimension while rhythm is experienced as moving along the horizontal. He then fuses and superimposes these discrete dimensions to develop a mutually interacting unity. In more general perceptual terms, the composer, in the purely auditory sphere, superimposes figural patterns and ground patterns.[33]

Arnold Schoenberg clearly refers to auditory experiences in his formulation of a principle of creative thinking in music:

> the last century considered . . . a procedure [such as mine] cerebral and thus inconsistent with the dignity of genius. The very fact that there exist classical examples proves the foolishness of such an opinion. But the validity of this form of thinking is also demonstrated by the . . . law of unity of musical space, best formulated as follows: *the unity of musical space demands an absolute and unitary perception.* . . . Every musical configuration, every movement of the tones has to be comprehended primarily as a mutual relationship of sounds, of oscillatory vibrations. . . . To the imaginative and creative faculty, relations in the material sphere are as independent from directions or planes as material objects are, in their sphere, to our perceptive faculties. . . . Our mind always recognizes, for instance, a knife, a bottle or a watch, regardless of its position and can reproduce it in the imagination in every possible position.[34]

For Schoenberg, as for Beethoven and Moore, there is the experience of mentally perceiving all aspects of an entity within the same space. Musical entities are independent of spatial constrictions for the composer because he freely superimposes and fuses them in a unified space.

Mozart reputedly used purely auditory imagery in his composing. That a homospatial process of superimposing prominent and subordinate themes and patterns occurred in Mozart's creating is suggested by observations based on manuscripts of his work such as the following one: "in the *Andante Cantabile* of the C Major Quartet (K 465) he [Mozart] adds a coda in which the first violin openly expresses what seemed hidden beneath the conversational play of the subordinate theme."[35] This observation was made by the Mozart scholar, Einstein, who intensively studied Mozart's musical creating through the manuscripts of his works and the construction of the works themselves.

Schoenberg was one of few composers leaving a well documented verbal account of successive steps in the composition of a particular musical work. Emerging from this is a concrete description of the use of a homospatial conception in a specific creation. After reporting the nature of some alternate versions of the beginning of his First Chamber Symphony, Schoenberg says:

> In all these cases there was no problem which one would call complicated. There was no combination of voices whose contrapuntal relation required adaptation, as in the [previously given] example from *Verklärte Nacht*. In these first notations, there were even no harmonic progressions which demanded control. There was at hand from the start a sufficient amount of motival forms and their derivatives, rather too much than too little. The task, therefore, was to retard the progress of development in order to enable the average good listener to keep in mind what preceded so as to understand the consequences. To keep within the bounds and to *balance a theme whose character, tempo, expression, harmonic progression, and motival contents displayed a centrifugal tendency:* this was here the task. [Italics added][36]

Schoenberg strove for and achieved this "centrifugal tendency." In order to experience such a tendency for the theme to move in an outward direction from a central core, it is necessary to experience all the discrete elements he mentions as moving together and occupying the same space. The point is not merely that this composer is using a spatial term; that could be merely a figurative expression, an analogy. The point is that the particular spatial term, "centrifugal," describes a feeling about the qualities of the theme that could only be derived from a homospatial conception of discrete aspects of the theme occupying the same space.

With respect to electronic music, much is so new and criteria so fluctuating that it is difficult to discuss the work of any particular composer without arousing a good deal of controversy. Moreover, specification of the spatial elements in this form of music is complicated by the inclusion in the creative process of visual factors connected to the physical wave properties of sound. Nevertheless, I shall quote an interesting observation made by the modern Israeli composer, Joseph Tal, because, despite its visual emphasis, it pertains to some of the particular spatial superimpositions in music I have discussed:

> We are now able to produce electronically the most rapid variations in time with a precision which has hitherto been unobtainable. These are added to the timbre characteristic of the basic tone and produce finally, *by a combination of vertical and horizontal relationships, a frequency structure where individual organisms are absorbed into serving the whole.*
>
> It follows from this suggestion that a systematic number of experiments may lead to a formulation of ideas from which the

composer may choose and elaborate suitable tone material. Such a sound, coming in this way from a number of sources, is indeed to be found in every score of Ravel and indeed, based on this tradition, we should gain sufficient knowledge and confidence to be able to find our way in a more or less intelligent manner in the new area of electronic music. [Italics added][37]

Here, in the electronic music laboratory, is the interaction and superimposition of spatial relationships with sound qualities to construct integrated wholes.

Although visualization is often absent from musical composing and creating, those composers who routinely employ visual imagery make use of a form of homospatial thinking. Beethoven, for instance, indicated a constant superimposition of auditory and visual imagery during composing in a confession made to his poet friend, Neate. While walking in the fields near Baden, Neate made a comment to Beethoven about his Pastoral Symphony and his power of painting pictures in music. Reportedly, Beethoven stated: "I have always a picture in my mind, when I am composing, and work up to it."[38] In stipulating the "working up" to a visual image, Beethoven describes not a synaesthetic experience, a mere association of sounds with visual imagery, but rather an active interaction between auditory and visual imagery in his mind, a superimposition of entities from discrete sensory modes. As Richard Wagner stated in an interview with his colleague, Englebert Humperdinck: "I see in my mind's eye definite visions of the heros and heroines of my music dramas. I have clear mental pictures of them before they take form in my scores, and while I am holding fast to those mental images, the music—the Leitmotives, themes, harmonies, rhythms, instrumentation—in short, the whole musical structure, occurs to me."[39]

Active or purposeful superimposition, fusion, and interaction of discrete entities—whether purely auditory, or auditory and visual, kinaesthetic, or other sensory modality together—is a criterial feature of homospatial thinking in music just as in visual and other arts. Because the superimposition and fusions are often very rapid and, for many composers, completely routine, the willful and intentional aspect tends to escape their notice. In conceiving such musical organizations as polyphonies, or even the simple concatenation of rhythmic patterns executed by multiple drums, the integration produced is not random or accidental, but willfully conceived. This is true whether the music is improvised, as in jazz, or carefully constructed before it is performed; in both cases, consistently successful integration is "composed" or made. In improvised music, the superimpositions and fusions are carried out in ongoing and split second fashion; in written music it is merely somewhat more leisurely done. Although John Cage and other proponents of so-called random music might insist that such willful intention is not necessary to produce worthwhile music, their position does not apply to musical creation as it is customarily understood—or else the type of integrations they produce exists on a different level than the one I am discussing here.

That superimposition of discrete entities is intentional is evident on careful reading of the following statement by Hindemith. This statement is frequently and erroneously quoted as a description of a mystical unconscious inspiratory experience, but, despite the sense of an extensive and comprehensive vision, the key emphasis in Hindemith's account is on the conscious and purposeful superimposition of the whole structure or form onto its discrete parts. Moreover, there is the suggestion of a superimposition of visual (seeing the form) and auditory (the sound details) elements within the same space.

> We all know the impression of a heavy flash of lightning in the night. Within a second's time we see a broad landscape, not only in its general outlines but with every detail. Although we could never describe each single component of the picture, we feel that not even the smallest leaf of grass escapes our attention. We experience a view, *immensely comprehensive and at the same time immensely detailed,* that we could never have under normal daylight conditions, and perhaps not during the night either, if our senses and nerves were not strained by the extraordinary suddenness of the event.
>
> Compositions must be conceived the same way. If we cannot, in the flash of a single moment, see a composition in its absolute entirety, with every pertinent detail in its proper place, we are not genuine creators. . . . Not only will he [the composer] have the gift of seeing—illuminated in his mind's eye as if by a flash of lightning—a complete musical form (though its subsequent realization in a performance may take three hours or more); he will have the energy, persistence and skill to bring this envisioned form into existence, so that even after months of work not one of its details will be lost or fail to fit into his photomental picture. [Italics added][40]

Suddeness and drama, even possibly some unconscious and mysterious factors, but the conscious use of homospatial thinking as well!

Literature

Homospatial thinking operates in numerous and diverse ways in literature. In addition to producing metaphors and integrating janusian formulations, this form of cognition operates in poetry to produce meaningful and effective rhymes, alliterations, and assonances. Entities which are connected or juxtaposed, such as the opposites in a janusian construct, words with similar graphic or phonetic properties, and words that are homographic homophones yielding double meanings are subjected to the superimposition and fusion of the homospatial process. In the case of some of these connections and juxtapositions, such as sound-alike or rhyming words, the initial coming together may be the result of a trained association process: the poet teaches himself to remember words with similar phonetic properties and they come to mind as associations to other words.[41] But the homospatial process is not associational; here again the principle is based on "ought," the words are superimposed or fused because the poet wills it. For emotional and/or aesthetic reasons, the poet wants to unify the words or to elaborate their intrinsic meanings and relations. After arriving at a juxtaposition of similar sounding words by association, he superimposes or fuses them in his mind and the resulting conception *generates wordings and ideas.*

In the creation of a poem about a scene on a beach, one of my research subjects had followed the line, "Or lathered magmas out of deep retorts," with the beginning of a new stanza, thus:

> Welling, as here to fill
> With tumbled rockmeal, stone froth, lithic fire
> The dike's brief chasm and the sill . . .

And there he stopped. He had earlier adopted a rhyme scheme based on the pattern ABABCC, and the line to be written would need to rhyme with the second line end word "fire." Not satisfied with any ideas involving such a rhyme, he stopped working on the poem that day. When he returned the next morning, he began thinking of the image of the beach, and of the ocean, and he thought of the word "spray." Deciding to change the word "fire" to "spray," he then searched for rhymes for the latter word and thought of "day." Next—and here the particular homospatial conception occurred—the words "day" and "spray" *together* produced an idea and image embodied in the following line, the line that became the fourth in the stanza:

> Weathered until the sixth and human day.

As he described the conception, the printed words "day" and "spray" were clearly superimposed upon one another and an image of day's brightness and the watery spray were also superimposed. Words and images are always mentally connected—for everyone—and these superimposed words and images produced the idea of "weather" and "weathering." Though it is not accurate to describe this conception sequentially, as it occurred virtually all at once, the biblical reference to "the sixth and human day," the reference to the Creation, developed from the image of the weathering by both spray and day (i.e., time). In addition to brightness, the connotation of day as

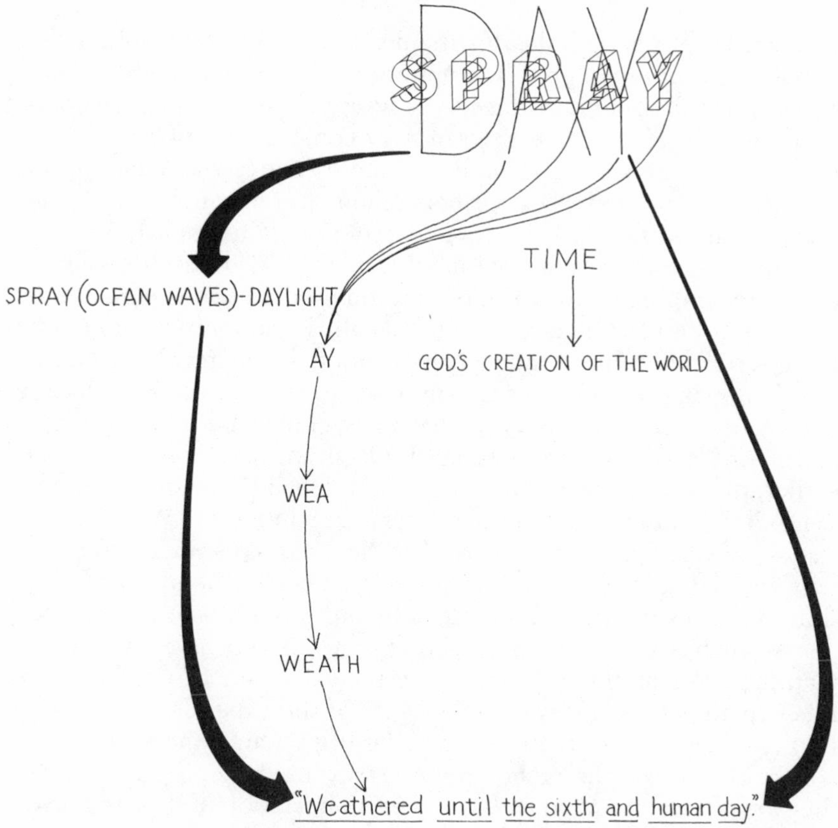

Fig. 42. Diagrammatic representation of the homospatial conception consisting of images of watery (ocean) spray and bright day (daylight), day as elapsed time, and of the printed words themselves led to the poetic line: "Weathered until the sixth and human day."

a temporal factor—the passage of days and of time—led to the idea of God's Creation in this context. Diagrammatically, the process could be described as shown on the accompanying figure (fig. 42).

Hence, the homospatial conception of day and spray superimposed and occupying the same space led to the construction of the entire line and to the introduction of the first reference to God's Creation in the poem. Though the poet had a dim idea of connecting the beach scene to this larger idea when he worked on the earlier portions of the poem, it only became a realization through the development of this line. It is hardly necessary to decide with certainty whether the Creation idea generated the homospatial conception or the latter generated the idea: the concrete realization of the idea, the poetic creation of this line, and the subsequent references to Creation in the poem were clearly made possible through the homospatial process.

A similar principle holds for the poetic use of homographs, homophones, and homographic homophones. Words such as "rifle" with two or more discrete meanings—the weapon and the act of searching—are notoriously used in the ordinary construction of puns. But in poetry such words are also used in a more serious way. Shakespeare, for instance, is often cited for his copious use of puns in his poetic dramas. But while Shakespeare and other poets frequently use puns in order to produce a humorous effect, they also use homophonic and homographic words for more profound and serious embodiment of aesthetic multiple meanings or so-called ambiguities. Sometimes these serious and humorous effects cannot be separated because the artist intends the same words or phrases to serve several purposes at once. Quite separate, however, are the psychological roots of the pun and of the aesthetically intended multiple meaning. As mentioned earlier, the pun is a technique of wit that depends, for its effect, upon what Freud called "rediscovering what is familiar."[42] When, for instance, the punster uses the word "rifle" in a context that calls attention to its double meaning, we laugh upon recognition of something we already know. The pun calls our attention to the fact that one word has two disparate meanings. Used as a joke, a pun is a manifestation of the primary process mechanism of condensation. It is experienced as pleasurable because of the experience of recognition and because of an attendant relief of psychic expenditure.

When homographs or homophones are used in poetry, however, they are often elaborated to develop an appreciation of the unfamiliar, an experience that may actually involve initial discomfort and an increased psychic expenditure. Depending on the context, little humor or relief may be involved. Generally, a creative poet uses the homophones or homographs in contexts that integrate the meaning with the sound or written form; the disparate meanings of the word are related to suggest identities of meaning paralleling the identities of sound and written form. This was demonstrated in the creation of "In Monument Valley" with the poet's use of the homophone "gait" where the motion of the horse was related to a figurative passing through the gate of heaven (chap. 3). In the case of the word "rifle," an effective poetic construction might emphasize the violence of the weapon and the violence of an act of searching or rifling through a drawer. When such an integration is produced, it is the result of homospatial thinking and the intentional superimposition of images suggested by the two meanings of the word. It does not result from condensation and primary process thinking. The difference can be characterized as follows: the punster is satisfied to call attention to a double meaning, to point it out and leave it alone so to speak; the creator, however, does something with these meanings, namely integrates them into an aesthetic whole. When the punster is also a creator, such as Shakespeare, he often uses the pun both as a joke and in an integrated, more serious way. In context, the pun produces comic relief or illustrates a speaker's character and also has a deeper impact. The first effect of producing laughter gives way to slight discomfort or thoughtful consideration. Note in *Macbeth,* for instance, the porter's wry punning comment on drink: "[it] equivocates him in a sleep, and, giving him the lie, leaves him" (act 2, sc. 3, line 34).

To return to metaphor, it is in production of metaphors that homospatial thinking plays one of its major roles in literary creation. Fortunately, unlike with visual and auditory metaphor, instances of literary metaphor require little exegesis or explanation. One bit of caution, however: although particular instances of literary metaphor are readily identified and agreed upon, there is nowadays a good deal of disagreement in psychological, philosophical, and linguistic quarters about the nature of metaphor in the general sense. And an even more important caveat: when discussing metaphors in literature, one must bear in mind the distinction between the tired metaphors and clichés of everyday language and the fresh and penetrating created metaphors in poetry and other types of literary art. Only in the construction of these latter types of metaphors does the homospatial process play a crucial role (N.B.: except, as with the integration of puns, it also integrates clichés into new metaphors).

Earlier in the book I cited the instance of a central literary image or metaphor (horse and rider in one accord) resulting from my research subject's homospatial thinking. Now I shall reproduce and discuss some documented material on metaphor creation from other poets who have not been subjects of mine. Although some of the works I shall examine would not be generally considered as effective or as valuable as "In Monument Valley," the particular metaphors discussed are, I believe, definite creations with artistic value in their own right. Moreover, as the following descriptions come from published material written by poets who were not my subjects, these are creative sequences free of any possible influence, even small or indirect, on my part.

In an appendix to the 1942 edition of the book, *An Anatomy of Inspiration* by Harding, the British poet Robert Nichols presented an account[43] of the thoughts and events connected to his writing of the following poem:

Sunrise Poem

The sun, a serene and ancient poet
Stoops and writes on the sunrise sea
In softly undulant cyphers of gold
Words of Arabian charactery;
And the lovely riddle is lovingly rolled
With sound of slumberous, peaceful thunder

Around the sky and sea thereunder
Toward my feet. What is here enscrolled?
Is it a poem or a story?
I cannot command this charactery,
But I think it is both and that it reads
This glorious morning as of old
When the first sun rose above the first sea,
As read it will while there is sea
And sun to scribe with quill of gold.
It is both a story and a poem,
A hymn as also a history
Concerning the mightiest of mages,
The best that has been or shall be
Writ for any throughout the ages,
Writ for any, whoever he be
Or the most scholarly of sages
Or the most awkward of those who plod,
For Greek, Jew, Infidel and Turk—
As it was written too for me—
One page, two eternal sentences:
"The Heavens declare the Glory of God
And the Firmament showeth His Handiwork."

With respect to the creation of the metaphorical first line (also the theme) of the poem, "The sun, a serene and ancient poet," Nichols describes the following sequence: while on a Mediterranean cruise, he had an unusual period of preliminary poetic productivity. Having many poetic ideas including fragments of lines, he wrote down some and some he totally discarded, but he did not actually complete a poem. Then one morning he awoke quite early and began to deliberate about whether to stay in his room until breakfast or to go on to the deck of the ship to see the sunrise. He had the following thought: "You're in fine fettle, so refreshed, that undoubtedly a poem will be waiting for you. By and large I'd say that it will probably be about the rising sun." Shortly, he decided to go on deck.

Standing on deck, Nichols noted that the sun was red but not so bright that he couldn't look at it; he also felt there was an amiable and "easygoing" quality in the scene. Soon, he began to experience feelings both of loneliness and excitement while looking at the reflection of the sun on the water, and, with that, a particular emotional sense of there being some form of writing on the water. His description of this emotional sense and the sequence leading up to the creation of the first line of the poem is as follows:

> I . . . apprehended that these figures *weren't* in a book but were, at that very moment, in the most literal sense *being written on the sea by the sun,* a being who was a poet. *I did not say to myself "the sun is a poet" but I felt the emotion such a person as*

> *myself might be expected to feel were he to find himself in the presence of a being both capable of doing what I now beheld being done and accustomed to doing it.* There was then a fractional pause, a halt in my attention as if that attention didn't wholly apprehend what was presented to it, the halt in fact that precedes recognition. . . . On an instant there was presented to my consciousness a favorite picture-postcard I had twice or thrice bought at the British Museum. Almost simultaneously there formed in my mouth the line
>
> "The sun an ancient, serene poet."
>
> The picture on the postcard—that of a poet, possibly Persian, seated on the ground, wearing a rose-pink turban, a green caftan and a little pair of black slippers, and gazing to the spectator's left—and the line were indissoluble.[44]

Thus, as Nichols described it, the initial line of this poem, a metaphor, was produced by a homospatial conception: the image of a poet, the sun, and the words comprising the poetic line were fused and were occupying the same space. Notice, for instance, that the word "serene" describes both the idea of the "easygoing" quality of the scene and a quality of the postcard poet's gaze. And the word "ancient" describes both a poet from an older civilization and the ageless sun. Notice, too, that the homospatial conception was not merely the result of undirected mental associations to the visual sensations of the scene: despite Nichols's use of passive grammatical constructions in the description, it is clear that he had an interpretative idea of a personage which led him to superimpose the image of the postcard poet onto the scene and to construct the line. A few lines further on in his essay, Nichols makes the guiding intentionality of his emotion clearer: "Did the postcard precipitate the line or the line the postcard? Neither. The emotion of being in the presence of an august personage engaged, as I beheld him engaged, precipitated both the line and the image."

For the poet, the homospatial conception produces the metaphor *and* its specific content. The superimposition and fusion of the postcard poet with the scene yielded not only the explicit equating of the sun and a poet, the structure of the metaphor, but suggested the particular words "serene" and "ancient" as content. It appears that the poet generally brings such images together into the same space, scrutinizes and savors them for interlocking features and similarities fitting *his emotional and cognitive orientation at the moment,* and then labels these in words to produce the metaphor. I realize, in saying this, that I seem to be describing a far more plodding, deliberate process than what Nichols describes as a dramatically sudden event. Further, Nichols's use of passive constructions such as "there formed" or "the emotion precipitated" may not seem to jibe exactly with my discussion of a willful, intentional sequence. I shall again emphasize, therefore, that I am analyzing a very complex though momentary event. All the steps I mentioned probably came together in a flash. Before describing the particular thoughts connected to the creation of the poetic line, Nichols explicitly stated that he had *intentionally* set out that morning to write a poem about the sun. His use of a passive grammatical construction rather than an active intention-connoting one need not be taken as a literal description of his thinking, but should be considered a stylistic device. Finally, when Nichols suggests that an "emotion" brought about this line and image, our knowledge of mental processes allows us to insist that conceptual thinking played a role as well.

The final form of the line he used is, of course, slightly different from the initial wording. In this regard, Nichols merely explained that he thought the wording "too jumpy" and he therefore changed the order of the adjectives. Many such judgments were made during the course of constructing the entire poem and other types of thinking also were applied. But overall, Nichols's description makes clear that neither the emotion and conception of the august personage alone, nor the mere association of the sun's reflection with writing, produced the initial metaphor. A supravening and superimposed image of the poet on the postcard was required. The indissoluble line and image he describes was a portion of the homospatial process.

Readers of poetry, literary critics, and psychologists analyzing a completed poem implicitly assume that metaphors are produced by an immediate experience involving perception of similarities through association or analogy. Or else they believe that a full-blown image of a particular scene comes to mind, seemingly out of nowhere, and this provides the structure and the content of the metaphor. For example, when such people are asked, as I have informally done, how they think the following metaphor "the road was a rocket of sunlight" was created, they invariably say something like the following: standing above a road on a sunny day, or, thinking about standing above such a road, the poet *noticed* or fancied he saw that the sun made the road look like the trail of a rocket. Or they suggest that the poet felt like a rocket while driving his car on a sunny road. When asked how the metaphor "the branches were handles of stars" was created, they generally say: walking in the country (or in a park) at night, the poet looked up at the trees and he *noticed* that the branches of the trees seemed to connect to the light points of the stars shining through them, or that he visualized such a scene.

These answers are incorrect. They are incorrect not because they are too simple or too unimaginative—some people elaborated the basic ideas in highly detailed and interesting ways—but because they are based on an incorrect assumption. This assumption is an automatic and intrinsic one and, aside from the people I have surveyed, it has been unquestioningly and unconsciously adopted throughout the history of art. For creativity research, it is a particularly insidious and confounding assumption that leads to frequent error. The assumption here is that the work of art is always created in the same way as it is experienced by a receiving viewer or reader. The answers as given derive from the associations instigated in the receiving reader's mind about the poetic scenes indicated by the metaphors. The answers are derived from the reader's perception of the impact of the metaphors. But the sequence and circumstances of metaphor creation are quite different from these perceptions; visualization of a particular scene or analogizing does not itself produce an effective metaphor. Because of homospatial thinking, a creative poet brings together elements on the basis of various types of conceptions. When actually creating the metaphor "the road was a rocket of sunlight," the creator was sitting at his desk and thinking about the alliterative properties of the words "road" and "rocket." He was also visualizing the shapes both of roads and of rocket trajectories and trails. Other conceptual as well as emotional factors brought the words and images to mind. Then, through a homospatial conception, he mentally superimposed the images (and, more vaguely, the words themselves) and fleetingly thought, "What connects road and rocket?"; "When do they relate to each other or look alike?" The answer came as, "in sunlight," and almost simultaneously the full metaphor, "the road was a rocket of sunlight," was conceived.

Similarly, "the branches were handles of stars" was created at a desk through superimposition and fusion of words and images. Attracted to the words "branches" and "handles" because of their assonance, their emotional and conceptual meanings, and their similarly elongated shapes, the creator mentally brought them together to fill the same spatial location. The connecting idea of "stars" was suggested both by the plausibility of branches and handles looking similar at night and by the sound qualities of the word. "Stars" is assonantal both with "branches" and with "handles"; mentally superimposing the two latter words emphasized and intensified the common "a" aspect and quality, and suggested the word "stars." After the full metaphor was created, the creator—like the reader—perceived and enjoyed such associations as the torchlike quality of the entire image, the sense of strength and supportiveness, connections between near and far, and the sense of branches reaching. He too visualized a scene of seeing the stars contiguous with the branches of a tree at night. All these associations convinced him that he had created an effective metaphor. Thus, a series of mental events, rather than the perceptions of similarities and contiguities in particular scenes, or of analogies among elements, served to produce these metaphors. Occurring so rapidly that the series of mental events sometimes seems to happen almost all at once, such a sequence is responsible for the creation of metaphor even when a particular scene seems to be the instigating factor. Even, for instance, when walking in the country or a park in the evening, a homospatial conception of a branch and handle occupying the same space is responsible for producing the effective metaphor.

A similar type of series of events was documented by the American publisher-poet Melville Cane. In his *Making a Poem,* an unusual book largely devoted to recounting instances of poetic creation,[45] Cane describes developing a poem entitled "The Dismal Month" as follows:

> The first half of the poem was actually written in the dismal month of March. My mood, if not dismal, was certainly one of impatience and dissatisfaction, as I looked back on too long a period of unproductiveness. With a calculated act of will I set aside a half-hour in the middle of a professional working day. Soon my habitual tensions and concerns disappeared; I had taken myself out of the city and found myself contemplating a country landscape. The date happened to be March 21, and as I noted that fact and looked out on the murky sky, I said to myself, wryly "This is spring."
>
> The point of view for a possible poem resided in that stray observation, which, translated and extended, came to this [transcribed in a notebook]:
>
> "A fine kind of spring! Not the standardized spring of the poets, but the last chapter of winter down-at-the-heels. Shabby green."
>
> "Shabby green" took hold. . . . Shabby green represented the color and shoddiness for my unspringlike season. Letting my fancy roam at will, I began to fill in the details, to picture the struggle of life breaking through the coils of inertia, really my own personal problem at that moment.[46]

The homospatial conception consisted of a superimposition of the imagined country scene and the murky sky outside the poet's window. While the poet does not use terms such as superimposition, occupying the same space, or others I have used to describe the homospatial process, his exposition makes clear that the phrase "shabby green" resulted from such merging and fusion of the images in his mind. Here are the first three stanzas of the poem he wrote:

THE DISMAL MONTH

Struggling to shake off
The clutch of sleep,
To strike off
Winter's irons,
Spring, imprisoned maid

Stirs, arises,
Bedraggled, disheveled,
Dead leaves sticking to her hair.

March is the dismal month of her delivery.

Cautiously,
In gown of shabby green
She picks her way unsteadily
Under lowering skies
Over ruts still frozen,
Through dregs of snow.[47]

Although I have included only the first half of this poem, the personification of spring, which is the central image or metaphor throughout, came, as he says, from filling in the "details" following the "shabby green" homospatial conception. It was not the result of an association or a remembrance regarding a particular element in a country scene, actual or imagined. The construction of the remainder of the poem consisted of a continual filling in of details generated by the tension in the original conception.

A particularly interesting aspect of this account is Cane's description of the emotional elements accompanying the homospatial conception. Here is a recounting in somewhat elaborated detail of some of the steps in the homospatial process, a process consisting of a complex interaction of many types of psychological phenomena, only one of which is the cognitive fusion of discrete entities. Embroiled in feelings of tension and discouragement, the poet initially conjures up a country scene in order, it seems, to become more relaxed and to write a poem. Then he brings himself back to his immediate surroundings by noting the date as demarcating the season of spring. The phrase "shabby green" not only fuses the visual images of the country scene and the murky city sky, but it also represents a fusion of the disparate aspects of his emotional condition: discouragement with hope, tension with relaxation, a sense of inertia with a sense of life. If we consider the psychological content of the words themselves, there are suggestions of the fusion of an aggressive and a sexual component I spoke of earlier as the psychodynamic basis of the homospatial conception. The word "shabby" suggests an unconscious aggressive aspect, while the word "green" suggests an unconscious libidinous impulse pertaining to nature and growth. In constructing the above stanzas, such images as the faintly erotic one of the imprisoned maid and the aggressive one of striking off winter's irons could have developed through a process of uncovering further unconscious sexual and aggressive content through the mirror-image function of homospatial thinking.

Cane also mentions the conjunction between his more extended conception of the poem, the representation of the struggle of life against inertia, with his own personal problem at that moment. For the poet, this conjunction between the self and its circumstances with the developing conception of a poem is directly analogous to visual artists' interaction with their materials described earlier. Indeed, as the poet proceeds with a particular poetic creation, there seems to be a complex type of superimposition of the image of the self with the material and vice versa: words merge with mental images and ideas, and there is mutual interaction and modification. All aspects of the words, their sounds and associated images, exert an influence as do all aspects of the mental image of the self. At the completion of a good poem, both the poet and the words or phrases he uses are literally altered and changed from what they were at the start. Thus, this is a comprehensive form of the homospatial process, involving all sensory modalities at once.

Such a comprehensive form of homospatial thinking operates in other arts as well. In the performing arts, actors experience a sense of fusion between the mental image of themselves and the character they portray, dancers experience such fusion and superimposition of their bodies and the "empty" space surrounding, and musicians a physical fusion with their music. And in other forms of literature besides poetry, this general type of homospatial thinking plays a role. While production of metaphor as well as creative use of homophony, alliteration, assonance, and even rhyme plays a role in all types of literary creation, homospatial thinking also tends to operate in broader ways in the creation of novels, short stories, and plays. Creating these latter forms of literature especially involves the continual interaction between the author's conscious image of himself and his materials, as well as fusions and superimpositions of scenes, sequences, and attributes of persons.

Data from my research subjects illustrate these phenomena in novels and plays. Arthur Miller described to me his initial idea for his play *Death of a Salesman* as consisting of the following: "the first idea was the image of the [salesman] character Willie moving around *inside his own head;* he was searching for, and checking on, various aspects and remembrances of his life much as one would search in a library. The first title for the play was to be *The Inside of His Head.*"[48] The initial conception or image therefore consisted of an entire man superimposed upon or occupying the same location as the entire inside of his own head.

A more complicated manifestation of the homospatial process, consisting both of fusions of scenes and of fusions of the author's self-image with the developing work, is contained in the following report.

It is based on a "natural" experiment performed with an outstanding American novelist engaged in creating a novel:

In the course of an interview series with this research subject, I introduced an unusual procedure. We had been working together from the time of the inception of the novel and, now that he appeared to be halfway through, I proposed the following: during the week's interval between our usual sessions, I would call him up before he started the day's work—he always started at the same hour—and ask that he write down everything he thought of in conjunction with constructing the first sentence for the novel that day. I would not tell him in advance which day I would call, because I did not want him to be specifically prepared either on the night before, or on arising that particular morning. We had good rapport; therefore I believed he would try to write what was on his mind without censorship or distortion. He consented to the procedure.

During the following week, I called him in the morning on a day selected by a random procedure. I merely stated on the phone, "Today is the day," and we engaged in no further conversation. When I met with him for our usual session later that week, he said he had done the task and he produced the material to follow. Although I had no idea of what I would find at the time—I had not then defined or discovered homospatial or janusian thinking—the following shows both fusion and superimposition of mental imagery and the author's attempt to "get himself into" or fuse himself with the work. The part of the novel he happened to be working on that day was the beginning of a new chapter, and it became a description of a college protest scene. I have edited this presentation of *his exact notes of his thoughts* only slightly for clarification of references:

"Read what was written yesterday—made some changes on page 129 of the manuscript—got lost in a fog while reading, remembered to write things down from now on—thought of speech to be given at the White House—returned to reading and became conscious of watching my thoughts: no good—changed the word 'intercepting' to 'bisecting' on page 132. At the end of the book will use phrase 'still too far to walk'—picture in mind of a street scene, strongly—mob scene in the novel *Day of the Locust.*

"Scene of the street between the old campus at the U. of California and the town of Berkeley—students rocking a street car—scene of a football rally. Fear of consequences but being drawn in [researcher's note: this refers both to the author himself and to the main character in the novel at this point]

—background scene of Durfee Hall and Battell Chapel at Yale comes together with Berkeley scene—Were these images put in my mind by reading an account of a riot 3–4 years ago?—See motorcycle policeman swerving into the crowd: his white crash helmet—start to read back over these notes.

"Get up and pull shade to shut out light from window—conscious of bird singing outside. Should I start this page or another one?

"Write down number of this chapter—Feel relieved about not going to Russia as originally planned.

"Set my hand up at the top of the paper [note: this is in order to "shut out" distraction and to focus]—Write: 'Down the center of Planique Street came the first surge of the riot.'

"What is John [the main character, a student] doing? How did he get there? Why do I see that particular spot so strongly? Memories of earlier pictures associated with the novel come in. Write second sentence: 'Six motorcycle policemen were sitting on their machines, abreast, blocking the throat of the street at the crossing with Fourth.'

"John will have come through an arch before the riot."

Having constructed the first as well as the second sentence for that day, the author made no further notes about his thoughts and continued to work on his novel. The experiment, as I had outlined it to him, was completed. In this written account of his thoughts on starting, which is surely as accurate and honest as it would be possible for any person to produce under the circumstances, there is a definite indication of the fusion and superimposition of two discrete images: the scene of the street between the old campus at the University of California and the town of Berkeley proper is fused with and superimposed upon the scene of the Durfee Hall-Battell Chapel area at Yale. And it is clear that this fusion and superimposition is immediately followed by—and therefore in all likelihood generated—the concrete idea of the motorcycle policemen, the substance of both the initial creation here and the second sentence he wrote. To recapitulate the sequence: it appears from the notes (this was later corroborated by the author himself) that he had a general notion of writing a riot scene before setting to work that day. In approaching that task, he thought first of a nonspecific street scene, and then he had a visual image of the Hollywood mob scene in the novel by Nathanael West, *Day of the Locust.* This image was succeeded by the image of the street at Berkeley. Up to this point, his mind was preoccupied with memories, nothing new had been generated, that is nothing that pertained directly to the novel as an entity, to its particular world. Only when he consciously experienced the Berkeley and Yale images together, occupying the same space, did he think of the motorcycle policemen and begin to articulate further the realm and world of the novel, its scenes and images.[49] Though the images were fused and superimposed, he continued to see discrete aspects of them as he elaborated the scene. In a later paragraph of the chapter, he wrote: "for some reason [John was] vividly conscious of the dirty stone of the heavy nineteenth-century buildings behind him," an inclusion of something from the Yale scene.

The broader type of manifestation of homospatial thinking, the author's superimposition and fusion of his self-image with his material, is also conveyed here in his orientation toward the main character and in his rather dramatic action of setting his hand at the top of the page as a barrier against distraction before he could actually begin writing. The author called my attention to this second matter himself. It could, of course, be merely considered a means of facilitating concentration. He seems to have been struggling at that point with the imposed and distracting task of having to write out his thoughts. In his difficulty, however, he became hypersensitive to the physical surroundings outside himself and, in discussing it with me later, he said that he put his hand at the top of the sheet in order to *separate both himself and the work from his surroundings.* He demonstrated the definite gesture with a slam of the side of his hand on his desk. The action, in other words, conveyed the sense of this author's blocking out the outside and putting himself in a space together with the work.

Creation of short stories, novels, plays, and poetry characteristically involves the types of homospatial thinking in this experiment. Creative writers tend to make use of visual imagery to a very high degree but not merely as the content of passive fantasies, reveries, or stock mental representations. In a questionnaire study of more than 100 fiction writers carried out by the editor Arthur Hoffman in 1923, for instance, eighty-one out of ninety-five responding reported a tendency to experience visual imagery.[50] None of the eighty-one reported habitually using stock or standard mental pictures (of such things as a church, student, cowboy, or a village) in their work, and only twenty-three reported having such pictures in mind to some degree or in certain circumstances. Although some of the writers surveyed in this study were producers of presumably not-so-creative slick magazine fiction, very highly creative authors such as Sinclair Lewis were also included in the group. Another particularly interesting feature of this study was the large number of writers reporting a heavy use of visual imagery in an era prior to current times, when there is an extraordinary and general influence of motion pictures and television on the use of the visual perceptual mode.

The writer's use of imagery, visual or otherwise, without resort to stock representations is really nothing new nor should it be surprising. Coleridge some time ago made a distinction between fancy and imagination, by which he meant that mere random, undirected, and standard ideas and images—fancies or, to use the modern term, fantasies—were not sufficient to produce art.[51] Active or constructive shaping—imagination—was required. And Freud, while he emphasized the important role of fantasy and daydreaming—and, by implication, imagery—in creative writing, also emphasized that the writer was able to shape and actively structure his fantasies through his special talents and abilities.[52] Freud could not specify the nature of these talents and abilities; homospatial thinking is one of them. The empirical and theoretical emphasis on imagery, but not on stock images, fancies, or fantasies alone, is supportive of homospatial thinking in literary creation. Creative writers report that they do not use stock or everyday images in their work, even though they, like everyone else, experience such images, because they convert images into literary creations through that cognitive process.

Related to the fiction writer's superimposition and fusion of his mental image of his self (all sensory modalities) with his materials are the homospatial processes operating in another significant aspect of literary creation, the construction of literary characters. Important in all types of literature, character creation is especially crucial in the writing of novels, short stories, and plays. It is well known that fiction writers often draw their characters from actual persons they have known. In a chapter entitled "Where Do Novelists Get Their Characters?" George G. Williams lists 100 well-known alleged connections between literary characters and real persons, ranging on an alphabetical list from Louisa May Alcott's parents and Mr. and Mrs. March in *Little Women* to Owen Wister's main character in *The Virginian* and Wister's friend, Colonel George R. Shannon.[53] But, just as creative fiction writers do not directly use standard or everyday sensory images in their work, so too they do not directly use, copy, or reproduce real persons. The process is neither a matter of copying, nor adding and combining parts, nor is it a matter of remembering snatches of conversations and incidental gestures. In creating a literary character, the effective writer has a full representation of a person or of persons in his mind including speech, actions, physical characteristics, and entire life history insofar as he knows it. As an ongoing process in time, this representation is superimposed and fused both with conscious representations of the writer's self and with action and representations emerging from the work in progress. The novelist

Elizabeth Bowen, while not explicitly describing this (homospatial) process, makes the following points about character creation:

> The novelist's perceptions of his characters take place *in the course of the actual writing of the novel.* To an extent, the novelist is in the same position as the reader. But his perceptions should be always just in advance. . . .
>
> (N.B.—The unanswerability of the question, from an outsider: "Are the characters in your novel invented, or are they from real life?" Obviously, neither is true. The outsider's notion of "real life" and the novelist's are hopelessly apart.). . . .
>
> The character is there (in the novel) for the sake of the action he or she is to contribute to the plot. Yes. But also, he or she exists *outside* the action being contributed to the plot.[54]

Bowen's assertions, although sometimes stated in other ways, are quite universally acknowledged and accepted by creative fiction writers. Superficially somewhat mystical perhaps, the remarks can be explained through an understanding of the function of homospatial thinking in character creation. Characters are neither from "real life" nor are they totally invented because they result from an interaction between the author's mental representation of real persons and his materials. The words, actions, and circumstances of the work in progress are superimposed and fused with the author's remembrance of real sequences and of real persons in order to produce literary characters. The author does not, for instance, decide in advance to construct a character who (1) looks like his wife, (2) talks like his mother, (3) acts like his mistress, and (4) is somewhat reminiscent of a childhood sweetheart. Moreover, it is not merely a matter of conscious decision making versus unconscious influences. Although psychoanalytic biographers have often retrospectively discovered that such combinations as just described—appearing like products of the unconscious primary process mechanisms of condensation—occur frequently in fiction, this does not mean that they result primarily from unconscious operations. The author is quite aware of having a real person in mind and of sometimes including actual remembered events, conversations, and actions in the fabric of his short story, novel, or play. He is also aware of altering such remembrances in relation to his constantly changing perception of what he has already written. While some aspects of the process are unquestionably unconscious—usually, of course, the inclusion within certain characters of parental qualities and behavior associated with unacceptable feelings—the continual superimposition and fusion of representations of real persons, of the self, and of the work in progress are always in consciousness. Because there is a conscious process of fusion, the characters are new integrations rather than combinations. Characters are neither the result of the unconscious combining function of condensation nor of some type of conscious combining operation. They are neither completely derived from persons in real life nor are they completely invented.

One author, for instance, was consciously aware of modeling a character after his own son. As he constructed scenes involving the character's interaction with the father in the novel, the author also thought about feelings and impressions pertaining to his own father. In writing the scenes, he brought together images of his son and himself, and images of himself with his own father. Moreover, the character in the novel had already been described as having experiences that were unlike both the author's own and those of his son. The discussions between the son and the father in the novel, therefore, resulted from a conscious merger and a fusion of words and ideas of the three types of images and persons: the author's son, the author himself, and the son character in the novel.

Another instance comes from the creation of *All the King's Men* by Robert Penn Warren. The narrator-character in that novel is named Jack Burden. In a retrospective discussion, Warren told me that he had decided to have the narrator of the novel be a character in the story in order to avoid having a removed, omniscient, and impersonal author relating the events, and also to provide a dramatic center, or "model" for the effect of the main figure Stark in filling some spiritual or psychological vacuum in others—the source of his power. He noted that while creating Jack Burden he had in his mind an actual young man he had known. Also, at one point in the writing, he said, he began to be concerned that the novel would lack a "moral center," that it might turn out to be merely a thriller. It was then that he gave Jack Burden a background as a graduate student of history who had decided to turn away from pursuing his doctorate [Warren: "Trying to find an indication of the point of the novel, I made up the story of the historic document of Cass Mastern. Jack, from a sense of contrast between the moral sense of this, his own family's document, and his own condition, gave up his doctorate. Or, at least, this was his alibi"]. Strikingly, at an important turning point or "moral center" of his own life Warren himself had decided to give up his graduate studies as well: during the period at Oxford, where he was taking a B.Litt., he had begun to write fiction as well as poetry and began to envisage a primarily literary career by which he could live, and so he resigned a fellowship at Yale which would have allowed him to return there to do a dissertation for the doctorate. He "swore" never to write even an article for a learned journal [Warren: "swore, perhaps—superfluously"].

That writers have not heretofore come forward to describe the process in these terms does not mean it is out of awareness. Introspection about the precise nature of mental events during the creative process is a hindrance and writers have wisely avoided it. Under the circumstances of my interviews with writers as research subjects, recall of thoughts in conjunction with a day's work in progress is high. There is sometimes a good deal of motivation to be open and cooperative, and clear memories of previous important creations arise. Consistently reported is a continuing awareness of images of real persons, and of thoughts and images about the material in progress in relation to images of the self. These images fuse and interact, and specific descriptions, dialogues, and elements of character are produced. Multiple discrete entities occupy the same space in the author's mind and the author integrates character, plot, and personal experience.

In the next chapter, some reported results from another type of empirical study of the literary creative process shall elucidate further the operation of homospatial thinking in the creation of literary character. And I shall attempt to clarify some differences between this particular psychological process and others with which it can be confused.

11

HOMOSPATIAL THINKING AS A PSYCHOLOGICAL PROCESS

Because homospatial thinking involves fusion, imagery, multiple sensory modalities, identity, and similarity, it can be confused with so-called primitive, pathological, and concrete modes of thought. Moreover, one of the characteristics of primary process thinking is the lack of ordinary spatial restrictions, so-called spacelessness. In dreams, this characteristic is manifested by the bringing together of concrete elements without regard to their ordinary locations, dimensions, conformations, or their integrity in space; there is defiance or exaggeration of the limitations and effects of gravity, size, and structure. Thus, flying, enormous feats of strength, or excessive exhaustion, as well as composite images of places, people, and things appear. Sometimes, as we well know, the composite images in dreams can be phantasmagoric. This primary process feature of spacelessness is mirrored in consciousness by homospatial thinking. Both operate to defy the ordinary restrictions of space but they function in a reverse cognitive and psychodynamic manner. The primary process characteristic functions to express wishes in concealed form, while homospatial thinking functions to unearth and reveal unconscious material as well as to integrate and unite concrete entities to produce both metaphors and abstractions. In homospatial thinking, discrete entities are usually superimposed and vague when occupying the same space; in dreams, entities tend to be brought together as vivid composites, that is, combination and compromise formation takes place.

Related to the mirror-image relationship between homospatial thinking and primary process spacelessness is the relationship of the former to the specific primary process mechanism of condensation. With condensation, multiple entities are brought together and compressed in order to discharge impulses in a concealed, distorted way. As this compression involves spatial representations, products of condensation bear some similarity to homospatial constructs. However, the product of condensation is always a composite; through compromise formation various aspects of multiple elements are combined. To elaborate on a distinction from the previous chapter, a character produced by condensation in a dream might have the red hair of the dreamer's mother, the voice of a childhood sweetheart, and appear in a circumstance connected to the dreamer's wife. The character produced by homospatial thinking might very well be a merger of these same three real persons but she (or he) would be a new integration of the three with derivations of particular characteristics rather than the characteristics themselves. While the purpose of the image produced by condensation in the dream is to represent the dreamer's wish—for timeless female care, for instance—in concrete and disguised form, the purpose of the homospatial process with respect to characterization is to create a new and valuable entity, as well as to begin to reveal the nature of underlying wishes and feelings.

As described earlier, the homospatial process also bears a mirror-image relationship with the primary process mechanism of displacement. With regard to sound similarities in poetry, for example, the homospatial process produces a shifting of emotional charge onto progressively more important psychological material; that is, content associated with unconscious wishes and affects comes progressively toward awareness. Displacement, on the other hand, uses sound similarities to shift emotional charge onto progressively less important material, and content progressively conceals unconscious wishes and affects.

Homospatial Thinking, Psychopathology, and Fusion

These distinctions made between homospatial thinking and primary process spacelessness, condensation, and displacement should also clarify the differentiation from psychopathological modes of thought, especially those in schizophrenia. Primary process mechanisms are usually considered to be operating prominently and significantly in schizophrenic symptomatology. Hallucinations, use of neologisms and word-salads, and various types of autistic communication and behavior appear to be identical with the products of condensation and displacement in dreams. As homospatial thinking is not a form of condensation or displacement, it—like janusian thinking—is not a form of schizophrenic cognition.

As homospatial thinking is, in some ways perhaps, more difficult to grasp than janusian thinking, I shall make some more specific differentiations. Homospatial thinking is not a hallucinatory experience, either visual or auditory, or of any other sensory type. There is no involuntary eruption of homospatial conceptions into consciousness as with hallucinations; the former are products of an active intentional process. Unlike hallucinations, which are vivid and realistic, the homospatial conception is vague and diffuse with only certain elements somewhat more vivid than the rest. And there is no question whatever about reality in the creator's mind. He is fully aware that he himself has produced, and is mentally manipulating, the images rather than their existing in a physical world before him.

Persons suffering from schizophrenia often appear to be communicating by means of metaphors, a matter that has received some attention in psychiatric literature.[1] By implication, the production of effective metaphors in this condition would suggest a capability for and a use of homospatial thinking. A subject for further elaboration and research, briefly the issue turns on whether the schizophrenic person is primarily aware of the figurative or of the literal meaning of a metaphorical expression. When saying, "spilled tea is anger," there is frequently a belief that a person's anger literally caused the tea to spill. This is not because schizophrenics cannot think abstractly. They most certainly can and do, and when they do they are, if predisposed, capable of homospatial thinking. But most often, they are focused on the concrete and literal meanings of their words and expressions. Here, the condensation mechanism predominantly holds sway.

With respect to other forms of psychopathology where there are intrusions as well as aberrant types of mental images, such as in hysteria, condensation rather than homospatial thinking is involved. And not only psychopathological forms of thought but psychopathological dynamisms are distinct from the psychological dynamisms of homospatial thinking. A particular case in point is the factor of fusion. In schizophrenia and other types of psychopathology, an excessively interdependent or interlocking relationship between parent (or parents) and child—symbiosis—is often implicated as a possible causative or attenuating factor. This interdependence is so extreme that young child and parent are psychologically virtually fused, a factor playing a role in the child's later difficulties in developing psychological boundaries between himself and all others, as well as his inability to distinguish categories. Other types of fusion that have been described are the narcissistic fusions associated with a wide diversity of psychopathological conditions.[2] Hellmuth Kaiser has described an underlying fantasy of fusion consisting of a wish to incorporate oneself or to be incorporated with another person, a fantasy that he believes to be the basis of all interpersonal and intrapsychic aberrations.[3] None of these types of fusions are involved in homospatial thinking. The homospatial process involves a fusion of the content of cognitive imagery and sensory experiences. Elements in the content can be, and usually are, representative of unconscious wishes and impulses, and when these elements are cognitively fused there is a concomitant fusion on other psychic levels as well. Neutralized and adaptive energy becomes available as a result. But the fusion of cognitive elements is not motivated by a "fusion fantasy," or a wish to reunite with a mothering figure or to regain a symbiotic relationship. Such fantasies and wishes *could be represented by the elements* in the homospatial conception but they are not the motivating force or the psychodynamic basis for the fusion of cognitive content. Elements are fused or otherwise brought together to occupy the same space because the creator intends them to be fused and to produce a creation.

Homospatial Thinking and Synaesthesia

Synaesthesia, a phenomenon in which "a stimulus presented in one sensory mode seems to call up imagery of another mode as readily as that of its own,"[4] has at times been linked to metaphor creation. With synaesthesia, music is "seen" and colors or other visual images are "heard" or "felt" or "tasted." Certain persons are especially endowed with this mode of perceiving, and it has been reported that mescaline and d-lysergic acid diethylamide (LSD) produce such synaesthetic experiences regardless of any previous endowment.[5] So dramatic and so stimulating are these experiences for the drug ingestors that the drugs are frequently touted as instigators and facilitators of creativity.[6] However, despite the rather dramatic qualities of this type of imagery and of the synaesthetic experiences during drug ingestion, no definite connections to creativity have been established. Although some musicians and other artists have occasionally used terms suggesting synaesthetic experiences, there are no data to suggest that such experiences played any direct role in their creations.

Primarily based on associational cognitive processes, synaesthesia is clearly distinct from homospatial thinking, an active process leading to integration. Also, synaesthesia involves only qualities of entities rather than entire entities or images of entire entities. It involves interchangeability of sensory modes rather than fusion or superimposition. Because synaesthesia derives from associations between experiences in different sensory modalities, such as a particular sound calling up a particular color sensation, it differs from homospatial thinking in involving sequential images. The color green, for instance, follows the appearance of the sound stimulus; the color and the sound do not occupy the same space.

Although some seemingly effective metaphors, such as "a yellow voice," appear on the surface to be direct products of synaesthesia, that may be primarily a serendipitous type of event. Such concatenations may result directly from synaesthetic experiences but, in relation to a context, the homospatial process may be required to render them into effective creations.

Homospatial Thinking and Mental Imagery

Imagination and creativity are so closely interrelated that often the terms are used as equivalent with one another. And the word "imagination" is based directly on the forming of mental images. That the homospatial process, as a major form of creative cognition, uses and depends on mental imagery to a very large degree should therefore be readily appreciated. However, it is important to clarify the nature of the relationship.

Because visual imagery is the sharpest and clearest, most readily arousable, and most widely experienced type of mental imagery, we tend to stress it. We tend to consider the characteristics of visual imagery as representing the characteristics of all types, and we use them for general laws. We study visual images, turn to them as examples, and check on them for verification. Moreover, visual imagery is the most specific and consequently the most readily communicated and validated type. In short, mental imagery as a category is often treated as though equivalent to visual imagery.

In the homospatial process, however, it must be emphasized that various types of imagery can be involved. As we have noted, auditory and kinesthetic imagery play an important role in homospatial thinking in music (and presumably dance) and poetry, and tactile imagery is involved in the process pertaining to materials in the visual arts. A capacity for thinking in visual imagery may not therefore be correlated with a capacity for homospatial thinking unless there exists some (so far unproved) general correlation between capacity in visual imagery and in other types. Indeed, a characteristic use of visual imagery could possibly function to reduce capacity to use other types of imagery and thereby to reduce homospatial cognition involving other sensory modalities. Homospatial processes depend for their function on the capacity to construct and to use some type of imagery.

Special types of facilities with visual imagery are not necessary factors for homospatial thinking. Special capacities to have vivid visual images, special eidetic faculties or special facility in remembering visual details are not intrinsic to the process. The images in a homospatial conception depend on the quality of the entities chosen by the creator, their fuseability and their relationship to the context in which the creator works. Homospatial conceptions are usually vague and diffuse, and an initial vividness of the images would not necessarily facilitate the production of an effective metaphor or other creation. Capacity to remember scenes or visual impressions may be of some general use in the visual arts, but it is not the same as the particular ability to use and fuse visual images. Eidetic images, which are reproductions of actual physical scenes, are not at all required for the homospatial process.

Special capacity with auditory and other nonvisual forms of imagery are, however, probably quite important in homospatial processes involving these other forms. Composers, for instance, surely have greater capacity to generate auditory images than the rest of us. The major issue is characteristic function and use. Special capacity with visual imagery is not ordinarily necessary because a tendency to think in visual images is already fairly highly developed in the general population. This is probably the result of a number of factors: developmental, evolutionary, and social. The intense contemporary bombardment of visual images from motion pictures and television surely plays a role. Only a reduced tendency to use visual imagery in comparison to the average, therefore, would be of pragmatic importance. Those who seldom think in visual terms would very likely seldom engage in the homospatial process. Those who frequently think in visual terms do not necessarily engage in homospatial thinking except perhaps by chance or because they apply their visual imagery creatively.

With respect to Coleridge's previously mentioned distinction between fancy and constructive imagination, mental images derived from ordinary everyday thinking, daydreams and fantasies, or directly from nocturnal dreams are the components of fancy. When used to anticipate or to apprehend an event or circumstance, or a series of events and circumstances, these images are components of imagination. Constructive imagination, the type we consider intrinsic to creativity, involves mental images subjected to the homospatial process. This process is an essential ingredient, or perhaps *the* ingredient, in constructive or creative imagination.

So-called concrete modes of thinking are usually considered more primitive or in some way inferior to the abstract, conceptual realm. Because the homospatial process depends on mental imagery and concrete elements in space, it might possibly be considered simplistic or even a low level of mental functioning playing a minor role in creation, especially intellectual creation. Because metaphors have a prominent concrete aspect and this process directly produces metaphors, it could be designated as merely a concrete or concretizing mode of thought. In order to demonstrate the high-level cognitive functioning of the homospatial process and also to provide further evidence for its salient role in literary creation, I shall report in an abbreviated way on an empirical study of mine (not yet published) pertaining to the function of homospatial thinking in the creation of literary character. Characterization is a major aspect of literary creation in plays, novels, short stories, and poetry as well. As the construction of a character is a complex matter occurring throughout the time of creation of a literary work, both the complete and the more abstract modes in which homospatial thinking operates can be appreciated.

The Creation of the Play "High Tor" by Maxwell Anderson

Maxwell Anderson's play *High Tor,* written and produced in 1936, was awarded the New York Drama Critics Circle Award for that year. Generally considered one of Anderson's best works, it is a humorous and somewhat whimsical drama concerning a young man's fight to preserve a Hudson River palisade called High Tor (Old English: *tor,* "hill" or "mound") from the encroachments of a local trap rock mining company. Highly lively and eventful, the critics' accolades described it as a "romp." Included in the play are ghosts of the palisade from an old Dutch ship who are modeled after the legendary Catskill mountain ghosts from Henrik Hudson's boat; bank robbers hiding out on the mountain; a pair of fatuous representatives of the local trap rock company, one a judge; a last surviving Indian of an extinct tribe; the young, long-patient girlfriend of the young male hero.

Maxwell Anderson was a distinguished and creative American dramatist who won many awards, including the Pulitzer Prize. Most notably, he was one of the few American playwrights to attempt high poetic drama. It has not been generally realized that the verse drama *High Tor* is an attempt at a modern restatement of Shakespeare's *Tempest.* Just as *The Tempest,* in one respect, concerned the confrontation of the old world with the new world of the Americas and with the future, *High Tor* concerns a similar but reversed confrontation. In the Anderson play, new world values emphasizing industrialization and materialism are confronted both by a young man wanting to preserve the natural life and ways of the past, and by ghosts from the old world. There are, moreover, many particular similarities in structure and content between the two plays, including an almost identical humorous sequence involving the seeing of a monster in the doubled set of protruding limbs and heads of two people sleeping under a common blanket. Because the play was clearly a literary creation and because original manuscripts were available, I undertook an empirical study of the creation of this work.[7]

In the earlier study of the creation of a play based on analysis of manuscript drafts, the study of O'Neill's *The Iceman Cometh,* I developed a methodology focused on textual errors and revisions by the author.[8] First draft revisions provide a written documentation of the dynamic, changing aspect of a work in progress. Study of revisions, therefore, is a reliable means for retrospective analysis of the process of literary creation. Furthermore, by extending the principle of unconscious and preconscious conflict as the basis for errors and slips of the tongue—one of Freud's most scientifically valid and widely accepted discoveries—to literary revisions as a related category, revisions become the means for understanding preconscious and unconscious influences operating during the creation of a particular work. Although Freud himself never extended his discoveries about slips and errors to the realm of literary revision, the basis for such an extension is the following: just as ordinary slips and errors represent a discrepancy between intent and execution—the person making the error wants to say or write the correct thing but doesn't—literary revisions also represent a similar discrepancy. An author has a particular aesthetic goal in mind and frequently he does not achieve it on the first try; hence, when he later recognizes a discrepancy between his intent and the execution, really an aesthetic mistake, he makes a revision or a change. Or, using a broader approach, constant change and revision focused on particular types of content or structure indicate an author's anxiety and conflict about those types of content or structure, regardless of whether a change is merely grammatical and lexical, or is more ambitious and aesthetic in nature.[9] Statistical analysis of revisions connected to written references to the central symbol of "the iceman" in O'Neill's play showed a significantly higher rate of revising in sentences containing direct references to "the iceman" than in all others, and content analysis of revisions indicated the nature of O'Neill's preconscious preoccupation and conflict. Content of revisions indicated O'Neill's preoccupation with the idea of a real rather than a symbolic iceman. Because, as indicated in other material from the play itself and from other documented sources, a real iceman was the same as an adulterer, the finding pointed to O'Neill's preoccupation with sexual matters and with a friend's suicide apparently precipitated by a wife's adultery.

In an attempt to develop a widely applicable approach to revision analysis, the manuscript of Anderson's *High Tor* was even more systematically investigated. All 2,439 sentences in the play were numbered sequentially, and presence or absence of revision (ranging from correction of pen slips and spelling errors to more extensive additions and deletions) was charted. On the basis of careful independent inspection of the sentences containing revisions, and on logical grounds, 61 separate categories or variables were developed for sentence classification. These variables were the following: length of sentence (three variables: short, medium, and long); character in the play speaking (15 characters or variables); character present on the stage (15 variables); early or late portion of the play (six variables: six scenes); linguistic factors (nine variables: presence of any of six specific personal pronouns; presence of a verb of giving or receiving, presence of a poetic metaphor); specific types of sentence content (13 variables: references to money, male-female relations, legal matters, death, religion or magic, darkness or light, age, food, occupation and work, play, violence or aggression, identity of persons or things, false or illicit matters). Every sentence in the play, revised or not, was scored on the basis of all 61 categories or variables. Scoring of sentences with regard to categories of sentence content and to the category of poetic metaphor was carried out by two raters working independently. The resulting data was assessed statistically to determine what categories were significantly associated with revision.

A major initial finding was that the dialogue of certain characters in the play or the mere presence of these characters on the stage was positively correlated with revision. Sentences spoken by these particular characters or in their presence tended to contain one or more revisions each, while other sentences did not. The association of revised sentences with these characters was statistically significant (chi-square $= 9.706$, $df = 1$, $p < .01$). The particular characters were the ghosts or dead persons in the drama. Further statistical calculations of chi-square associations were then made, grouping the individual characters into two larger categories of living and dead characters. On the basis of this second calculation, findings were that the following categories or variables were all significantly associated with revision: dead characters speaking or on the stage, longer (both medium and long) sentences, presence of poetic metaphors, verbs of giving and receiving, references to darkness or light, and references to death. Sentences having any or all of these characteristics tended to be highly revised in the first-draft manuscript of the play.

The findings of associations between revision and longer sentences, presence of poetic metaphors, verbs of giving and receiving, and references to darkness and light are all of interest but I shall focus here only on the statistical associations having the most definite content implications, the association between revision and the dead character categories and the association between revision and references to death. The associations with the categories of reference to darkness or light and of verbs of giving and receiving do, in fact, also have a connection to the meaning of these findings but the connection is too involved and is unnecessary for this summary.

According to the psychological rationale for the study of revision patterns described above, the association with dead characters and with references to death in sentence contents indicated that the playwright was preoccupied with death during the writing of the play. Alternatively, of course, one could say that the dead characters were merely hard to create, their lines difficult to formulate, and that constructing sentences referring to death in a play is always difficult. But, keeping to the idea that the reason for Anderson's consistent revising here was a conflict and preoccupation about death, I reasoned that someone very close to him had probably died at or around the time the drama was created. This I made as a prediction of what

I might further find out about Anderson despite the fact that it was primarily a comical rather than a tragic play. And after some extensive detective work—nothing but a very brief biography exists and Anderson gave out very little personal information during his lifetime—I discovered that his father died three months before he began writing *High Tor*.

After establishing this connection, a connection supporting the hypothesis that revision patterns indicate an author's personal preoccupations (there was a similar construction in the O'Neill study), I looked again at the content of the play. The young hero of the play, Van Van Dorn, is at the beginning briefly described as having inherited the High Tor palisade from his father. Later it is clear from the dialogue that Van Dorn's father has died shortly before the action of the play begins. Thus it appeared that the hero of the play was definitely based, in one aspect at least, on Anderson himself.

Although direct connections such as this between authors and their heroes are usually assumed to be universally present in literature, such is definitely not the case. There would be no reason to assume a priori that this particular feature was derived from the author's life. Moreover, the connection to the author definitely does not itself account for the creation of the Van Dorn character. For one thing, Van Dorn is a hunter who lives alone on High Tor and spends his time living as he pleases. One of the reasons he will neither sell the palisade to the trap rock company nor marry his extremely patient girlfriend is that he wants to continue living in the woods just as he has done up to that point. But Anderson himself did not at all live that way, nor was he reputed to be as aggressive as the Van Dorn character; also, Anderson was married at the time he wrote the play. There was, I discovered, a living person named Van Orden who lived on the real mountain in New York State named High Tor and it can surely be assumed that Van Dorn was partly derived from him. Young Van Orden inherited and held on to the mountain for a time.

In order to gather further information about Maxwell Anderson, particularly any information pertinent to the writing of the play, I made contact with Quentin Anderson, the playwright's oldest son. Enormously helpful to me from the first, when Mr. Anderson learned that I was interested in *High Tor*, he directed me to a 1952 novel entitled *Morning, Winter and Night*.[10] This novel, it is not generally known, was written by his father under the pseudonym of Michaelson. The pseudonym, it seems, was motivated both by the highly autobiographical material in the novel and by the need or desire to include explicit sexual scenes and sexual slang that might in 1952 have affected or hurt his literary reputation. Quentin Anderson believed that the novel was based on actual experiences in his father's life. Through this book and the findings of the revision study, the creation of the Van Dorn character, among other things, could be explicated and clarified.

The story concerns a year spent by Maxwell Anderson, then twelve years of age, on his grandmother's farm. This grandmother was, according to Quentin Anderson, a very important person in his father's life, often being described by the father as the person who virtually brought him up. Focused a good deal on the young Maxwell Anderson's relationship to his grandmother, the novel also vividly recounts his painful awareness as a boy of the onset of puberty and his first sexual experience during that particular year. But a major event in the story is the death of an old man living in the grandmother's house. This man, referred to as the "old coot," appears throughout the story only to be somewhat of a handyman, living in the house on the grandmother's good graces as he does precious little work. A climactic revelation, then, is that this same man actually had once been the grandmother's lover and with her he had fathered her beloved child who died in infancy. Much of the final portion of the novel is devoted to the details of this man's death and burial. In a final scence, the old man lies dead in his coffin while, due to circumstances, the young Anderson and his girlfriend engage in a strange attempt to have intercourse in the same room. The attempt fails.

The specific connection to the characterization in the play *High Tor* is that the "old coot" was, like Van Dorn, a hunter. Throughout the novel, in fact, this man is pointedly described as going and coming as he pleases and living a good part of the time alone in the woods, just as Van Dorn does. Most important, it is strongly and quite dramatically emphasized that the "old coot" stubbornly held on to his way of life, never marrying the grandmother and never giving up his long trips to go hunting. These characteristics are point for point the same as those of Anderson's character in *High Tor.* Not only is Van Dorn devoted to hunting and living as he pleases, but he significantly temporizes about marriage. And the main dramatic focus of the play is Van Dorn's stubborn refusal to give up his land and way of life. That the "old coot" was himself important in Anderson's life is unmistakable from the descriptions and climactic events in the autobiographical novel.

The revision patterns indicating Anderson's preoccupation with death during the writing of the play point both to his father's death and the (psychologically connected)[11] death of the "old coot." The life history information and circumstances indicate that at least three distinct persons came together in the character of Van Van Dorn: Anderson himself, the real owner of the mountain High Tor named Van Orden, and the hunter-lover of Anderson's grandmother. Anderson's conscious and intentional bringing together of the three persons is indicated by the following considerations: (1) Van Dorn is exactly in Anderson's own circumstance at the start of the play: he has just lost his father; (2) Van Dorn has the "old coot's" occupation as well as his personality characteristics described explicitly sixteen years later in the novel of 1952; (3) not only is Van Dorn's name almost the same as Van Orden, but among Anderson's literary effects[12] there is a newspaper clipping concerning the man who owned and lived on the real mountain, High Tor; (4) Anderson himself had earlier been, according to his son, actively involved in a dispute with a power company about his own land. This dispute was analogous in many ways with Van Dorn's dispute with the trap rock company.

That the bringing together of the three persons was a continual process of fusing or superimposing them throughout the writing of the play rather than a mere labeling and combining of certain specific traits is demonstrated by a detailed consideration of the manuscript. Throughout the play, Van Dorn behaves as though he were all three persons together. Stubbornly holding on to the land just as the "old coot" hunter would, his relationship to the female ghost, the captain's wife, is also very much like the basic relationship of the young Anderson to his grandmother. His abiding love of the land and of his Dutch ancestry, however, is also totally unlike the "old coot" and is more related to qualities of the real owner of High Tor, who held onto the mountain and whom Anderson knew. Or, as far as loving the land is concerned, this was also a feature of Anderson himself.

The phenomenon of fusion of three discrete persons, sometimes producing abstract conceptions of the character's moral stance and nature and sometimes producing new and concrete qualities and behaviors, is demonstrated in the ongoing and unfolding events of the play. At one point in the original manuscript there is an indication of a dramatic shift: in writing the end of the second of three acts, Anderson tried three quite different versions, the only place throughout the writing he vacillated so extensively. The three different versions reflected his indecision about whether to have Van Dorn give in and sell the palisade to the trap rock company, a crucial issue in the story. Clearly, the "old coot" never would have. Also, there is some concern about how the girl would have viewed his action, a factor probably more of concern to Anderson himself. In the final version used, Van Dorn tells his young girlfriend he will sell the Tor if she stays with him. This, a new and more softened position, leads to a selling of the land in the last act with a climactic philosophical pronouncement about the future activity of the trap rock company: "Nothing is made by men but makes, in the end, good ruins." The creative solution, in other words, developed during the writing of the play. Anderson had not decided beforehand when or how the Tor would be sold or, perhaps whether it would be sold at all. Van did not follow the "old coot's" way, but out of a fusion of three discrete persons, Anderson was enabled to produce a vibrant, new and integrated character.

To recapitulate the probable sequence: as Anderson was preoccupied with his father's death before and during the writing of *High Tor,* an early idea for the play very likely consisted of the ghosts of the Hudson palisades. Now, while ghosts are assuredly dead, it is of interest that there is much discussion in the early portion of the play (and in the first formulations on the manuscript) of their wish to be alive or to go back to a previous state. Although this is not in itself remarkably new, it does suggest, along with the overall structure of the drama—a romp involving both the dead and living—that the idea of portraying life and death simultaneously was an early conception in Anderson's mind. Ghosts could be considered "living dead." This, of course, would be a janusian conception. With respect to the Van Dorn character, therefore, the initial conception would also have been janusian: the dead hunter together with the living playwright as well as the living owner of High Tor in one character simultaneously. In conjunction with this janusian conception, the homospatial process then operated throughout the writing of the play, fusing and superimposing images, sequences, and actions. In this way, the homospatial process played a significant role in the creation of a dramatic character.

Because of the nature of the real persons fused and superimposed—the writer himself, the living owner of the property, and the old man whose characteristics are explicitly described, and because of the handling of the characterization in the play—the character's finding a new solution, the process of fusing or of homospatial thinking seems to have been an ongoing, conscious intentional one, operating together with high-level logical and critical mental faculties in creating the *High Tor* drama.

12

TIME, SPACE, AND CAUSALITY

I have presented the evidence and described the mirror-image processes; the task is now to understand and to establish the nature and extent of what has been achieved. Have we indeed discovered the cause or causes of creativity? How do the mirror-image processes operate, precisely, to produce creations? Considering the matter of arousal in the creative process emphasized earlier, what is the evidence for such arousal and how does it function in created products? Are there other qualities of the mirror-image processes, beside their arousal function, that lead to the production of creations?

I shall, in this and the following chapter, be concerned with the answers to all these questions. To some extent, the full answers await further empirical research, but something needs to be said now about the nature of the mirror-image processes in relation to creations and to creativity. Their role and their extensiveness must be pinned down and clarified more precisely. In these two chapters, therefore, I shall relate the mirror-image processes to the factors intrinsic to the definition of creation that I stipulated in the introduction to this book, the factors of newness and of value. Some of the relations have already been outlined or implied earlier, particularly in chapters 3 and 8, and those I will primarily expand or make explicit. Others that may be surprising I shall spell out for the first time now. I have held some of this back because of the logic of the exposition, but I will also confess that I have exerted some prerogative to reserve a few surprises for the end. My purpose has neither been to outrage nor to irritate but really to render the discussion somewhat isomorphic with its subject matter. As suspense is the stock-in-trade of the creative artist, am I not obliged, in a scientific analysis of his work, to do him the slight homage of following his precepts? A request for indulgence.

One word of warning, however: the discussion in this chapter might, for the scientific reader, seem too philosophically oriented both in tone and in terminology. Though I believe, and I hope to show, that so-called philosophical matters are important with respect to creativity,[1] I am also aware that some find such matters tedious and digressive. These latter I urge to skip to the next chapter now, perhaps to return later to this one after digesting the material at the end. The philosophically minded may consider this chapter long overdue and may have skipped to here already.

While there are many ways of defining creations and creativity, I have chosen to be guided by what are perhaps the most stringent definitions of all; creations are both *new* and *valuable* and creativity is the state or capacity through which a new and valuable entity or quality is brought into being. Consequently, I have focused fairly steadily on creations that are generally considered to be among man's most valuable achievements, those in art, science, religion, philosophy, and other intellectual endeavors. I admit it is not necessary to be so stringent about the matter; one could provide some suitable criteria for what is valuable that encompass a far broader range of activities. Sheer productivity could be considered valuable, and in the narrow sense that people produce particular things that never existed before, one could start with the assumption that productivity and creativity are synonymous. Also, internal psychological experiences are new and valuable for the person experiencing them. There are creative cooking, creative discourse, and creative performance in sports, physical labor, and other areas. However, such broad criteria for the valuable seem too relative and intangible, and I have deemed it difficult to obtain a scientific consensus about them. Consequently, I have been left with a definition of creations and creativity that comes close to excluding everything but the achievements of genius. Genius stands virtually alone as the unchallenged perpetrator of creations; only the products of genius are widely accepted as unquestionably valuable and truly new. As Kant said, "Genius is the talent (or natural gift) which gives the rule to Art."[2] The relationship between genius and the new and valuable is actually reciprocal: when a product is hailed as being an unquestioned creation, its author or producer is designated as a genius. To some extent, the matter is completely circular and tautological; I bring in the word "genius" only to highlight the nature of the task I must consider. One way of asking the question here could be: have we found the cause of genius?

To some extent, I have tried to meet the challenge of such a question by citing the works and testimony of unquestionable geniuses such as Einstein, da Vinci, Michelangelo, Rembrandt, Picasso, Darwin, Freud, Pasteur, Poincaré, Nietzsche, Kierkegaard, Sartre, O'Neill, Beethoven, Mozart, and others. But I seriously doubt if my severest critic or the strictest methodologist would require that I limit my discussion of creation and creativity to the works and acts of the very few such as these. Moreover, the idea of genius as the only true creator goes beyond the requirements of a strict definition of creativity and of creation, because the term "genius" suggests certain factors of genetic endowment, extraordinary intellectual capacity, and the repeated production of highly valued thoughts and works. Such factors need not enter if we focus merely on the production of any single creation and on creativity either as a potential for, or a state of, bringing forth creations.[3] After all, it is hardly necessary to answer all the questions about genius or to be limited to considering the extraordinarily high levels of success associated with genius; nor is it actually clear that genetic endowment or extraordinary intellectual capacity is required for every type of creating.[4] More to the point in the present consideration is the question of whether we can speak of finding the "cause" of creativity in any sense, whether it be the workings of genius, creativity taken broadly, or the appearance of a single creation. For in raising the question of finding the cause of creativity, we are confronted with the problem of the "new" and of "newness" as intrinsic to the definition of a creation.

Causation and Newness

Creations are new; to create is to bring forth something new. While it is common and lexically accurate to use the word "creation" merely to refer to something made or brought into being, we are not interested in that elemental use of the term in our researches. Shoes, automobiles, and other more advanced products of our impressive technological age are surely all made and are brought into being, but, unless they are individually or categorically unusual and unique in some way, they are seldom classified or studied as creations. We make further demands: seldom are we satisfied for an unusual entity to be merely different; to be studied and appreciated as a creation, we expect it to be unprecedented. It is the unprecedented aspect of an entity "brought into being" that captures our imagination and, along with the entity's value, leads to the honorific designation of "creation." For the term has been used to describe the beginning of the world and of life, and we tend to believe that both the initial creation and creations made by humans share an essential attribute of newness.

New; think about the word "new." What is the sense in which we mean it here? In what way is something new? I have connected "new" with the quality of being unprecedented but surely alternate meanings and interpretations come to mind: (1) Nothing is really new under the sun; things that seem to be new are merely reappearances of past substances or forces (remote, obscure, or forgotten). (2) Things are merely new in a particular context; something that already existed in another context is brought to our awareness or into our sphere, and therefore seems to be new. For the native bushmen of Australia, almost everything in the civilized world is considered new, including what has existed for centuries. (3) New things result from combinations and recombinations of things that existed before. Perfectly respectable are all of these alternate interpretations of "new," and all provide an approach to much that is considered new in human experience. Scientific discoveries may surely appear to be new as a result of these factors and a good deal of what appears as new in artistic and intellectual creations also results from one or other of them. Possibilities for shifting contexts are almost limitless in art, and, a far cry from the naiveté of the native bushmen of Australia, sophisticated art audiences have been exposed to newness resulting from a shift of context throughout the history of art. Shift to a classical mode during the Renaissance, a shift to primitive modes during modern times, and the more specific context shifts in the experiments of the dadaists in the 1920s, and the continuing present emphasis on "found" art (natural objects presented in the artistic context) come immediately to mind. Moreover, all of these alternate interpretations produce no difficulty with respect to the problem of finding a cause of creativity. They all refer to traceable factors that can account for the appearance of the new.

If we accept these interpretations of the manifestation of newness in art, in science, and in other areas of tangible creating, both the homospatial and janusian process decidedly do cause many aspects of creations. For, inducing surprise in an observer or producing the unexpected—effects intrinsically linked to both processes—are the critical features underlying all three interpretations of the manifestation of the new. If what is new depends on already existing factors being combined or recombined, or reappearing, or appearing in another context, or all three, then surprise and the unexpected play a very important role. We call something new either because we are surprised to see it appear in an unfamiliar context, or we never expected it or knew it existed, or it is the unanticipated result of a combination or recombination of known factors. Indeed, important aestheticians and psychologists give the element of the unexpected a prominent place in their theories of art.[5] And scientific discoveries are often called creations because they are so completely unanticipated and surprising.

Both of the mirror-image processes of thought lead directly to surprising and unexpected effects. What could be more surprising than the simultaneous antitheses resulting from janusian thinking? How could one be taken more immediately off guard than by an assertion that the complete opposite or antithesis of an inviolately held belief, fact, or proposition is true? And then, not only is the opposite or antithesis of the inviolate original considered to be true and valid, but its truth does not actually challenge the validity of the original! In like manner, what could be more surprising than the manipulations of the homospatial process? When, in our experience, do we ever find two or more discrete entities occupying the same space? When, except in the creative process, is it ever imagined? Nothing in human experience can compete with janusian and homospatial thinking for producing the element of surprise. Two tenets of human experience and thought that have been held throughout history and culture are (1) something cannot be true and not true at the same time; that is, contradictions always invalidate one another; (2) two or more things cannot at once occupy the same space.

Although janusian and homospatial formulations do not, as I have emphasized, necessarily appear directly in creations, their transformations and ultimate effects retain an implicit and intrinsic element of surprise. Literary tragedies, for instance, arise from a janusian formulation of antithetical elements, such as freedom in slavery, pride in humility, or triumph in defeat. When these antithetical qualities are revealed and elaborated as a tragic novel or play unfolds, there is always an element of surprise, the culmination and overall impact of the suspenseful journey the creator has given us.[6] Effective metaphors resulting from homospatial thinking or from janusian and homospatial thinking operating together always produce surprise when first encountered and often continue to do so on later encounters. Think, for example, of what would have been the initial impact of metaphors such as "black holes in space" or Marianne Moore's famous "the lion's ferocious chrysanthemum head"[7] with their overtones of impossible contradiction and equivalence. The more one thinks of a literal equivalence between a lion's head and a chrysanthemum flower or of actual holes in outer space—overtones and implications that must have played a role in their initial impact—the more surprises and interesting connotations appear.

Both homospatial and janusian thinking produce effects that satisfy interpretation 2 and 3 (above) of the new as combination or recombination of the old, or as the result of shifts of context. Although I have emphasized the integrating rather than the combining function of homospatial thinking, there is no necessary contradiction. Combining is not the same as integration, but the former is still included in the latter. Some degree of combining occurs in producing integrations and therefore the bringing together of previously existing discrete entities in a homospatial conception, and of previously existing opposites and antitheses in a janusian conception, involves combinations or recombinations of the old in the sense of the interpretation 3. Shift of context also is involved. For example, the logical understanding of the janusian formulation leading to "In Monument Valley" is that horses are, in a sense, both human and not-human. This does not arise from the ordinary context of horses defined merely as animals; the formulation arises only when shifting to the context of how horses spend their lives. For the metaphor "the road is a rocket of sunlight," the road can be seen as this rocket only when shifting to the context of the driver in the speeding car, or from a hill above the road, or from the perspective and context of a war-weary soldier.

Less intrinsically linked to the mirror-image processes is the first interpretation of the new as the reappearance of past substances or forces. Only if we focus on the mirror-image process function of unearthing unconscious material could this interpretation apply. By definition, the Unconscious contains the old, the hidden, and the forgotten or repressed; shared very old and forgotten material reappearing could seem new. Physical and cultural events, facts, and experiences that reappear would, however, not necessarily be included. According to some, the basis of poetry and presumably its newness derive from the "revaloration" of words, reinvesting words with older and more fundamental meanings. With this definition, metaphorization and the mirror-image processes, which make use of literal, concrete, and unconscious qualities of words, could be primarily responsible. For that matter, if metaphors are viewed as interesting and new because they reveal hidden connections between known objects, events, and ideas—a view I consider quite limited—the mirror-image processes would also be primarily involved. Hidden connections usually involve unconscious material and the mirror-image processes function consistently and effectively to unearth such material.

If we use the stricter and more literal definition of the new, the new as the completely unprecedented,[8] the matter of designating the factors responsible for creations—the cause of creativity—becomes far more complicated. Nevertheless, it is necessary to come to grips with the dilemma. For there are surely types of creations that appear to be unprecedented, not in the sense that every single feature is new but in their significant aspects. Every creation must have known or familiar aspects—with the possible exception of creations attributed to a deity—or it would not be understood or recognized. Moreover, much of the value accorded to creations derives from their effective representation of the familiar. Both artistic and scientific types of creations must faithfully present known internal or external reality. Science reproduces exactly both the past and current state of events and laws, and art represents the qualities of sounds or movements or sights or words, the manifestations and functions of ethics and morality, the role of thoughts and feelings and social forces, and the appearance of the changeable and the inevitable. Nevertheless, in designating something as a creation, we suggest that it is in some way or in some respect truly unprecedented and new. We suggest there is, in some fashion, complete discontinuity from the past. This newness may consist of a new particular factor such as a new sound, a new value, or a new perception of reality. It may, as Hausman suggests, consist of the full presentation of a new form, a form that initiates a new class of entities. In art, such far-ranging newness is most clearly exemplified by the works of Homer, Cervantes, Haydn, Beethoven, Cézanne, Braque, Joyce, Strindberg, Picasso, Schoenberg, and other innovators. This issue is not semantic; regardless of definitions and terms used to discuss creations, we must acknowledge our intrinsic belief in a real or actual unprecedented aspect, and, in many if not all cases, our realization to some degree of what appears as actually or truly new. Surprise is not enough to account for what appears as truly new.[9] For one thing, surprise does not explain the impact. We do not return to a work of art, or relisten to a piece of music, or go again to a well-known play primarily because we want to recapture an earlier experience of surprise, but we do return to such works partly in order to re-experience our initial sense of their newness or novelty.

Over and beyond the experience of newness in the observer or audience, we must consider the newness experienced by the creator. After all, the observer could be deceived; regardless of his belief about the unprecedented nature of a particular creation, he may merely not know enough to be able to detect all its forerunners and precedents. A creation may initiate a new form merely through chance or through selection as a result of complicated but knowable sociological or physical factors. Accidental chisel markings on a sculpture could, for instance, become the herald of a new approach during the proper social and critical climate. We need to turn to the creator, but that too produces a dilemma. Creators constantly tell us, in public statements and elsewhere, that they often do not know the sources of their creations; they experience leaps of thought and a sense of discontinuity in the creative process. In the midst of a train of thought, an idea comes that seems to have no connection with what went before.

Discontinuity is the source of the dilemma. Complications result both from the creator's experience of discontinuity during the course of the creative process and from the discontinuity from the past required for the appearance of something truly new. Complications particularly arise with respect to cause and causation. Causes depend on continuous processes; if a break or discontinuity occurs within a process, it becomes difficult, or perhaps impossible, to identify a cause. If something is truly unprecedented and new, it lacks or is discontinuous with antecedents. And a causative factor must be antecedent to, or in some way contiguous with, the entity it produces.[10] Put another way: if we were to know the cause of a phenomenon, we would then be in a position to predict its occurrence. For having in our possession a sure knowledge of what has produced the phenomenon, we should be able to predict what will produce it again. But if creations are truly unheralded and new, they are intrinsically unexpected and therefore unpredictable. More important, if there is real discontinuity in the creator's thought during the creative process, we can never predict the occurrence of creative ideas.

In making this point, I am for the present ignoring many distinctions and relationships that would add richness and specificity to the discussion, such as: cause as both a necessary and sufficient condition; cause in relation to correlation; a creation as totally new in distinction to new only in certain aspects; predicting the necessary conditions for the appearance of a creation versus predicting the precise nature and qualities of the creation. I am also ignoring the enormous number of elements, in art especially, that are fully and clearly continuous with antecedents. Much of art is a direct product of experience and a direct reflection of nature and of experience. But this does not account for the new. I will return to some of these matters, but for now I want to press on and examine some direct implications of the dilemma about the cause of creativity.

As I said, cause depends on continuous processes and this is a source of difficulty. What, then, do we mean by "continuous processes" or, for that matter, any type of continuity? Continuity refers to nothing other than continuity in time and space. A causative factor is either continuous or contiguous in space with the entity it produces or it is closely associated or continuous in time. Or, cause and caused are continuous both in time and in space. Time and space. We have arrived at the most basic factors we know. Causality, creativity, everything in experience, must eventually be related to these two basic factors. Let us then look at time and space, each in turn. Particularly, we shall look at the mirror-image processes in relation to time and space and see if we can answer the question raised at the beginning of this chapter.

Time

There seem to be virtually as many approaches to the matter of time as there are years in recorded history. There are distinctions made between clock time and real duration; cosmic and human time or physical and psychological time; actual and possible becoming. There is time considered as motion, time as duration, time as only an abstraction, time as change, time as aging. There are concerns about measuring time appropriately and there are attempts to reverse time, speed it up, or slow it down. The list goes on and on, but in an interesting development during the current century, philosophers have turned their attention directly to the terms applied to time. They have decried the tendency, in Western thought especially, to spatialize time, that is, taking metaphorical terms derived from spatial relations such as long and short, near and distant, and using them in a literal way to define qualities of time. Since Einstein's discovery of relativity, physicists and philosophers have been particularly interested in relationships between time and space, and they have raised important questions about a real space-time continuum and about the irreversibility of time.[11]

I do not propose to enter here into any of these intriguing questions and approaches to time. Nor do I intend to develop a definition of time that will necessarily satisfy the many issues, metaphysical and scientific, raised in the various approaches. I will merely emphasize some aspects of time that pertain particularly to causality, elemental aspects that can still be considered as intrinsic to time. As the philosopher-scientist Waismann, in a modern paraphrase of Saint Augustine, said: "The queer thing is that we all seem to know perfectly well 'what time is,' and yet if we are asked *what* it is, we are reduced to speechlessness."[12]

The first aspect of time I will discuss is *sequence,* or succession. Intrinsic to time, both as an experience and as a notion, is the appearance of sequence. Events clearly follow each other; something comes first and another comes after. We distinguish between these: before and after; then and now; now and later; past, present, and future. We observe sequences in complicated events, not merely noticing that one drop of water falls before another but seeing that long series of events precede and follow one another. Though we sometimes project a sequence onto the elements in a static object, say, when viewing a painting, we are aware (when challenged) of the differences between such a mentally projected sequence and an actual physical or perceived succession.

The second is *repetition.* Although events may never occur in exactly the same form twice, repetition is intrinsic to time. If the sun did not rise and set repeatedly, we might have observed other regularities defining the passage of time. Without such regularity and repetition, in fact, we would not have developed a sense of time as continuous passage. Some would emphasize change rather than repetition—that it is the change from light to darkness that denotes passage of time. And surely the occurrence of physical change and aging is one of the most dramatic and poignant aspects of our experience of time. There is no need for contention: both change and repetition are important. But repetition is critical to passage, measurement, and causality. Without repetition, there would be no sense of one event causing another nor would there be any way of determining a cause or even a correlation.

Sequence and repetition are important aspects of time, and both are critical to causality. Both are also decidedly present in the creative process. The creator produces various aspects of his work sequentially and much repetition occurs. There is repetition within the work being created and repetition in his life experience. Time passes, and no one would doubt that it takes some time to produce a creation. Yet it is constantly reported, by creators in every field, that there are experiences of timelessness when actively engaged in creating. How can we understand this?

The generally accepted explanation pertains to attention and concentration. During the course of the creative process, the creator is often deeply absorbed in his work. Light, sounds, even human presences, are completely ignored. If they do intrude on the creator's consciousness because they are sudden, sharp, or persistent, the creator often rouses from his absorption quite slowly and with difficulty and he experiences the change as distinctly distracting or even irritating. Sometimes he experiences an abrupt awareness of his surroundings and of external presences, and there is a transitory feeling of strangeness as he readjusts. One of the first things he does, even while responding to the intrusion, is to check the time on his watch, or to note outside conditions of light or darkness, or to ask what the time is. He has clearly been unaware of, or lost track of, time. That is, he has lost track of measured time, and frequently he has also lost track of duration and of the sense of time's passage. The amount of time passed almost invariably surprises him.

Loss of awareness of time's passage of this type is an experience of timelessness but it is not unique to the creative process. Any type of work or play involving deep or undivided attention and concentration can produce it. Rapt absorption in a work of art of any kind, is particularly accompanied by such a sense of timelessness. Very likely —limited data about the matter exist—a more prolonged and intense type of absorption and concentration occurs during the creative process than during other forms of activity, including active aesthetic contemplation. The factor of arousal, which I shall discuss more fully in the next chapter, may play a part in producing the intensity. The seclusion and isolation that often is necessary for creative work enhances absorption and intensity, but this interrelationship becomes somewhat circular. The need for absorption and intensity may require seclusion and isolation or the need for seclusion and isolation may produce absorption and intensity as a by-product. Serving purposes in the creative process such as facilitating inner expression or symbolic thinking, the former may incidentally induce the latter. In either case, a sense of timelessness results.[13]

The loss of the sense of time's passage is only one aspect of the timelessness involved in the creative process. Seclusion, intense concentration, and aroused involvement account for the subjective sense of timelessness to some extent, but there is a unique suspension of time during the creative process that is more specific than this. More than a loss of the sense of time's passage, there is an abrogation and a transcendence of the intrinsic elements of time mentioned: sequence and repetition. This transcendence occurs in janusian thinking. For the creator engaged in the janusian process conceives of opposites or antitheses *simultaneously,* not successively or in sequence. Through simultaneity both repetition and sequence are transcended. When two or more elements are conceived as operating simultaneously, they come neither before nor after. Nothing in this is repeated, but all occurs at once. When two or more elements operate simultaneously, they are outside of the continuing process of repetition, change, and flux we refer to as "time"; the janusian conception is *out of time.*

Earlier (chap. 7), I quoted Mozart's description of his experience of hearing the parts of a musical composition *all at once* and that striking description very well illustrates the complex simultaneity in the creative conception. While we have no way of knowing definitely whether Mozart was referring to opposites and antitheses occurring simultaneously, the report conveys the type of time transcendence phenomenon involved in the janusian conception. Not merely a matter of fancied simultaneity—multiple elements seeming to sound or to occur at once—nor a matter of ambiguity tolerance—permitting or actively considering alternative ideas or perceptions in consciousness —janusian conceptions intrinsically involve concomitant conflicting components. When the creator conceives of opposites and antitheses operating simultaneously, he brings complex sequences into a single moment and a single conception. Such unusual experiences as actually hearing extended musical sequences all at the same time account in part for the complexity of Mozart's and others' creations. When Einstein conceived of a man both falling and at rest at the same time, he brought many sequences together: the man falling, objects near him falling, the man at rest, objects near at rest, magnetic fields, conducting circuits, and so on. The janusian conception does not merely consist of two or more concrete elements appearing at once, but, because opposites and antitheses are abstractions, it necessarily consists of repeated phenomena operating simultaneously. Usually, it also consists of simultaneous sequences. Through this simultaneity time stands still; in standing still, it is transcended.

In conceiving of oppositions and antitheses operating simultaneously, the creator goes beyond the bounds of time. To say that it will rain tomorrow and it will simultaneously not rain tomorrow invalidates temporality. If the statement is interpreted as meaning that it will rain tomorrow at one point in the day and it will not rain tomorrow at another point, this would be designating and conceiving a succession of events. It would not be the structure formulated at the moment of the janusian idea. To say that the sun will rise tomorrow and it will simultaneously not rise tomorrow goes outside of temporality. A conception that the sun rises and, on the same day, that it also does not rise is beyond the bounds of time; factors of logic, information, interpretation, and elaboration translate it into temporal terms.

I say that time is transcended rather than merely negated because, as I have repeatedly pointed out, the creator is in full possession of his logical and rational faculties during the course of the janusian process. He goes beyond time at the moment of the formulation, but he also casts it into meaningful, highly effective, and temporal-connoting terms. Just as opposites and antitheses facilitate transcendence of current ideas and knowledge, simultaneity facilitates transcendence of time. In bringing together opposites, extremes, and polarities, the creator brings together the outer limits of what is known or he moves from the known to the unknown through one of the few means available to the human mind.

The sense of timelessness in the creative process is, therefore, a special one. It is due not merely to intense concentration but to the characteristics of the janusian process, with the specific formulations that are produced along the way. Janusian formulations are out of time, out of sequence and repetition, and the janusian process produces discontinuity.

Space

As with time, there are myriad approaches and considerations with regard to space.[14] A particular confusion arises even in learned discussions because of the common tendency to think of space in terms of an empty area rather than the all-inclusive "expanse in which all material objects are located and all events occur."[15] Even when focusing exclusively on the latter sense of the term, philosophers and scientists alike have a good deal of difficulty arriving at a consistent definition of the nature of space. In recent years, these thinkers have reconceptualized space in a manner consistent with non-Euclidean formulations and with discoveries about the nature of the cosmos and the universe. The perspective on relativity has replaced Newtonian notions of absolute space. For psychology, a particularly important development has been an emphasis on experiential properties of space such as the idea of "lived space" developed by the philosopher Merleau-Ponty.[16] These philosophical perspectives have, among other things, shown the pitfalls of traditional preconceptions such as describing the psychological experience of space in terms of "inner" and "outer." Space, as an experienced psychological entity, is not delimited by the bodily integument, skin or other body boundaries. Therefore the differentiation between "inner psychological space" and "outer physical space" is always figurative with respect to experience and physical reality. Possibly useful as a heuristic device, the differentiation and the terms "inner" and "outer" must be applied carefully and cautiously, particularly in the formulation of psychological theory.

For the present discussion, I shall adopt an elemental and basic view of space that derives from psychological experience and seems to cut across diverse approaches and definitions. Particularly, the conceptualization pertains both to causality and to the psychological phenomena in the creative process with which we are concerned. It is the view of space proposed by Henri Bergson, as follows: "it is scarcely possible to give any other definition of space; space is what enables us to distinguish a number of identical and simultaneous sensations from one another; it is thus a principle of differentiation."[17] When we speak of space in relation to causality, this seems ultimately the definition we must have in mind. Our knowledge of space derives from *differentiation,* and the recognition of spatial contiguity between entities or factors also depends on their prior differentiation. For a causative factor to appear or to be understood as contiguous in space with the entity it produces, these entities must first be recognized as different. Moreover, effective or operative differentiation of spatial attributes of elements depends on multiple types of *sensation;* we require both tactile and kinesthetic senses, for instance, to experience spatial depth.

Space is closely associated with differentiation and sensation just as time is associated with sequence and repetition. And differentiation and sensation, like sequence and repetition, are consistent features of the creative process. The creator constantly experiences multiple types of sensations during the course of his work, and he incorporates immediate and remembered sensations into the product. He differentiates sensations as well as objects in his environment and he constantly differentiates words, forms, ideas, objects, and sensations in carrying out his work. Yet the creator characteristically experiences a sense of spacelessness during the course of the creative process, just as he experiences a sense of timelessness. Perhaps less dramatic than losing track of time, there are definite though fleeting senses and feelings of disconnectedness, loss of awareness of surroundings and location, and sometimes even a sense of floating and of diffusion. Though intrusions do not usually instigate questions such as "where am I?" nor any checking of location routine analogous to the checking of a watch,[18] the sense of spatial disorientation following an intrusion is often keen.

When, for instance, creative thinking goes on during the driving of an automobile—a very frequent occurrence for some creators—there is sometimes a marked loss of the sense of location and surroundings. While involved in the creative task, driving is carried out automatically, sometimes for miles on end, until there is some distraction or intrusion—sharp curve, honking horn, construction work, another car rapidly approaching an intersection—and a concomitant sense of sharp return to awareness of location and surroundings. When losing track of space in such a manner during driving, the driver is usually amazed afterward at how far he had come without realizing it, how he had managed to drive without noticing where he was or what was around him, and often he then takes great pains to establish his current exact location. Immediately after an intrusion, he checks for road signs, familiar landmarks, or he even stops the car and consults his maps. As with the loss of track of time, he knows that he has passed through space, distance, and location, but he has lost track of it. He has lost track of differentiation and sensation, and he has experienced a sense of spacelessness. When sitting at his desk or walking in the woods, he also loses track of surroundings and location in a similar way, and sometimes he experiences other more general feelings of spacelessness.

Absorption and intense concentration play an important role; these factors induce spacelessness as well as timelessness to some degree. But the homospatial process is a cardinal factor inducing the sense of spacelessness. Because it brings one or more entities into the same spatial location, this process induces subjective experiences of lack of differentiation and of spacelessness. This form of thinking transcends the intrinsic elements of space. As space is a principle of differentiation, the initially undifferentiated elements and sensations in a homospatial mental conception are not within space, but are, in perhaps the only way available to the human mind, beyond the spatial dimension. Just as the janusian formulation is out of time, the homospatial conception is outside of space or spatiality. Just as the janusian formulation transcends sequence, the homospatial conception transcends differentiation. Moreover, the homospatial conception is out of space or spatiality in a double sense: not only does it transcend the principle of differentiation, but in totally filling the space, or the field, of consciousness, it also transcends space. When space is totally and diffusely filled, there are no longer any internal locations or boundaries. Once the filling reaches the limit of a spatial enclosure, it is on the outside—at least in part—of that enclosure. This filling of mental space or the field of consciousness is one of the factors responsible for the dizzying sense of spacelessness often accompanying homospatial conceptions. It sometimes allows the creator to plumb the very limits of spatial experience.

The subjective feelings of spacelessness and timelessness characteristically experienced during the creative process are therefore chiefly products of homospatial and janusian processes. Neither spacelessness nor timelessness in creativity results merely from intense absorption and concentration nor, incidentally, do either need to result in any way from a mystical type of experience nor the taking of psychedelic drugs, as some have alleged. While drug ingestion and mystical experiences are said characteristically to induce feelings of spacelessness or timelessness, these do not appear to be connected, or directly related, to the processes I have just described.

Cause and Creativity

The janusian conception is out of time or temporality and the homospatial conception is outside of space or spatiality. Operating within the creative process, the janusian and homospatial processes produce discontinuity—in time and in space respectively. As cause is dependent on continuity in space and time, we seem to have come as close as possible to factors operating within the creative process that produce a disruption in causal connection and sequence, a disruption that is associated with the appearance of creations and of creativity.

Also, we can now see that the spacelessness and timelessness characteristic of dreaming are, in an additional way, mirror images of the spacelessness and timelessness in the creative process. Spacelessness and timelessness in dreams function essentially to preserve the past. These features allow the dreamer to express wishes from various portions of his life in a condensed and disguised manner. Such wishes are thereby kept and preserved in their original form and they neither develop nor change. Timelessness and spacelessness in the creative process, on the other hand, are intrinsic to radical change and creation.

Can we now turn back to the question at the start of this chapter and say that, with the discovery of these two processes, we have found the cause of creativity? We are perilously close to a conceptual tangle. Surely it is fair to say that the homospatial and janusian processes account for many phenomena associated with creating and with creativity. Surely we can now assert that both processes are major *conditions* for the appearance of a creation and that they set the stage for the appearance of the new. Both of these thought processes together allow the creator to move from what exists and what is known to the limits of knowledge, spatiality, temporality, and experience, and therefore to move into the realm of the unknown. He moves from the familiar to the unconceived, the new, and sometimes the decidedly strange; possibilities for simultaneous antitheses and oppositions allow for unlimited formulating of previously unimagined ideas and entities. If, say, we were ever to derive a clear notion of soul or mind or even behavior, we might find a way to formulate meaningful notions of antisoul, antimind, or antibehavior, existing or operating or having validity at the same time. Or, with respect to temporality, physicists have already begun to formulate ideas of time both running forward and, with the same characteristics and regularity, running backward.

The homospatial process allows for innumerable formulations of previously unimagined ideas and configurations of physical reality. Think, for a particularly mind-bending example, of what might be derived and discovered about the nature of the universe if one were able to conceive all the discrete elements fused and superimposed and the entire dimension of physical space as totally and diffusely filled. It is entirely likely that only through progressing in such ways from the realm of the known can human consciousness and intelligence reach into the realm of the new and unknown.

In designating janusian and homospatial thinking as major conditions for creation, it is difficult to say how close we have come to a cause. These surely appear to be necessary conditions, but cause in a strict sense is a matter of conditions that are sufficient as well as necessary. Can these processes account for all the created qualities of a particular work, theory, or discovery? Can we predict that a creation will always result or, more reasonably, occur with significantly greater frequency than would be expected by chance alone? In part the answers must await definitive empirical research. Also, there are other aspects of creations to be accounted for than those I have indicated so far, and I shall attempt to outline those in the next and final chapter. But a general and inclusive answer arises from what I have already discussed and, though this answer still leaves traces of a conceptual tangle, I shall state it now and return to it more fully another day.

Insofar as the specific elements in a janusian or a homospatial conception—the specific opposites, antitheses, and discrete entities—are unique to a particular creator, there are unique aspects of resulting creations that cannot be predicted. Thus, Shakespeare chose the opposites, antitheses, and discrete entities that he used for *Hamlet,* and the precise appearance of all the specific qualities of Shakespeare's *Hamlet* could not be predicted. Einstein chose a man falling from the roof of a house, and neither that instance nor all the elaborations and ramifications of Einstein's general theory of relativity could have been predicted. We can, however, describe some of the structure necessary for the appearance of such creations. We can state that we know what is necessary for the appearance of the new. Homospatial and janusian thinking transcend the dimensions of space and time, respectively, and are conditions for the discontinuity with contiguous or antecedent factors that occurs whenever the truly new appears. These thought processes are conditions for producing creations. When they are employed, we can expect with a fair amount of certainty that a creation will appear.

13

GODDESS EMERGENT: CREATIVE PROCESS AND CREATED PRODUCT

Creation involves intense motivation, transcendence of time and space, concentration, and the unearthing of unconscious material. The creative process is the mirror image of dreaming with special types of structurally and functionally reflecting and obverse cognitive operations producing creations. Dreams keep the dreamer asleep but creative processes and resulting creations arouse both creators and recipients. We value creations because they enlighten us, arouse us, excite us, awaken us, and enlarge our understanding of and our participation in waking life. With opened eyes, we are more adapted to the past, present, and future.

The picture of the goddess emerging is admittedly somewhat refined and abstracted. Missing are the richly detailed and concrete depictions of lives transformed and organized in the substance of creations, the day-to-day shaping and revising, the feats of memory and to some extent of intelligence, and the intense and rewarding love of materials including paints, sounds, words, formulas, test tubes, optical and electronic equipment, flow sheets, and ideas. That there is such diversity and richness in creation is one of the reasons I have conjured it all in the form of a goddess. No picture, especially a scientific one, could capture all the rich and diverse aspects of products that so directly incorporate the essences of life and of lives. Thinking of applying the model of creation as a mirror-image process of dreaming to all the concrete instances one knows about is, without copious psychological data, quite difficult. With respect to the matter of day-to-day shaping, thinking, and revising in the creative process, however, I want to make explicit a general conclusion arising from the account of the creation of the poem presented in early chapters. The mirror-image functions—janusian and homospatial thinking and others—operate throughout the course of the creative process from beginning to end. By and large, janusian thinking operates early during what has been called the inspiration or illumination phase, as distinct from the elaboration, working out, or verification phases later. But it also occurs later and during working out periods as well. Homospatial thinking occurs early, late, and throughout. Actually, the temporal distinction made between inspiration and elaboration in the creative process is an incorrect one; these phases or functions alternate—sometimes extremely rapidly—from start to finish. Both janusian and homospatial thinking, therefore, operate during the long sequences of revising, shaping, and working out.

The rich details and the range of capacities associated with the emergence of the goddess should be borne in mind in the discussion to follow. Although specific backgrounds, motivations, and skills are required for creating in a particular field, I shall now be concerned with general aspects of creation in relation to resulting creations. I shall focus on the relationship between the mirror-image process of dreaming through which the goddess emerges from the mind of the waking and aroused creator and the nature and qualities of the prized and valued creation, the goddess herself. In relating the mirror-image processes to created products and creations, I hope to show some of the reasons for their wide operation in diverse types of creative processes. I shall be concerned not only with the new but with the valuable aspect of creations. Summarizing and elaborating suggestions made throughout this book, I also shall enter, in a broad way, into the domain of the psychology of art. Though I have rather scrupulously avoided this area up to this point—because, as I have emphasized, the creative process can be misunderstood when focusing primarily on the effects of its products—the psychological impact of the product does need to be taken into consideration. Factors in the creative process must have a connection to the nature of the product.

The creative process, as I have described it, consists of the creator struggling actively and adaptively to achieve certain goals. He works intentionally to produce a creation, although initially he may describe or formulate the task only in such terms as finding the best solution to a problem, capturing light on a canvas in the best way possible, or making an important "statement" about the nature of the world. Once he decides on making something, a painting, play, theory, or crucial experiment, he has directly begun the creative process, as I have defined and used this term throughout. During the course of the creative process, the creator predominantly uses abstract thought processes but to some degree he also unearths unconscious material. Although he is focused on the details and exigencies of the task, and therefore pays little attention both to the nature and structure of his thought processes and of the unconscious material unearthed, these factors determine important aspects of the product. Unearthing of unconscious material is not volitional in the same sense as deciding to create. The creator is always aware of wanting to find something out—the artist creator often is specifically aware of wanting to find out something about himself—but unearthing unconscious material is not a predominate goal. Creators intend to produce a creation in a particular medium and they are consciously concerned about the stringencies of the medium—the scientific principles or the artistic rules and principles regarding color, composition, word use, content, and so on.[1]

The Creative Process and the Unconscious

Although creators are seldom manifestly or consciously concerned with uncovering their unconscious wishes, thoughts, and feelings, they derive some indirect gratification from this aspect of the creative process. Artists, for instance, often return to the same theme or image repeatedly in their works and, while they may not work through or resolve elements of unconscious conflict, they often arrive at some form of insight. Subjects of mine have reported a knowledge of searching for an adequate father, concern with ambivalent feelings toward a brother or a mother or a son, and concerns about heterosexual and homosexual feelings reflected in particular productions and throughout the corpus of their art. Visual artists also become focused on both content and formal factors having important psychological roots. The process of moving toward insight or uncovering unconscious material is gratifying in itself, regardless of the outcome.[2] Thus, it must properly be considered an unconscious, preconscious, or semiconscious goal of the creative process in art.

The unconscious material uncovered by the artist during the creative process is often incorporated, somewhat transformed, into the art work and this is one of the factors in the aesthetic appeal. Reassurance, identification, and insight, as well as a stirring of basic wishes, motivations, and emotions, seem to play a role. The appearance of what are usually frightening feelings and impulses in publicly exhibited form and the knowledge that the artist and other human beings share such feelings and impulses is reassuring to the recipient audience. There is also a heightened sense of recognition and an identification with the universal feelings and impulses presented; these produce a sense of expansion and a relatedness between the audience and the work, between the audience and the creator, and among the members of the audience sharing the experience. The audience may, in addition, experience an upsurge of their own unconscious feelings and impulses and, despite some anxiety, come away with newly achieved insights. Much has been written about the aesthetic appeal of the presentation of unconscious material in art and I shall not repeat it here.[3] Moreover, as I shall clarify later, the process of uncovering rather than incorporation of unconscious content into the work of art is very likely the more critical factor in aesthetic appeal.

A common error in many psychoanalytic theories of art, that is, theories that relate aesthetic appeal to unconscious factors,[4] is the tendency to focus primarily on the content rather than the structure of artistic works. Thus, a good deal of attention is paid to the appearance of themes and plots embodying the Oedipus complex[5] as well as various types of symbolizations and manifestations of forbidden sexual and aggressive material. When structure is considered, it is almost invariably explained in terms of being a direct manifestation of the primary process mechanisms of condensation, symbolization, and displacement. Metaphors and rhymes are usually considered to be based on displacement, characters based on condensation, and images on symbolization.[6] According to such theories, whether explicitly stated or not, the structure of a work of art must have the same basis and psychological function as the structure of dreams. Carried somewhat further, manifestations of the artist's primary process thinking in works of art would appeal to, or reverberate with, the recipient audience's constant substratum of unconscious and primary process thinking during waking life.

The first aspect of the formulation, the idea of dream structure and artistic structure having the same function, is surely incorrect taken by itself because artistic structure has many functions other than impulse expression and disguise. Moreover, if art derived its power primarily from its resemblance to dreams, we might well have dispensed with art some time ago and only reproduced, viewed, and contemplated dreams themselves. The second aspect of the formulation, however, has merit and empirical support; there is good reason to believe, on the basis of clinical and experimental evidence, that art stimulates unconscious processes and has its impact on both a conscious and an unconscious level. Extensive clinical work with patients in psychoanalysis has yielded constant indications that particular art works stimulate deep unconscious concerns.[7] Psychological experiments have also demonstrated "symbolic" or unconscious sexual arousal in response to artistic works.[8]

The impact of art on an unconscious level is primarily due neither to the appearance of dream processes in art nor merely to the representations of unconscious material in the content of art works. Rather, it is the mirror-image factor in creativity that plays a crucial role. As mirror-image processes of dreaming, the types of thinking described here function to instigate the unconscious appeal of art. Because of the similarity—not the identity—between these operations and certain aspects of dreams and of primary process mechanisms, a work of art interacts directly with unconscious levels in the audience or viewer. Because the artistic work embodies qualities derived from such processes as homospatial and janusian thinking, it resonates with the primary process mode. A characteristic feature of dreams and primary process operations, for example, is equivalence of opposites. In the service of impulse discharge and disguise, primary process thinking uses and represents opposites interchangeably in dreams and in unconscious thinking. Consequently, when opposites are presented as overtly or tacitly incorporated in a work of art because of the operation and instigation of janusian thinking, there is an effect on an unconscious level. For the recipient audience, there is a resonance and recognition at the level of primary process and unconscious thinking. The structure and/or the content of the presentation in the work of art is deeply familiar and, for many reasons, both stimulating and gratifying. Presentation of opposites together in a work of art is isomorphic with, rather than equivalent to, unconscious material and primary process representations. Opposites are meaningfully and plausibly presented together and the wish fulfillment of dreams is thereby connected to the realm of reality. Plausible connections among opposites go beyond the magical equivalence of opposites in dreams and the unconscious. One can have things "both ways" or many ways at once in a work of art and satisfy the demands of rationality and reality as well. Thus, presented or suggested juxtapositions of opposites in artistic works, regardless of the specific opposites involved, appeal on an unconscious level. When the specific opposites have personal meaning to the recipient audience, the impact is even greater. For example, in O'Neill's title for his play, *The Iceman Cometh,* the catchy simultaneous opposition of the biblical and therefore sacred word "cometh" with the mundane or profane "iceman" is a grammatically and aesthetically plausible construct. The phrase has nowadays even become widely adopted as pithy metaphor. As I have shown in another work on that play, numerous other simultaneous oppositions arising from the context of the play are represented in this title, including the coming of Christ and the antithetical coming of bleak salvationless annihilation or death, and the coming of Christ and the antithetical sexual "coming" or orgasm of an adulterous iceman. The particular juxtaposition of a sexual and a religious coming has, for those who see it develop in the play, the effect of a rather direct interaction with an unconscious level. The equivalence of the coming of bleak annihilation or death with Christ's coming is less wish fulfilling but it nonetheless stimulates plausible intellectual debate and resonates, for several people, with particular personal conflicts.

Not only do the compressed juxtapositions of particular opposites contained in such a title as *The Iceman Cometh* interact directly with the unconscious level, but broader, more sweeping oppositions emerging from the substance of a tragedy have a similar impact. In a temporally extended literary work, the juxtaposition of such opposites as cruelty and tenderness in the tragic hero, ambition and debasement, love and hate, pride and humility, is a cumulative effect. These oppositions, while conceived simultaneously by the creator, gradually unfold in the completed work. Reader or audience re-experience the initial juxaposition either along the way or by the time they reach the end portion of the work, and there is unconscious resonance.

Embodiments and derivatives of homospatial thinking in a work of art also interact directly with unconscious levels. Both in dreams and in primary process thinking, spatial restrictions and spatial dimensions are characteristically ignored and distorted. The literary or linguistic, the auditory, and the visual metaphors derived from homospatial thinking all evoke, appeal to, and otherwise stimulate the wishes and experiences of that spaceless and isomorphic unconscious level. On the basis of clinical evidence, linguistic metaphors invariably have unconscious significance[9] and it is reasonable to assume that other types of metaphors also have unconscious significance in art. Metaphors represent and embody obliterated boundaries and they thereby evoke the boundariless unconscious world. Particular discrete entities in the homospatial process producing the metaphor have—just as particular opposites within the janusian process—particular impact and personal meaning. Metaphors such as "spiteful sun" or "smiling sun" can, and often do, have the unconscious (and uncanny) impact of the sun seen as an actual smiling or spiteful human face. A metaphor such as "a tower of emptiness" will, for several, evoke unconscious sexual feelings and conflicts. Visual and auditory metaphors with nonlinguistic or nonspecific content will, if viewed and heard intently, produce subjective experiences reminiscent of the spacelessness of dreams and of the vividness resulting from the spatial compressions and distortions of the primary process. Fusion of elements in metaphors and in other aspects of artistic creations is particularly interactive with the unconscious level because it is isomorphic with primitive wished-for fusions of the self with others, such as the narcissistic fusions mentioned earlier. And as the homospatial process produces meaningful connections in art through rhymes, rhythms, double meanings, assonances, and alliterations, the primary process uses the same kind of sound similarities and ambiguities.

Neither homospatial nor janusian thinking, it should be emphasized, are exact mirror images of particular primary process qualities or operations. Janusian thinking roughly mirrors equivalence of opposites and homospatial thinking mirrors so-called spacelessness and certain aspects of condensation and displacement. Janusian formulations sometimes inversely resemble condensations in that extensive areas of opposition are juxtaposed and compressed. Also, abstract symbolization in art, which is sometimes traceable to homospatial and janusian thinking and sometimes is an independent mirror-image function, is roughly the reverse of primary process symbolization. While concrete entities and situations are used as symbols representing abstractions in art, abstract symbols are used by the primary process as representations of the concrete.

In sum, although homospatial and janusian thinking are not primary process or unconscious operations, the creations they produce do evoke and interact with unconscious levels. Although the creative process is not a form of regression or a type of unconscious functioning, created artistic products have definite unconscious effects and appeal. Works of art represent and incorporate unconscious material and they resonate with the unconscious level of the viewer or audience. Consequently, they both reassure and stimulate some degree of anxiety. Contrary to some prominent artistic and psychological convictions and beliefs, the unconscious material in art does not result from a direct outpouring of unconscious derivatives during the creative process, a direct outpouring that is subsequently or concomitantly disguised by various types of formal aesthetic devices or by undefined or standard types of ego processes. The janusian and homospatial types of thinking are both ego processes. These ego processes are themselves focused on formal aspects of a work of art; they have a good deal to do with determining formal structures, and they also serve to unearth unconscious material that is incorporated into the content of the work. In addition, some aspects of the formal structure of a work of art resemble unconscious primary process mechanisms and such formal aspects thereby interact with and stimulate unconscious modes and associated contents. The creative process does not consist of an upsurge of unconscious material held in check or made appealing through formal devices; the focus on form is present throughout. Form itself stimulates unconscious processes.

Anxiety and Arousal

In everyday life, the interaction between conscious and unconscious processes is a highly complex matter. And surely this interaction is no less complicated in art. At times, as we have learned from clinical and psychotherapeutic explorations, an upsurge into conscious waking life of material derived from unconscious sources is fraught with intense discomfort and anxiety. At other times when material from unconscious sources enters consciousness in the form of insight, there is considerable relief. Depending on the mode and circumstances, presentation of a word, an idea, or a situation touching on a person's unconscious feelings and conflicts may instigate intolerable anxiety and feelings of aversion. Or a fairly similar presentation may be reassuring and even stimulating as well as instigating feelings of attraction. Much depends on circumstances and mode of presentation, but some things are certain: anxiety is closely linked to unconscious processes and the balance between discomfort and attraction is a very delicate one.

Both quantitative and qualitative factors play a role. Anxiety is adaptive for human beings because, at a minimum, it alerts us to the presence of danger and prepares us physiologically to respond. Under general circumstances, most people characteristically experience anxiety as an alerting reaction that leads to learning and mastery over danger. For others, anxiety may characteristically be too intense and, rather than mastery, there is flight or inaction and failure.[10] When material from unconscious sources comes into consciousness accompanied only by mild or moderate anxiety, insight and subsequent mastery often occurs; when there is a large amount of anxiety, the experience may be overwhelming. This delicate balance is a factor both in the creative process and in the reactions to works of art.

I have already outlined some of the roles anxiety plays in the creative process. To some degree, anxiety is defended against and kept out of consciousness. Unconscious material is presented indirectly and in conjunction with abstract and other types of thought processes, much as it is in everyday life. Janusian thinking, in its initial phases and disassociated from the homospatial process, operates in conjunction with a defense mechanism, negation, which—like all defenses—protects against upsurgence of unconscious material and overwhelming anxiety. But this defense is more revealing than other defenses and the overall progression instigated by the mirror-image process is toward unearthing unconscious material, an unearthing that must engender a good deal of anxiety along the way. In addition to the empirical data presented earlier in this book, and other confirmation from my research interviews with writers documented elsewhere,[11] the proposition that anxiety is engendered during the creative process has been subjected to the following experimental verification.

In two separate experiments, one carried out with creative high school students and the other with the proven highly creative writers who have been my research subjects,[12] a special procedure was employed to assess the presence of anxiety during various phases of the creative process. Words and phrases from the manuscripts in progress of an author's own completed poem or short story were used to construct a special word association test. This test was administered to the author in a special session. Measurement of anxiety in connection with particular words and phrases was based on time of word association response, or "latency" of response. Under instructions to respond to a word or phrase stimulus with the first word that comes to mind, responses taking greater amounts of time indicate more conflict and anxiety than faster ones.[13] Deleted words and phrases from the manuscript were used as stimuli representing early phases of the creative process and substituted words and phrases represented a later phase. Successive manuscript revisions were tested and compared. All words and phrases were chosen randomly and, in order to control for recognition and other factors, words and phrases from other sources were also used. The results from creative high school students were compared to noncreative or less-creative matched controls writing short stories in the same classes.[14] No controls for the prominent writer group were used.

On a theoretical basis, it is reasonable to expect that most persons will, in carrying out any form of personal or emotive writing, manifest greater anxiety in connection with early deleted material in their writings and less anxiety in connection with material that is substituted later. Roxon-Ropschitz has provided some clinical evidence for this with patients writing notes and literary pieces.[15] Disguise and defensiveness, along with straightforward correcting for errors and with emotional conflict, presumably play a role in revision. And indeed, the control group of high school students attempting creative writing showed much greater latencies and therefore greater anxiety with responses to their own deleted words and phrases than to their own substituted phrases and words from successive manuscript revisions. The creative high school group, on the other hand, showed significantly greater latency of response and greater anxiety with responses to their *substituted* and *later used* words and phrases from successive manuscript revisions. Moreover, the group of proven creative writers (all poets) also demonstrated greater anxiety, as measured by latency of response, with their substituted or later used words and phrases from successive revisions than with all other types of stimuli.[16]

These preliminary experimental results tend to support the observations from my research interviews that the creative process involves increasing anxiety as it progresses. The creator engages in a task that makes him increasingly anxious as he pushes onward. And, as we know, he does this again and again, usually taking up another creative task as soon as he has finished the last one. Why? There are several answers to this question, but I shall focus primarily on one of them, a biological factor relating to both the creative process and the created product.

Anxiety is closely related to arousal, both physiologically and psychologically. Which one of the two factors is more basic is difficult to determine definitely at the current state of our knowledge. Generally, there is an admixture of the two factors; while arousal may be the more general undifferentiated state that initially gives rise to anxiety, experientially there is a quantitative factor in the interrelationship between the two. Moderate anxiety is virtually synonymous with arousal. We feel aroused when anything stimulates (at least) a moderate degree of anxiety; anything that arouses us can also make us moderately anxious.[17]

In chapter 2, I pointed out some of the ways anxiety and arousal are experienced as gratifying in both the aesthetic experience and the creative process. Crucial are both the manner of generation and the extent to which these factors are produced. Merely instigating arousal and anxiety, regardless of the manner and degree, is not necessarily gratifying in creation or in aesthetic experience. As a mirror image of dreaming, the creative process is more stimulating and arousing than ordinary modes of experience and the created product can instigate fairly elevated levels of anxiety as well. But neither the process nor the product produce overwhelming anxiety, for just as nightmares wake the dreamer and force him to end the dream, too much anxiety forces both the creator and the audience to abandon the creation.

In a major treatise on the psychology of art, Berlyne has set down an impressive amount of evidence indicating that arousal is a key factor in aesthetic appeal.[18] Generation of arousal by a work of art is, according to Berlyne, related to "collative variables" of novelty, expectations, complexity, conflict, ambiguity, and multiple meaning, as well as other psychophysical and ecological variables. In addition, he cites evidence that too much arousal is uncomfortable and that there are arousal limiting and modulating factors contributing to aesthetic appeal. He distinguishes between phenomena he describes as "arousal jags" and as "arousal boosts," a distinction based in part on the role and type of relief of arousal factors. Arousal jag refers to "a kind of situation in which an animal or a human being seeks a temporary rise in arousal for the sake of the pleasurable relief that comes when the rise is reversed."[19] Arousal boost, which somewhat overlaps with arousal jag, refers to pleasure derived directly from moderate increments of arousal, a pleasure that is independent of subsequent relief and reversal. Underpinning Berlyne's formulations are some relatively recent neurophysiological discoveries regarding the mammalian brain, particularly the functioning of the reticular formation and the presence of what appear to be primary and secondary systems for reward and gratification.[20] Based on Olds's experiments with rats under conditions providing for electrical self-stimulation of the brain, the postulated primary and secondary reward systems are complex types of neurophysiological functions. Direct production of pleasure results, it appears, from electrical stimulation of the primary system. Stimulation of the secondary system, however, operates indirectly by releasing the primary system from the inhibiting effects of an organized aversion function. Berlyne's postulate, then, is that this primary reward system is also stimulated by a moderate arousal increase, the arousal boost, while increase of arousal followed by relief, the arousal jag, brings the secondary reward system into play. Relief or reduction of arousal inhibits the aversion system and thereby indirectly releases the gratifying effects of the primary reward system.

I cannot go into Berlyne's extensive documentation and experimentation pertaining to the importance of arousal in the psychological response to art. It should be clear, however, that his formulations regarding moderate arousal, arousal boost, and arousal jag apply equally appropriately to anxiety. Terms such as moderate anxiety and increase and relief of anxiety could be readily and consistently substituted into these formulations. Although Berlyne's commitment to an information theory approach causes him to focus heavily on stimulus complexity as an instigator of arousal, there need be no conflict with the emphases on unconscious sources of arousal and anxiety I have presented. In short, both anxiety and arousal generated during the creative process and the related anxiety and arousal stimulated by resulting products, works of art, have intrinsic psychophysical and psychodynamic properties connected with gratification.

Moderation, modulation and control seem to be key factors relating the anxiety and arousal generated during the creative process to the appeal of the work of art. Though the creative process characteristically involves a progressive uncovering of unconscious material with attendant anxiety, the progression, as we have seen, is slow, gradual—an arousal boost—and highly controlled. Indeed, in the early phases of the creative process, and in janusian thinking, defenses play a prominent role. Both the janusian and homospatial processes focus strongly on formal aspects of the evolving work, such as contrast, conflict, irony, paradox, unity, and such a focus on evolving form and structure serves to hold anxiety in check. Only mild to moderate anxiety is experienced. When material derived from unconscious sources eventually enters more fully into the creator's consciousness, there is usually relief of earlier diffuse anxiety and and arousal—the arousal jag—primarily because the creator is at that point more prepared to understand and incorporate what he is experiencing. Both the adaptive fusions of the homospatial process and the ego reinforcement due to progressive mastery and accomplishment during the course of creating facilitate this preparation. Because of adaptive fusions and mastery, there is also anxiety followed by relief all along the way. It is difficult to spell out the exact ongoing details of the delicate balances between discomfort and relief, attraction and aversion, throughout the process of creation, but it is certain that the creator cannot be overwhelmed by the anxiety involved. When he is, progress is severely retarded. In some cases, work continues but the product shows the marks of incoherence and extreme distortion resulting from the overwhelming anxiety of its creator. It is the mirror-image and primarily secondary process nature of the creative process that functions to keep anxiety within bounds; when primary process thinking holds sway, the creator has already become overwhelmed and, should the work continue, the resulting product shows the disagreeable effects.

For the audience of the work of art, the structure imparted by the mirror-image processes and the amount and explicitness of unconscious material presented in a work of art are factors in the degree of arousal and anxiety experienced. Appearance of unconscious material can be reassuring but, in the delicate balance, a good deal of anxiety can be stimulated. The structured, implicit, and moderate amount of unconscious material in effective works of art stimulates only moderate levels of arousal and anxiety. Mirror-image processes merely resemble primary process mechanisms; hence, they interact with unconscious levels and stimulate and unearth rather than discharge unconscious material, producing only moderate anxiety and arousal. When material derived from unconscious sources is presented directly in the work of art, the creator's insight about this material is usually presented as well. There is arousal boost and arousal jag. When primary process thinking and a more direct presentation of unconscious material predominate in a purported work of art, there is often intolerable anxiety and discomfort, and aversion results. Despite both the seeming freedom and the acceptance of the ramifications of the Oedipus theme and other unconscious material in modern-day art and culture, in fact, such aversion still occurs. The outright failure of such modern films as George C. Scott's *The Savage Is Loose,* an explicit portrayal of mother-son incest, and of Elmer Rice's last play, *Cue for Passion,* an explicit rendition of the Oedipus theme in *Hamlet,* was certainly due in some degree to such aversion. In most cases, the source and nature of the anxiety experienced remains unconscious; sophistication and psychological defenses require that we not acknowledge fear in art—or, for that matter, in life.

In addition to the controlled and moderate unearthing of unconscious material, the mirror-image processes instigate arousal in another way. For the creator, the formal conceptual attributes of the initial products of janusian and homospatial thinking are arousing and dramatic. Homospatial conceptions initially involve rather dramatic fusions and janusian formulations, the bringing together of extremes and polarities. Unmodified, such conceptions entail a high degree of cognitive strain and tension and are highly stimulating and arousing. Used in their initial form directly in a work of art, janusian formulations particularly might produce an experience of excessive arousal and adversion. Or there would be another type of reaction to excessive arousal and anxiety—laughter and derision. Slogans such as "War is

Peace" and other Orwellian "double think"[21] ideas or Mrs. Malaprop's humorous mixing of extremes, such as "our retrospection will be all to the future,"[22] are useful within the particular artistic creations to illustrate the anaesthetization of the populace and Mrs. Malaprop's character, respectively. These phrases are not themselves artistic creations because they are not modulated and integrated into a context indicating they could have plausibility or meaning. They are artistic devices illustrating human foibles within a creation and they function to produce excessive arousal, aversion, and release in laughter along the way.

A work of art based on constant juxtaposition of polarities of good and bad, of extremes of political ideology, of primary colors exclusively, often produces aversion, derision, or the reaction to excessive and persistent arousal we experience as boredom. So too, constant fusion and lack of differentiation can be wearisome and boring. Within the creative process, however, the aroused creator modifies initial extremes and fusions, sometimes at the moment or else immediately after he thinks of them. Janusian formulations are integrated through the homospatial process, and discrete new elements are separated out of homospatial fusions. Throughout the creative process, other types of modifications and other elaborations occur, and the original conceptions appear in the final product usually much transformed. This transformation of extremes and fusions results in a product that still conveys, in modulated form, attributes of the highly arousing original conceptions.

With this introduction of the formal conceptual attributes of the mirror-image processes, I can now turn to other types of created products beside artistic ones and consider more general aspects of the relationship between the creative process and creations. While anxiety and arousal play a role in scientific and other types of creation, it is a rather subtle and recondite one. Therefore, the function of anxiety and arousal in other fields is best considered within the more general context to be elaborated next.

Specification, Symmetry, Encapsulation

Earlier, in the chapter on opposition (chap. 8), I pointed out some salient features of opposites in comparison with contrasts and differences. Opposites bear a reciprocal relationship with one another and they are more sharply distinct than are contrasts and differences. Opposites represent definite points on a scale or in a dichotomy and they are therefore more *specific* than other related entities. Thus, "cold" and "hot" are more easily identified in diverse contexts and located more specifically on diverse temperature scales than are either "cool" or "warm." Opposites, and antitheses as well, represent sharp contrarities and extremes and are therefore clear reference points.

This quality of specification may be particularly important for the scientist but it is also enormously useful for any creator in the task he faces.

Though creating by human beings is surely not a matter of bringing forth something out of nothing, there are analogies between human creation and those mysterious and universal events that have given the word "creation" such honorific significance. For the human creator surely faces some type of chaos at the start. Knowledge and experience, despite the notable backlog of achievement stored up by civilized man, are always essentially the "blooming, buzzing confusion" characterized by William James. For artists and scientists as well as others, the task of creating is always, to some degree, the bringing of order to some area of knowledge and experience where chaos and the blooming, buzzing confusion reigned before. Small as it may seem in the face of such an enormous undertaking, the specification and organization provided by formulating and designating the opposites and antitheses pertinent to a particular area of knowledge and experience greatly help in the task of creation. For the scientist and theorist, designating salient opposites and antitheses is an important aid in conceptualization. Though he may move away from and modulate formulations structured in such terms, in early phases they are extremely valuable. And they are no less important for the experimentalist within any field, because crucial experiments are seldom performed without a previous formulation of clear and specific, if not exclusive, alternatives. For the artist, designating opposites and antitheses seems, as I said earlier, to function as his only method of arriving at absolutes, absolute truth or absolute aesthetic categories, in what appears to be a relativistic world. Saying this, I do not mean to indicate that I *know* that everything is relative, nor that every artist necessarily believes that, but I mean that designating opposites and antitheses is one of the important methods available to the human mind for formulating absolute categories. Absolutes are always extremes. Every absolute has an opposite, and designating opposites is a way of suggesting and defining immutable or absolute factors. To say that human behavior can be described as either good or as its opposite, bad, implies an absolute standard. To say that maleness and femaleness are opposites, as we well know today, also implies adherence to absolute standards. Akin to the scientist, the artist may transform and otherwise modify the extremes he begins with, but they help him to start and they remain as underpinnings in final creations.

The creative process progresses from the formulation and specification of polarities, dichotomies, and extremes toward modulation. Rather than using diffuse or moderate elements and relationships at the start, and for some distance along the way, the creator is willing to deal with the risks of contradiction and conflict. He modifies and shapes the conflicting extremes in forming a creation. To leave things overtly as extremes would be uncreative. As reality seldom consists of extremes, his product would have little connection to the natural world. In the process of creation, there is a compromise between the needs of formulating along the way and the requirements of reality.

I have throughout this book given numerous examples of oppositions and antitheses conceived in the early phase of theory building and of artistic creation. Here, I want merely to point out a connection between opposition and creation that implicitly suggests a verification of the principles I have just described. In their accounts of the creation of the world and of the creation of all things, virtually all of the pre-Socratic philosophers described some type of separating out and interplay between various opposites: hot and cold, wet and dry, bounded and unbounded, fire and water, earth and sky. And creation myths throughout the world and throughout the ages have very frequently emphasized formation of opposites of various types.[23]

Such ubiquitous connecting of opposition with the creation of the world does not, of course, necessarily point to an underlying fact about the nature of reality or about the origins of the world. Just because so many have postulated the idea does not mean it is intrinsically true. But the consistent connecting of opposition and creation could arise from a psychological fact. Human beings may have unwittingly connected opposition and world creation because they have, in their own creative activities, started with opposites.

Looking, for instance, at the account in Genesis as a product of human minds, such a factor seems to be operating. From the first words, the Creator is described as formulating and separating the oppositions of "heavens" and "earth."[24] There is "darkness upon the face of the deep," and the Creator produces light; next, He separates the light from the darkness and calls the light, "Day," and the darkness, "Night." Immediately following, He separates the waters above from the waters below. Then, gathering the waters below into one place, He creates the "dry land." The sequence of oppositions is dramatic. Hardly an accidental sequence, it seems to represent a projection of human thought processes onto the first creation. Considering it a product of the mind of men, some might relegate it to a dualistic or more primitive mode of thinking characteristic only of ancient precivilized times. However, without even considering the importance and any particular metaphysical interpretations of these lines, the durability of the passages throughout the history of Judeo-Christian civilization suggests acceptance at periods of highly sophisticated levels of thought.

Formulations of opposites are an aspect of the janusian process, and such formulations function in creating to bring specificity out of undifferentiation and chaos. The specificity achieved during the process of creation, though it is later modulated and transformed, helps to determine the eventual shape, clarity, and order of the created product. These resulting qualities are intrinsic to the value we accord to creations in art, science, or any field; they help provide definition, communicability, vividness, and comprehension. Formulating opposites and antitheses is not, of course, the only possible means of producing specificity. But janusian thinking is a sure, clear way of developing specificity, specificity that combines with other functions in imparting value to creations.[25]

Another function of the janusian process is the production of symmetry. When opposites or antitheses are brought together, the elements in the resulting conception are symmetrical. In the pure case, opposites or antitheses are totally reciprocal with each other, reversed or in conflict in one significant feature but in all aspects equal and fully matched. Thus "odd" and "even," "always" and "never," "Democrat" and "Republican," "north" and "south" are fully equal aspects of the contexts or the scales in which they are opposed: numbers, time, American political parties, compass direction, respectively. Earlier, of course, I emphasized that it is very difficult to establish perfect reciprocity in the case of a particular set of opposites primarily because of the difficulty in limiting words and concepts to any one context. Also, I emphasized the importance of the difference between opposites rather than the similarity. Nevertheless, the matching and the similarity must now be brought into focus because, regardless of whether it is possible to describe and define full reciprocity in any one particular case, the symmetrical quality of janusian formulations is clear and apparent. To say, for instance, that odd and even are the same would incorporate the entire world of numbers symmetrically; neither side of this janusian equation can have more numbers than the other. And this symmetrical quality, or, if you will, this thrust toward symmetry, is an aspect of janusian thinking that contributes to the construction of creations.

In science, symmetry characteristically plays an important role in conceptual model building. Scientific theories constantly move in the direction of formulating symmetries regarding each and every aspect of the physical world. Thus, there are levo and dextro molecules and compounds, dominant and recessive genes, anabolic and catabolic processes, and so on. Whether this tendency is derived from a deep intuition into the structure of the world, an anthropomorphic type of projection of the symmetrical qualities of our bodies onto the physical world, or an aesthetic feeling is not clear. Following the principle of constructing symmetrical models, however, has resulted in a great deal of scientific advance. An interesting case in point concerns the theory of the "conservation of parity," the postulate that the laws of nature applied equally to both left and right particles. When the Nobel Prize–winning physicists Lee and Yang produced evidence disproving and overthrowing this theory, there was consternation and shock throughout scientific circles. In recent years, however, new theories and new evidence have developed which seem to point to another more inclusive principle of symmetry in the physical world. Janusian formulations, as they may postulate the simultaneous existence of heretofore unknown opposites and antitheses, facilitate the discovery of new symmetries.

In art, the symmetries formulated initially in the janusian process often function to impart fundamental balance and proportion to a completed work. Such balance and proportion also seems valuable in science, where theories that are elegant and aesthetically pleasing often seem to be the most salient and useful, and this could well be a major factor in the scientific creator's use of janusian thinking. It must be said, however, that symmetry alone does not impart value to a work of art, and an exclusive focus on symmetry in science also can be misleading.[26] In modern times, there has been a tendency in the visual arts especially to emphasize asymmetrical rather than symmetrical forms.

Essentially, the symmetrical thrust is an ordering principle, helping to give form and balance to the substrata of knowledge and experience that are bases of art and science as well as other pragmatic and theoretical fields. Janusian thinking, as it operates characteristically in early phases of creation, produces an overall order even when there is asymmetry in the completed work. Aspects of janusian formulations may be transformed into asymmetries. These aspects may function side by side with other processes oriented to asymmetry or, in cases where antitheses are not completely reciprocal, there may be some degree of asymmetry at the start. Regardless of the particular asymmetrical details in a creation, there is almost invariably a sense of overall balance, proportion, and order, whether it be the feeling of equipotent forces in a tragic conflict in literature, alternation between rest and motion in music, congruence between the bounded and unbounded in the visual arts, or coordination in various aspects of a scientific theory. The symmetrical structure of the janusian formulation leaves its mark.

Both symmetry and specificity are constant properties of opposites and antitheses, taken together or in sequence. Because of the simultanenous opposition and antithesis in janusian formulations, however, there is also a distinct tension among the elements. Both the symmetry and specificity, therefore, are in dynamic states; there are forces tending toward diffusion and reduction as well as toward elaboration and enhancement of these characteristics. Properly speaking, there is dynamic symmetry and dynamic specificity. Generative of other forms and formulations during the creative process, the dynamic specificity and symmetry produce constant shifts of affective and conceptual tensions and relationships. In art especially, the dynamic factor contributes to a constant interaction among elements that is retained in the final creation. Dynamic symmetry and specificity, rather than static balance, harmony, and fixed meaning, characterize the artistic work. Beyond this, the simultaneity of opposition and antithesis in the janusian process relates to another creative function of this form of cognition, the function of encapsulation.

Although encapsulation potentially involves highly complicated enfoldings within protected boundaries, the janusian process only serves to provide the basis and structure for this phenomenon. The encapsulation function of the janusian process is best understood by focusing on opposites and antitheses as polarities or extremes. Polar opposites, such as liberty and slavery, good and bad, hard and soft, top and bottom, are the limits, respectively, of their categories: restraint, value, consistency, vertical direction. More complicated polarities, such as radical and reactionary, are the limits of complex dimensions of human ideation and behavior: politics, ideology, Weltanschauung, artistic preference. Regardless of the nature of the dimension or context, polarities are, by definition, the limits, and reference to polarities helps to define a context. Thus, we ask: "What is temperature?" and both our usual association and our answer are: "hot and cold, a scale from hot to cold." And: "What kinds of ideology are there?" Answer: "They range from radical to reactionary." Or: "What is vertical direction?" Again: "Going from down to up or vice versa." Of course, many variations on these answers are possible, but my point is that our understanding of a context, category, or dimension is inextricably connected to limits. Asked in the reverse way: "What are hot and cold?", the succinct answer would be: "The limits of temperature." Or, "What are radical and reactionary?" and a specific succinct answer would be: "Extreme types of ideology." And: "What are up and down?" Answer: "Verticality." Reference to limits and polarities, in other words, implies an entire dimension.

Reference to limits is one of the most economical or concise ways to concretize and define a field or dimension.[27] Knowing the limits provides a basis for storing and extending knowledge. Given a knowledge of the content of both the radical and reactionary points of view on a topic, many variant positions can be deduced. The limits clarify the nature and content of intermediary factors. With respect to encapsulation, referring to limits can stimulate associations to information and experiences pertaining to any or all the phenomena involved in an entire dimension. By bringing together polarities and limits simultaneously in a janusian formulation—even though they are in conflict—an entire dimension potentially is encapsulated. An entire system is suggested. And one of the reasons the creator engages in janusian thinking is that, consciously or unconsciously, he is attempting to accomplish just such a goal—he is attempting to encapsulate a dimension or, in a sense, a world. When Einstein, for instance, brings motion and rest into a unitary conception, he is attempting to encapsulate the entire domain of gravitation and electromagnetic induction. When the artist brings human and beast into a unitary conception, he is attempting to encapsulate the world of sensate living things. Although particular polarities can refer to more than one context, little difficulty for the creator is produced. The scientist knows the context he is concerned about and the artist is quite pleased when a particular set of polarities defines and suggests several contexts at once.

With respect to opposition and antitheses based on cut or dichotomy rather than on polarity, the principle of encapsulation also applies. While left and right or man and woman may not necessarily be polarities, a set of such opposites does define a context, a dimension, and a world. Rather than defining limits only, opposites based on dichotomy define the halves of a dimension or context in a general way. Within the creative process, such opposites might be brought together first and the contents of their encapsulated type of world or dimension later elaborated. As there is such ready shifting between oppositions of dichotomy and oppositions of scale—left and right halves thought of as left end and right end, for instance—the difference can either be negligible or it can be used by the artist creator to formulate and work with more than one type of context. When an artist visualizes a scene for a landscape painting, left and right, for him, may encapsulate both the context and the contents of the scene entirely. And a poet may conceive both that left and right hands and that radical and reactionary are the same.

In scientific creation, the structure of encapsulation is, along with symmetry and specification, an exceptionally valuable tool. The scientist brings an entire dimension of knowledge into a unitary conception—Darwin brought the entire domain of adaptation and maladaptation together when reading Malthus[28]—and he thereby pinpoints and resolves basic questions. He formulates underlying polarities and dichotomies in an area of confusion, brings specificity and symmetry through particular salient opposites and antitheses, and through encapsulation his solutions incorporate and circumscribe the total context. Adaptation and maladaptation encapsulate evolution of living things and potentially apply to all evolutionary processes. In such fashion, scientific and other intellectual systems are created and developed.

For the artist, encapsulation functions to compress[29] his world of absolutes produced through the specificity and symmetry of opposites and antitheses. Bringing together the limits, halves, and polarities of a dimension of experience through a janusian conception, the artist suggests the contents and defines his realm. The resulting images, structures, and concrete objects are rich in suggestion and ramification throughout the realm, both for the artist himself and his audience. When an iceman and Christ are equated, the implications and ramifications extend throughout an entire domain bounded by sex and religion. For the artist especially, the more opposites and antitheses included, the greater are the ramifications and the worlds potentially encompassed.

To some extent, encapsulation, along with multiple opposition and antithesis, introduces ambiguity into artistic creations. Among modern critics, ambiguity has been heavily emphasized as a factor in aesthetic appeal. While production of such ambiguity could surely be considered to be one of the functions of janusian thinking, a particular caution about the term "ambiguity" must be stressed in connection with literature and with art. Aesthetic ambiguity could not consist merely of indefinite or indeterminate meaning. Such ambiguity would be merely confusing and incomprehensible, and consequently of little value. Structured and defined ambiguity suggesting and yielding multiple meanings is the valuable, or the aesthetic, factor. Such definition and structure is not overt but implied, and consequently there is a quality both of indeterminacy and of control. Because of the specificity of opposites and antitheses, there is definition within the ambiguities derived from the janusian process. There is creation rather than diffusion and disarray. The type of ambiguity developed, a specific and controlled type of ambiguity, contributes to the ordering and richness of artistic creations. Burgeoning out in the final product is the compressed, specific, symmetrical world encapsulated in the janusian process.

Unity and Fusion

The ordering features of janusian thinking have much to do with the process of separating out and creating out of chaos. More is involved, however, to produce the fully separated and organized entity we esteem as a creation. With art especially, we use the term "creation" because the art product is virtually a living breathing object, fully formed and distinct with all its parts interacting, nourishing, and enhancing each other. The outstanding art work has what is called "organic unity," a quality well highlighted by Emily Dickinson when she asked her sometime mentor, T. W. Higginson, "my verse . . . do you think it breathed . . . ?"[30] Although many factors surely come into play to produce such perfect lifelike unity as Dickinson asked about, the homospatial process functions importantly in the production of organic unity in works of art. Through the homospatial process, discrete entities are fused and superimposed without losing their distinctiveness; they continue to interact and relate to one another. Both particular opposites and antitheses forming the encapsulations of the janusian process and other types of discrete entities are integrated into unified artistic images, conceptions, and metaphors. Horse and human are fused as the central unifying image of a poem. The coming of an iceman and a Bridegroom (Christ) are fused into the metaphor "the iceman cometh," a metaphor that embodies the central unifying conception of a play—that men need illusions about sex, faith, hope, and salvation but deception and death are the only realities. Fusion of particular rhymes, and sound similarities relate meanings with poetic images, producing unified form and content within a poem. In music and the visual arts, discrete sound patterns and visual entities are fused and superimposed to produce compositions in which elements interact and relate throughout. Unification in all forms of literature of the factors of concrete events of plot, values, and characterizations results from the fusion of author's self-image, images of other real persons, and plot constructions. And throughout all art forms, abstractions are rendered into related and interacting concrete forms through the homospatial process.

Metaphors, both the particular linguistic, auditory, and visual ones, and the more general type characterizing an entire work of art, exemplify the unity produced through the homospatial process.[31] As shown in chapters 9 and 10, metaphors are unities consisting of discrete and oftentimes disparate elements that interact and relate to each other within a larger context or a whole. The metaphor "the branches were handles of stars" has an impact as a whole unified phrase, suggesting a feeling of upward striving or an image of tapers and torches, and, at the same time, the particular elements—branches, handles, and stars—interact with each other and call our attention to particular qualities of sound, shape, and meaning. So, too, the play *Hamlet* and the character Hamlet can both be considered to be metaphors: they each have an impact as a whole. Also, there are the discrete interacting qualities of contemplation and action arising from defined sequences within the play, and the character Hamlet has discrete interacting features. Moreover, like all metaphors, both the play and the character Hamlet have no literal meaning; they are figurative representations of reality rather than direct or literal copies. The metaphor "the branches were handles of stars" surely does not indicate an actual equation of branches and handles; it represents an idea or experience. So, too, Hamlet, though he seems quite real in the play, is not the product of a tape-recorded transcript; he, like any artistic product, represents far more than the literal facts portrayed.

Auditory and visual metaphors also have representational qualities because they are derived in some way from real sounds and sights. As sounds and sights are far less specific than words, however, representation is more diffuse. By and large, auditory metaphors are unities derived from the context of a particular work; they are fusions and superimpositions of patterns appearing in the particular work although these patterns also relate to, and to some degree represent, other works of music and other sounds and rhythms. But the differences between the various types of metaphors are matters of degree rather than of kind. Linguistic metaphors are highly referential and therefore they, more than auditory metaphors, relate to phenomena outside the work. Thus, also more than other types of metaphors, linguistic metaphors can be understood and to some extent appreciated outside of a particular work. Reference and representation, however, are not primarily responsible for their aesthetic effect. Just as with other types of metaphors, linguistic metaphors unify discrete and disparate elements in the work itself. They represent other elements in the piece as well as specific elements in reality, and they derive their fullest power as unifiers within the particular context of the work. The general Hamlet metaphor I described can only be fully appreciated by reading or by seeing the play.

Because metaphors both relate discrete and disparate elements in a work of art and are intrinsically related to the context of the work, they play a crucial role in producing organic unity. This unity is organic in a double sense: first, metaphorical elements are in a dynamic relationship with each other; they modify, interact, and relate within a larger whole. In this, they are quite analogous to the nourishing, enhancing, and interacting qualities we associate with organisms. Second, because metaphors are never literal, can never be understood as purely literal or as purely referential statements or structures, they do not have a one-to-one correspondence with reality. As noncorresponding and nonliteral statements, metaphors are sharply distinct and separated from reality. Thus, they help separate the work of art from the reality outside and around it, the world of actual sounds, sights, and doings. With this separation, metaphors help impart boundaries to the work of art, boundaries that are not merely the frame around a painting nor the beginning and end of a play, novel, or musical work, but psychological and aesthetic boundaries. They form an integument around the artistic work analogous to the skin and other boundaries separating and defining a living organism; they separate the work from everything in its environment and interrelate with—nourish and are nourished by—other elements within the work.

When metaphors are developed from the encapsulation structure produced by the janusian process, the janusian and homospatial processes function concomitantly. By fusing and superimposing encapsulated elements and boundaries developed from janusian thinking, the homospatial process imparts integration and organic unity. In a sense, the homospatial process animates the boundaries and encapsulations derived from janusian formulations by interrelating them within a larger whole, a particular or a general metaphor. The oxymoron type of literary metaphor, for example, "penniless rich palms" of Hart Crane,[32] is an obvious example of the results of janusian and homospatial thinking operating close together. And, as Beardsley and others have so cogently shown, most literary metaphors have implicit oppositional and antithetical properties.[33] Explicit simultaneous antitheses, such as those displayed by many oxymorons, tend to be too arousing and therefore less effective in art. Implicit simultaneous opposition or antithesis, as produced by a more extensive fusion within the homospatial process, is a stimulating and vital feature of numerous literary metaphors. And auditory, visual, and other types of metaphors, including the larger metaphor of an entire artistic work, also often have oppositional and antithetical qualities.

Fusion, as Dewey and other aestheticians have suggested,[34] is a salient feature of artistic works and an important factor in aesthetic value and appeal. That homospatial thinking and other related thought processes account for much of the fusion experienced in connection with works of art is highly likely, but this is a topic for further research. I must restrict my discussion about this highly fascinating area to one aspect of the aesthetic experience of fusion that seems directly traceable to the effects of the homospatial process, what Straus called "homogenization of space."

In a remarkably insightful and provocative article concerning the nature of spatiality, Straus pointed out that all perceptual experience has spatial aspects.[35] With particular reference to the auditory sphere, he developed a distinction between the spatial characteristics of noise and music. Noise, he said, puts us in mind of particular locations in space while music does not; music therefore homogenizes space. When we hear a noise, we are distracted; we turn to find the source of it and we are put in mind of a specific location, a particular source from which the distracting sound arises. When we hear music, we know that it is produced by an instrument or by instruments in a particular place, but, in distinction to the experience with noise, we do not search nor are we expressly mindful of definite and distinct location. Music homogenizes space in the sense that it seems to fill uniformly all space in our immediate environment. Moreover, music seems to penetrate our bodies and to fill our consciousness, obliterating all felt distinctions between inner and outer space and producing a sense of uniform continuity everywhere. The quality of distance between the hearer and the source of music is overcome.

Straus went on to state that all forms of art produce a similar experience: "art is able to overcome apartness and distance and to create a second world by proclaiming the harmony of appearances."[36]

His analyses and formulations regarding music and other types of art are surely cogent and meaningful for anyone who has introspectively contemplated the nature of the aesthetic experience. Although Straus himself made no explicit distinction between the effects of good and bad art, we can most assuredly consider that the homogenization of space and the overcoming of distance he described are connected *only* with successful creation. There is nothing intrinsic in merely producing musical tones or rhythms, nor merely putting visual forms on a canvas, working on novels, and the like that would automatically produce such experiences. Therefore, to extend his analysis, this homogenization of space can be explained on the basis of a fusing of elements in a good work of art, a fusing that obliterates boundaries and separations. In listening to a good musical composition, fusions of discrete patterns of sound and rhythm—not only tones or other individual elements—lessen the distance and homogenize space. In viewing a good painting, the viewer's awareness of the fusion of background and foreground, of sides, and of juxtaposed patterns of shapes, textures, and colors, intensifies and brings to consciousness an exciting sense of the painting transcending the boundaries of the canvas and the frame, filling the surrounding space, and "moving" toward the viewer.[37] In a complex way, literary metaphors and other fusions in literature produce a similar overcoming of the sense of distance.

Though a good art work is bounded and unified, it also has these properties of transcending its boundaries, interacting with the consciousness of the viewer or audience, and overcoming the sense of distance. In this respect, art is also analogous to a living organism, for, while we are aware of the separateness and integrity of a living being —particularly, of course, another human—we also experience variations in our sense of distance from others. Human interactions may also be said sometimes to "homogenize" space and sometimes to emphasize distinctness and separateness.

Fusions in art to some degree, and unity in art to a larger degree, are the result of homospatial thinking. In scientific creations, the factors of fusion and unity seem not to play as important a role as in art except that, to reemphasize a connection, scientific theories often have definite aesthetic qualities, qualities intentionally sought by scientific creators. The unifying function of homospatial thinking seems actually to be most apparent during the course of the scientific creative process rather than in the direct construction of the final product. While working out early ideas and constructions, the homospatial process helps the creator to develop unities between abstract formulations and the world of concrete phenomena. Abstract ideas are translated into spatial or concrete terms, or spatial phenomena are fused to yield abstract ideas as in the example of Poincaré's and Hadamard's discoveries. Janusian formulations are integrated, and specific metaphors are produced which aid in conceptualization and scientific model building. Such metaphorization is also important for creative thinking in philosophy, engineering, politics, advertising, and business, to mention some other fields particularly.

Scientific creations do not derive their value primarily from attributes of organic unity or fusion but they do, at times, manifest an amazing degree of unity, or similarity at least, between the structural properties of human thought and perception and the structure of nature. Left- and right-sided molecules, positive and negative electricity, matter and antimatter, are cases in point.

Articulation and Freedom

In the process of creation, the progression from chaos and the blooming, buzzing confusion to a formed new and valuable entity, there initially is separation of specific elements and then a unification. In the overall sequence, janusian thinking with its specification function bears the brunt of separating out specifics in the early phase. Next, homospatial thinking, through fusion and superimposition, effects a major proportion of the integrations and unifications. The janusian and homospatial process each also have both separating and unifying aspects; both operate independently and together as well as in somewhat different sequences. Symmetry and the encapsulation aspects of janusian formulations produce an aggregating effect that tends toward unification; the unifying function of the homospatial process serves to organize and thereby to give distinctness and boundaries to both portions and the whole created product. Boundaries and limits are also defined by the particular opposites and antitheses involved in janusian formulations.

Whatever the sequence or the particular aspects responsible, and beyond the functions only of the homospatial and janusian processes, the creative process in any field is best characterized in terms of bringing together and separating. The creative process is a matter of continual separating and bringing together, bringing together and separating, in many dimensions—affective, conceptual, perceptual, volitional, physical—at once. There is differentiation, diffusion, redifferentiation, connecting, and unifying at every step of the way. All these functions produce entities that are independent and free from the initial chaos.

Best describing this phenomenon is the term "articulation." The term is appropriate in many different ways. First, as generally used, to articulate is to make something, give it form, or bring it into being; therefore, the term overlaps to some degree with "to create." Second, the root meaning of articulation is "joint," such as a joint between two bones in the body. The nature of a joint, though it may not be apparent without some thought and consideration, is to be *both* a connector and a separator at once; a joint both connects and separates bones or other objects. This quality of the joint is reflected in the use of the word "articulate" to apply to a style or characteristic of speaking and presentation. When a person is described as articulate, or as speaking articulately, the essential meaning is that he speaks *both* fluently and clearly. He both joins his words or ideas together into a smooth and flowing production, and he differentiates and separates his words and ideas clearly so that they can be readily understood.

The creative process is a process of articulation. To recapitulate the model: "The earth was without form and void, and darkness was upon the face of the deep . . . and God said, 'Let there be light'; and there was light. And God saw that the light was good; and God separated the light from the darkness. God called the light Day, and the darkness he called Night. And there was evening and there was morning, one day" (Gen. 1:2–5). In the description, light is first formulated as the opposite of darkness. Both light and darkness then coexist simultaneously until they are further separated. Next, they are brought together in the context of a day. Such bringing together and separating and bringing together—articulation—characterizes all phases of the creative process. Beginning with undifferentiated knowledge and experience, the creator proceeds through differentiation and joining, expansion and constriction, stray pathways and returns, diffusions and sharpenings, fantasy and reality, world visions and narrow technical concerns, cultural concerns and individual preoccupations, art styles and personal styles, arousal and ratiocination, abstraction and concretion, breaking and making. Always, as there are factors and processes tending toward diffusion and expansion, there are equally strong factors and processes directed toward differentiation and joining.

A particular case in point, an illustration of the pervasiveness of articulation, is seen in the handling of errors during the creative process. Creative people, I have found, handle errors in such a characteristic way that it is fair to label this as a special mark of creativity. Whereas most people carrying out a very difficult task, as creating unquestionably is, tend to be rather careful, controlled, and constantly wary of making errors, such is not the case with the highly creative. While engaged in the creative process, they feel free to range far and wide, take chances and think thoughts that invariably lead to some error. Characteristically, when such errors appear, there is not a good deal of distress and consternation, but a virtually immediate attempt at articulation. Misses and mistakes are, if possible, joined into a whole. Significant elements in the error, ranging from a slip of the paintbrush to the growing of mold on a petri dish, are separated out, and an attempt is made to articulate them into the corpus of the work in progress and, at the same time, to join each together. In other words, the error may be incorporated into the work or, if it is suggestive, it may lead the entire work into completely new directions.

Such an approach to errors and mistakes could in part be classified as a type of flexibility of thinking, an attribute that has long been known to be a general characteristic of creative people. Also, there is a willingness to learn by experience and to consider the significance of wrong results, capacities that are very advantageous for creating or for any type of high-level intellectual pursuit. Articulating errors during the creative process, however, consists of more than these types of capacities and approaches. Not only is it seeing how an error changes an initial conception or belief, there is a special allowing of, almost a courting of, errors and mistakes. There is sometimes even some pleasure connected with their appearance because of past successes. They are not purposely introduced, but as soon as they appear the creator engages in an active process of making in which errors are transformed into something else.

The creator's willingness to articulate whatever arises, to commit errors and to range far and wide in any direction during the creative process, connects to and, once again, mirrors, the experience of dreaming. Dreams appear also to be extraordinarily free forms of thinking in which anything happens and any image can appear. In distinction to the virtually limitless freedom of the creative process, however, there are definite limits and restrictions in dreaming. Representations in dreams appear free and wide-ranging but the underlying forces producing these representations are not at all free. When, as mentioned earlier, dreams come too close to revealing unconscious wishes and impulses, they are abruptly terminated and we wake up. In this respect, the creative process is a good deal less restricted. Because of the structural control of the mirror-image processes and because of the creator's willingness to articulate anything that comes up, he can often explore more perilously close to forbidden unconscious wishes and impulses. And he can tolerate considerably more anxiety in waking life than is possible during dreaming. Consequently, his entire range of thinking is freer. As the creative process unearths unconscious material to some degree, it is much less restricted by unconscious processes—unconscious factors exert their effect on consciousness because of being unconscious—than are dreams.

The mirroring similarity and reversal with respect to the range and freedom of thinking are paralleled with regard to arousal. Although dreams seem to be very stimulating and arousing while we are dreaming, they cannot actually be arousing to any degree or intensity because we would then be awakened. In the creative process, on the other hand, a good deal of arousal is possible because it is carried out completely in a waking state. When too much arousal occurs during creating, it leads to a desire or an attempt to escape including drowsiness or a wish to sleep—on the basis of recent dream research there is also perhaps a need to dream at such times—but sleep seldom is easy to achieve under such circumstances. Termination of the project or further articulation are often the only alternatives.

I have characterized the creative process as arousing and anxiety inducing and emphasized a progression toward unearthing unconscious processes. In relating arousal to moderate levels of anxiety, I have said little about other affects or impulses that can be included in the aroused state such as sex, love, anger, curiosity, attraction, aggression, and indeed the entire gamut of functions associated with stimulation and activation. All, depending on the type and the content of a particular process of creating, are, at different times, variously involved. Curiosity, for instance, could be said to arise out of a diffuse, alerted state of anxiety, both before and during the creative process. The creator is curious because of a diffuse feeling of mild or moderate anxiety that alerts him to the need for information or action. Sexual impulses aroused during the creative process might induce conflictual anxiety because they are forbidden or because they require discharge. Or the alert, moderately tense state connected to creating gives rise to feelings of attraction and the need for sexual discharge. Little documentation of the manifestations and permutations of these factors is possible because little is known about the complex interrelationships of particular emotions, alerting and arousal, and particular impulses. With respect to the general emotions and motivations of the creative process, however, one matter surely returns yet again from the early portions of this book: why does the creator seem to court anxiety? Why does he engage in an activity and a process during which he could readily be overcome with anxiety when most people avoid such risks?

In emphasizing the progression toward uncovering unconscious processes, I have throughout this book drawn no sharp distinctions between artistic creators and scientific or other types of creators. This may, for some, have been surprising or possibly outrageous. The artist's search for personal truth and insight is readily apparent; both the artist and his audience are interested in confronting and understanding, to some degree at least, an internal psychological world. In insisting on the uncovering of unconscious processes in other types of creating, I have depended on a basic psychological dictum, as follows: it is highly unlikely that anyone would pursue a task or a problem to the degree that is characteristic of scientific and other types of creation unless that problem *had some special personal meaning.* All human choices have, to some extent, an unconscious and personal basis, and with most activities the choice also often relates to other, more significant goals. With creative activities, however, the characteristically intense type of absorption in a particular task, the creator's intense devotion and concern, indicates a significant personal connection. The scientific creator, for example, is interested in discovering something about external reality, and he, like the artist, often wants the rewards of success and recognition for their own sake. But he chooses a task or problem in the first place and is enabled ultimately to clarify or to solve it partly because of its personal meaning. Incorporated into the final scientific solution is little resembling a personal insight, or even a representation of unconscious material as in art, but some unearthing occurs. Recall, if you will, Einstein's statement about the problem he had chosen: "The thought that one is dealing here with two fundamentally different cases was, for me, unbearable." Surely Einstein was not given to overdramatization nor to hyperbole, and the passion indicated by this remark was authentic. Why was this situation unbearable? Without more extensively detailed knowledge about Einstein, we cannot know or even guess. But returning to his solution, we must note the stipulating of an observer falling from the roof of a house. Falling is surely connected with gravitation but the image of a person falling from a roof also seems affectively charged. We cannot know, but the particulars of creative scientists' thought are rich in such suggestive references. The unearthing of unconscious processes seems to have little to do with the value of the resulting scientific creation except perhaps in some structural way that currently is unclear, but it is of value to the creator. He experiences arousal and a sense of progression during the creative process. All creators court the anxiety of creation for deep and personal gains.

Earlier in this book, I emphasized the function of arousal as a preliminary to the attainment of control. In science and other fields besides art, arousal in the creative process also results from the especially dissonant and disjunctive cognitive, physical, and interpersonal tasks involved. Given the creator's personal involvement in such tasks, the tasks themselves generally consist of the most complicated, difficult, and challenging matters in the sphere of human experience. If this were not so, we would not accord the high degree of positive value we do to achievements designated as creations in those fields. Control is therefore involved in a double sense. All creators court the anxiety connected with the internal psychological effects of creative processes in order to experience gratifying effects such as Berlyne's arousal boost and arousal jag, and to experience a psychological sense of control. Also, nonartistic creators especially confront anxiety-producing tasks and problems in the physical environment in order to attain control over that environment. Such control, the mirror image of the control over internal wishes in dreams, is only one aspect—an important one—of the creative process overall. For control is not necessarily progressive; one may merely use control to stay in the same place. In the overall progression of the creative process, control gives way to articulation.

Articulation within the creative process also pertains both to the world of external physical reality and to internal psychological experience. As the creator separates and joins materials and elements in the external world, he articulates internal factors as well. Because articulation produces freedom and independence from chaos, the outcome of this articulation is a measure of freedom in both spheres. The ultimate achievement of the creative process is freedom..

This is not to say that the creative process is a form of psychotherapy. The articulation of internal psychological experience does not in any major way constitute a therapeutic process. The psychological insights achieved, as I have described them throughout, are relatively minor ones or they are somewhat distorted. Seldom does the creator apply them actively or systematically to his personality and his life.[38] By and large, the major form of psychological insight occurring during or after the creative process, in art especially, consists of the artist's dim or overt recognition that the material with which he had been dealing related, in some type of significant way, to his own unconscious concerns. He realizes that the "problem" of a poem or painting, or the anger expressed in a piece of music, was his own. Or he realizes that the discovery he was seeking was also some discovery about himself. When the creator has a significant psychological problem, it is touched on and emerges to a small or large extent during the creative process. But it is not worked through as it is in therapy, and the creator often returns to it again and again in subsequent works.

Progression itself, however, the progression toward uncovering unconscious processes, is beneficial. Regardless of whether meaningful personal insight is ultimately achieved, the uncovering progression involves an internal freeing up and a movement away from the stifling effects of the creator's own past. Unconscious material, steeped in distortions based on past experience, exerts an enslaving effect on the creator, as well as on all of us, because of its inaccessibility. During the progressive unearthing of this unconscious material in the creative process, there is an articulation consisting both of separating away the past and of bringing together of present with past. To the degree that this articulation is successful, to the extent there is some separation from the enslaving hidden impact of past experience on present behavior and thought, as well as some bringing together of a meaningful continuity of past and present, some psychological freedom is achieved. The bringing together of the continuity of past and present involves a sense of continuity of identity. Psychological freedom consists of breaking away from the need to repeat the past in the present; it also consists of being able to accept and even to value aspects of one's self that are rooted in the past and are unchanging. These latter help to define and to establish a person's individuality and uniqueness. While the creative process in itself does not produce such psychological freedom, there is a definite and consistent movement in that direction. Regardless of where the creator starts from, regardless of the degree of psychological freedom he possesses, there is always—given the inevitable residua and conflict within the human psyche—a need for more. And the struggle toward psychological freedom is one of the hallmarks of the creative process. It justifies the risks and anxieties involved.

Basic to the value and appeal of art is the creator's struggle toward freedom. All great works of art reflect this struggle, all great works of art incorporate the energy and dynamism of the progression toward this goal. Worlds attempted to be conquered but not quite, truths begun to be revealed but never fully, and conflicts stated but not resolved are overriding characteristics of the works we return to and remember. The masterpiece reminds us of our dreams, but it goes beyond them. It reawakens the unconscious stuff of which dreams are made, brings the images and feelings into the fringes of our consciousness, and gives us glimpses of the underlying meanings and truths. But it never embodies them fully worked out, nor does it resolve their nagging tension. The great work shows us that the world we perceive has both separations and unifying relationships, that our feelings are both distinct and fused, and that our relationships to others are characterized both by total separateness and by being—almost joining—together. But none of this is static or complete, there is a constant struggle with appearances and with past experience—the past experience of the artist himself and the shared past experience of the race—and an attempt to overcome and move on. In *Hamlet,* for example, we are exposed to a man dealing with, among other things, an unconscious oedipal conflict and matricidal and patricidal impulses. The embodiment of such universal conflicts and unconscious impulses is certainly one of the bases of its touching universal chords. But the touching of these chords alone is not the basis of the play's appeal; it is Hamlet's struggle to free himself, his vacillation between the demands of his inner world based on antecedent experience and his understanding intellect focused on the present. Faced with the inevitability of death and punishment because of inner compulsion and external circumstances, he struggles to overcome and, in the end, he must succumb. We remember his death, and are saddened and moved by it, but we return to see the play or reread it, or think about it over and over again, not because of the reaffirmation of the universality of the oedipal conflict or the inevitability of death but because of Hamlet's (and Shakespeare's) struggle. We read or go to re-experience the ironies, the contradictions, the paradoxes, and the fusions in the structure of the play and in the poetry. We are interested in feeling and perceiving words, the flow of time, concrete and abstract spatial elements brought together and separated, and we experience both the rigid diffuseness of our unconscious world and the artist's attempt to use it, to structure it into connections and separations and, by so doing, overcome it.

In painting, even the most representational painting, the creator's struggle for freedom is incorporated. Forms, colors, and objects—all rich in unconscious associations—are juxtaposed and rearranged, producing separations and fusions not seen in ordinary perceptual experience. Rembrandt's faces in his self-portraits alternately seem to look more inward than outward, to look more outward than inward, to fuse with their surroundings, to resemble his father (or another significant person) more and less. Light and shade are in continual dynamic tension with each other. Each portrait bears the marks of struggle, struggle with forms and colors and with what they represent internally as well as struggle with the limitations imposed by nature. The face of Leonardo's *Mona Lisa* takes on the qualities of harshness and softness representative of that painter's ambivalent view of women, but the smile in the creation is a fusion and an attempt to understand, alter, or otherwise develop the view. Remembered landscape scenes in the painting take on human qualities of harshness or softness, but also human separateness from nature is emphasized.

Composers also struggle for psychological freedom. Their struggle is primarily related to structural rigidities of time and of space, and of the Unconscious. Composers deal directly with dynamic factors of tension, separateness, and fusion, separating sound patterns from old associations and bringing them together, producing expectations and inhibiting them. To the extent that music is representational, it represents our basic struggle with separation, tension, and fusion in nature and in human relations. Music and dance also relate significantly to kinesthetic sensations, the movement of our bodies in space and the degree of restriction or freedom we experience or feel. To the extent that music is representational or symbolic of particular emotions and feelings, the composer struggles to define and fuse such represented emotions and feelings in order to clarify and express and/or to develop and overcome them.

The artist's struggle for psychological freedom is embodied in his work and we, his audience, participate in the struggle as well. Vicariously, we empathize with the dynamic forces embodied in the work. Touched are our own unconscious concerns, conflicts, and processes and, to the degree that the artist achieves some relief from the unearthing process, we experience some relief as well. But, more often than not, the work of art stimulates us to begin, or to continue, our own struggle for psychological freedom. On the one hand, experiencing unconscious material and structures reminiscent of dreams in a work of art is reassuring. Externalized, embodied, and shared are our images of sleep and our forbidden and frightening impulses and emotions. On the other hand, unconscious material and the perceptual and cognitive characteristics of artistic structures, imparted by the mirror-image and other processes, produce moderate anxiety and arousal. Effective art arouses us and makes us anxious in this way; we remember it, we talk about it, and we apply it to our lives. We articulate and develop the unconscious and conscious processes embodied in the work. Anxiety is one of the most powerful motivating factors we know; it instigates patients to seek therapy, others to seek power or safety, and all of us to savor, re-experience, and think about art. We are, moreover, aroused by the creator's struggle for freedom, his exposition and definition of values, and his perceptions and reorderings and restructurings of experience. We follow his model and his achievements, and we adopt and learn from his values, his conceptual formulations, and his perceptions about nature and the world. The work of art stays with us and, as we articulate its impact—separate and bring together all the facets, intellectual and emotional—we are also engaged to some degree in a struggle for psychological freedom, freedom from our own unconscious distortions and the stifling aspect of past experience.

Newness itself is anxiety provoking to us all. While we inevitably seek newness and novelty—indeed it seems to satisfy a basic need of which the emotional component is, in all likelihood, arousal—we are always somewhat discomforted in the face of it. Accepting newness and clear-cut novelty always requires some type of realignment of previous feelings and conceptions as well as habits, an experience most human beings find in some measure difficult.[39] Because they almost invariably present something new or suggest a new organization of perception, knowledge, and experience, artistic creations induce anxiety on this basis. This anxiety in turn stimulates our own progression toward intellectual as well as psychological freedom. Moreover, as confrontation with newness promises mastery of the unknown, the greater is the freedom to be attained.

Beside their emotional and psychological impact, the particular values imparted by artistic creations stimulate freedom and independence both from the external environment and from internal psychological struggles. When the work of art embodies particular perspectives on death, tyranny, human relations, or even political processes, it helps us to formulate our own values and perspectives. To the degree that the perspectives are meaningful and adaptive—as they are in enduring works—they help to give us independence and freedom from the cloying entanglements of social interchange, the limitations of a restricted perception of nature and of natural processes, and they guide us to regulate internal psychological forces in accordance with reality and with our own freely formed goals. We learn from art, both in a general way and from the particulars it gives us. We learn the details of history, of diverse experiences outside our ken, of the world of nature and civilization, and of undertakings tried and failed.

Scientific creation, of course, teaches also. Science bestows extensive information about our environment and also tangible products that contribute directly to freedom and independence. More than art, in fact, science frees us from dependence on our physical environment, and particular creations enable us to adapt both broadly and narrowly to this environment in the most effective way possible. Through scientific advance we adapt to the physical world by changing it to suit our needs. The scientific creator's struggle for freedom, however, is not experienced by an audience or recipient as is an artist's. When we sense the concordance with unconscious processes present in some scientific theories, such as the ideas antimatter, quarks, and of "strangeness" and color in subatomic particles, we may experience a twinge of both assurance and discomfort, but we prize scientific creation for the potential freedom it imparts us—even though we may not understand it immediately or directly partake of its effects—with respect to our environment.[40] Newness in scientific creations induces anxiety, just as it does in art. Often this newness has such far-reaching implications—the Copernican view of the universe, Darwin's concept of evolution, Einstein's theories of relativity, Freud's psychoanalysis—that it induces significant reformulation of each individual's conception of himself, including a new struggle for psychological freedom. Acceptance of the Copernican view, for instance, though it evolved gradually and did not occur in the span of an individual lifetime, eventually required each person's reappraisal of the notion of the centrality of man; it also required less absolute reliance on authorities who had insisted on the latter notion.

The motivation toward freedom of the creative person, scientific or artistic in type, is displayed in the daring nature of his thinking. Not satisfied merely with extant formulations, systems and knowledge, the creative scientist drives toward the new. He defies the laws of ordinary logic and is willing to conceive the apparently illogical or inconceivable. He is willing to conceive and to entertain the simultaneous validity of a postulate or body of knowledge that is as far from the known and accepted as possible, the antithetical or opposite postulate or body of knowledge. He is willing to conceive and tolerate mental images that defy the accepted data of the senses, conceptions that bring two or more discrete entities into the same space. Although I do not know how particular conceptual opposites or specific sensory representations of discrete entities are chosen—especially by the scientist, the artist tends to develop an antithetical context or to choose particular representations because of his personal interest and understanding of social and moral concerns—I suspect that the motivation toward freedom is important. I suspect the scientist struggles to free himself from the tightly constructed and highly elaborated content and structure of his domain of interest. He searches either for essential oppositions and discrete entities underlying enormous complexity or else for more extended—grander, if you will—ones. Thus, Einstein's breakthrough conception was free of the highly elaborated particular substance and data of both gravitation and electromagnetic induction. It involved the essential elements, from both domains, of a person falling and of motion. It also contained Einstein's magnificent addition of the element of rest and the simultaneous manifestation of rest with motion. Darwin's breakthrough conception consisted of going beyond Malthus's presentation of the negative effects of population growth. He very likely conceptualized the maladaptive essence of the struggle indicated, and with daring freedom he conceived the never-before-postulated grand antithesis and the idea that this noxious circumstance was at the same time adaptive. These constructs of Einstein and Darwin are the quintessence of simultaneous opposition in that they contain both conflict and harmony. In our current ignorance of direct or reciprocal connections between a motive to freedom and cognitive operations, it is necessary only to emphasize the continuing stimulation and self-propelling power of such dynamic constructions. And despite our ignorance of the enormous panoply of particular sources of wisdom and intellect transmitted within great works—the scope and intricacy of the novel, scientific theory, philosophical exegesis, painting, or sonata—we can focus on the relationship between freedom and the overall genesis, development, and structure, the created aspect of these achievements.

Creation and freedom are inextricably connected because a creation in any field is a testification to, and an embodiment of, freedom and independence. Creations always stand apart from nature. They derive from nature, they represent nature, and they refer to it, but they are independent entities. The work of art is a unity unto itself, and the scientific creation stands above and outside of nature with its own internal coherence. The work of the creator is the result of free and independent thinking; regardless of whether the product is a work of art, a scientific discovery or theory, or another type of creation, it bears the stamp of his uniqueness. Watson and Crick's discovery of the double helix structure of DNA bears the characteristics of Watson and Crick's unique formulation; others would have described it differently, or even emphasized different aspects, such as the single-strand functioning more recently uncovered. And Einstein's general theory of relativity is surely Einstein's alone. Each person carves out the particular dimensions of the blooming, buzzing confusion he or she will articulate. Freedom itself resembles creation—it always consists of separateness along with bringing together or connectedness. As human beings, we are neither free nor independent unless we observe, and are mindful of, our contacts and connections with others and with nature. And we must be mindful of our intrinsic separateness, uniqueness, and individuality. When we glimpse the goddess emerging from the head of the creator, it must remind us of the nature of our freedom.

NOTES

References to the works of Sigmund Freud are to the *Standard Edition of the Complete Psychological Works,* translated and edited by J. Strachey et al. (London: Hogarth Press), with original publication date, and year and volume number of the Hogarth edition.

Introduction

1. A. E. Housman, "I think it best not to make any alterations . . . as it makes the public fancy one is inspired," from a letter to Grant Richards, July 24, 1898, quoted in: G. Richards, *Housman* (London: Oxford University Press, 1941), p. 22.

2. Throughout this book, the term "process" refers to an organized series of actions or events directed to some end, in distinction particularly to isolated acts or behaviors. Processes are functions of some type of system. The creative process is distinct from the creative person or agent as well as the created product. The creative process is a function of the creative agent and it results in the created product.

3. Broadly, intrinsic value is the type attributed to works of art, while instrumental value is the type connected to pragmatic usefulness and science. See C. I. Lewis, *An Analysis of Knowledge and Valuation* (LaSalle, Ill.: Open Court Publishing, 1946), for further elaboration and discussion of these terms.

4. Sheer productivity is also to be distinguished from creativity. One may, for instance, produce numerous books, journal articles, or paintings and few, if any, would be either new or more than minimally valuable. Although prolific producers are sometimes called creative, prolixity is better classified as a type of achievement than a form of creativity.

5. Seneca, *Tranquility of Mind,* trans. W. B. Langsdorf (New York: Putnam's, 1900), pp. 90–91. As Aristotle's remark is not retrievable in the original, the statement is usually quoted in Seneca's Latin rendition: *Nullum existat magnum ingenium sine mixtura dementiae fuit* (Seneca, *Dialoquorum Libri IX–X.* [Turin: C. B. Peravia, 1948], p. 37).

6. There are some recent well-known examples, among poets especially, but the list would include: the artists Hieronymus Bosch, Vincent van Gogh, Wassily Kandinsky, Albrecht Dürer; the scientists James Faraday, Isaac Newton, Tycho Brahe; the composers Robert Schumann, Hugo Wolf, Camille Saint-Saëns; the writers Johann Hölderlin, August Strindberg, Arthur Rimbaud, Edgar Allan Poe, Charles Lamb, Guy de Maupassant, Theodore Roethke, Ezra Pound, T. S. Eliot, Virginia Woolf, Hart Crane, Sylvia Plath, Jonathan Swift, Lewis Carroll (Charles Dodgson), William Blake, Ernest Hemingway, Charles Baudelaire; and the philosophers Arthur Schopenhauer and Friedrich Nietzsche. For bibliographic references on these persons (particularly artists), see A. Rothenberg, and B. Greenberg, *The Index of Scientific Writings on Creativity: Creative Men and Women* (Hamden, Conn.: Archon Books, 1974). To those who would spontaneously argue with this list, I would emphasize that the fact of psychosis need in no way detract from the greatness or significance of each of these person's works.

7. As with any type of human function, it is difficult to separate out a clear-cut process solely directed toward creation. Many behaviors and functions overlap. For analytic purposes, however, I shall throughout this book discuss the creative process as though it were an ongoing and separate phenomenon. Postulated overlappings are, of course, considered in methodologies adopted and in conclusions.

8. A. Rothenberg, "Poetry and Psychotherapy: Kinships and Contrasts," in *Poetry the Healer*, ed. J. Leedy (Philadelphia: Lippincott, 1973), pp. 91–126.

9. See esp. A. Rothenberg, and C. R. Hausman, *The Creativity Question* (Durham, N.C.: Duke University Press, 1976). For a comprehensive bibliography of scientific research on creativity, see Rothenberg and Greenberg, *Index: Creative Men and Women,* and also A. Rothenberg, and B. Greenberg, *The Index of Scientific Writings on Creativity: General, 1566–1974* (Hamden, Conn.: Archon Books, 1976).

10. E. Frenkel-Brunswik, "Intolerance of Ambiguity as an Emotional and Perceptual Personality Variable," *Journal of Personality* 18 (1949):108–43; T. W. Adorno; E. Frenkel-Brunswik; D. J. Levinson; and R. N. Sanford, *The Authoritarian Personality* (New York: Harper & Row, 1950).

11. S. Mednick, "The Associative Basis of the Creative Process," *Psychological Review* 69 (1962): 221.

12. A. Koestler, *The Act of Creation* (New York: Macmillan, 1964). Koestler has recently postulated a "Janus principle" as the general characteristic of organismic systems, or what he calls "holons." This particular principle consists of manifesting "both the independent properties of wholes and the dependent properties of parts" and has little direct connection to his theory of creative action. See Koestler, *Janus: A Summing Up* (New York: Random House, 1978).

13. E. DeBono, *Lateral Thinking: A Textbook of Creativity* (London: Ward Lock Educational, 1970).

14. M. Wertheimer, *Productive Thinking* (New York: Harper, 1945).

15. J. P. Guilford, *The Nature of Human Intelligence* (New York: McGraw-Hill, 1967); J. P. Guilford and R. Hoepfner, *The Analysis of Intelligence* (New York: McGraw-Hill, 1971).

16. See N. Frye, *Fearful Symmetry: A Study of William Blake* (Princeton, N.J.: Princeton University Press, 1947); S. T. Coleridge, *Biographia Literaria* (1817), ed. J. Shawcross (London: Oxford University Press, 1973), esp. 1: 197 ff., 2:12–13, 219–63.

17. K. Burke, *Permanence and Change* (New York: New Republic, 1935).

18. To my literary readers who may be bothered by the mixing of mythological metaphors, Athena for creations and Janus for a phenomenon within the creative process, let me say I have done so intentionally. An unmixed designation of metaphors might run the risk of being considered a purely poetic (in this context, an unscientific) account of creation. Moreover, to adopt a particular myth consistently entails a risk of suggesting that whatever material I present was intrinsically known to the ancients, i.e., incorporated implicitly in the particular myth. I do not think that such is the case, either implicitly or otherwise, and would therefore not like to suggest it. It is of some interest, within a limited framework of citing ancient wisdom, that the god Janus was considered by the Romans to be the *creator* of the world and was the god of beginnings and of communication. It is also of some interest that the Greek goddess Athena, and her Roman counterpart, Minerva, were each goddess of wisdom, a factor surely related to creativity, in their respective cultures. Furthermore, both Janus and Athena (or Minerva) also functioned primarily as protectors in time of war: Janus was also god and protector of doorways and Athena was also the protector of fortresses. This could suggest an implicit connection between wisdom or creativity and protection against destruction and violence.

Chapter 1

1. In view of a long literary tradition relating humans and animals, this idea may not at first seem strikingly original. A fuller understanding of its implications and structure, spelled out in chap. 3, however, should demonstrate its originality.

2. The use of the term "manifest content" follows Freud's distinction between the experienced and reported, or manifest, elements in the dream and the underlying meaning, or latent content, of these elements.

3. Note also a more tacit connection: the grandmother's hands are blunted with the last joints missing from the fingers and therefore they are constructed like the single-joint ends of a horse's leg, ending in the hoofs.

4. The subject and I had worked together for some time when these dreams occurred and he had become skilled in analyzing his own dreams. Although I believe our work together contributed to his impressive self-analysis, an analysis I consider to be accurate as far as it goes, I must add that the subject himself had always shown extraordinary capacity and insight with respect to dream analysis. While such capacity seemed to be related to his poetic gift and his proficiency with symbols and images, I would not generalize about it. I would not consider—there is no evidence from my work with other poets—that this capacity for dream analysis is necessarily related to poetic creativity.

5. See S. Freud, "The first short dream is often the conclusion of a second longer dream—the first is the 'dependent clause' and the second, the 'principal clause' " ("The Interpretation of Dreams," 1900, [London, 1964], 4:315).

6. Findings in recent sleep research have suggested other psychological and biological functions of dreams as well, but the wish-fulfillment function has not been at all disproven. Recent theories of dreaming as a discharge or restorative function, in fact, support a wish-fulfillment function. See chap. 2 below for further discussion.

7. See further discussion of psychological analysis of art in the following chapter and *passim.*

8. This thought and image will be described further in chap. 3.

9. An example from the completed poem "In Monument Valley" is the phrase "Hell's Gate." He pointed out to me that it related to the German word *hell,* meaning "light." See chap. 3 for other connections with the word "hell."

10. In another work I have discussed, and presented evidence for, the emotional importance of literary revisions (see A. Rothenberg, "The Iceman Changeth: Toward an Empirical Approach to Creativity," *Journal of the American Psychoanalytic Association* 17 [1969]:549–607). Further discussion and data pertaining to this issue will be presented here (see chaps. 4, 11, and 13).

11. E. Bishop, "Cirque d'Hiver," in *The Complete Poems* (New York: Farrar, Straus & Giroux, 1969), p. 34.

12. Note the possibility that the city of Troy mentioned in the poem, which the poet specifically meant to have a double reference to both the ancient seaside site of the Trojan war and the North American, northern hemisphere city of New York State, therefore has the dual characteristics of being both on the seaside and in the north, as does the place in the dream.

13. Elizabeth Bishop was, at the time of this dream, living in Brazil. Hence, there is a further indication of a direct connection between Bishop and the grandmother.

14. That is, before Freud provided a key to the understanding of the incoherency (see chap. 2).

15. This should not be construed to apply merely to the so-called confessional poetry of poets such as Lowell, Plath, Berryman, Hughes, and Sexton. While some critics have pointed out that the work of these poets seems to be particularly concerned with unconscious material related to dreams, I am not referring to such a particular style but to a universal characteristic of the creative process. See A. Alvarez, *The Savage God* (New York: Random House, 1972), for an interesting discussion of this group of poets.

Chapter 2

1. If creations are considered to be entities that are truly new, i.e., radically different from any antecedents, their appearance is an intrinsic mystery, i.e., it cannot be explained. Explanation implies prediction and, as the truly new is unprecedented and therefore unpredictable, it cannot be explained. See C. R. Hausman, *A Discourse on Novelty and Creation* (The Hague: Martinus Nijhoff, 1975); for a review of others arguing similar positions and a critique, see Rothenberg and Hausman, *Creativity Question,* pp. 3–26; also see chap. 12 below.

2. V. G. Hopwood, "Dream, Magic and Poetry," *Journal of Aesthetics and Art Criticism* 10 (1951–52):152.

3. See references to Blake and Coleridge in P. Bartlett, *Poems in Process* (Oxford: Oxford University Press, 1951). Also see Novalis, *Schriften* (1798); J. P. Richter, "Uber die naturliche Magie der Einbildungskraft," *Leben des Quintus Fixlein, Samtliche Werke,* 33 vols. (G. Reimer, 1840), 3:235 ff.; F. Nietzsche, *The Will to Power,* trans. and ed. W. Kaufman and trans. R. J. Hollingdale (New York: Random House, 1967), pp. 419–53, 539–43.

4. Throughout this book, I shall refer to and discuss primary process thinking as defined by Sigmund Freud in chap. 7 of "The Interpretation of Dreams" (1900). See also D. Rapaport, *Organization and Pathology of Thought: Selected Sources* (New York: Columbia University Press, 1951), for an analysis and appraisal of primary process thinking.

5. M. Bonaparte, *The Life and Works of Edgar Allan Poe* (London: Imago, 1949), p. 651.

6. Famous examples are E. Jones, *Hamlet and Oedipus* (New York: Norton, 1949; rev. ed., New York: Doubleday, 1954); H. Sachs, *The Creative Unconscious* (Cambridge, Mass.: Sci-Art Publishers, 1942, 1951); D. Schneider, *The Psychoanalyst and the Artist* (New York: International Universities Press, 1950). One of the earliest literary critics to develop a theory of poetry as analogous to dreams was F. C. Prescott (see *Poetry and Dreams* [Boston: Four Seasons, 1912]). Recent literary critics have modified Prescott's position and have produced some interesting works of criticism (see F. C. Crews, *The Sins of the Fathers: Hawthorne's Psychological Themes* [New York: Oxford University Press, 1966]; S. Lesser, *Fiction and the Unconscious* [Boston: Beacon Press, 1957]; N. Holland, *Psychoanalysis and Shakespeare* [New York: McGraw-Hill, 1964, 1966]). For a comprehensive bibliography of scientific writings on art and artists, many of which treat the work of art as analogous to the dream, see Rothenberg and Greenberg, *Index: Creative Men and Women.*

7. S. Freud, "Creative Writers and Daydreaming" (1908 [1907]) (London, 1959), 9:143–53.

8. S. Freud, "Jokes and Their Relation to the Unconscious" (1905) (London, 1960), vol. 8.

9. His basic position, from which he never really strayed, is famously summed up as follows: "Before the problem of the creative artist, analysis must, alas, lay down its arms" (S. Freud, "Dostoevsky and Parricide" [1928 (1927)] [London, 1961], 21:177).

10. See E. Kris, "The Psychology of Caricature," for the first use of the term, and "On Inspiration" and "On Preconscious Mental Processes" for detailed elaborations; all are in his *Psychoanalytic Explorations in Art* (New York: International Universities Press, 1952).

11. M. Graf, *From Beethoven to Shostakovich* (New York: Philosophical Library, 1947).

12. J. J. Montmasson gave dreaming an important role in imaginative work of any kind, including that of science (*Invention and the Unconscious,* trans. H. S. Hatfield [New York: Harcourt Brace, 1932], pp. 43 ff. W. B. Cannon reported that a great discovery by the Nobel Prize winner, Otto Loewi, apparently occurred in a dream (*The Way of an Investigator* [New York: Norton, 1945], p. 60.) Kekulé's discovery of the structure of the benzene ring is usually also cited as an instance of a scientific breakthrough resulting from a dream. Although Kekulé himself used the term "dream" *(Traum)* in admonishing

his colleagues to creative thinking, the full context and correct translation of his remarks requires some significant modification of the traditional interpretation of his account (for references and further discussion, see n. 13, chap. 5 below). The misconception about Kekulé's account has an important bearing on the point I am making here. His report of the discovery of the benzene ring does bear out that there is a similarity between dream process and creative thinking, but the obverse factor—the mirror-image relationship—has not previously been considered or recognized.

13. H. Poincaré, *Science and Method*, trans. F. Maitland (New York: Dover Press, 1952).

14. Cannon, *Way of an Investigator.*

15. G. Wallas, *The Art of Thought* (New York: Harcourt, Brace, 1926).

16. Plato, *The Ion*, trans. Lane Cooper, ed. E. Hamilton and H. Cairns, in *Plato: The Collected Dialogues* (New York: Bollingen Foundation, 1961), p. 220.

17. I. Kant, *The Critique of Judgment*, trans. J. C. Meredith (London: Oxford University Press, 1952), esp. pp. 188 ff.

18. Nietzsche, *Will to Power*, pp. 420 ff.

19. B. Blanshard, *The Nature of Thought* (Atlantic Highlands, N. J.: Humanities Press, 1964), vols. 1 and 2, esp. 2:166–211.

20. In this section I shall continue to discuss artistic creativity as the general model; creativity in science and other fields will be considered later.

21. According to the classical formulation of primary process thinking, it occurs in infants prior to the development of reality testing and other ego functions. It is designated as "primary" because it is first in the human developmental sequence. Consequently, it is identified as an early or primitive mode of cognition.

22. Kris, *Psychoanalytic Explorations*, p. 312.

23. P. Noy, "A Revision of the Psychoanalytic Theory of the Primary Process," *International Journal of Psychoanalysis* 50 (1969):155–78.

24. G. J. Rose, "Creative Imagination in Terms of Ego 'Core' and Boundaries," *International Journal of Psychoanalysis* 45 (1964):75–84.

25. See D. W. Winnicott, "Transitional Objects and Transitional Phenomena" (1951), in his *Collected Papers* (New York: Basic Books, 1958); A. H. Modell, "The Transitional Object and the Creative Act," *Psychoanalytic Quarterly* 39 (1970):240–50; W. Muensterberger, "The Creative Process: Its Relation to Object Loss and Fetishism," in *Psychoanalytic Study of Society* (New York: International Universities Press, 1962), 2:161–85.

26. S. Arieti, *The Intrapsychic Self: Feeling, Cognition and Creativity in Health and Mental Illness* (New York: Basic Books, 1967). Also see more recently, Arieti, *Creativity: The Magic Synthesis* (New York: Basic Books, 1976), esp. p. 12.

27. For Freud, fully coherent linguistic statements and constructs were converted by means of primary process operations into the disrupted, incoherent visual representations in dreams. See J. G. Schimek, "A Critical Reexamination of Freud's Concept of Unconscious Mental Representation," *International Review of Psycho-analysis* 2 (1975):171–87, for an excellent critique, based on information from developmental psychology, of this aspect of Freud's formulation of primary process operation. See also, M. Edel-

son, "Language and Dreams: The Interpretation of Dreams Revisited," *Psychoanalytic Study of the Child* 27 (1972):203–82, for a discussion of the analogies between Freud's dream theory and the linguistic theory of Noam Chomsky. Some years ago, at a conference at Austen Riggs Center in Stockbridge, Mass., Erik Erikson pointed out that Freud's method of psychoanalysis contained a significant element of bias against visual perception and thought: asking the patient to lie on a couch where he and the analyst could not see each other's faces denied the importance of the visual mode.

28. Though some will argue that dreams reveal as well as conceal, the primary thrust is toward censorship. All representations, including symbols of any type, could be said to have a double nature and to reveal as well as conceal. From the perspective of psychological function, however, the relative degree of the two factors of revelation and concealment is absolutely critical. The fact of a thrust toward censorship follows from Freud's discovery that the function of dreams is to keep the dreamer asleep; wishes are expressed in censored form. This discovery has not been superceded or overturned (see Freud, "The Interpretation of Dreams"; W. Dement, "The Biological Role in REM Sleep," in *Sleep Physiology and Pathology,* ed. A. Kales [Philadelphia: Lippincott, 1969], pp. 245–65; J. G. Salamy, "Sleep: Some Concepts and Constructs," in *Pharmacology of Sleep,* eds. R. L. Williams and I. Karacan [New York: Wiley, 1976], pp. 53–82). A recent erudite attempt at challenging the wish fulfillment and disguise principles from a neurobiological viewpoint (R. W. McCarly and J. A. Hobson, "The Neurobiological Orgins of Psychoanalytic Dream Theory," *American Journal of Psychiatry* 134 [1977]:1211–21; and Hobson and McCarley, "The Brain as a Dream State Generator: An Activation-Synthesis Hypothesis of the Dream Process," *American Journal of Psychiatry* 134 [1977]:1335–48) is unsuccessful because it fails to take the guardian of sleep discovery adequately into consideration. Moreover, in their emphasis on patterns of neuronal generation as responsible for dreams, the authors do not adequately explain their postulated interaction between neurophysiological and psychological effects. They state that there is an integration of "disparate sensory, motor and emotional elements via condensation, displacement and symbol formation" (p. 1346), but outside of postulating a mysterious isomorphism with the "state of the nervous system during dreaming sleep" (p. 1347), they do not explain why the particular mechanisms of condensation, displacement, and symbol formation function at all. This challenge to psychoanalytic dream theory therefore comes back full circle to rely on the basic contribution of psychoanalysis, i.e., explication of the dream mechanisms, to the understanding of dreams.

29. Recognizing that psychological and biological functions are not necessarily distinct, I make the distinction here for the purpose of expository clarity.

30. Dement, "Biological Role of REM Sleep," pp. 245–65. For a recent assessment see Salamy, "Sleep: Some Concepts and Constructs," pp. 71–73.

31. Throughout this book I shall use the term "unearthing" to refer to bringing unconscious material *close or closer* to awareness without necessarily bringing this material directly or fully into awareness.

32. D. E. Berlyne, *Aesthetics and Psychobiology* (New York: Appleton, Century, Crofts, 1971).

33. See C. Darwin, *The Descent of Man*, 2d ed. (New York: Appleton, 1892), esp. chap. 3.

34. S. Freud, "Introductory Lectures on Psychoanalysis, Part III" (1916–17) (London, 1964), 16:377.

35. Some may see this explanation as the traditional Aristotelian one emphasizing pity and terror. To set the record straight, the factor of anxiety arousal and resolution is more complicated and, very likely, also more basic than pity and terror together. For one thing, anxiety arousal enters into both emotions.

36. Freud quoted the common expression *Träume sind Schäume* (dreams are froth) as representative of the scientific viewpoint of that and earlier times (Freud, "Interpretation of Dreams," p. 133).

37. See discussion in L. L. Altman, *The Dream in Psychoanalysis* (New York: International Universities Press, 1969), pp. 1–4.

38. S. Freud, *Die Träumdeutung* (Leipzig: Franz Deuticke, 1900), title page. Although Freud specified in *Gesammelte Schriften* 3 (1925):169, that "this line of Virgil (*Aeneid*, VII, 312) is intended to picture the efforts of the repressed instinctual impulses" (trans. J. Strachey et al.), he nevertheless used it as a general motto for the whole volume on dreams. This motto also embodies his basic approach to psychology, i.e., gaining insight into the higher mental processes such as normal development, consciousness, adaptive behavior, and creativity through studying the "lower" ones: abnormal functioning, the unconscious, everyday mistakes, and the dream.

39. There is growing tendency among psychoanalysts, and psycholinguists as well, to emphasize the revelatory aspects of symbols and of dreams. This must be considered an "after the fact" position. We now understand dreams and symbols because we have many more tools to do so. Only rarely can it be said that the dreamer's motive is primarily communication; dreams are a more "royal road to the Unconscious" than waking life primarily because the complexities of consciously motivated activities are absent. Waking activities are, now that we have the tools for understanding, also royal roads to the Unconscious.

40. M. Kanzer, "The Communication Function of Dreams," *International Journal of Psychoanalysis* 36 (1955):260–66; A. Roland, "The Context and Unique Function of Dreams in Psychoanalytic Therapy: Clinical Approach," *International Journal of Psychoanalysis* 52 (1971):431–39; J. Klauber, "On the Significance of Reporting Dreams in Psychoanalysis," *International Journal of Phychoanalysis* 48 (1967):424–32; M. S. Bergmann, "The Intrapsychic and Communication Aspects of the Dream," *International Journal of Psychoanalysis* 47 (1966):356–63.

Chapter 3

1. See discussion of the role in inspiration in creativity in A. Rothenberg, "Poetic Process and Psychotherapy," *Psychiatry* 35 (1972):238–52.

2. Throughout this book, I use the term "process" to apply to the creative thought patterns because, in all cases, there is an extended sequence consisting of selecting and designating either opposites or discrete entities, posing them simultaneously, fusing them, etc., and applying these conceptions to the creative task.

3. Note the distinct difference between this formulation and the "regression in the service of the ego" of Ernst Kris. Kris states that the creator shifts between primary process and secondary process thinking. Primary process productions are modified by the secondary process *after* they appear (Kris, *Psychoanalytic Explorations,* esp. pp. 291–318).

4. Some might want to insist that this earlier image of rocks as simultaneously alive and dead was the original janusian thought. I have no quarrel with such a point and it simply starts the janusian process at an earlier phase of the creation of the poem. The poet himself, when reading over the section above after I had written it, suggested that the structure "Hot pumice blew . . . causing the Elephant Rock to howl" was a formulation of an inanimate production of the animate and was therefore an instance of the type of thinking I was describing.

5. The precise relationship between cognitive functions and affect or feelings as well as psychological defenses against affects has not yet been satisfactorily worked out in any current psychological theory, including psychoanalysis. Whether cognition is always accompanied by affect, whether cognition and affect are two aspects of a single process, or whether it is appropriate to postulate an integration of the two processes that does away with the distinction entirely has not yet been settled. Although there is a good deal of disagreement about the most appropriate formulation among these alternatives, there is general agreement that the old sharply drawn distinction between cognition and affect—in common parlance, between thought and feeling or between intellect and emotion—is incorrect. Cognition and affect are clearly highly interrelated. See J. C. Harper et al., eds., *The Cognitive Processes: Readings* (Englewood Cliffs, N.J.: Prentice-Hall, 1964), esp. part 5, "Cognition, Motivation and Personality," pp. 387–582; S. J. Korchin, "Anxiety and Cognition," in *Cognition: Theory, Research, Promise,* ed. C. Scheerer (New York: Harper & Row, 1964); J. S. Antrobus, ed., *Cognition and Affect* (Boston: Little, Brown, 1970); J. C. Mancuso, *Readings for a Cognitive Theory of Personality* (New York: Holt, Rinehart, & Winston, 1970). A full description of janusian thinking, as well as the other thought processes discussed in this work, requires the settling of problems such as this one. It also requires the elaboration of a more complete theory of the relationship between thought and personality than is currently available. Certainly, such a task cannot be attempted here.

6. S. Freud, "Negation" (1925) (London, 1961), 9:235–42.

7. Anna Freud, in her classical work on ego defenses, did not even include negation as one of the ten familiar and prominent defenses; see A. Freud, *The Ego and the Mechanisms of Defense* (New York: International Universities Press, 1946). As an exception to the general psychoanalytic neglect of this defense, David Rapaport gave it some attention in his seminal work *(Organization and Pathology of Thought).* Also, Jacques Lacan, the psychoanalytic innovator, developed an aspect of his own theory from Freud's article on negation; see J. Lacan, "Réponse au Commentaire de Jean Hyppolite sur la 'Verneinung' de Freud," *La Psychoanalyse* 1 (1956):41–58; also in *Ecrits* (Paris: Editions du Seuil, 1966), pp. 381–99.

8. In distinction to other defenses, the person using negation often recognizes its defensive function fairly readily, even when it is not pointed out by another person.

9. This process is often mistakenly attributed to the defense of projection. The writer is considered to be projecting his inner feelings onto the *characters* he has created. But such a formulation overlooks the psychological reality of the situation and, like primary process theories of creativity, tends to overlook the creative person's rationality and his clear grasp of distinctions during the creative process. The writer does not project his inner feelings onto his characters as though they were real people. He knows they are fictional and are products of his own mind at all times. But he does attribute what he writes to aesthetic necessity alone and he negates any direct relationship to himself. In an unpublished experiment carried out by Eugene Shapiro and myself, results conclusively demonstrated that literary works are not analogous to projective tests, projection is not a major or a primary factor in literary creation (A. Rothenberg and E. Shapiro, "Psychological Approaches to Literature," in prep.).

It is also incorrect to label the major mechanism as either intellectualization or rationalization on the basis that the concept of aesthetic necessity is used as a justification. For one thing, writers acknowledge that this phase is related in some way to unconscious processes and therefore defensive justification alone could not be involved. Rather than mere justification, there is an active *negation* of any direct congruence between the specific contents of the material and the specific contents of the writer's own Unconscious.

10. A. Rothenberg, "Autobiographical Drama: Strindberg and O'Neill," *Literature and Psychology* 17 (1967):95–114.

11. Rothenberg, "Poetic Process and Psychotherapy."

12. Eric Plaut has called my attention to the possibility that the defense of ego splitting operates in conjunction with janusian thinking. Ego splitting was defined by Freud: "Two psychical attitudes have been formed instead of a single one—one, the normal one, which takes account of reality, and another which under the influence of instincts detaches the ego from reality. The two [contrary attitudes] exist alongside of each other" ("An Outline of Psychoanalysis" [1940 (1938)], 23 [London, 1964] 202; see the remainder of the discussion on pp. 202–4 and see also S. Freud, "Splitting of the Ego in the Process of Defense" [1940 (1938)], 23 [London, 1964] 275–78). Although Freud only sketched out the nature of this defense, it has received a good deal of attention by modern theorists of the borderline states such as Otto Kernberg and Margaret Mahler. Primarily, it functions in a rather holistic way to involve large segments of the psychic structure, and it consequently has a major role in borderline states and psychosis. Although it could be involved initially in stimulating an orientation toward janusian thinking in particular creative persons, or more fleetingly in the initial development of specific janusian formulations by a broader range, it functions primarily to produce psychopathological structures and symptomatology. In this splitting defense, the "two attitudes persist side by side throughout their lives without influencing each other" (Freud, "Outline," p. 203), a point also emphasized by Kernberg. Splitting therefore would not allow for the creator's awareness of contradiction in janusian formulations, nor for the unearthing of unconscious material. As a psychopathological defense, splitting bears the same type of mirror-image relationship to creative functions as do other psychopathological mechanisms (see discussion here, chap. 6). As an initiator of an orientation to

janusian thinking as well as a fleeting instigator of particular janusian formulations, splitting functions in a manner similar to ambivalence (see discussion here, chap. 9). See also O. F. Kernberg, "Borderline Personality Organization," *Journal of the American Psychoanalytic Association* 15 (1967):641–85; M. S. Mahler, "A Study of the Separation-Individuation Process, and Its Possible Application to Borderline Phenomena in the Psychoanalytic Situation," *Psychoanalytic Study of the Child* 26 (1971):403–25; J. F. Masterson, "The Splitting Defense Mechanism of the Borderline Adolescent: Developmental and Clinical Aspects," in *Borderline States in Psychiatry*, ed. J. E. Mack (New York: Grune & Stratton, 1975), pp. 93–102.

13. His achievement of insight could not be attributed to my presence except in a small way; he frequently had such insights on his own, and he and I were merely discussing the poem in a general fashion, not exploring any underlying meanings.

14. I think the improvement in the poem throughout the stages of revision I have presented and the aesthetic power of these lines is self-evident without further elaboration. I think all would agree that the stillness coming both from the horse and the star is consistent with the body-soul overtones of the poem, that this construction conveys a sense of unity and peace, and that other aspects of the changes are highly effective. But to go into any further critical and aesthetic discussion at this point would clearly be diversionary, if indeed it is necessary.

15. See A. Roe, "A Study of Imagery in Research Scientists," *Journal of Personality* 19 (1951):459–70; F. C. Bartlett, "The Relevance of Visual Imagery to the Process of Thinking," *British Journal of Psychology* 17 (1927):23–29; P. McKellar, *Imagination and Thinking* (New York: Basic Books, 1957), and "Three Aspects of the Psychology of Originality in Human Thinking," *British Journal of Aesthetics* 3 (1963):129–47; A. Paivio, *Imagery and Verbal Processes* (New York: Holt, Rinehart & Winston, 1971). For a philosophical account and an assessment, see E. Casey, *Imagining* (Bloomington: Indiana University Press, 1976).

16. Clearly, the reference to space in this context is to the subjective experience of inner space in the mind. The expression, "imaginary space in the mind" conveys the sense of what I am referring to, but I have avoided it because of the possibility of a confusing tautology. Homospatial thinking is a component of artistic imagination and, therefore, it would be confusing to use the term "imaginary" in any part of a definition. The most accurate description psychologically is that the homospatial experience fills, or totally occupies, consciousness.

17. I refer to the mother and grandmother interchangeably because I think it is clear that they have equal psychological importance here, at least as far as the wish to be cared for is concerned. The grandmother was a constant presence throughout his childhood and was a direct object of the poet's longings. That there are differences in his orientation to his mother and grandmother will become clearer in the next chapter, but we are not interested in pursuing a detailed analysis or reconstruction of the poet's life, his unconscious contents, or the psychodynamic structure of his personality in this book. By the same token, the wish-fulfilling memory of the summers with the three women could be a screen memory for infancy, but this deeper psy-

chodynamic sheds no further light on the matter being discussed, nor does it in any way invalidate the analysis.

18. In this discussion we are entering into an especially complicated theoretical area because the use of homophones enters into punning. Freud extensively analyzed the psychological structure of puns and proposed that they were products of a process he called "joke work," a process similar to dream work; see Freud, "Jokes and Their Relation to the Unconscious." In chapter 10 below, I shall take up this theoretical issue more fully, but I must emphasize here that I am discussing not the construction of a pun but how a homophone is used in the creation of a poem.

19. Freud's explanation (see ibid.), stated here, of the psychodynamics of the pleasure derived from puns is, I believe, quite correct.

20. The process through which the "Hell's Gate" phrase was finally arrived at seems also to have been influenced by janusian thinking. First designated as a heavenly gate, the nether region may also have been in the poet's mind at the same time. He did, in any event, shift from heaven directly to its opposite in these versions; no intermediary was formulated at all. It is quite common for janusian thinking or aspects of the janusian process to operate in concert with homospatial thinking.

21. H. Hartmann, E. Kris, and R. Lowenstein, "Notes on the Theory of Aggression," in *The Psychoanalytic Study of the Child* (New York: International Universities Press, 1949), vols. 3 and 4:9–36; H. Hartmann, *Essays in Ego Psychology* (New York: International Universities Press, 1964); A. Solnit, "Aggression: A View of Theory Building in Psychoanalysis," *Journal of the American Psychoanalytic Association* 20 (1972):435–50.

22. Freud, "Creative Writers and Daydreaming," p. 153.

23. Kris, *Psychoanalytic Explorations.*

24. G. J. Rose, "Narcissistic Fusion States and Creativity," in *The Unconscious Today,* ed. M. Kanzer (New York: International Universities Press, 1971), pp. 495–505.

25. "The general assumption is that under certain conditions the ego regulates regression, and that the integrative functions of the ego include voluntary and temporary withdrawal of cathexis from one area or another to regain improved control" (Kris, *Psychoanalytic Explorations,* p. 312).

Chapter 4

1. I shall give as much information in this account as seems necessary to clarify material pertaining to the poem. Details about specific relationships and circumstances will, however, be omitted.

2. The possibility arises, of course, that the stipulated process of unearthing the unconscious seen in the creation of this poem was stimulated entirely by the poet's relationship to me. However, I have previously reported another empirical study of the creative process, carried out totally in my absence and the absence of any psychiatrist, where the characteristic of unearthing unconscious processes was clearly present; see Rothenberg, "The Iceman Changeth." I should also point out that, whatever my role in the process, it is the concomitance of unearthing the unconscious and the successful creation of a poem that must be explained.

3. I have discussed the relationship between insight and inspiration in some detail elsewhere; see my "Poetic Process and Psychotherapy." The data pre-

sented here provide a more elaborate documentation and confirmation of the previous suggestions and propositions.

4. Monument Valley, Arizona, does have a rock formation named the Two Sisters.

5. After reading the foregoing material as documented here, the poet agreed that it was all quite plausible and probable. As the nature of our relationship was not a psychotherapeutic one, there was no need or possibility to pin down these connections further.

6. In a strict use of the term, a symbol is a substitute for something else which it may or may not superficially resemble. I have here used the expression "figurative representation" in lieu of "metaphor" in order to avoid confusion when I later refer to artistic metaphors specifically. In a broad sense, however, figurative representations can be considered equivalent to metaphors. Metaphors, or the here-designated "figurative representations," both represent other entities and integrate elements of these entities into their content. There is today much interest and discussion about such definitions and distinctions; see esp. L. C. Knights, and B. Cottle, eds., *Metaphor and Symbol* (London: Butterworth, 1960).

7. During that day, he had formulated the lines (as still part of the last three stanzas):

> A gentle broken horse
> For all he knew it could have been I who first
> Broke him, rode him, abandoned him.
> When I went off to study or to war.

8. The reference to that time period continued with various alterations, through successive versions. Different aspects swing back and forth, as follows (numbering of versions is mine):

> 1. One summer dusk a year or two after the war
> 2. One spring dusk before I went to war
> 3. One spring dusk during a lull in the endless war
> 4. One spring twilight during a lull in the war

See also previous note.

9. Despite the lag of several days, the appearance of Bishop in the dream is appropriately considered day residue; in fact, it could also be considered residue connected to the poet's having temporarily, and probably uncomfortably, abandoned the poem for a few days.

10. It is not yet clear exactly how this particular process operates in other creative endeavors besides poetry and imaginative literature. Sound similarities and identities play an important role in musical creation; see chap. 10 below for a discussion of how homospatial thinking functions in pattern superimposition in music. Pattern superimposition would involve sound similarities and identities in a manner analogous to creative rhyming and alliteration in poetry.

11. Many other psychological themes, e.g., yearning and loss, are suggested in the data presented but they are not pertinent to the discussion of the creative process here. The dream analyses also do not include all the connections and elaborations of a complete presentation of data and an exploration, but such a presentation would be digressive.

12. Beardsley uses the word "incept" for this initial idea, a good term, I think; see M. Beardsley, "On the Creation of Art," *Journal of Aesthetics and Art Criticism* 23 (1965):291–304. Also, see chap. 5 below.

13. Note that the Garden of Eden idea, as represented in a reference to giving the horse an apple core, is antithetical to the idea of being at death's door; pleasure and gratification are opposed to death and punishment. The qualities of the setting in the poem are therefore simultaneously antithetical, another janusian formulation introduced at a very early stage of the writing of the poem.

14. Freud's essay, "Creative Writers and Daydreaming," has been rightly criticized for focusing only on escapist and hack writing in discussing the role of fantasy in literary creativity. It is partly because of this error that psychoanalysis has come to be identified with a view of art as a manifestation of regressive primary process thinking and wish fulfillment. Although Freud was certainly right to emphasize personal roots in creativity and the importance of fantasy and wish fulfillment at some level, he neglected the qualitatively different psychodynamics of good art I am discussing here ("Creative Writers and Daydreaming," pp. 141–54).

15. See Rothenberg, "The Iceman Changeth," a study in which the process of revision is seen as a feature providing both an understanding of the creator's unconscious processes and the means whereby a literary work is improved and given aesthetic value.

16. The reference to Shoup and his farm, a real person and a real place, escaped deletion because it was not connected to any immediate personal or psychological concern and because it had a specific aesthetic purpose. This purpose was not changed or contradicted by the overall aesthetic and psychological thrust of the final poem. Shoup's farm was included initially because it gave particularity and contemporaneity to the mythic allusion to Troy. The personalized reference to a particular farm and person known to the poet was an intentional aesthetic device designed to contrast with, to establish continuity with, and to heighten the immediacy of the ancient Trojan war. The real Shoup's farm was located near Troy, N.Y., a factor introducing the connection into the poet's mind. The inclusion of such incidental personalized references in order to enhance the overall aesthetic effect does not at all contradict the general point made here about the concealing aspect of literary revision.

17. Here, the philosophical question arises of whether this shift from description and documentation represents actual discontinuity with the past and radical newness (see n. 1, chap. 2 above, and chap. 12 below). The author's constant act of separating himself and his immediate preoccupations and concerns from the object he is creating is, I think, an intensive and profound one and thereby warrants consideration as a core feature of the production of radical newness. As I discuss below in chap. 13, such separating concomitantly involves a bringing together; the author also continually connects the material to real experience and to the natural world during this phase of the process.

Chapter 5

1. Pertinent to this discussion is the fairly recent proposition advanced by T. S. Kuhn in *The Structure of Scientific Revolutions* (Chicago: University of Chicago Press, 1970) that science advances through the development of

paradigms. Kuhn distinguishes between normal scientists and those who develop paradigms producing revolutionary advances. Normal scientists follow paradigms until they are no longer productive or heuristic; at that point, a new paradigm is produced and normal scientists proceed to test it out and apply it. While I am not specifically concerned with formulations about scientific progress here, Kuhn's account of the making of scientific paradigms roughly parallels the concept of creativity in science outlined in these pages.

2. Though it has become somewhat fashionable to doubt the authenticity of the apple story, two of Newton's contemporaries, Pemberton and Stukeley, both report that the first idea occurred while Newton was sitting alone in the garden; see H. Pemberton, *A View of Sir Isaac Newton's Philosophy* (Dublin, 1728). Stukeley's famous account is as follows: "After dinner, the weather being warm, we went into the garden and drank thea, under the shade of some appletrees, only he and myself. Amidst other discourse, he told me, he was just in the situation, as when formerly, the notion of gravitation came into his mind. It was occasion'd by the fall of an apple, as he sat in a contemplative mood. Why should that apple always descend perpendicularly to the ground, thought he to him self. Why should it not go sideways or upwards, but constantly to the earths centre? Assuredly, the reason is, that the earth draws it . . ." (W. Stukeley, *Memoirs of Sir Isaac Newton's Life,* 1752 [London: Taylor & Francis, 1936], pp. 19–20).

3. F. Darwin, ed., *The Autobiography of Charles Darwin and Selected Letters* (New York: Dover, 1958), pp. 42–43 (repr. of 1892 ed.).

4. Poincaré, *Science and Method,* pp. 52–53.

5. J. Hadamard, *The Psychology of Invention in the Mathematical Field* (Princeton, N.J.: Princeton University Press, 1949), p. 81.

6. See numerous examples presented in the following: Montmasson, *Invention and the Unconscious;* Koestler, *Act of Creation;* R. M. Harding, *An Anatomy of Inspiration* (Cambridge: W. Heffer & Sons, 1940); Wallas, *Art of Thought.*

7. H. von Helmholtz, "An Autobiographical Sketch (1891)," in *Selected Writings of Hermann von Helmholtz,* ed. R. Kahl (Middletown, Conn.: Wesleyan University Press, 1971), p. 474.

8. R. Dubos, *Pasteur and Modern Science* (Garden City, N.Y.: Anchor Books, Doubleday, 1960), p. 114; Cannon, *Way of an Investigator,* pp. 59–60; C. F. Gauss, *Works,* vol. 5 (Gottingen: W. F. Kaestner, 1863–1933), p. 609; reported by S. Chandrasekhar in E. Fermi, *Collected Papers* (Chicago: University of Chicago Press, 1965), 2:927.

9. "Mein geistiges Auge, durch wiederholte Gesichte ähnlicher Art geschärft, unterschied jetzt . . . von mannigfacher Gestaltung" (A. Kekulé, *Berichte der Deutsche Chemische Gesellschaft* [1809], 23:1306 [above translated by Meredith Nunes; see n. 13 below for the entire passage]).

10. "Hypnopompic" refers to the semiconscious state preceding awakening; "hypnagogic" refers to a similar state prior to falling asleep. Visual imagery frequently occurs in both states.

11. Wallas, *Art of Thought.*

12. Of course, we must remember that unconscious factors play a role in all thinking. Here we are discussing the heightened influence or activity of unconscious processes characteristic of all creative thinking.

13. In Japp's initial translation of the lecture (F. R. Japp, "Kekulé Memorial Lecture," in *Memorial Lectures Delivered before the Chemical Society;* also listed as: W. H. Perkins, ed., *Chemical Society Memorial Lectures, 1893–1900* [London: Gurney & Jackson, 1901], pp. 97–169) in which Kekulé described his discovery, the word *Halbschlaf* is given as "a doze." The following is Kekulé's entire original account in German:

> Da sass ich und schrieb an meinem Lehrbuch; aber es ging nicht recht; mein Geist war bei anderen Dingen. Ich drehte den Stuhl nach dem Kamin and versank in Halbschlaf. Wieder gaukelten die Atome vor meinen Augen. Kleinere Gruppen hielten sich diesmal bescheiden im Hintergrund. Mein geistiges Auge, durch wiederholte Gesichte ähnlicher Art geschärft, unterschied jetzt grössere Gebilde von mannigfacher Gestaltung. Lange Reihen, vielfach dichter zusammengefügt; Alles in Bewegung, schlangenartig sich windend und drehend. Und siehe, was war das? Eine der Schlangen erfasste den eigenen Schwanz and höhnisch wirbelte das Gebilde vor meinen Augen. Wie durch einen Blitzstrahl erwachte ich; auch diesmal verbrachte ich den Rest der Nacht um die Consequenzen der Hypothese auszuarbeiten.
>
> Lernen wir träumen, meine Herren, dann finden wir vielleicht die Wahrheit:
>
> "Und wer nicht denkt,
> Dem wird sie geschenkt,
> Er hat sie ohne Sorgen"
>
> aber hüten wir uns, unsere Träume zu veröffentlichen, ehe sie durch den wachenden Verstand geprüft worden sind. [Kekulé, *Berichte,* pp. 1306–7.]

Although Kekulé does use the German world for dream, *Traum,* in his comments to his colleagues about the event as follows, "Let us dream, gentlemen," the full context of his remarks is seldom cited and includes: "take care not to make our dreams known before they have been worked through by the wakened understanding" (translations by Meredith Nunes). He may therefore have been using the word *Traum* in a figurative sense to connote free and daring thinking. As for the actual description of the content of his thought, the following passage indicates a homospatial process whereby two discrete entities are superimposed or fused and occupy the same space: "My mind's eye, sharpened by repeated visions of similar art, distinguished now greater structures of manifold form: long rows, sometimes more closely fitted together, all twining and turning in snake-like motion. But look! What was that? One of the snakes seized hold of its own tail, and the whole form whirled mockingly before my eyes (trans. by F. R. Japp, modified by M. Nunes)."

The atoms are first visualized as strung out in twisting and twining rows with a snakelike *quality.* Immediately following that, a snake is visualized as seizing its own tail. The context makes clear that he saw both the atoms in rows and a snake as occupying the same space because, after describing the snake's action, he says that a single "whole form" ("conformation" per Japp) whirled before his eyes. In his mind's eye ("my mental eye" per Japp), he visualized a snake and rows of atoms together and soon he had articulated a new identity, the structure of the benzene molecule.

A janusian formulation also contributed to the creative result. The circular structure of the benzene molecule was derived from the snake seizing its own tail. As a snake can only seize with its mouth, opposite aspects of the snake, head and tail, were present simultaneously in the initial conception. As I have stated previously, homospatial and janusian thinking often operate conjointly to produce creations. Although we cannot be certain, because of the ambiguity about Kekulé's state of consciousness, whether the process consisted only of a mirror image of dreaming or whether there was also an element of dreaming itself, the key cognitions took the form of homospatial and janusian conceptions.

14. For an interesting history and an extensive documentation of the numerous contributors to the ultimate solution, see R. Olby, *The Path to the Double Helix* (Seattle: University of Washington Press, 1974). Although the book clearly reveals that Watson, like all other creative scientists, stood on the shoulders of gaints, it is important to note that Olby's account does not differ from Watson's on any salient point.

15. J. D. Watson, *The Double Helix* (New York: Atheneum, 1968), pp. 125–26.

16. This essay came to my attention long after I discovered janusian thinking and other processes in literary creativity.

17. A. Einstein, "The Fundamental Idea of General Relativity in Its Original Form" (circa 1919, trans. by Gerald Holton), manuscript, Einstein Archives, Institute for Advanced Study, Princeton, N.J.; acknowledgment to Otto Nathan, Trustee of the Estate of Albert Einstein, and to Helen Dukas for permission to quote this essay, and to Professor Holton for permission to use his translation. Holton has published other portions and versions of the above translation in *Thematic Origins of Scientific Thought: Kepler to Einstein* (Cambridge, Mass.: Harvard University Press, 1973), pp. 363–64; and "Finding Favor with the Angel of the Lord: Notes Toward the Psychobiographical Study of Scientific Genius," in *The Interaction Between Science and Philosophy*, ed. Y. Elkana (New York: Humanities Press, 1975), pp. 369–71.

18. Kris, together with Abraham Kaplan, uses the term "stringencies" to apply to the possible modes of dealing with a problem; clearly, there are quite a large number of such stringencies in science in comparison with art. The creative scientist must be aware of and capable of applying all, or most, of the appropriate stringencies; E. Kris and A. Kaplan, "Aesthetic Ambiguity," in Kris, *Psychoanalytic Explorations*, pp. 243–72.

19. An interesting suggestion, and an observation completely coordinate with the analysis I am presenting here, is to be found in an analysis by Gerald Holton, the Einstein scholar. Holton points out the existence of polarities in Einstein's personality and cites both his sensitivity to polarities in science and his talent for dealing with antitheses. Einstein's interest in the polarity between the Faraday and Maxwell-Lorentz theories, according to this, was an instance of his special sensitivity to such types of problems. Holton's observations are quite fruitful and are especially gratifying because they were arrived at independently; they were not published at the time I first described janusian thinking (G. Holton, "On Trying to Understand Scientific Genius," *American Scholar* 41 [1971]:95–110).

20. "I shall never believe that God plays dice with the world," he said; quoted in P. Frank, *Einstein: His Life and Times*, trans. G. Rosen (New York: Knopf, 1947), p. 208. One can respect this as a religious belief, but certainly it is also a strongly emotional "nonobjective" position for a man of science.

21. Routinely, in psychoanalytic treatment, scientists and other intellectuals reveal the emotional and unconscious roots of their interest in a particular research area and a particular type of conceptual problem. Moreover, applied psychoanalytic research on creative people frequently gives plausible evidence of such connections; see Rothenberg and Greenberg, *Index: Creative Men and Women,* for bibliographic references. For an interesting attempt at arriving at some of the unconscious bases of Newton's thought, see F. E. Manuel, *A Portrait of Sir Isaac Newton* (Cambridge, Mass.: Harvard University Press, 1968). For references to cognition and motivation research, see chap. 3, n. 5, above.

22. Sidney Blatt suggested to me that Einstein's thinking of the idea of falling from a roof could have represented an unconscious suicide wish. It could also have represented an unconscious wish to fly. A wish to fly often represents a deeper wish for free and uninhibited sexuality and sexual gratification.

23. Einstein's description of a person falling from the roof of a house suggests a homospatial conception along with a janusian one. It is well known that Einstein's thinking was highly visual in nature; he reported that himself; see Hadamard, *Psychology of Invention,* pp. 142–43, and Wertheimer, *Productive Thinking.*

24. Darwin, *Descent of Man,* p. 41.

25. H. Gruber and P. H. Barrett, *Darwin on Man* (New York: Dutton, 1974), p. 105. This is an excellent analysis which correctly discusses scientific creative thinking as a sequence of processes rather than a single act. The author of the theoretical section (Gruber) recognizes the overall thrust of Darwin's idea, but misses the factor of simultaneous antithesis.

26. Darwin, nevertheless, accorded Wallace full acknowledgment.

27. "Letter by A. R. Wallace to A. Newton, 1887," in F. Darwin, *Autobiography,* p. 200.

28. The translation of the passage here by Maitland is later than Halsted's frequently quoted one (H. Poincaré, *The Foundations of Science,* trans. G. B. Halsted [New York: Science Press, 1913], p. 387). The reflexive verb form *s'accrocher* that Poincaré himself used (*Science et Méthode* [Paris: Flammarion, 1924], pp. 50–51) is literally translated as "to fasten together as in crocheting." The Maitland rendition here of "coalesce" seems more appropriate than Halsted's previous one of "collide." The only questionable aspect of Poincaré's statement, questionable with respect to being a description of homospatial thinking, is his use of the word *combinaison,* i.e., "combination." New identities or integrations of previously discrete entities result from homospatial thinking, while "combinations" are additive results. Whether the discrepancy is significant or whether Poincaré was following common usage and referring broadly to a bringing together that would include either or both combination and integration cannot, unfortunately, be ascertained.

29. Quoted by R. Hart, "Reminiscences of James Watt," in *Transactions of the Glasgow Archeological Society* (Glasgow: James MacNab, 1868), 1:4.

30. For an account of this history, see R. H. Thurston, *A History of the Growth of the Steam Engine* (Ithaca, N.Y.: Cornell University Press, 1939).

31. E. Benedictus, "Les Origines du verre Triplex," *Glaces et Verres* 201 (1930):9–10; phrases quoted from this article were translated by Brenda Casey.

32. This type of thinking was also characteristic of Sigmund Freud, see A. Rothenberg and W. Sledge, "The Creative Thinking of Sigmund Freud" (in preparation).

33. Quoted in R. Dubos, *Louis Pasteur: Free Lance of Science* (Boston: Little, Brown, 1950), pp. 95–96.

34. Ibid., pp. 99–100.

35. Dubos, *Pasteur and Modern Science*, pp. 113–14. The collaborator mentioned was Pasteur's nephew, Adrien Loir, who, as an early teacher of René Dubos, conveyed the story to him (personal letter from Dubos, July 9, 1975).

36. See aspects of Koestler's, Montmasson's, Harding's, and Hadamard's interpretations: Koestler, *Act of Creation*; Montmasson, *Invention and the Unconscious*; R. M. Harding, *Towards a Law of Creative Thought* (London: Kegan, Paul, Trench, Trubner Co., 1936), esp. the account of James Watt, pp. 140–44; Hadamard, *Psychology of Invention*.

37. R. Feynman, interviews by C. Weiner, 1966–1977; Oral History Collection, American Institute of Physics, New York, N.Y., p. 259.

Chapter 6

1. See Bartlett, "Dreams and Visions," *Poems in Process*, pp. 62–77.

2. Kuhn, *Structure of Scientific Revolutions*, esp. pp. 174–210.

3. A number of scientific discoveries have occurred at a point in the discoverer's life when he had suffered an important setback or loss. Metchnikoff discovered phagocytosis after having lost his position at the university (see B. M. Fried, "Metchnikoff's Contribution to Pathology," *Archives of Pathology* 26 [1938]:700–16; Freud discovered the "key" to dream interpretation after having a disappointing experience relating to one of his patients (see E. H. Erikson, *Identity: Youth and Crisis* [New York: Norton, 1968], pp. 197–204); Semmelweis discovered the cause of puerperal sepsis when his admired teacher died of an infection contracted while performing an autopsy (see W. J. Sinclair, *Semmelweis: His Life and His Doctrine* [Manchester: University Press, 1909], pp. 48–50).

4. See discussion of creativity in an idiot-savant in D. S. Viscott, "A Musical Idiot-Savant; a Psychodynamic Study, and Some Speculations on the Creative Process," *Psychiatry* 33 (1970):494–515.

5. Some aestheticians, such as Benedetto Croce, propose that the creation occurs completely in an artist's mind. This proposal, like claims by artists that a creation occurred all at once in a dream, ignores the critical making and creating that occurs during writing, painting, experimenting, etc.; see B. Croce, *Aesthetic As Science of Expression and General Linguistic*, trans. D. Ainslie (London: Macmillan, 1909). Also, for data regarding the creator's interest in discovery, see J. W. Getzels and M. Csikszentmihalyi, "The Creative Artist as an Explorer," in *Human Intelligence*, ed. J. McV. Hunt (New Brunswick, N.J.: Transaction, 1972), pp. 182–92; J. W. Getzels and M. Csikszentmihalyi, *The Creative Vision: A Longitudinal Study of Problem Finding in Art* (New York: Wiley, 1976).

6. Beardsley, "On the Creation of Art," p. 291.

7. Freud, "Creative Writers and Daydreaming," p. 150.

8. Ibid., pp. 152–53.

9. The psychological circumstances here can best be understood in the

context of the functioning of repression. A common instance is losing or forgetting some article of importance, such as a key or valuable paper. The more one strives to find such an article, the more difficult it is to find. This is because one is struggling directly against repression, the repression that caused the forgetting in the first place. When, however, one turns to another task or else rests in some way, the location of the lost article eventually comes into consciousness. The explanation is that, through rest or distraction, the ego has become strengthened and therefore repression is relaxed because the anxiety or conflict producing the need for repression is either lessened or else can be more easily faced. So, too, the creator is blocked on a problem because some conflict or anxiety is involved in its unconscious meaning or structure. He turns away from the task and, when in a relaxed ego state, he overcomes the anxiety and solves the problem through creative cognitive processes. Another contributory factor may be that the time lapse and distraction allows for inessential elements of the problem to drop away. It should be emphasized that the explanation here sharply contradicts the classical formulation of an "incubation" phase in the creative process (see Wallas, *Art of Thought*).

10. Although metaphors are often quoted out of context, a full appreciation of them usually involves some knowledge of their original meaning. Thus, we cannot appreciate "iron curtain" without at least knowing that it applies to a state of partial hostility between people or nations. Restoring metaphors to a context is one of the goals of poets who revivify clichés and dead metaphorical expressions.

11. See Rothenberg, "Autobiographical Drama," for a formulation of O'Neill's oedipal competition with Strindberg as a factor in literary influence; see also H. Bloom, *The Anxiety of Influence* (New York: Oxford University Press, 1973), for some elaborations and further applications of this type of phenomena.

Chapter 7

1. I am referring, of course, to Taoism and Buddhism as theological systems that have commanded the greatest number of adherents in the Orient. While adherence to specific beliefs is difficult to establish, especially in modern day China, the popular folk religion in that country has been largely based on Confucianism. Confucianism, in turn, has depended on Taoism for its theological underpinnings and exegesis.

2. Hans-Joachim Schoeps, *The Religions of Mankind,* trans. R. Winston and C. Winston (New York: Doubleday, 1966), pp. 40 ff.

3. The Judeo-Christian idea of God and Satan is generally considered to have occurred sequentially. Biblical historians often point out that the Hebrew word for the evil one, Shatan, appears late in sacred writings, long after the monotheistic conception of God was well established. But there is also evidence that an ill-defined supernatural principle of evil was contained in the earliest Judaic formulations, long before the name Shatan was actually used. If this is so, and the original Jewish conception of monotheism was really the product of a single thinker such as Abraham, or the Egyptian Ikhnaton, then the monotheistic idea itself consisted of the conception of the simultaneous presence of good and evil in a single supernatural force, and was a product of janusian thought.

4. Quoted in Chang Chung-yuan, *Creativity and Taoism: A Study of Chinese Philosophy, Art, and Poetry* (New York: Harper & Row, 1970), p. 31.

5. See Schoeps, *Religions of Mankind*, p. 178, for this formulation of Nirvana, a generally accepted one.

6. See D. T. Suzuki, *The Zen Doctrine of No-Mind*, ed. C. Humphreys (London: Rider & Co., 1969), p. 52.

7. See R. E. Allen, ed., *Greek Philosophy: Thales to Aristotle* (New York: Free Press, 1966), pp. 25–56.

8. C. K. Ogden, *Opposition* (Bloomington: Indiana University Press, 1932, 1967).

9. F. Nietzsche, *Ecce Homo* (1908), trans. C. Fadiman (New York: Modern Library, 1927), p. viii.

10. Ibid., pp. 96–97.

11. In view of Nietzsche's frequent references to his own poor health at the time he achieved these germinating ideas, there is an interesting shift to the opposite here. As Nietzsche manifestly identified himself with Zarathustra, this could have been a janusian formulation of both poor health and great healthiness simultaneously. His health was very bad throughout the period of conceiving and writing *Zarathustra*. After the event described in the quotation above, he wrote, "For a few weeks afterwards I lay ill in Genoa. Then followed a depressing spring in Rome, where I escaped with my life" (Ibid., p. 101). The conception of "great healthiness" for Zarathustra could specifically have resulted from defensive operations of reversal or turning to the opposite, overcompensation, and denial in fantasy. Such defensive operations do not preclude the possibility of a janusion formulation which, although it is a cognitive event, has a range of defensive and emotional concomitants (as do all cognitive events). If, however, it were solely a defensive operation and Nietzsche did not consciously conceive poor health and "great healthiness" simultaneously, it would *not* be a janusian formulation. Only an emotional predisposition to thinking in opposites would be operating.

12. Ibid., p. 107. In this passage, the rhetorical interrogatory form has been converted to the indicative. As is clear from reading Nietzsche's words in context, the above construction accurately represents the essence of the "Zarathustra type" idea.

13. Ibid., p. 102.

14. Ibid.

15. S. Kierkegaard, Journal IV, A108, 1843, quoted and translated by W. Lowrie in Editor's Introduction of S. Kierkegaard, *Fear and Trembling* (Princeton: Princeton University Press, 1941), pp. xii–xiii. Of interest is Kierkegaard's reference to "divine madness," the term Plato used to describe creativity. In his linking of a simultaneous antithesis to a concept applying to creativity, Kierkegaard seems intuitively to be following the same line I have formulated here.

16. Coleridge, *Biographia Literaria*, 2:262.

17. W. Blake, *The Marriage of Heaven and Hell* (ca. 1790), p. 3, reproduced in facsimile, with an introduction by Clark Emery (Coral Gables, Fla.: University of Miami Press, 1971).

18. M. Ernst, "Inspiration to Order," in *The Painter's Object*, ed. and trans. M. Evans (London: G. Howe, 1937), p. 79.

19. This, I believe, is a factor in a widespread tendency of philosophers and psychologists to study and discuss creativity through a focus on visual art. Writers, of course, face an "empty" or blank page when they start to write and composers face silence, but both the connection between emptiness and definite spatial factors is lacking and the contrast between absence (no words, no sounds) and presence (literature, music) is less marked and is experienced less.

20. Even the dramatic visual effects produced by the psychedelic drugs, if they were to be structurally useful in the way described, would not be sufficient to produce art. Conception *and* execution are requisite.

21. Quoted in E. Protter, ed., *Painters on Painting* (New York: Grosset & Dunlap, 1971), p. 41.

22. J. Albers, interview by Brian O'Doherty on National Educational Television, 1962; Center for Cassette Studies Tape no. 27605, Audio Text Cassettes, 8110 Webb Avenue, North Hollywood, California 91605.

23. H. Moore [Untitled], in *Unit 1,* ed. H. Read (London: Cassell & Co., 1934), p. 29.

24. H. Moore, interview by Donald Carroll, England; Center for Cassette Studies Tape no. 29818, Audio Text Cassettes, 8110 Webb Avenue, North Hollywood, California 91605.

25. As music involves motion and rest in a prominent way, it should be no surprise that composers often allude to such ideas.

26. P. Klee, *The Thinking Eye: The Notebooks of Paul Klee,* ed. J. Spiller (New York: G. Wittenborn, 1961), p. 51.

27. Ibid., p. 50.

28. Chang Chung-yuan, *Creativity and Taoism,* see esp. pp. 199–238.

29. K'ung Yen-shih, in *The Secret of Painting,* quoted in ibid., p. 212.

30. Shen Tsung-ch'ein, in *The Study of the Painting of Chieh Chou,* quoted in ibid., p. 218.

31. J. Albers, *Interaction of Color* (New Haven: Yale University Press, 1963), p. 32.

32. Albers, "Interview by O'Doherty."

33. Focused on a single geometric shape as they were, the *Homage to the Square* paintings as a group also emphasized and enhanced diversity of color and of color effect.

34. Vincent van Gogh, *Further Letters of Vincent van Gogh to His Brother* (London: Constable, 1929), p. 166.

35. Michel E. Chevreul, *De la Loi du contraste simultané des couleurs et de l'assortiment des objets coloriés* (1839); trans. by C. Martel as *The Principle of Harmony and Contrast of Colors, and Their Application to the Arts* (London: Bohn, 1860).

36. See John F. A. Taylor, *Design and Expression in the Visual Arts* (New York: Dover, 1964), pp. 177 ff.

37. Quoted in C. R. Leslie, *Memoirs of the Life of John Constable,* ed. A. Shirley (London: Medici Society, 1937), p. 118.

38. Ibid., p. 394.

39. Quoted in English translation from Redon's journal and letters in R. Goldwater and M. Treves, *Artists on Art* (New York: Pantheon, 1945), p. 361.

40. P. Mondrian, "Plastic Art and Pure Plastic Art," in *Circle,* ed. J. L.

Martin, B. Nicholson, and N. Gabo (London: Faber & Faber, 1937), p. 46. Note that Mondrian's designation "same value but of a different aspect and nature" corresponds to the definition of opposition presented here in chapter 8.

41. See K. Clark, *Leonardo da Vinci* (Cambridge: University Press, 1939); see also P. Taylor, ed., *The Notebooks of Leonardo da Vinci* (New York: New American Library, 1960). An example of Leonardo's janusian thinking is the following: "The motions of a dead thing will make many living ones flee with pain and lamentation and cries—*of a stick, which is dead*" (from Taylor, p. 180).

42. Richter described this drawing as follows: "they are back to back because they are opposed to each other; and they exist as contraries in the same body, because they have the same basis, inasmuch as the origin of pleasure is labour and pain, and the various forms of evil pleasure are the origin of pain" (J. P. Richter, ed., *The Notebooks of Leonardo da Vinci* [New York: Dover, 1970], 1:353).

43. A. Conti, "Leonardo pittore," *Conferenze Fiorentine* (Milan: 1910), pp. 108–9.

44. Clark, *Leonardo da Vinci*, p. 118.

45. Attributed by Eugene Muntz to an important nineteenth-century critic whose nom-de-plume was Pierre de Corlay (E. Muntz, *Leonardo da Vinci: Artist, Thinker, and Man of Science* [London: William Heinemann, 1898], 2: 155–56).

46. H. Keller and B. Cichy, *Twenty Centuries of Great European Painting* (New York: Sterling, 1958), p. 103.

47. W. Gaunt, *A Guide to the Understanding of Painting* (New York: Harry N. Abrams, 1968), pp. 246–47. Gaunt uses the term "contrast" as synonymous with "opposite," not in the broader sense discussed here in chapter 8 below.

48. Taylor, *Design and Expression*, p. 95.

49. See A. H. Barr, Jr., *Picasso: Fifty Years of His Art* (New York: Museum of Modern Art, distrib. by Simon & Schuster, 1946), p. 272.

50. I am grateful to Rudolf Arnheim for his scholarship and his penetrating work, *Picasso's Guernica: The Genesis of a Painting* (Berkeley: University of California Press, 1962). This book first brought these sketches to my attention and it contains many valuable insights, although Arnheim's analysis is not the same as the one I am presenting here.

51. Up to this point, my description follows that of Arnheim. The material following is my own.

52. An unintentional but striking affirmation of the presence of a simultaneously opposed spatial orientation is provided by the content of a controversy between two leading interpreters of the painting, Anthony Blunt and Rudolf Arnheim. In his book on the painting (*Picasso's Guernica* [New York: Oxford University Press, 1969]), Blunt takes issue with Arnheim as follows: "Some writers, e.g. Rudolf Arnheim, *Picasso's 'Guernica,'* Berkeley, California, 1962, p. 19, identify the setting of the painting as the interior of a room, but, summary though the drawing of the buildings is, there is no question they are intended to show exterior walls, and the electric light could be a street lamp just as well as a hanging light in a room" (p. 59, note). Rather than taking sides and opting for a street lamp or a hanging light, we must surely consider that both of these trained and perceptive observers are correct in part:

the scene is both an interior and an exterior. Despite their training and perceptiveness, neither Arnheim nor Blunt would necessarily notice this simultaneous opposition unless prepared to see it.

53. Quoted in Barr, *Picasso* (italics in the original).

54. Frank L. Wright, "Organic Architecture Looks at Modern Architecture," in *Seven Arts*, ed. F. Puma (New York: Doubleday, 1953), p. 68.

55. Quoted in R. Erickson, *Sound and Structure in Music* (Berkeley: University of California Press, 1975), p. 105.

56. Hans Mersmann, "Versuch einer musikalischen Wert ästhetik," *Zeitschrift für Musikwissenschaft*, 17 (1935):40 (passage translated by Meredith Nunes).

57. Langer reinterprets Mersmann's assertion, substituting the term "ambivalence" for expression of opposites, and Epperson endorses her term rather than Mersmann's; see S. Langer, *Philosophy in a New Key* (Cambridge, Mass.: Harvard University Press, 1942), pp. 243–45; G. Epperson, *The Musical Symbol* (Ames: Iowa State University Press, 1967), pp. 73 ff. It is not clear whether these later authors merely prefer the term "ambivalence" because of its psychological connotations. Epperson emphasizes conflict in the ambivalence, "the simultaneous push-pull of conflicting forces" (p. 307) and therefore continues to suggest polarity. Neither of the two later authors take any issue whatsoever with the idea of simultaneity, however; "ambivalence" therefore refers, at the very least, to expression of a simultaneously double or multiple entity. I was not aware of Mersmann's formulation when I first discovered janusian thinking and was therefore quite interested to find such a specification and an indirect support for its operation in music from an independent and sophisticated source.

58. L. Bernstein, *The Unanswered Question* (Cambridge, Mass.: Harvard University Press, 1976).

59. In its initial and still essential meaning, counterpoint, that major musical mode of Western music in the sixteenth and seventeenth centuries surviving into modern times, is considered to be the sounding of two or more opposite voices simultaneously. Sometimes used interchangeably with the term "polyphony" to refer merely to multiple different voices together, true counterpoint seems to consist of the construction of simultaneous opposition. Many rules for constructing counterpoint in musical composition have, of course, been formulated, but the creative composer has usually been distinguished by his own special contrapuntal effects. Although it is often difficult to ascertain whether clear-cut opposition or antithesis is involved because the form has become so elaborated and familiar, the creative composer's capacity to contruct effective contrapuntal themes within the context of an entire piece may require janusian thinking, and the specification and bringing together of opposites.

60. M. Graf, *Die innere Werkstatt des Musikers* (Stuttgart: Verlag von Ferdinand Enke, 1910), p. 206.

61. A. Schmitz, *Beethovens zwei Prinzipe: Ihre Bedeutung fur Themen und Satzbau* (Berlin: Ferd. Dummlers Verlagsbuchhandlung, 1923), pp. 3–11.

62. In the next chapter, I draw a distinction between contrast and opposition. However, in the case of music, where opposition is totally based on context, it is justifiable to equate contrast and opposition.

63. Bernstein, *Unanswered Question,* pp. 41–42, figs. 112–25.

64. W. A. Mozart, a letter, quoted in E. Holmes, *The Life of Mozart* (London: Dent, 1912), p. 256. This statement is taken from Mozart's only extant reference to his processes of creating. Although Holmes indicates he has seen the letter, first published by the critic Rochlitz in vol. 17 of the *Allgemeine Musikalische Zeitung,* and therefore vouches for its authenticity, some experts have raised questions about Mozart's authorship; see ibid., p. x; see also H. Mersmann, ed., *Letters of Wolfgang Amadeus Mozart,* trans. M. M. Bozman (London: Dent, 1928). Mersmann states the letter is a *bona fide* Mozart (p. vii).

65. S. T. Coleridge, *The Friend: A Series of Essays* (London: William Pickering, 1850), 1:166. Coleridge is specifically referring to a work of Cimarosa, a composer he calls "Mozartish." I was unaware of this passage and Coleridge's use of the Janus metaphor at the time I discovered the janusian process, and again it seems a type of independent support from a major creator. Coleridge's use of the phrase "a female Janus" is of double interest because, in posing the opposite sex designation for the traditionally male god Janus, he enriches the metaphor by means of his, the poet's, own janusian thinking.

66. See Hindemith's description quoted in chap. 10 below. Schubert indicated he composed a complete song in a single flash; quoted in Harding, *Anatomy of Inspiration,* p. 71.

67. Claudio Monteverdi, Preface, *Eighth Book of Madrigals:* Madrigali guerreri ed amorosi, 1638; quoted in S. Morgenstern, ed., *Composers on Music* (New York: Pantheon, 1956), p. 22. In addition to other deletions for the sake of readability and clarity, I have deleted the translated word "although" in the sentence describing the agitato style as sixteenth notes sounding together with the voice in slow tempo; otherwise this statement, put in a negative way, might be confusing for those not familiar either with the musical issues involved, or with Monteverdi's music.

68. See A. Schoenberg, *Style and Idea* (New York: Philosophical Library, 1950).

69. Ibid., p. 105.

70. Interestingly, Bernstein maintains that Schoenberg's actual musical pieces were not as successful and, by implication, not as creative as was Schoenberg's theoretical impact. Alban Berg, Schoenberg's disciple, wrote more pleasing music than Schoenberg, according to Bernstein, because he composed pieces that were both nontonal and tonal at once; see Bernstein, *Unanswered Question,* pp. 301 ff.

71. I. Stravinsky and R. Craft, *Conversations with Igor Stravinsky* (Garden City, N.Y.: Doubleday, 1959), *Memories and Commentaries* (Garden City, N.Y.: Doubleday, 1960), *Expositions and Developments* (Garden City, N.Y.: Doubleday, 1962), *Dialogues and a Diary* (London: Faber & Faber, 1968), *Themes and Episodes* (New York: Knopf, 1966); I. Stravinsky, *Stravinsky: An Autobiography* (New York: Simon & Schuster, 1936), *Poetics of Music,* trans. A. Knodel and I. Dahl (Cambridge, Mass.: Harvard University Press, 1947).

72. Stravinsky, *Poetics of Music,* pp. 36–37.

73. R. Sessions, *The Musical Experience of Composer, Performer, Listener* (Princeton: Princeton University Press, 1950), pp. 50, 52–54.

74. It seems likely that he did not want to be confusing or digressionary by mentioning this; or else he considered it unimportant.

75. See J. L. Mursell, *The Psychology of Music* (New York: Norton, 1937), p. 274.

76. See Harding, *Anatomy of Inspiration*, p. 76.

77. L. B. Meyer, *Emotion and Meaning in Music* (Chicago: University of Chicago Press, 1956, 1961).

78. It might be considered that kinesthetic experience is closer to visual experience than it is to auditory in that one can "shut off" motion, i.e., stand still. However, the experience of continued internal motion, heartbeat, etc., subjectively disrupts such a state.

79. Aristotle, *The Poetics*, trans. W. H. Fyfe (Cambridge, Mass.: Harvard University Press, 1932); Coleridge, *Biographia Literaria*, 2:12; C. Brooks, "The Language of Paradox," in *The Language of Poetry*, ed. A. Tate (Princeton, N.J.: Princeton University Press, 1942), p. 37; Burke, *Permanence and Change*, pp. 71–168.

80. R. Graves, *On English Poetry* (London: William Heinemann, 1922), p. 13; M. Beardsley, "The Metaphorical Twist," *Philosophy and Phenomenological Research* 22 (1962):293–307; M. Black, "Metaphor," *Proceedings of the Aristotelian Society* 55 (1955):273–94; Hausman, *Discourse on Novelty and Creation*, esp. pp. 85–123.

81. Joseph Conrad, Preface to *Nostromo*, *Nostromo* (London: Dent, 1918), p. ix.

82. These passages are from Anthony Trollope, *Autobiography* (New York: George Munro, 1883), pp. 75 and 77. In the account here, Trollope's ironic comments about the poor wisdom of his intentions have been deleted, as they clearly refer to his disappointment about the extent of the book's sales. *The Warden* was, nevertheless, his first popularly successful novel.

83. "Herefordshire" is emended from the 1883 edition, according to *The Oxford Trollope* (1950). The 1883 edition has "Worcestershire."

84. V. Woolf, *A Writer's Diary*, ed. L. Woolf (New York: Harcourt, Brace, 1954), pp. 139–40.

85. Rothenberg, "The Iceman Changeth."

86. Quoted in T. Cole, *Playwrights on Playwrighting* (New York: Hill & Wang, 1960), p. 232, from an interview in the newspaper *La Nacion*, Buenos Aires, November 30, 1933, translated by Joseph M. Bernstein.

87. C. Bonnefroy, ed., *Conversations with Eugene Ionesco* (London: Faber & Faber, 1970), pp. 72–73.

88. A. Rothenberg, "Word Association and Creativity," *Psychological Reports* 33 (1973):3–12, and "Opposite Responding as a Measure of Creativity," *Psychological Reports* 33 (1973):15–18.

89. J. B. Carroll, P. M. Kjeldegaard, and A. S. Carton, "Opposites vs. Primaries in Free Association," *Journal of Verbal Learning and Verbal Behavior* 1 (1962): 22–30.

90. Numerous ways of categorizing word association responses are possible. Classification schemes have ranged from the highly complex and intricate one developed by Gardner Murphy ("An Experimental Study of Literary vs. Scientific Types," *American Journal of Psychology* 28 [1917]:238–62), which includes categories such as contiguity, similarity, opposites, subordination, supraordination, and cause and effect, to the relatively simple differentiation of paradigmatic and syntagmatic used by modern psycholinguists (see n. 24,

chap. 8, below). For further information about the types of schemes and the difficulties of establishing satisfactory categories, I refer the interested reader to Phebe Cramer, *Word Association* (New York: Academic Press, 1968). In spite of the diversity of possible classifications and the difficulty in designing any one scheme that is generally suitable, opposite responding is relatively easy to identify empirically and, in all word association research, opposite responding is scored either as a separate category or is subsumed under a more general one. For example, the paradigmatic classification mentioned, which is based on substitutability, subsumes both synonym and antonym (or opposite) responses.

91. Two testers, Judith G. Scott and the late Jane Glassman, administered the tests for the entire group. Subjects were randomly assigned to each of the testers in order to control for possible influence of the testers' personality or technique on results obtained. Statistical assessment indicated insignificant overall difference between the results obtained by the two testers.

92. The usual list contains 100 words for statistical convenience. The standard Kent-Rosanoff word "chair" was replaced by the word "fair" for this test, so 100 words actually were presented, but ninety-nine were scored. The word "fair" was used because it had an unequivocal opposite, "unfair." Because it was not a standard stimulus word, however, responses to this word were scored separately and results reported here do not include these scores.

93. Measurement of the time from the presentation of the stimulus to the beginning of each response was obtained both by a stopwatch carried by the tester and by electronic measuring of response times directly from the tape recording. Only electronic time measures are reported in the results; the stopwatch was held by the tester during the experiment primarily to keep the subject aware that responses were being timed.

94. Previous classification study described in Rothenberg, "Word Association and Creativity"; this article also gives further description of the characteristics of the creative group.

95. Responses that were neither opposites nor primaries were classified as "others," but these scores are of little pertinence here and will not be reported.

96. That rapidity of opposite response is not a function of Marbe's Law, i.e., common responses are given more rapidly than uncommon ones on word association tests, is demonstrated by the time difference between all opposite responses here and the highly common nonopposite primaries.

97. Should the question arise of whether the testers implicitly encouraged or willingly stimulated opposite responding, let me add and emphasize that neither of the two testers were informed of the experimental hypothesis.

98. See Rothenberg, "Opposite Responding," for specification of empirical criteria on which these calculations are based and for further information about procedure.

99. As a test for creative potential, cautions pertaining to this procedure must be emphasized. It is extremely important that the subject be put at ease and that every effort be made to encourage his reporting his first association. Excessively delayed responses to the word stimuli should be discarded, and retesting of these words or of the entire list should be done. Only then can the aversion to giving popular responses be minimized.

Chapter 8

1. See J. J. Katz and J. Fodor, "The Structure of a Semantic Theory," *Language* 39 (1963):170–210; D. A. McNeill, "Study of Word Association," *Journal of Verbal Learning and Verbal Behavior* 8 (1966):548–57. McNeill emphasizes a minimal contrast feature for verbal opposites to account for word association results. He does not discuss the conceptual factor of opposition and, by omission, would seem to suggest that the verbal feature of minimal contrast is the major factor in opposites. See also discussion in H. H. Clark, "Word Associations and Linguistic Theory," in *New Horizons in Linguistics* ed. J. Lyons (Baltimore: Penguin Books, 1970), pp. 275–76.

2. *Webster's New Dictionary of Synonyms* (Springfield, Mass.: Merriam, 1968).

3. Medium is not specifically different from tall because it is different from short as well.

4. Primarily this position has been at times taken in various oriental philosophies, Buddhism, Taoism, and Hinduism. The idea that opposites flow into one another has been adopted and forwarded by numerous mystics and mystical orders in both the Western and the Eastern world. See also an experimental study of similarity in opposition, T. F. Karwoski and J. Schachter, "Psychological Studies in Semantics: III. Reaction Times for Similarity and Difference," *Journal of Social Psychology* 28 (1948):103–20.

5. There is nothing to suggest that a misapprehension problem would arise later because of the mother's "mislabeling" of the child's behavior with this word. The child constantly hears words applied to him which he does not understand or are inappropriate at the time and no later difficulties in apprehension seem to occur.

6. G. Kreezer and K. M. Dallenbach, "Learning the Relation of Opposition," *American Journal of Psychology* 41 (1929):432–41.

7. B. Inhelder and J. Piaget, *The Early Growth of Logic in the Child,* trans. E. A. Lunzer and D. Papert (New York: Norton, 1964), pp. 146–47.

8. Ibid., p. 149.

9. For an excellent review, see R. J. Wales and R. Grieve, "What Is So Difficult about Negation?," *Perception and Psychophysics* 6 (1969):327–31.

10. J. Piaget, "Principal Factors Determining Intellectual Evolution from Childhood to Adult Life," in *Factors Determining Human Behavior,* Harvard Tercentary Conference (Cambridge, Mass.: Harvard University Press, 1937), pp. 32–48.

11. D. R. Entwisle, *Word Association of Young Children* (Baltimore: Johns Hopkins Press, 1966). Opposite-evoking stimulus words and opposite responses were, as in my own word association studies reported in the last chapter, those defined in Carroll et al., "Opposites vs. Primaries."

12. Entwisle, *Word Association,* p. 71.

13. Children's averages computed from Entwisle's figures; see Carroll et al., "Opposites vs. Primaries," and Rothenberg, "Word Association," for adult averages.

14. W. G. Perry, *Forms of Intellectual and Ethical Development in the College Years* (New York: Holt, Rinehart & Winston, 1970). Using an open-ended interview approach along with independent judges' ratings of tape recorded interview content, Perry and his associates defined and documented

nine positions or forms of intellectual and ethical development in college students. These positions progressed from the first stage of simple dualistic thinking—knowledge, conduct, and values are categorized into sweeping and unconsidered differentiations such as right and wrong, ingroup and outgroup—to the appreciation and recognition of relativism and, finally, the making of "commitments" or affirmations and choices within a relativistic world. Though focused on ethical as well as intellectual parameters, the findings and theory have pertinence to theories restricted particularly to cognitive development, as discussed here.

15. The terms "scale" and "cut" were introduced by Ogden *(Opposition)*.

16. For an extensive discussion of Kant's antinomies, see N. K. Smith, *A Commentary to Kant's "Critique of Pure Reason"* (New York: Humanities Press, 1962).

17. See Allen, *Greek Philosophy*, p. 9.

18. Paul Roubiczek, *Thinking in Opposites* (London: Routledge & Kegan Paul, 1952).

19. See, for discussion of opposition in Eastern religions, C. J. Bleeker, and G. Windengren, eds., *Historia Religionum*, vol. 2, *Religions of the Present* (Leiden: Brill, 1971), pp. 242–43, 372, 466–67, 508–9.

20. Carroll et al., "Opposites vs. Primaries," pp. 22–23.

21. R. D. Wynne, H. Gerjuoy and H. Schiffman, "Association Test Antonym Response Set," *Journal of Verbal Learning and Verbal Behavior* 4 (1965):354–59.

22. In another, more complicated, study, Wynne and associates varied instructions and sequence of stimulus presentation in order to assess practice effects in opposite response. They found that the frequency of the subjects' opposite responses increased after repeated testing and concluded that opposite responding resulted from the subjects' desire to expend the least conceptual effort. Again, however, they have assumed that a subject consciously employs some strategy to attain a goal other than that explicitly stated by the tester (R. D. Wynne, H. Gerjuoy, H. Schiffman and N. Wexler, "Word Association Variables Affecting Popular-Response Frequency," *Psychological Reports* 20 [1967]:423–32).

23. J. Deese, *The Structure of Associations in Language and Thought* (Baltimore: Johns Hopkins Press, 1965).

24. McNeill, "Study of Word Association." The shift referred to here is a so-called paradigmatic shift, at the ages of eight and nine. This shift is described in Entwisle's study cited earlier; it includes but is not synonymous with the increase in opposite responding at these ages. Paradigmatic responses on the word association test are those that can be substituted for the stimulus; they fall within the same syntactical category. Syntagmatic responses, in distinction, form a unit with the stimulus; they are usually associated in a syntactical sequence with the stimulus word. For example, "red" is a paradigmatic response to "green," while "grass" is a syntagmatic one. Paradigmatic responses characteristically increase at the expense of syntagmatic ones at ages seven, eight, and nine.

25. H. R. Pollio, R. Deitchman and S. Richards, "Law of Contrast and Oppositional Word Associates," *Journal of Experimental Psychology* 79 (1969):203–12.

26. Ibid., p. 211.

27. Ibid.

28. See, e.g., N. Chomsky, *Aspects of the Theory of Syntax* (Cambridge, Mass.: M.I.T. Press, 1965); N. Chomsky and M. Halle, *The Sound Pattern of English* (New York: Harper & Row, 1968); N. Chomsky, *Studies on Semantics in Generative Grammer* (The Hague: Mouton, 1972).

29. See n. 1 above.

30. E. L. Thorndike, and I. Lorge, *The Teacher's Word Book of Thirty Thousand Words* (New York: Teachers College Press, 1944).

31. I had been interested in developing and extending the definition of opposite responding used in the Carroll et al. experiment, because those experimenters had not included many responses that seemed to be logically opposite the stimulus. That was the reason for the particular design used here but it has little pertinence to the present discussion.

32. The definition used in the instructions covers only scalar or quantitative opposition, and only a continuum and poles are indicated. This was done intentionally because qualitative or cut opposition is harder to define and most people give the quantitative definition when asked to explain opposition. Because the experimenter was present when the ratings were done, subjects were able to ask questions and any confusions about the definition were resolved. The results, of course, show that subjects actually used both a qualitative and quantitative definition of opposition.

33. The persons judging the sour-not sweet and the man-male pairs as opposites seem merely to have been careless and unthinking in these particular cases. That these judgments did not represent a general misunderstanding of the instructions nor a special pressure on these raters to respond quickly was determined by the following two assessments: (1) other ratings for these raters did not show any consistent feature indicating misunderstanding; (2) these raters spent the same amount of average time on the entire rating task as did others.

34. It is worthy of note that the influence of linguistic usage on the production of dichotomous categories often appears as a confounding factor in Koestler's theory of creativity discussed earlier. Many of his examples of two mutually incompatible but self-consistent modes are based on his defining a dichotomous linguistic context in which differences are overstressed and appear as incompatibilities, much as dichotomy leads to the appearance of opposition above. For example, he recently referred to incompatibility between motions of tides and motions of the moon in Kepler's discoveries, and to arithmetic and music in Pythagoras's constructions of harmony and, in a joke, to the code of sexual morality and the logic of the division of labor. In bringing two entities together in a single context in such fashion, they can appear to be incompatible rather than being merely different from one another. See especially Koestler, *Janus*, pp. 109–64.

35. See Hausman, *Discourse on Novelty and Creation*, for a meaningful discussion of the familiar and unfamiliar in creations; see also, W. W. Gordon, "On Being Explicit about Creative Process," *Journal of Creative Behavior* 6 (1972):295–300. Gordon uses the terms "familiar" and "strange" with respect to metaphors, although in a different sense than used here.

36. I do not, by any means, intend to suggest that metaphor or art in gen-

eral needs to be rendered comprehensible in logical or prosaic terms in order to be appreciated; I am emphasizing only an intuition and a sense of understanding.

37. Holton, "On Trying to Understand Scientific Genius," p. 107. See also, L. von Bertalanffy on the opposites in science in *Problems of Life* (New York: Wiley, 1952), pp. 176–204.

38. Holton, "On Trying to Understand Scientific Genius"; see also chapter on Bohr in Holton, *Thematic Origins of Scientific Thought*, pp. 115–61. For Kuhn, see his, *Structure of Scientific Revolutions*.

39. Exploring such matters as opposition between colors, tones, and values is, in fact, a traditional concern of artists as seen in the remark of van Gogh (quoted in chap. 7 above, n. 34).

40. A. Rothenberg, "On Anger," *American Journal of Psychiatry*, 128 (1971):86–92.

41. Kuhn, *Structure of Scientific Revolutions*.

42. See esp. R. Jakobson, and M. Halle, *Fundamentals of Language* (Grauenhage: Mouton, 1956), and C. Lévi-Strauss, *Structural Anthropology* (New York: Basic Books, 1963 [vol. 1], 1976 [vol. 2]). The brilliant achievements of Lévi-Strauss demonstrate almost single-handedly the conceptual value of formulating oppositions as discussed below in chap. 13. By categorizing cultural practices and beliefs into opposites and opposite patterns, he has been able to provide profound understanding of intra- and inter-cultural relationships. As a methodology, structuralism has been criticized because of its exclusive use of binary opposition. Multiple opposition and the broader perspectives on opposition discussed here could possibly enrich the structural approach.

43. In this consideration, mathematical symbols would be included as a type of language.

44. See, e.g., D. M. Ferguson, *Music as Metaphor* (Minneapolis: University of Minnesota Press, 1960). I assume the reader is familiar with the ever-prevalent argument between those who reject any referential element in music, any suggestion that music refers to anything beyond itself, and those who relate music to visual experiences, memories, historical events, etc. Most music aestheticians today come down hard against referential and so-called extramusical approaches.

Chapter 9

1. Freud, "The Interpretation of Dreams."

2. W. Sledge and I have identified numerous instances of simultaneous antithesis in Freud's formulations. Freud's brilliant analysis of the nature of the uncanny as comprised of two antithetical aspects, "*heimlich*" or familiar and "*unheimlich*" or unfamiliar, is an especially noteworthy instance of a janusian conception; see S. Freud, "The 'Uncanny' " (1919) (London, 1955), 17:217–52.

3. As I discuss in the final chapter here, the operation of janusian thinking in producing artistic creations and their aesthetic appeal supports and lends increased weight to Freud's formulation about primary process.

4. S. Freud, "The Antithetical Meaning of Primal Words" (1910) (London, 1957), 11:153–62. Freud based this analysis on the work of a German philologist, Karl Abel.

5. C. Lévi-Strauss, "The savage mind is logical in the same sense and in the same fashion as ours, though as our own is only when it is applied to knowledge of a universe in which it recognizes physical and semantic properties simultaneously" (*The Savage Mind* [Chicago: University of Chicago Press, 1966], p. 268).

6. See *The Collected Works of C. G. Jung* (Princeton, N.J.: Princeton University Press, Bollingen Series, 1966), esp. *The Psychology of the Unconscious,* vol. 7; *Psychological Types,* vol. 6; *The Structure and Dynamics of the Psyche,* vol. 8.

7. Some others who have strongly emphasized the importance of reconciliation of opposites, in art and/or in life are Coleridge (probably the first), Eli Siegel, and Cyril Connolly. For Coleridge's discussion of poetry as a reconciliation of opposites, see esp. chap. 14 in *Biographia Literaria.* The English critic Connolly said the following: "To attain . . . truth we must be able to resolve all our dualities [opposites]" (*The Unquiet Grave* [London: Hamish Hamilton, 1945], p. 85). Siegel, who founded a movement called "Aesthetic Realism" states as a manifesto: "The resolution of conflict in self is like the making one of opposites in art," and "All beauty is a making one of opposites, and the making one of opposites is what we are going after in ourselves"; see, e.g., E. Siegel, *The Aesthetic Method in Self Conflict* (New York: Definition Press, 1965), *Psychiatry, Economics, Aesthetics* (New York: Definition Press, 1946).

8. See G. W. F. Hegel, "The Science of Logic," in *The Encyclopedia of the Philosophical Sciences,* trans. W. Wallace (London: Oxford University Press, 1965). For a good discussion of Hegel's dialectic, see J. N. Findlay, *Hegel: A Re-Examination* (New York: Collier Books, 1962).

9. S. Plath, "Three Women," *Winter Trees* (London: Faber & Faber, 1971), p. 50.

10. The consideration here should also clarify the relationship of janusian thinking and syncretism. Syncretism, the attempted reconciliation or union of different or conflicting principles, practices, or parties, usually involves logic, compromise, or a process of accretion such as the gradual incorporation of tenets and rites from different religions into a single religion. While janusian thinking could play a role in developing a particular syncretic result, syncretic thinking and approaches proceed along many and varying paths. Also, Arieti's theory of creativity as a "magic" synthesis of primary and secondary process does not take into consideration the difference between integration, which is more intrinsic to creativity, and synthesis (see Arieti, *Creativity*).

11. Connections between sex and death have a long mythopoetic history. McClelland has discussed these connections in the theme of the harlequin figure which he traces to a time prior to the commedia dell'arte in the eleventh century. Also, he cites earlier connections in Greek mythology; see D. W. McClelland, "The Harlequin Complex," in *The Study of Lives,* ed. R. W. White (New York: Atherton Press, 1963), pp. 94–120. Also, Professor Toby Olshin has called my attention to the widespread tendency among Renaissance poets, particularly John Donne, to equate sexual orgasm and death in both punning and serious contexts. This long-standing mythic and literary background has not detracted from the impact of new constructions equating sex and death.

12. Koestler's emphasis is on dualistic factors both in the concept of bisociation and in his recent use of the metaphor of the god, Janus. He focuses on a two-faced god rather than on opposition (*Janus*).

13. See L. Festinger, *A Theory of Cognitive Dissonance* (Evanston, Ill.: Row, Peterson, 1957). Cognitive dissonance consists of a relation of discrepancy or lack of fit between two items of knowledge or conceptions held at the same time. Festinger emphasized that such discrepancy produced discomfort and a motivation toward reduction or resolution. This motivating effect of cognitive dissonance applies to the stimulating quality of janusian formulations, the motivation and instigation to consider further and to seek further information when exposed to such formulations. With the simultaneous antitheses and oppositions, there could hardly be a form of cognition that is manifestly more discrepant or dissonant.

14. E. Bleuler, *Dementia Praecox or the Group of Schizophrenias,* trans. J. Zinkin (New York: International Universities Press, 1950), p. 53.

15. Ibid.

16. See earlier psychodynamic formulations about the author of "In Monument Valley"; see also Rothenberg, "The Iceman Changeth," and "Poetic Process and Psychotherapy."

17. Bleuler, *Dementia Praecox*, p. 54.

18. In referring to absence of figurative intent, I do not mean to invoke the complicated and controversial issue of whether schizophrenics think concretely rather than abstractly, nor do I mean to propose a systematic formulation about figurative thinking in schizophrenia. It is well known that persons suffering from schizophrenia do think abstractly, sometimes "overabstractly," and that they are also capable of speaking and thinking both figuratively and metaphorically. I have suggested some formulations about schizophrenic production of metaphors elsewhere (A. Rothenberg, "Poetry in the Classroom," *American Poetry Review* 3 [1974]:52–54), and a full discussion of the matter must be postponed for other communications.

19. T. Lidz, *The Origin and Treatment of Schizophrenic Disorders* (New York: Basic Books, 1973), p. 59.

20. Ibid., pp. 85 ff.

21. "Overinclusion" was first introduced by Norman Cameron; see his "Schizophrenic Thinking in a Problem-Solving Situation," *Journal of Mental Science* 85 (1939):1012–35.

Chapter 10

1. Needless to say, the oxymoron is only one type of metaphor, and sometimes a rather banal type as well.

2. I have not, and shall not, systematically discuss here such art forms as dance, theatre, film, or the opera. This is not because such forms are less important but only because all are partly covered through consideration of the broader areas of visual arts, music, and literature. All, particularly dance creation, in which homospatial thinking plays a large role, deserve extensive further comment and consideration.

3. V. C. Aldrich, "Visual Metaphor," *Journal of Aesthetic Education* 2 (1968):73–86, and "Form in the Visual Arts," *British Journal of Aesthetics* 11 (1971):215–26.

4. Aldrich "Form in the Visual Arts," p. 223. References to Aldrich's overall philosophy of art involving first, second, and third orders of formulation are deleted in the quotation. The visual metaphor concept clearly is an autonomous one.

5. This effect is apparent even though looking at this photograph of the sculpture; it is far stronger when viewing the sculpture itself.

6. Anton Ehrenzweig, the brilliant and discerning art teacher, also had recourse to this diagram in his attempt to show the limitations of the traditional gestalt figure-ground formulation as applied to art. Ehrenzweig formulated an unconscious "dedifferentiated" perception to account for artistic "seeing." A suggestive concept, possible points of contact with the processes I am describing are altered and weakened by the emphasis on *unconscious* perception. The homospatial process is conscious, as should be evident after applying the visualizing principle to the Rubin profiles; see Ehrenzweig, *The Hidden Order of Art* (Berkeley: University of California Press, 1967).

7. Albers, *Interaction of Color,* p. 73.

8. Ibid., p. 72.

9. Ibid., p. 44.

10. Some controversy exists about whether this is an actual scene of Florentine countryside or merely, as Kenneth Clark states, a typical da Vinci background. Regardless, it is not a scene that would have been directly seen and copied from such a room as in the painting. Its particular visual features are the important issue, whatever the source; see Clark, *Leonardo da Vinci,* pp. 118–19. Anna Maria Brizio takes the following position: "It is not a real landscape, but a kind of geological composition in which, in the stratification of the rocks, in the shape of the waters, the temporal stratification of centuries past is reflected" ("The Painter," in *The Unknown Leonardo,* ed. L. Reti [New York: McGraw-Hill, 1974], p. 24).

11. Both Freud and Neumann, the discerning explicator of the Jungian aesthetic, focused extensively on this cartoon and painting and both emphasized psychological factors pertaining to the content rather than the formal perceptual effect. Neumann saw the archetypal image of the Great Mother in these forms and Freud saw the two mothers of Leonardo's childhood (E. Neumann, *Art and the Creative Unconscious: Four Essays,* trans. R. Manheim [New York: Harper & Row, 1959]; S. Freud, "Leonardo da Vinci and a Memory of His Childhood" [1910] [London, 1957], 11:59–138). In passing, Freud even gauchely criticized the fusion and the artistic form as follows: "One is inclined to say that they are fused with each other like badly condensed dream-figures, so that in some places it is hard to say where Anne ends and where Mary begins. But what appears to a critic's eye as a fault, as a defect in composition, is vindicated in the eyes of analysis by reference to its secret meaning [i.e., the two mothers]" (p. 114).

12. Brizio, "The Painter," p. 44.

13. H. Moore, "The Sculptor Speaks," *Listener* 18 (1937):338.

14. Quoted from a letter written by Oskar Kokoschka to Professor Tietze (ca. 1917–18), in E. Hoffman, *Kokoschka: Life and Work* (London: Faber & Faber, 1947), p. 158.

15. Quoted in J. Cladel, *Rodin the Man and His Art: With Leaves from His Notebook,* trans. S. K. Star (New York: Century, 1917), p. 108.

16. Michelangelo Buonarroti, Sonnet 15 and Madrigale 12, quoted in J. A. Symonds, *Life of Michelangelo* (London: John C. Nimmo, 1893), 1:110.

17. C. Oldenburg, *Notes in Hand* (New York: Dutton, 1971), p. 47.

18. C. Oldenburg, *Drawings and Prints* (London: Chelsea House, 1969), p. 24.

19. Ibid., p. 126.

20. Klee, *The Thinking Eye*, pp. 328–30.

21. M. Beckmann, From a lecture given at the New Burlington Galleries, London 1938, quoted in Protter, *Painters on Painting*, p. 211.

22. H. Matisse, "La Chapelle du Rosaire," quoted and translated in A. H. Barr, *Matisse: His Art and Public* (New York: Museum of Modern Art, 1951), p. 288.

23. W. Hogarth, *The Analysis of Beauty* (London: J. Reeves, 1753), p. 113, and pp. 119–20.

24. A. Gleizes and J. Metzinger, "Cubism," in *Modern Artists on Art*, ed. R. L. Herbert (Englewood Cliffs, N.J.: Prentice-Hall, 1964; orig. pub. 1912 by Figuière).

25. Moore, "Sculptor Speaks."

26. Moore [Untitled], in *Unit 1*.

27. See the architect Bertrand Goldberg's use of this term and a related term, "kinetic space," in J. W. Cook, and H. Klotz, *Conversations with Architects* (New York: Praeger, 1973), pp. 122–46, esp. pp. 130–31, "kinetic space," and p. 142, "multiuse space."

28. Ibid., p. 203.

29. Some of this controversy derives from what recent philosophers have pointed to as a Western tendency to spatialize time (see chap. 12 below). As music is primarily temporal, figurative spatial terms applied to music produce serious conceptual problems, particularly when they become reified and are used as though such dimensions directly apply. Moreover, there is a tendency to think of space in music as equivalent to something static, stationary, or abstracted, in distinction to the dynamic, moving, concrete quality of time. This, I believe, is an invalid polarization of attributes and it derives in part from conceptualizing space solely in visual terms. Erwin Straus has developed an excellent analysis of the phenomenology of space in music in which he posits that music "homogenizes" space; it is experienced as overcoming a boundary between inner and outer space and fills the distance between the hearer and the source. While I think Straus's discussion is valid, and strongly recommend a careful reading of it (E. Straus, "The Forms of Spatiality," in *Phenomenological Psychology* [New York: Basic Books, 1966], pp. 3–37), it cannot be used as a basis for the consideration of space in music specifically, because the homogenization he describes occurs in other art forms as well. I shall discuss his analysis later in chap. 13 in discussing homospatial thinking and the basis of its creative effect. For the definition of space used throughout the remainder of this chapter, see chap. 12.

30. The model for the definition of the nature of metaphor must be the linguistic metaphor. As used here, visual and auditory metaphors differ from linguistic metaphors only because the latter, being composed of words, have clear and specific referents.

31. L. van Beethoven, From a written conversation with Louis Schlosser (1822 or 1823), in *Beethoven: Letters, Journals and Conversations,* trans. and ed. M. Hamburger (New York: Pantheon, 1952), p. 194.

32. Quoted in M. Agnew, "Auditory Imagery of Great Composers," *Psychological Monographs* 31 (1922):282.

33. A student of mine has suggested that the musical staff represents vertical and horizontal relationships in music together. Such a formulation, though it could conceivably incorporate a hitherto undefined intrinsic psychological factor in music, is essentially restrictive because it tends to identify the spatial aspect of music with the purely visual matter of notation. The perceptual laws discussed in this section apply both to visual and auditory experience and are more basic than the visual notation scheme. Moreover, many alternative notation procedures not using vertical and horizontal are possible for music.

34. Schoenberg, *Style and Idea,* p. 113. Deletions in this quotation of Schoenberg's reference to Swedenborg's heaven and an absence of absolute direction in musical space are made for the purposes of clarity.

35. A. Einstein, *Mozart: His Character, His Work* (New York: Oxford University Press, 1945), p. 156.

36. Schoenberg, *Style and Idea,* p. 162.

37. J. Beckwith and U. Kasemets, *The Modern Composer and His World* (Toronto: University of Toronto Press, 1961), p. 117. The word "combination" used in this context suggests interactions rather than a compromise or reconciliation of the horizontal and vertical relationships.

38. A. W. Thayer, *The Life of Ludwig van Beethoven* (New York: Schirmer, 1921), 2:316.

39. Quoted in A. M. Abell, *Talks with Great Composers* (Garmisch-Partenkirchen: G. E. Schroeder, 1964), p. 184.

40. P. Hindemith, *A Composer's World* (New York: Doubleday, 1961), pp. 70–71. I have referred to Hindemith's comprehensive image earlier in the chapter on janusian thinking. For janusian thinking to be involved, it would be necessary to assume that Hindemith was also referring to simultaneity of opposing temporal orientations. While it is difficult to ascertain such a reference in the above, it is, in any event, quite common to find both janusian and homospatial thinking operating conjointly in a particular aspect of the creative process.

41. I use the expression "remember" advisedly here; it is a shorthand formulation used merely in the service of an uncluttered exposition. There are many reasons for the poet's great storehouse of sound and sight associations to words, including a possible inherited capacity and an intense interest in and sensitivity to words. Moreover, poets often carry out a directed association procedure, writing out—on the margins of their manuscripts—all the rhymes to a particular word that they bring to mind.

42. Freud, "Jokes and Their Relation to the Unconscious."

43. R. Nichols, "Birth of a Poem," in R. M. Harding, *An Anatomy of Inspiration,* 2d ed. (Cambridge: W. Heffer & Sons, 1942), pp. 105–26.

44. Ibid., pp. 110–11.

45. M. Cane, *Making a Poem* (New York: Harcourt, Brace & World, 1962). Numerous examples of both janusian and homospatial thinking abound in

this book. See especially the origin of the metaphor "tree of time" in a homospatial conception superimposing twelve apples onto twelve tones of the clock (pp. 49–51) and the origin of the poem "Humbly, Wildly" in the janusian conceptions of boiling as "both hot and cold" and water as "both responsible and irresponsible" (pp. 31–38).

46. Ibid., pp. 60–61.

47. Ibid., p. 59; see pp. 59–60 for remainder of poem.

48. Miller wrote the following in the introduction to his collected plays: "The first image that occurred to me which was to result in *Death of a Salesman* was of an enormous face the height of the proscenium arch which would appear and then open up, and we would see the inside of a man's head. In fact, *The Inside of His Head* was the first title. It was conceived half in laughter, for the inside of his head was a mass of contradictions. The image was in direct opposition to the method of *All My Sons*—a method one might call linear or eventual in that one fact or incident creates the necessity for the next. The *Salesman* image was from the beginning absorbed with the concept that nothing in life comes 'next' but that everything exists together and at the same time within us; that there is no past to be 'brought forward' in a human being, but that he is his past at every moment and that the present is merely that which his past is capable of noticing, and smelling and reacting to" (*Arthur Miller's Collected Plays* [New York: Viking, 1957], p. 23). The passage represents the matter essentially as Miller did to me personally. What is of some additional interest, however, is the shift of emphasis and consequent omissions. In the above passage, Miller doesn't mention his conception that Willie, the salesman, was inside his *own* head. He stresses in the written passage the stage setting and the abstract meaning of the idea. This emphasis is clearly appropriate here as Miller is discussing the aesthetic issues in the play, not recounting the steps in the creative process to a researcher.

49. The author's use of the passive grammatical construction "comes together" with respect to the Berkeley and Yale scenes is more equivocal than an active construction such as "I brought together," but the latter type of phraseology is seldom applied to personal mental events. Nevertheless, it is certain that this author was consciously searching for ideas and he *intended* to construct a scene from the images in his mind. Moreover, he is not describing a process of free association nor a regressed state of consciousness. These assertions and my formulations in the text have been corroborated by the author himself after reading the material here.

50. A. S. Hoffman, *Fiction Writers on Fiction Writing* (Indianapolis: Bobbs-Merrill, 1923).

51. Coleridge, *Biographia Literaria*, 1:50 ff.

52. Freud, "Creative Writers and Daydreaming."

53. G. G. Williams, *Readings for Creative Writers* (New York: Harper, 1938), pp. 181–87.

54. E. Bowen, *Collected Impressions* (New York: Knopf, 1950), p. 251.

Chapter 11

1. E. Caruth and R. Ekstein, "Interpretation within the Metaphor: Further Considerations," *Journal of Child Psychiatry* 5 (1966):35–45; R. Ekstein and J. Wallerstein, "Choice of Interpretation in the Treatment of Borderline and

Psychotic Children," *Bulletin of the Menninger Clinic* 2 (1957):199–207. The schizophrenic use and production of metaphor is a complicated matter, and is a topic in my "Creativity: Pure and Applied," in progress.

2. G. J. Rose, "Fusion States," in *Tactics and Techniques in Psychoanalytic Therapy*, ed. P. L. Giovacchini (New York: Science House, 1972).

3. See L. B. Fierman, ed., *Effective Psychotherapy: The Contribution of Hellmuth Kaiser* (New York: Free Press, 1965), esp. pp. 117–41, 208–10.

4. Definition by M. D. Vernon in *Visual Perception* (London: Cambridge University Press, 1937), p. 205. The discussion following here is not meant to pertain to the use of the term synaesthesia in the literary movement associated with Baudelaire, Rimbaud, and Huysmans, as I am concerned with the psychological process rather than with any particular aesthetic approach or the advocacy of a particular aesthetic idea.

5. See P. McKellar, *Imagination and Thinking* (New York: Basic Books, 1957), pp. 60–64, 192–93.

6. R. E. L. Masters and J. Houston, *The Varieties of Psychedelic Experience* (New York: Holt, Rinehart & Winston, 1966).

7. Original manuscript written by Anderson is at the Beinecke Rare Book Library, Yale University. It consists of a legal-size ledger book in which the play is written on the recto sheets with some revisions on the verso sides. I acknowledge my gratitude to Donald C. Gallup, curator of the Yale American Literature Collection, for making the material extensively available to me. Some later revisions by Anderson are also deposited at the University of Texas Library at Austin. Help with method and statistics on this study was provided by George F. Mahl and with statistics by Barry Cook.

8. Rothenberg, "The Iceman Changeth." The methodology was in part devised as a means of empirical study of literary creation in which an interviewer or observer could not exert any inadvertent influence.

9. In an experimental study by Bruce Nagle and myself using latency of reaction time on a word association test as an anxiety measure, subjects showed significantly higher levels of anxiety when presented with words connected to their own revisions than to other words from their own and others' writings ($p < .05$; A. Rothenberg and B. Nagle, "The Process of Literary Revision," in prep.; see also B. Nagle, "The Process of Literary Revision: A Study of Its Psychological Meaning in the Writing of Normal, Emotionally-Disturbed and Creative Individuals," M. D. Thesis, Yale University School of Medicine, 1969).

10. J. N. Michaelson, *Morning, Winter and Night* (New York: William Sloane Associates, 1952).

11. The novel clearly indicates oedipal overtones between young Anderson and his grandmother. The "old coot" was therefore also a displaced type of father figure.

12. These effects are at the University of Texas Library at Austin.

Chapter 12

1. For that matter, I think it is patently true that philosophical matters are important for all scientific discourse.

2. Kant, *Critique of Judgment*, p. 188.

3. The reader will be aware by now that there will be no direct or extended

consideration of genetic, social, or personality factors involved in the capacity to use the mirror-image processes. A direct formulation of the features of a creative personality or of environmental factors in creativity is beyond the scope and purpose of this book.

4. There is, in fact, some evidence that high or very high intelligence, as measured by standard intelligence tests, is not required for various types of creation. Standard intelligence tests primarily measure verbal intelligence, however, and this could account in part for these results, especially in connection with creation in the visual or nonverbal arts. For rather extensive research, as well as controversy, about this and related matters, see the following: J. W. Getzels and P. W. Jackson, *Creativity and Intelligence* (New York: Wiley, 1962); F. Barron, *Creative Person and Creative Process* (New York: Holt, Rinehart & Winston, 1969), pp. 39–51; M. A. Wallach and N. Kogan, "Creativity and Intelligence in Children," in *Human Intelligence*, ed. J. McV. Hunt (New Brunswick, N. J.: Transaction Books, 1972), pp. 165–81; M. A. Wallach and N. Kogan, "A New Look at the Creativity-Intelligence Distinction," *Journal of Personality* 33 (1965):348–69; M. A. Wallach and C. W. Wing, *The Talented Student: A Validation of the Creativity-Intelligence Distinction* (New York: Holt, Rinehart & Winston, 1969).

5. See J. Dewey, *Art as Experience* (New York: Minton, Balch, 1934); Meyer, *Emotion and Meaning in Music*, and more recently, *Explaining Music* (Berkeley: University of California Press, 1973). Also, for an excellent discussion of surprise and the unexpected in psychological and aesthetic theory, see Berlyne, *Aesthetics and Psychobiology*, pp. 143–49.

6. The Aristotelian definitions of tragedy as based on reversal, along with recognition and suffering, support this.

7. M. Moore, "The Monkey Puzzle," in *Collected Poems* (New York: Macmillan, 1951), p. 80.

8. Hausman has used the terms "novelty proper" and "radical novelty" to refer to this stricter or more pure understanding of newness. Hausman's incisive analysis of the problem of newness in creation is an important background for the discussion here (Hausman, *Discourse on Novelty and Creation*).

9. Berlyne makes this point by citing a passage from the philosopher Home in which Home states that surprise depends on the unexpected while novelty can be appreciated even when it is expected. Home uses the example of a traveler to India who expects to see an elephant but is still moved to wonder when seeing it because of its novelty. Although this distinction between the surprising and the novel is valid, the example is actually not appropriate. We expect to find novelty when confronted with a work of art, seeing a play, etc., but we may still be surprised about the specific details of the novel entity (see Berlyne, *Aesthetics and Psychobiology*, p. 146). On the teleology of surprise, see Rothenberg and Hausman, Introduction, *Creativity Question*.

10. From the time of Aristotle, several types of causation have been recognized and emphasized. For a concise review and discussion of types see H. L. A. Hart and A. M. Honoré, *Causation in the Law* (Oxford: Clarendon Press, 1959), especially pp. 1–78. I shall not engage here in a discussion of these alternate types of causation, because the concept of efficient causation I have outlined is of primary interest to the scientist. For the same reason, I shall only focus on antecedent causation rather than teleological causation. Moreover, formula-

tions about creativity in terms of teleology have their own difficulties. See Rothenberg and Hausman, *Creativity Question*.

11. See R. M. Gale, ed., *The Philosophy of Time* (London: Macmillan, 1968); M. Capek, ed., *The Concepts of Space and Time* (Boston: Reidel, 1976).

12. F. Waismann, "Analytic-Synthetic," in Gale, *Philosophy of Time*, p. 55. Also, see St. Augustine, *Confessions* (New York: E. P. Dutton, 1936), p. 262.

13. The presence of the subjective state of timelessness during the creative process has been a major consideration in regression theories of creativity such as that of Kris (see his *Psychoanalytic Explorations*). Withdrawal of cathexis from the external world, according to Kris, facilitates the upsurgence of regressive primary process modes of thought. And timelessness, a cardinal feature of id and other unconscious processes, holds sway. Such a formulation ironically recreates a problem facing Freud, Kris's direct mentor, in his approach to the interpretation of dreams. For Freud raised the question of whether the pictorial and other representations in dreams resulted primarily from the suspension of conscious perceptual processes during sleep. Resolutely, he pointed out that the need for discharge of unconscious processes, the expression of wish fulfillment, rather than suspension of conscious perception was primary. With respect to the creative process, I follow Freud's type of resolution rather than that of Kris. Janusian thinking, for reasons indicated here, is responsible for the timelessness in creativity, rather than withdrawal of cathexis from the external world and subsequent regression. Janusian thinking is again not a manifestation of regression and primary process thinking, but it directly produces an effect of timelessness.

14. See Capek, *Concepts of Space and Time*.

15. *The Random House Dictionary of the English Language*, unabridged ed. (New York: Random House, 1967), p. 1362.

16. M. Merleau-Ponty, *Phenomenology of Perception*, trans. C. Smith (London: Routledge & Kegan Paul, 1962), pp. 243 ff.

17. H. Bergson, *Time and Free Will* (New York: Macmillan, 1912), p. 95.

18. It is interesting that, other than compasses and highly technical gadgets which we do not regularly use, there are no everyday instruments for this purpose.

Chapter 13

1. Some contemporary artists consider art and the representation of unconscious contents to be synonymous. In their attempts at attaining a direct outpouring of unconscious material through personally directed free association or drugs, they often are going about unearthing unconscious material in the wrong way.

2. It is doubtful that the artist is driven to work on the same themes over and over only because he cannot work them out and therefore must repeat them. This explanation would be appropriate if art were merely a symptom of psychological illness and, like all symptoms, bound to be repeated. But good art, as we know, shows progression of theme, both within a single work by a particular artist and in the corpus of his productions. In the light of this, and the other evidence presented throughout this book, the emphasis should be on the gratifications of progressing toward insight (see section below, "Articulation and Freedom," and Rothenberg, "Poetic Process and Psychotherapy").

3. Lesser, *Fiction and the Unconscious*; N. Holland, *The Dynamics of Literary Response* (New York: Oxford University Press, 1968); F. Crews, ed., *Psychoanalysis and Literary Process* (Cambridge, Mass.: Winthrop Publishers, 1970).

4. To some extent, the above critique applies to Jungian as well as Freudian theories of art. Jung talked about the artist's use of autonomous complexes to structure the content of the Collective Unconscious, but never explained the nature of these complexes very fully. As the Jungian theory of dreams differs from the Freudian, however, the above comments applying to condensation and displacement do not apply to Jung's conceptions. See the following by C. G. Jung: "Psychology and Literature," *The Collected Works of C. G. Jung*, vol. 15, ed. H. Read, M. Fordham, G. Adler, and W. McGuire, trans. R. F. C. Hull (New York: Pantheon Books, Bollingen Series, 1966), pp. 84–105; *Psychological Types* (New York: Harcourt Brace, 1946), reprinted in *The Collected Works of C. G. Jung*, vol. 6, ed. H. Read, M. Fordham, G. Adler and W. McGuire, trans. R. F. C. Hull (Princeton, N.J.: Princeton University Press, Bollingen Series, 1971); "On the Relation of Analytic Psychology to Poetic Art," *British Journal of Psychology* 3 (1923):213–31, reprinted as "On the Relation of Analytical Psychology to Poetry," in *Collected Works*, vol. 15. See also Neumann, *Art and the Creative Unconscious*, for a theory of art based on Jungian psychology.

5. Or Jungian archetypes.

6. See, e.g., Arieti, *Creativity*. Although Arieti postulates a "tertiary process" as responsible for creativity, he considers artistic structures to be derived from primary process mechanisms.

7. See R. Novey, "The Artistic Communication and Recipient: *Death in Venice* as an Integral Part of a Psychoanalysis," *Psychoanalytic Quarterly* 33 (1964):25–52; S. Schreiber, "A Filmed Fairy Tale as a Screen Memory," *Psychoanalytic Study of the Child* 29 (1974):389–410; E. Buxbaum, "The Role of Detective Stories in a Child Analysis," *Psychoanalytic Quarterly* 10 (1941): 373–81; J. L. Rowley, "Rumpelstilzkin in the Analytical Situation," *International Journal of Psychoanalysis* 32 (1951):190–95; S. Freud, "The Occurrence in Dreams of Material from Fairy Tales" (1913) (London, 1958), 12:279–87.

8. See review of such experiments by M. A. Wallach, "Thinking, Feeling and Expressing: Toward Understanding the Person," in *Cognition, Personality and Clinical Psychology*, ed. R. Jessor and S. Feshbach (San Francisco: Jossey-Bass, 1967), pp. 141–72. See also review of experimental work pertaining to unconscious factors in art in H. Kreitler and S. Kreitler, *Psychology of the Arts* (Durham, N.C.: Duke University Press, 1972), esp. pp. 286–93.

9. H. M. Voth, "The Analysis of Metaphor," *Journal of the American Psychoanalytic Association* 18 (1970):599–621.

10. Of course, in the face of overwhelming danger from some threatening source in reality, such as a predatory animal, flight might well be the only appropriate response.

11. Rothenberg, "Poetic Process and Psychotherapy."

12. A. Rothenberg and B. Nagle, "The Process of Literary Revision;" and A. Rothenberg, "Anxiety in the Creative Process," manuscripts. So far thirty-one subjects have participated in these experiments.

13. The use of latency of response on word association as a measure of anxiety is well established; see C. G. Jung, *Studies in Word Association* (Lon-

don: William Heinemann, 1918), reprinted in *Collected Works,* vol. 2 (1973); D. Rapaport, "The Word Association Test," in *Diagnostic Psychological Testing* (Chicago: Year Book Publishers, 1946), 2:13–84. For the principle of using the word association technique to measure anxiety associated with written documents, I am indebted to George F. Mahl, personal communication, and G. F. Mahl and L. McNutt, "Disturbances in Written Language as a Function of Anxiety," manuscript.

14. Creativity ratings were made by teachers, and also independently by Robert Penn Warren and by James Moffett (educator and designer of curricula in the language arts), both of whom have had considerable experience with assessing creativity in students.

15. I. Roxon-Ropschitz, "The Act of Deleting and Other Findings in Writings of Neurotics," *Psychiatry* 9 (1946):117–21.

16. For all three groups, creative and control high school students and proven creators, mean latency of responses to words from other sources roughly paralleled mean latencies in that group's lower latency of response category (either deleted or substituted).

17. Cultural factors surely play a role as well. In Anglo-Saxon culture, the nonresponsive steady mode is prized and sensations of arousal are viewed with suspicion or outright guilt. In such cultures, there is anxiety about becoming or feeling aroused.

18. Berlyne, *Aesthetics and Psychobiology.*

19. Ibid., p. 136.

20. The terms "primary system" and "secondary system" should not be construed to have any connection to primary and secondary process thinking discussed throughout this book.

21. G. Orwell, *1984* (New York: Harcourt Brace, 1949).

22. R. B. Sheridan, "The Rivals," in *Twelve Famous Plays of the Restoraiton and Eighteenth Century,* ed. C. A. Moore (New York: Random House, 1933), p. 849.

23. See M. L. von Franz, *Creation Myths* (Zurich: Spring Publications, 1972), esp. pp. 61–86, 150–69; Allen, *Greek Philosophy;* Bleeker and Windengren, *Historia Religionum,* vols. 1 and 2.

24. "Heavens" or "sky" and "earth" are generally rated as opposites in most experiments and rating tasks. Quotations here are from the Revised Standard Edition of the Bible.

25. Specificity in janusian thinking sharply distinguishes it from perception of incongruities (see Burke, *Permanence and Change)* or bringing together of habitually incompatible modes (see Koestler, *Act of Creation, Janus)* mentioned earlier. More precisely, the distinction from both Burke's and Koestler's formulations is that both incongruity and incompatibility are potential aspects of the janusian process. They are—so to speak—way stations toward the construction of simultaneous antitheses.

26. See discussion by Albert Solnit, regarding the problem of exclusive reliance on symmetry in theory building in psychoanalysis, particularly with regard to the theory of aggression. Solnit, "Aggression."

27. Pollio et al. (see n. 25, chap. 8) also refer to opposites as defining a dimension in their notion of "conceptual convenience." However, opposition is too abstract, and the types of oppositions discussed here especially are too

extensive and complex to be considered only as convenient memory storage factors. Moreover, janusian formulations characteristically engender cognitive strain rather than qualities of ease and convenience.

28. See Gruber and Barrett, *Darwin*, pp. 105 ff. for Gruber's discussion of this point.

29. I abjure using the word "condense" in this context because of its use in connection with primary process, and because of the specific differences between janusian thinking and primary process condensation I have already described. It is compression rather than condensation because elements are kept discrete in janusian thinking, not combined or entered into compromise formations.

30. E. Dickinson, letter to T. W. Higginson, April 15, 1862, in T. H. Johnson and T. Ward, eds., *The Letters of Emily Dickinson*, (Cambridge, Mass.: Harvard University Press, 1958), 2:403.

31. It should be emphasized that here, as throughout earlier portions of the book, the idea of metaphor is used in the sense of an effective, vital entity. It is not used to connote the merely figurative or nonliteral entity that also is commonly designated as metaphor.

32. H. Crane, "Voyages II," *The Complete Poems and Selected Letters and Prose of Hart Crane*, ed. B. Weber (Garden City, N.Y.: Doubleday, 1966).

33. Beardsley, "Metaphorical Twist"; Hausman, *Discourse on Novelty and Creation*; M. Black, *Models and Metaphors: Studies in Language and Philosophy* (Ithaca: Cornell University Press, 1962); Burke, *Permanence and Change*.

34. See S. C. Pepper, "The Concept of Fusion in Dewey's Aesthetic Theory," *Journal of Aesthetics and Art Criticism* 12 (1953):169–76. Also see M. Beardsley's discussion in his *Aesthetics: Problems in the Philosophy of Criticism* (New York: Harcourt Brace, 1958), pp. 299 ff., of what he calls the fusion theory of art which he attributes to Walter Abell and a considerable group of followers.

35. Straus, *Phenomenological Psychology*. Actually, Straus contends that all perceptual experience is "controlled by modes of the spatial," but I will here adopt only a more limited form of that assertion.

36. Ibid., p. 17.

37. Such viewing of art does connect the artistic product with the creative process. It could be legitimately described as creative perception in its own right.

38. Here I am not referring to cognitive insight about, e.g., knowledge, values, religion, or reality.

39. So-called novelty seeking is often motivated by anxiety about serious commitment either to the old or to the new.

40. When scientist peers hail a new discovery or theory as a creation, they may vicariously appreciate, or imagine, their colleague's struggle for freedom.

INDEX

Pages where illlustrations occur are marked by an asterisk.